Programming with VisualAge® for Java™ Version 3.5
Third Edition

OSAMU TAKAGIWA, FREDERIK HAESBROUCK,
VERONIQUE QUIBLIER, AND SARAH POGER

PRENTICE HALL PTR
UPPER SADDLE RIVER, NEW JERSEY 07458
www.phptr.com

ISBN 0-13-066494-4

© **Copyright International Business Machines Corporation 1998, 2001. All rights reserved.**
Note to U.S. Government Users — Documentation related to restricted rights — Use, duplication or disclosure is subject to restrictions set forth in GSA ADP Schedule Contract with IBM Corp.

Third Edition (April 2001)

This edition applies to Version 3.5 of VisualAge for Java, Professional Edition, for use with the Windows NT or Windows 2000 operating systems.

Comments may be addressed to:

IBM Corporation, International Technical Support Organization
Dept. QXXE Building 80-E2
650 Harry Road
San Jose, California 95120-6099

When you send information to IBM, you grant IBM a non-exclusive right to use or distribute the information in any way it believes appropriate without incurring any obligation to you.

Published by Prentice Hall PTR
Prentice-Hall, Inc.
Upper Saddle River, NJ 07458

Prentice Hall books are widely used by corporations and government agencies for training, marketing, and resale.
The publisher offers discounts on this book when ordered in bulk quantities. For more information, contact Corporate Sales Department, Phone 800-382-3419; FAX: 201-236-7141;
E-mail (Internet): corpsales@prenhall.com
Or write: Prentice Hall PTR, Corporate Sales Department, One Lake Street, Upper Saddle River, NJ 07458.

Take Note!
Before using this information and the product it supports, be sure to read the general information in Appendix C, "Special notices," on page 367.

Printed in the United States of America
10 9 8 7 6 5 4 3 2 1

ISBN   0-13-066494-4

Pearson Education LTD.
Pearson Education Australia PTY, Limited
Pearson Education Singapore, Pte. Ltd.
Pearson Education North Asia Ltd.
Pearson Education Canada, Ltd.
Pearson Educación de Mexico, S.A. de C.V.
Pearson Education—Japan
Pearson Education Malaysia, Pte. Ltd.
Pearson Education, Upper Saddle River, New Jersey

Contents

Figures xi

Tables xvii

Preface xix
The team that wrote this redbook xix
Comments welcome xx

Chapter 1. Introduction to the environment 1
VisualAge for Java product family 1
    VisualAge for Java Professional Edition 2
    VisualAge for Java Entry Professional Edition 4
    VisualAge for Java Enterprise Edition 4
    VisualAge for Java Entry Enterprise Edition 5
    Updates to VisualAge Java 5
Building your first applet 5
    Let's get started! 7
    SmartGuide 8
    The Workbench 12
    Modifying your applet 14
    Creating an animated applet 15
    Changing the properties of the applet 16
Building your first application 17
    Running a program as an applet and application 20
    The VisualAge for Java Source View window 21
The VisualAge for Java Scrapbook 22
    Using the Scrapbook 22
    Scrapbook context 25
    Correcting errors in the Scrapbook 25
    If your Scrapbook page remains busy 27
Customizing VisualAge for Java 28
    Workbench Options 28
Building your first servlet 31

Chapter 2. Organizing your code 41
Projects in VisualAge for Java 41
    Adding features 42
Packages in VisualAge for Java 42
The Workbench 43
    The Workbench Projects page 44
    The Workbench Packages view 46

Using types from other packages.	48
The Workbench Resources page	50
The Workbench Classes page	50
The Workbench Interfaces page	52
The Workbench All Problems page.	52
Full source code edit	55
Code Assists	56
Importing and exporting with VisualAge for Java	57
Importing into VisualAge for Java	58
Exporting from VisualAge for Java	60

Chapter 3. Migrating to Java2 . . . 65
The Fix/Migrate SmartGuide	65
The repair process	68
Migrating your servlet and JSPs.	70

Chapter 4. Beginning the ATM project . . . 73
Problem domain	73
Building the ATM model	75
Use cases	76
ATM state diagrams	78
Analysis class diagram	82
Design class diagrams	84
Interaction diagram	89
Overall architecture	91
The big picture	91
GUI client	92
Browser client	93
Database access.	94
Example implementation	95
Detailed steps implementing the first class	96
Reusing existing method to create a new method	101
PrimaryKey class hierarchy.	102
Creating an inner class	103
Persistency based on HashMaps	105
Finder methods	105
Implementations of the state diagram	106
Test application	107

Chapter 5. Creating servlets . . . 109
Overview of Java servlets	109
The Java Servlet API	113
Building the ATM application servlets	116

Chapter 6. Creating JSPs 129
Java Server Pages 129
How Java Server Pages work 130
JSP interactions 131
Invoking a JSP by URL 132
    Calling a servlet from a JSP 132
JSP 0.91 and 1.0 133
Designing the JSP model 134
    Model-View-Controller (MVC) 134
    Servlet based modeling 135
Building the ATM application 138
    JSP tags 140

Chapter 7. Creating GUI applications 143
Abstract Windowing Toolkit and Java Foundation Classes refresher 143
Visual Composition Editor 144
    The Beans Palette 146
    Modification of the Beans Palette 147
    Visual Composition Editor toolbar 149
    The free-form surface 149
Working with beans in the Visual Composition Editor 150
    Adding beans 150
    Customizing Beans 151
    Naming beans 154
    Beans List 155
    Factory and variable 155
Visual Programming in action 156
    The ATM classes created 157
    Building the CardBean class 159
    Building the CardBeanHome class 164
    Building the BankAccountBean class 167
    Building the ATM application 169
    Connections 175
    Connection properties 177
    Creating connections 178

Chapter 8. Versioning your code 183
introduction to versioning 183
    Program elements 184
Workspace versus repository 185
    The workspace Is only a cache 186
    Backup or restore the workspace 187
    Clean workspace copy 188

Multiple workspaces on one repository 189
Backup or restore the repository 189
Workspace versus repository continued 190
Version control 191
Editions and versions 191
Consequences of versioning 193
How to version elements with VisualAge for Java 194
Apply this to the ATM application 197
Methods, a special case 197
Importance of versioning your code regularly 198
Fields and inner classes 199
Versioning resource files 199
Using editions 201
Method edition tab 201
Comparison result window 203
Merging compared elements 205
Types edition tab 209
Packages edition tab 210
Projects edition tab 211
Replacing current edition 213
External versioning systems 216
Import and export effects 217
Import and export with Java files 217
Import and export with repository files 218
Repository Explorer 222
Purging and restoring elements 225
Compacting a repository 226
Go To tools 228
Solutions 228

Chapter 9. Testing and debugging the Web application 231
VAJ Debugger 231
The debugger 231
The Debug Page 231
The Breakpoints Page 236
The Exceptions Page 241
External Debug 243
Generating a Class Trace 245
Performance and the Class Trace option 245
Inspectors 245
The Inspector window 246
WebSphere Test Environment (WTE) 249
Start the WebSphere Test Environment 250

Testing JSPs under WebSphere Test Environment. 254
    VisualAge for Java configuration for JSPs 254
    Running a simple JSP. 255
Debugging servlets and JSPs 257
    Debugging a servlet 257
    JSP Execution Monitor 259
    Debugging JSP generated source code 261
    Debugging JSP without importing. 262
Persistent Name Server. 262
WebSphere Test Environment — advanced configuration 265
    Types of resources 265
    Resource locations 265
    The key configuration files 266
WebSphere Test Environment — multiple Web applications. 270
    Configuring multiple Web applications 271
    Using the ServletEngineConfigDumper servlet. 273

Chapter 10. Using relational databases 275
JDBC 2.0 275
    DataSource versus DriverManager. 278
Queries and result sets 278
Stored procedures 279
Updating the database 279
Using SQLJ inside VisualAge for Java 280
Data access beans. 281
Making the ATM persistent. 285
    Prerequisites. 285
    Creating tables 286
Making the card class persistent 287
Creating the Select beans 288
    Card Select bean 288
    Card Select All bean 299
    CardAcctSelect 299
Modify beans 300
    Card Insert 301
    Card Delete. 303
    Card Update 304
    Card Visual Composition Editor View 306
    Modifying related methods 306
Data Access Beans with an application 309

Chapter 11. Internationalization 311
Java Internationalization Framework 311

Locales 311
Resource bundle. 314
Internationalization in VisualAge for Java 316
Building a language panel 320
LanguagePanel view. 320
Creating the resource bundles 321
Dynamically changing the locale 323
Loading resource bundles. 323
Retrieving resources from resource bundles 324
Finishing the LanguagePanel 324
Formatting dates and times. 328
Other internationalization considerations 331
Using predefined formats 331
Internationalization in the Web environment 336
Character codes on the Web 337

Chapter 12. Deploying the Web application 341
Before you start 341
Using WebSphere Application Server 342
Deploying a Web application. 343
Planning for multiple Web applications 348
Deploying a JSP 349
Deploying an application 349
Include Referenced Types 350
Deploying an applet 352
Web browsers. 352
CLASSPATH or CODEBASE 352
Applet Tags. 353
Deploying the ATMApplication applet 355
Deploying supporting code 355

Appendix A. JSP tag syntax. 357
JSP tag syntax summary 357
WebSphere specific tags 359

Appendix B. Using the additional material 363
Locating the additional material on the Internet 363
Using the Web material 363
System requirements for downloading the Web material. 363
How to use the Web material 364

Appendix C. Special notices 367

Appendix D. Related publications. 371
IBM Redbooks 371
IBM Redbooks collections 371
Other resources 372
Referenced Web sites 372

How to get IBM Redbooks 373
IBM Redbooks fax order form 374

Glossary 375

Abbreviations and acronyms 383

Index 385

IBM Redbooks review 391

Figures

1. The VisualAge for Java Welcome dialog box 7
2. The Quick Start dialog box. 8
3. The Create Applet SmartGuide 9
4. The Properties page of the Create Applet SmartGuide. 10
5. The Events page of Create Applet SmartGuide. 11
6. The Code Writer page of Create Applet SmartGuide 12
7. The Workbench 13
8. Your first applet running in the Applet Viewer 14
9. Class Properties window for the HiThere class 16
10. Creating the HiAgain Application 17
11. Application Attributes 18
12. The VisualAge for Java Console 20
13. The Source View window. 21
14. Launching the Scrapbook in VisualAge for Java 23
15. Evaluating Java Code in the Scrapbook 23
16. Console output for the loop executed in the Scrapbook 24
17. Using operators in the Scrapbook 25
18. An error message in the Scrapbook window 26
19. Using the Code Assist facility. 27
20. Workbench Options 29
21. The Servlet SmartGuide 32
22. Servlet SmartGuide Import Statement window 33
23. Servlet attributes 34
24. HiHttpServlet Source View. 35
25. Starting the WebSphere Test Environment 37
26. WebSphere Test Environment Control Center 38
27. Console window when starting the WTE Servlet Engine. 39
28. HiHttpServlet Output 40
29. The Workbench toolbar 43
30. Workbench Projects page 45
31. Workbench Packages page 47
32. Create Class SmartGuide: Import statement dialog box 49
33. Workbench Resources page 50
34. Workbench Classes page 51
35. Workbench Interfaces page. 52
36. Workbench All Problems page. 53
37. Warning Dialog: Undefined Variable 54
38. Source View. 56
39. Code Assists 57
40. Importing Java Files into VisualAge for Java. 59

41. Importing from another repository 60
42. The Export SmartGuide 61
43. Exporting to a Jar file 63
44. How to start the Fix/Migrate SmartGuide. 66
45. The Fix/Migrate SmartGuide window. 67
46. Fix/Migrate SmartGuide- Excluded packages- 68
47. ATM use case diagram 77
48. ATM state diagram. 79
49. Sub state Diagram of ATM In Use State 80
50. Analysis class diagram 83
51. ATM related part of the design model 85
52. Design class diagram related to primary keys 86
53. Transaction 87
54. TransactionAbortedException diagram 88
55. Sequence diagram for the 'get money' scenario 90
56. Architectural diagram. 92
57. Specify BigInteger as superclass. 97
58. Second page of 'Create new class' SmartGuide for Money 98
59. Skeleton method in class browser. 100
60. Overview of communication between Web browser and servlet 111
61. Multiple requests reaching the servlet 113
62. Workbench after creating the eight servlets. 118
63. ShowATMServlet in the Web browser 123
64. InsertCardServlet in the Web browser. 125
65. EnterPINServlet in the Web browser 126
66. EnterPINServlet in the Web browser — invalid PIN 126
67. ChooseAccountServlet 127
68. ChooseActionServlet 127
69. EnterAmountServlet. 128
70. ChooseActionServlet — View Transaction History selected by user. . . . 128
71. The JSP processing life-cycle on first-time invocation. 131
72. Sample JSP including a servlet 133
73. Sample JSP forwarding processing to a servlet 133
74. Model-View-Controller design 135
75. Servlet-only model 136
76. Servlet-JSP model 137
77. The Visual Composition Editor. 145
78. Nonvisual Bean Icons 146
79. The Beans Palette with Swing 147
80. Modifying the Beans Palette 148
81. Modify Palette dialog box. 148
82. Selection and Choose Bean tools on the Palette. 150
83. Choose Bean Dialog 151

84. Property sheet of a JTextField bean 152
85. Bean pop-up menu for class and variable 154
86. The finished ATM Applets 156
87. Classes defined in com.ibm.itso.sg245264.atm.memory package 157
88. Classes defined in com.ibm.itso.sg245264.atm,database package 158
89. Add package window. 159
90. Create Class SmartGuide 160
91. Create Class SmartGuide — Attributes window 161
92. BeanInfo window for CardBean Class 162
93. Create Class CardBeanHome -— Attributes window 165
94. Create class BankAccountBean — Attributes window. 167
95. Create the ATMApplication Applet. 169
96. Create ATMApplication — Applet Properties window 170
97. The Beans List. 171
98. JAppletContentPane Property sheet 172
99. Choose CardBeanHome Bean 173
100.Choose CardBean bean 174
101.The ATMApplication View. 174
102.ATMApplication connection view. 180
103.The ATMApplication applet view 181
104.Versionable program elements 184
105.Interaction between IDE components, workspace, and repository 185
106.Exit dialog of VisualAge. 186
107.Basic state diagram for editions 192
108.Project browser menu bar 195
109.Popup menu for a package expanded on the Manage option. 195
110.Versioning dialog window 196
111.Dialog to specify the name of each sub-element 196
112.'Show edition names' — toggle. 197
113.Using the popup menu on a method to go directly to its edition tab 201
114.Edition tab in method browser showing a list view of available editions . 202
115.Hierarchical view of the editions on the edition tab 203
116.Comparison result window in action 204
117.Replace with Alternative option to merge source 206
118.Shadow objects are unchangeable warning 207
119.The two versions of the 'Compare With' popup menu submenu. 208
120.Edition tab in class browser. 209
121.Edition tab in Package Browser 210
122.Edition tab in project browser 212
123.'Replace Wtlh' submenu available from many places. 213
124.Replacement dialog for a class element 214
125.Replacement Dialog for resource files 215
126.Add To Workspace from the edition popup menu 215

127. Create package SmartGuide. 216
128. Export to a repository file, second page of SmartGuide 219
129. Specify the packages and the editions to export. 220
130. Import from resource file dialog. 221
131. Repository Explorer e on package tab 223
132. Repository Explorer showing the available projects 224
133. Confirmation before purging elements 225
134. Restore purged items 226
135. Cannot compact the repository while there are open editions 227
136. Compacting will remove open editions and will create a backup 227
137. Go To dialog 228
138. Solutions are manipulated in the Repository Explorer 229
139. Popup menu for solution list 229
140. Solution export dialogs 230
141. Debug Page Toolbar. 232
142. Debugger option 233
143. Running programs in the Debugger 234
144. Watches window 235
145. Evaluation window. 235
146. Breakpoints Page toolbar 236
147. Breakpoint in the Paint Method 238
148. Conditional Breakpoint Configuring Dialog Box 240
149. Breakpoint Configuring Dialog Box: Printing Diagnostics 241
150. Exceptions. 242
151. External method breakpoint dialogs 244
152. An Inspector window 246
153. Changing the Value of a Field. 247
154. Evaluating Code in the Context of an Object 248
155. WebSphere Test Environment 249
156. WebSphere Test Environment Control Center 250
157. WebSphere Test Environment Class Path 251
158. Servlet Engine Console Status 252
159. HiHttpServlet output 253
160. The default_app.webapp: JSP 1.0 configuration. 255
161. The default_app.webapp: JSP 0.91 configuration. 255
162. Very simple JSP response 256
163. Very simple JSP source 256
164. Debugging the HiHttpServlet. 258
165. ServletEngineRunner threads 259
166. JSP Execution Monitor options 260
167. JSP Execution Monitor window 261
168. JSP settings 262
169. Persistence Name Server settings 263

170. Persistence Name Server console 263
171. DataSource configuration 264
172. Servlet engine configuration 274
173. Add a JDBC driver to the workspace classpath 277
174. dialog during translation process. 280
175. Workspace SQLJ menu 281
176. SQLJ Properties window. 281
177. Relationship between the select and modify objects. 284
178. CreateTable class 286
179. Change the VCE palette to the data access beans. 287
180. Choose the Select data access bean 287
181. Properties window for the Select bean 288
182. New database access class 289
183. Connection Alias Definition 290
184. New SQL Specification 291
185. SQL Assist SmartGuide — Tables 292
186. SQL Assist SmartGuide — Condition 1 293
187. SQL Assist SmartGuide — Columns 294
188. SQL Assist SmartGuide — SQL. 295
189. Specify Parameter Values. 296
190. SQL Execution Result Set. 296
191. Created SQLs 298
192. SelectAllSQL Result 299
193. CardAcctSelectSQL 300
194. Modify Bean 301
195. SQL Assist SmartGuide — Insert 301
196. SQL Assist SmartGuide — Insert Value. 302
197. Insert 302
198. SQL Assist SmartGuide — Delete 303
199. SQL Assist SmartGuide — Update Values 304
200. SQL Assist SmartGuide — Update Statement. 305
201. Card Visual Composition Editor 306
202. CardQuery Applet — Visual Composition Editor 310
203. AllLocaleList connections 313
204. AllLocaleList applet 314
205. Externalizing strings 317
206. String externalization editor. 319
207. The LanguagePanel in the Visual Composition Editor 321
208. Externalizing the SelectLanguageLabel 322
209. LanguagePanel connection. 327
210. Running LanguagePanel. 328
211. LanguagePanel View2 329
212. LanguagePanel Output with dates and times 331

213. setting up converter manually 338
214. Show Config Servlet 339
215. Web Application name 344
216. Parent Servlet Engine 344
217. Add a Servlet -— Select the ITSO Web Application 346
218. Select ATM.jar. 346
219. Specify the Servlet class 347
220. WebSphere Standard Administrative Console 348
221. Exporting the ATM to a jar File 351
222. Testing the ATM Application 351
223. Class diagram 365
224. JavaDoc 366

Tables

1. Object-oriented terms ... 6
2. Default VisualAge for Java projects and their contents ... 42
3. .Toolbar icon descriptions ... 44
4. JSP conversion map ... 71
5. Terms used ... 109
6. The stages of the servlet life-cycle ... 114
7. Methods used to request a servlet ... 116
8. All servlets needed for the ATM application ... 117
9. Scope ... 120
10. Differences between workspace and repository ... 191
11. Accessing relational data in Java ... 275
12. Summary of data access beans ... 282
13. Summary of JSP tag syntax ... 357
14. IBM extensions to JSP for variable data ... 360
15. WebSphere scripting language extensions (XML format only) ... 361

Preface

This IBM Redbook provides you with sufficient information to effectively use the VisualAge for Java Professional Edition Version 3.5 environments to create, manage, and deploy Web-based applications using methodologies centered around servlets, applets, Java Server Pages, and JavaBean architectures.

This book is intended to be read by anyone who requires both introductory and detailed information on software development in the Java and Web-based application environment using applets, servlets, and Java Server Pages. We assume that you have a good understanding of Java and some knowledge of HTML.

We describe the Java development though the VisualAge for Java product. Following this, we cover Java applications, Java applets, servlets, and JSP programming, and 3-tier application design concepts. Using the knowledge developed in these chapters, we then provide detailed information on the development environments offered by VisualAge for Java. These chapters will assist you in using the features offered by these tools, such as integrated debugging, the WebSphere Test Environment, and publishing of Web site resources.

The team that wrote this redbook

This redbook was produced by a team of specialists from around the world working at the International Technical Support Organization San Jose Center.

Osamu Takagiwa is an Advisory I/T Specialist with the IBM International Technical Support Organization, San Jose Center. He writes extensively and teaches IBM classes worldwide on all areas of Application Development. Before joining the ITSO 4 months ago, Osamu worked in IBM Japan as an I/T Specialist.

Frederik Haesbrouck is a Java Architect working for his company FreWare bvba in Belgium. He graduated as a computer scientist at the University of Ghent in 1995. After some experience as an employee of different firms including Alcatell Bell, IBM Belgium, and eXpanded Media, he started working as an independent Java Architect contractor all over.

Veronique Quiblier is an Application Development Specialist with IBM Technical Sales for EMEA. She has 15 years of experience in the field of application development.

Sarah Poger is a programming manager with SunGard Futures Systems in Chicago, Illinois. She has over 5 years of application development and architecture experience, primarily in the finance sector. She is currently working on several Internet applications targeted for brokerage firms.

Thanks to the following people for their invaluable contributions to this project:

Ueli Wahli
International Technical Support Organization, San Jose Center for his ongoing support in all aspects of application development and redbook publishing

John McLean
Program Director Language Products, IBM Silicon Valley Lab

Comments welcome

Your comments are important to us!

We want our Redbooks to be as helpful as possible. Please send us your comments about this or other Redbooks in one of the following ways:

- Fax the evaluation form found in "IBM Redbooks review" on page 391 to the fax number shown on the form.
- Use the online evaluation form found at `ibm.com`/redbooks
- Send your comments in an Internet note to `redbook@us.ibm.com`

Chapter 1. Introduction to the environment

VisualAge for Java product is IBM's integrated, visual development environment for building Java applications, servlets, applets, and Java Beans. VisualAge for Java supports the complete cycle of Java program development. Using the true rapid application development (RAD) capability provided by VisualAge for Java, you can shorten the development life cycle of your applications and improve their time to market.

VisualAge for Java is a comprehensive, best-of-breed Java tool for creating e-business applications that target the IBM WebSphere software platform for e-business — the industry's most flexible and reliable e-business foundation for the rapid development and delivery of a brave new world of e-business applications. The ability to rapidly build, test, and deploy e-business applications sets VisualAge for Java apart from its competition.

In this chapter you will find a short description of the VisualAge for Java product family and an overview of VisualAge for Java Version 3.5. You will learn the basic terms that you need to understand to create your first program. Before you finish reading this chapter, you will have your first Java program up and running on the Web!

VisualAge for Java product family

VisualAge for Java Version 3.5 is available in four editions:

- VisualAge for Java Professional Edition
- VisualAge for Java Entry Professional Edition
- VisualAge for Java Enterprise Edition
- VisualAge for Java Entry Enterprise Edition

This book covers the VisualAge for Java Version 3.5 Professional Edition and the VisualAge for Java Version 3.5 Entry Professional Edition, without describing the features of VisualAge for Java Enterprise Edition and VisualAge for Java Entry Enterprise Edition.

IBM also has several other offerings related to VisualAge for Java, including:

- VisualAge Developer Domain (VADD)

    VisualAge Developer Domain (VADD) is Java developer's central access point for products, JavaBeans, tools, tech tips, demos and samples, product support, and product updates. In addition, VADD gives you access to an ever-expanding technical library of Java information, including newsletters, IBM Redbooks, technical articles, white papers, IBM Systems

Journal articles, product documentation, FAQs, presentations, and educational opportunities. VADD is also a great place for you to exchange information with a worldwide community of Java developers through the forums and newsgroups. VADD offers you different access levels, depending on your needs.

You can learn more about VisualAge Developers Domain at:

>   www.software.ibm.com/vadd

- WebSphere Application Server

  IBM WebSphere Application Server is an e-business application deployment environment built on open standards-based technology. It is the cornerstone of WebSphere application offerings and services. The Standard Edition lets you use Java servlets, Java Server Pages and XML to quickly transform static Web sites into vital sources of dynamic Web content. The Advanced Edition is a high-performance EJB server for implementing EJB components that incorporate business logic. The Enterprise Edition integrates EJB and CORBA components to build high-transaction, high-volume e-business applications.

VisualAge for Java Professional Edition

VisualAge for Java Professional Edition is an integrated visual environment that supports the complete cycle of Java program development. VisualAge for Java gives you everything you need to perform the development tasks. described below. The IDE includes:

- Incremental compiler

  Changes to your code are compiled "on-the-fly" as you work with individual methods and class declarations. Errors in your code are immediately flagged so that they can be fixed while you are concentrating on that part of the code.

- Repository-based environment

  All of the code in the development environment is stored in a *repository*. This repository enables incremental compilation and provides for very powerful search capabilities. The code that you are working with is stored in a *workspace*. Version management is built into the repository, and versions or *editions* of code are automatically stored when you change any *program element* (method, class, package, or project) in your workspace.

VisualAge for Java Professional Edition is a single-user, repository-based environment. If you work as part of a development team, you may want to consider using VisualAge for Java Enterprise Edition.

- Project-based development

    VisualAge for Java provides *projects.* The basic Java environments provide only the concept of a package to organize your work. In VisualAge for Java you organize your packages in projects.

- Source code editor

    A full-featured syntax editor, which helps you write error-free source code.

- Advanced coding tools such as automatic formatting, automatic code completion, fix-on-save, and suggested corrections feature

- An integrated debugger

- A Visual Composition Editor, which enables you to develop your application visually

- A JavaBean creation tool to create 100% pure Java beans that you can use with the Visual Composition Editor

New powerful features that come with Version 3.5 of VisualAge for Java Professional Edition include:

- Full Java 2 SDK, Standard Edition, V1.2.2 support
    - JDK 1.2.2
    - Swing 1.1

- Fix/Migrate SmartGuide assists with Swing 1.0.3 ->Swing 1.1 Migration

- Full source code editing

    The new option Open Source View provides you with another way to view entire source in editor. Code assist is available in source view. The file format/order is preserved. The editor-oriented programmers should like this!

- Improved inner class support

    You can Browse/Edit inner classes/methods like normal classes/methods in IDE.

- Manage non-Java artifacts from Resources view

    Non-Java artifacts are not stored in repository. They are managed based on date/time stamp when resources are released

- Enhanced code formatting

- Servlet SmartGuide generates servlets, JSP files, and prototype HTML

- All Problems page filtering

    Filter warnings/errors on All Problems page
- New WebSphere Test Environment Control Center

    You can Start/Stop Servlet Engine, Start/Stop Persistent Name Server (PNS), Set JSP Execution Monitor Settings and Define Data Sources

VisualAge for Java Entry Professional Edition

The VisualAge for Java Entry Professional Edition provides the same functions as VisualAge for Java Professional, with a limit of 750 Java types (classes and interfaces).

To download VisualAge for Java, Entry Professional Edition, Version 3.5 you must be a registered user of VisualAge Developer Domain and logged in. Registration is free.

VisualAge Developer Domain(VADD) Web site:

    www.software.ibm.com/vadd

VisualAge for Java Enterprise Edition

VisualAge for Java Enterprise Edition is an enterprise-aware, Java application development environment for teams of Java developers. Use it to extend existing server data, transactions, and applications to e-business.

In addition to the functions in the Professional Edition, VisualAge for Java V3.5 Enterprise Edition supports:

- Updated Enterprise Access Builder (EAB) functionality that consolidates connectors at a JDK 1.2.2 level and positions customers for compliance to the emerging Java 2 Platform, Enterprise Edition JCX API.
- Enhanced Enterprise Access Builders (CICS TS, IMS, Encina, MQSeries, TXSeries, Host-On Demand, and SAP R/3) that provide more connectivity than any other Java IDE.
- Test client generation that speeds testing of server side Java code (EJB components). Also generates clients to Enterprise Access Builders connectors.
- Enterprise JavaBeans components. Generation of and complete support for the EJB specification, through wizards, persistent mapping tools, dependency management, and improved test and advanced deployment tools.

- XMI Toolkit for integration with the Rational Rose product, and other XMI-based UML modelling tools.
- Interface definition language (IDL) development environment and improved support for multiple object request brokers (ORBs), which can now be loaded into and unloaded from the development environment.

VisualAge for Java Entry Enterprise Edition

The VisualAge for Java Entry Enterprise Edition provides the same functions as VisualAge for Java Enterprise Edition, with a limit of 750 Java types (classes and interfaces).

To download VisualAge for Java, Entry Enterprise Edition, Version 3.5, you must be registered user of VisualAge Developer Domain and logged in. Registration is free.

VisualAge Developer Domain(VADD) Web site:

```
www.software.ibm.com/vadd
```

Updates to VisualAge Java

Updates to the different editions of VisualAge Java are provided at the VisualAge Developer Domain (VADD) Web site:

```
www.software.ibm.com/vadd
```

Building your first applet

Now that you have an idea of the capabilities of VisualAge for Java, you can build your first applet.

Before starting, you should familiarize yourself with the terms in Table 1. If you are not familiar with any of the terms in Table 1 or you are new to the Java language itself, first read some of the resources listed in "Locating the additional material on the Internet" on page 363.

Table 1. Object-oriented terms

Term	Definition
Class	A template for creating objects. A class defines the behavior and properties that are common to all objects of that class.
Interface	A specification of behavior that a class must provide if it implements the interface.
Object	An instance of a class. An object shares the behavior of all objects of the same class, but each object can have a different state.
Applet	A special kind of class introduced in Java. Its instances usually run in a Web browser such a Netscape Navigator. Contrast with *Application*.
JApplet	If you want to use Swing components in the applet, use JApplet as the super class rather then Applet.
Swing Set	Swing Set = JFC (Java Foundation Classes) JFCs are building blocks that are helpful in developing interfaces to Java applications. They allow Java applications to interact more completely with existing operating systems.
Application	In Java programming, a self-contained, stand-alone Java program that includes a static main method. It does not require an applet viewer. Contrast with Applet.
Attribute or field	A data variable held by a class.
Access modifier	In Java the access modifiers are public, private, protected, and default or package.
Method or Message	Objects communicate with each other by sending messages. When an object receives a message, a corresponding method, defined in the class definition, is invoked to perform the required task.
Package	A collection of Java classes that typically serve a common purpose. This is Java's way of organizing classes into logical entities that are easier to maintain and understand than a huge set of classes at the same level.
Server	The computer that hosts the Web page that contains an applet. The .class files that make up the applet, and the .HTML files that reference the applet reside on the server.
Servlet	Server-side programs that execute on and add function to Web servers. Java servlets allow for the creation of high-performance, cross-platform Web applications.

Let's get started!

Before you go any further, you must have VisualAge for Java installed on your computer. Your first Java class is a simple applet that displays the text of your choice in the applet's window. You launch VisualAge for Java by double-clicking the **IBM VisualAge for Java** icon in the IBM VisualAge for Java folder or selecting **Start→Programs→IBM VisualAge for Java for Windows→IBM VisualAge for Java**.

If this is the first time you have started VisualAge for Java, a dialog box will inform you that some features are being installed. Next, the Welcome to VisualAge dialog box (see Figure 1) is displayed. The Welcome to VisualAge dialog box is shown when you start the VisualAge for Java IDE, unless you deselect the checkbox at the bottom of the window. Click **Close** to close the dialog box.

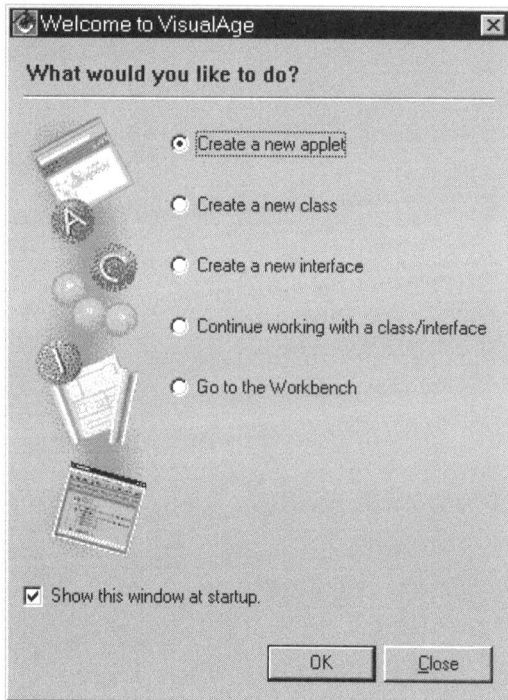

Figure 1. The VisualAge for Java Welcome dialog box

A different dialog, the Quick Start, can also be used to start. The Quick Start is available from the **Workbench→File** menu (see Figure 2).

The Workbench window opens the first time you start VisualAge for Java. The Workbench is where you usually create and manipulate your classes. From the Workbench you can launch the Quick Start window. Open the Quick Start now, by selecting **File→Quick Start** from the menu bar.

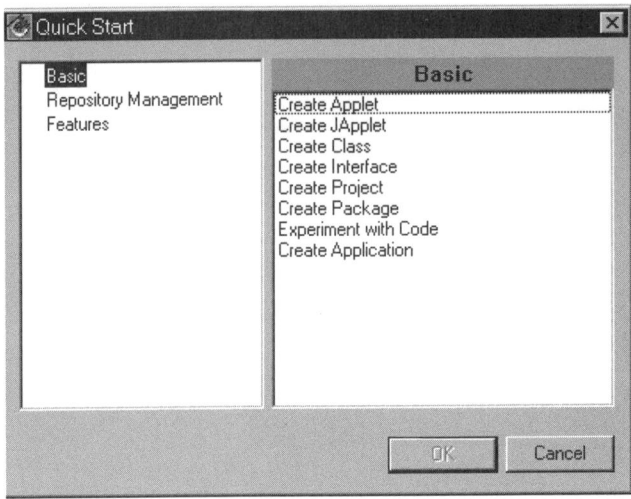

Figure 2. The Quick Start dialog box

Using the Quick Start dialog, you can select from three options:

- **Basic:** Create a new Applet, JApplet, Class, Interface, Project or Application, or experiment with code.
- **Repository Management:** Compact the repository.
- **Features:** Add or Delete features to your environment.

You are going to create an applet, so select **Basic→Create Applet** and click **OK**.

SmartGuide

VisualAge for Java uses SmartGuides (which are similar to Wizards in other products) to help you create Java applets, servlets and applications. Clicking the **OK** button on the Quick Start window opens the Create Applet SmartGuide (Figure 3), which guides you through the process of creating your new applet class.

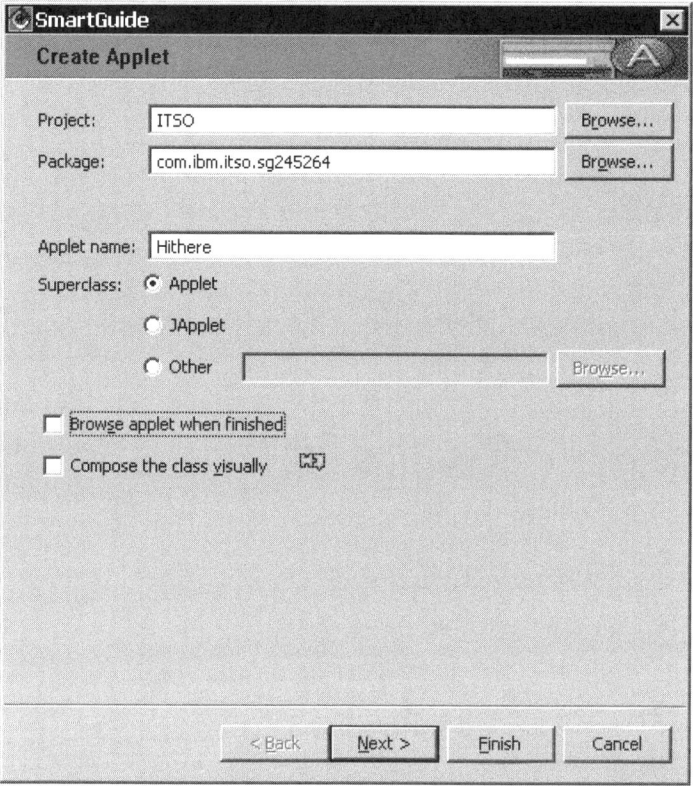

Figure 3. The Create Applet SmartGuide

To create your applet, fill in the text fields (Project, Package, and Applet name) as shown in Figure 3. Leave **Applet** selected as **Super class.** This means that java.applet.Applet class is used as your Super class. Deselect the **Browse applet when finished** and **Compose the class visually** checkboxes. We discuss Visual Programming in Chapter 7, "Creating GUI applications" on page 143.

Click the **Next** button to access the second page of the SmartGuide. Note that the project is a folder which provides a way to organize your Java and related codes. We also discuss this in Chapter 2, "Organizing your code" on page 41.

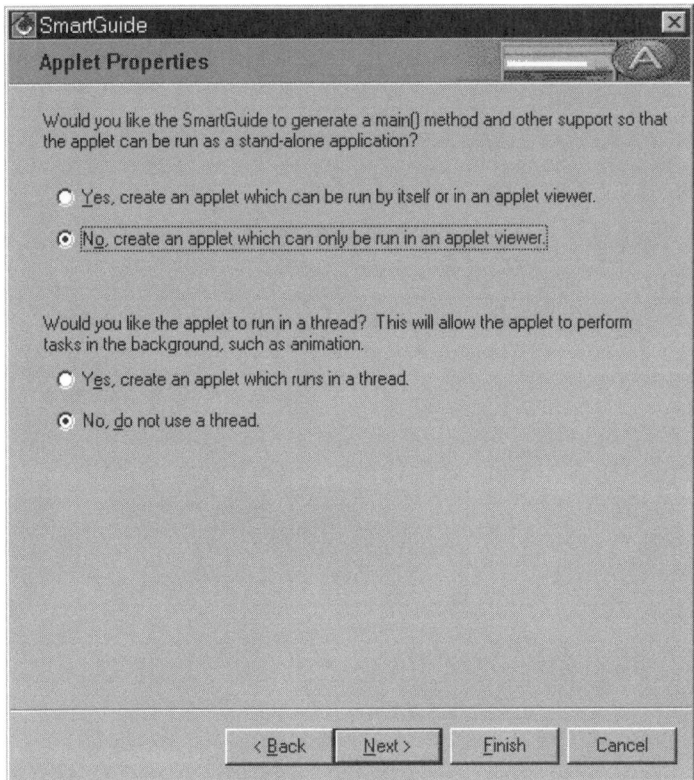

Figure 4. The Properties page of the Create Applet SmartGuide

These options are:

- Create for main method, which creates a Frame window class and instantiates your applet inside.
- Your applet can contain threads. You also can add thread programming manually.

Leave the default selections (see Figure 4) and click the **Next** button.

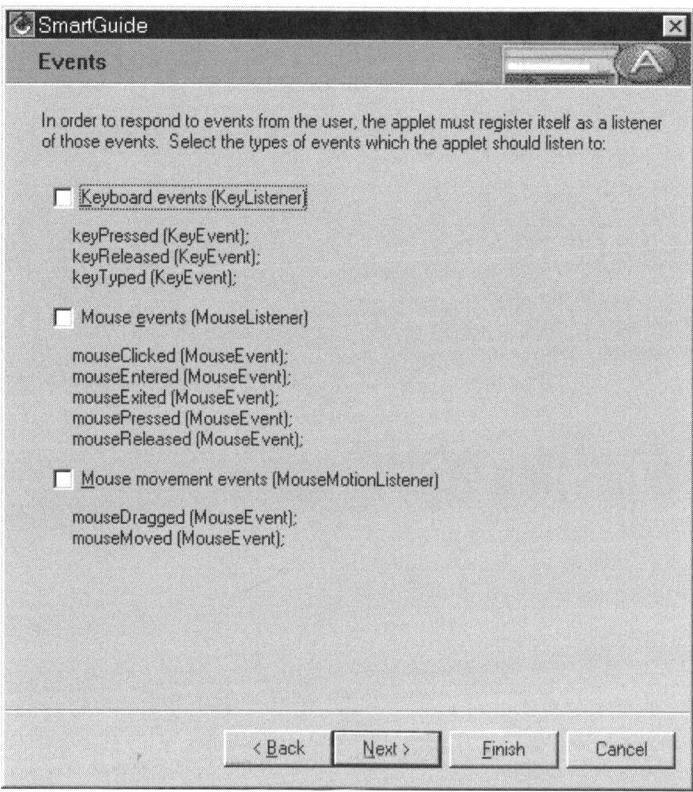

Figure 5. The Events page of Create Applet SmartGuide

These options creates an event-handler method in your applet class. As your first applet does not use any events, just click the **Next** button (Figure 5).

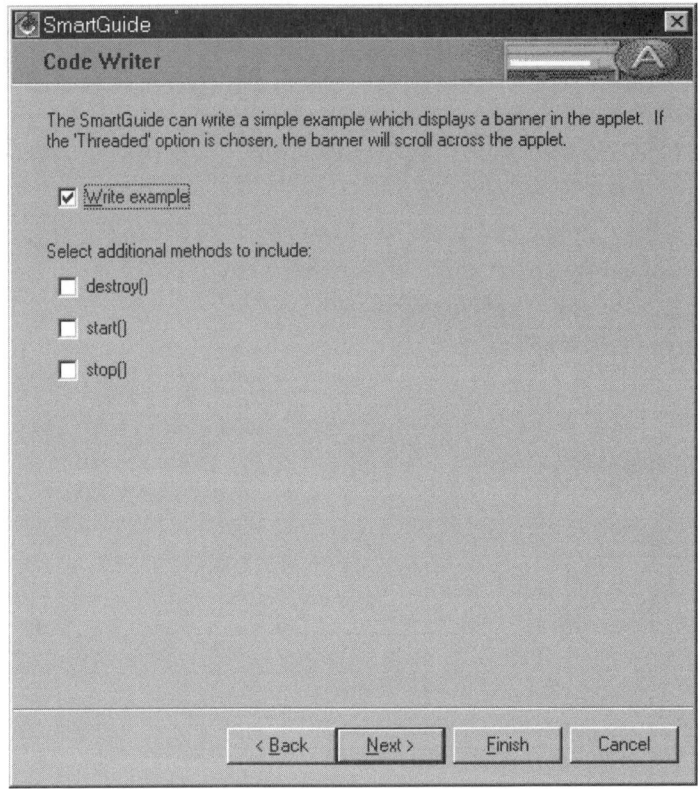

Figure 6. The Code Writer page of Create Applet SmartGuide

Select the **Write example** checkbox and click the **Finish** button as shown in Figure 6. VisualAge for Java now creates the code needed for your new applet. The dialog closes and lets you work with the Workbench window (see Figure 7).

Believe it or not, you have just created your first applet with VisualAge for Java! Now you can use the WorkBench to examine and run your applet.

The Workbench

The Workbench is the main control center of the VisualAge for Java IDE. From the Workbench, you can access projects, packages, and classes; and you can modify and test your code with just a few mouse clicks.

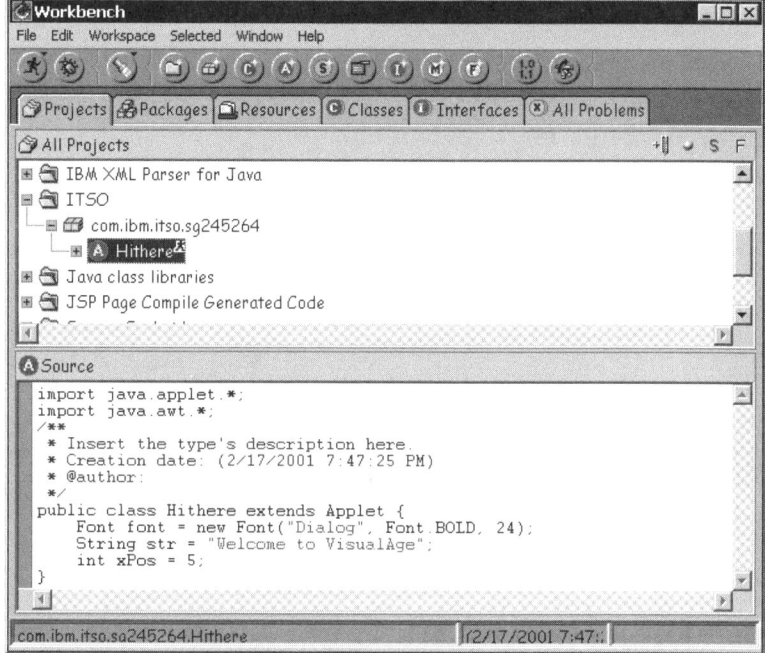

Figure 7. The Workbench

To test your newly created applet, click the plus sign next to your project and your package to expand them and then select the **HiThere applet**. Select **Selected→Run→In Applet Viewer** from the menu bar of the Workbench to run the applet. You can also run your applet by clicking the **Run** button (the left-most button with the picture of a person running).

The Applet Viewer opens and runs your applet (Figure 8). The Applet Viewer is a utility that lets you test your applets without having to use a Web browser. You may have to resize the window to see the complete message.

Figure 8. Your first applet running in the Applet Viewer

Congratulations, you have built and tested your first applet with VisualAge for Java!

Modifying your applet

To modify the applet to show different text, select your class in the Workbench. The class definition of the applet is displayed in the Source pane of the Workbench window and looks like this:

```
import java.applet.*;
import java.awt.*;
/**
 * Insert the type's description here.
 * Creation date: (11/16/2000 11:54:36 PM)
 * @author:
 */
public class HiThere extends Applet {
    Font font = new Font("Dialog", Font.BOLD, 24);
    String str = "Welcome to VisualAge";
    int xPos = 5;
}
```

To change the text "Welcome to VisualAge" to any string you like, just type over the text. Save your changes by selecting **Edit→Save** from the menu bar. VisualAge for Java compiles the code immediately, and you can test the result by again selecting **Selected→Run→In Applet Viewer** from the menu bar.

You do not even have to close the Applet Viewer to see the changes! Change and save the text, then select **Applet→Reload** from the menu bar of the running Applet Viewer.

This simple example shows how VisualAge for Java can help you create Java programs. You did not have to edit, save or compile any file. You simply changed the code generated automatically by VisualAge for Java, saved it, and ran it. This reduced development time is a reality, thanks to the incremental compiler, which compiles changes to your code on the fly when you save it.

Creating an animated applet

Now that you are becoming more familiar with the VisualAge for Java IDE, it is time to create your second applet. With VisualAge for Java, it is easy to create applets that scroll text from one side of the applet to another.

This time you create a new class without using the Quick Start. Instead, expand the Programming ITSO project by clicking on the + (plus sign) and then select the `com.ibm.itso.sg245264` package. Next, click on the **Create Applet** icon (the one with the capital A on it) on the tool bar of the Workbench. The SmartGuide appears again, requesting you to fill in information about your second applet. Because you selected the package, the Project and Package fields are already filled in (if not use the same names as in your first applet). Enter `HiThereAgain` in the *Applet Name* field and make sure the **Browse applet when finished** checkbox is not selected. Click the **Next>** button to access the **Applet Properties** page. Select the **Yes, create an applet which runs in a thread** radio button, and click the **Next** button. From the **Events** page, just click the **Next** button. Select **Write example** checkbox from the **Code Writer** page and click the **Finish** button.

Run the applet by selecting it in the Workbench and then selecting **Selected→Run→In Applet Viewer** from the menu bar.

Your application should show a marquee text scrolling from left to right. You have just built an animated applet.

Changing the properties of the applet

An HTML applet tag is required to run an applet within a browser, and within that tag there are some required fields. VisualAge for Java automatically creates the applet tag for you. If you want to change any of the properties or add new ones, you open the Properties window for the class. Select the **HiThere** class in the Workbench and then select **Selected→Properties**. The window shown in Figure 9 appears.

The first time you ran your HiThere applet (Figure 8 on page 14), the applet size was not perfect. On the Applet page of the Properties window, change the *Width* to 300 and the *Height* to 100 and run your applet again. In the other pages of this window you can set the Class path for the applet (where the Applet Viewer looks for external classes) and see other properties of the class. If this class were a Java application (which you are about to build), you could set the command line parameters here.

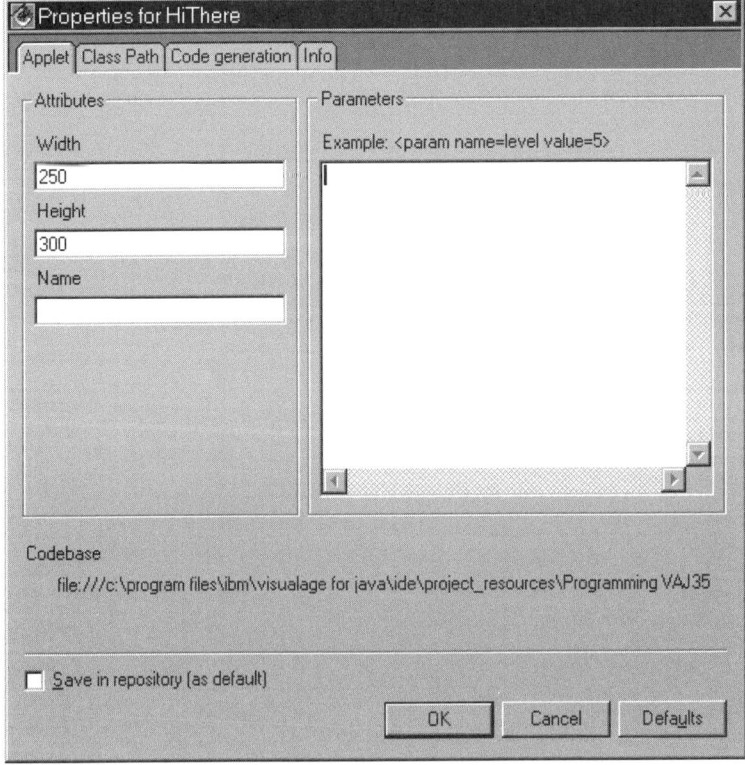

Figure 9. Class Properties window for the HiThere class

16 Programming with VisualAge for Java Version 3.5

Building your first application

In this section you create a Java application that prints a string to the VisualAge for Java Console. The Console is a window that displays messages sent by your application to the standard output of the operating system and where you enter input for your applications. To create a class that can be run as an application, without the Applet Viewer or a Web browser, you have to implement a method called main in your class.

Now start creating your application. In the Workbench, select the package you created (com.ibm.itso.sg245264), then select **Selected→Add→Class** from the menu bar. Enter HiAgain in the **Class Name** field (see Figure 10).

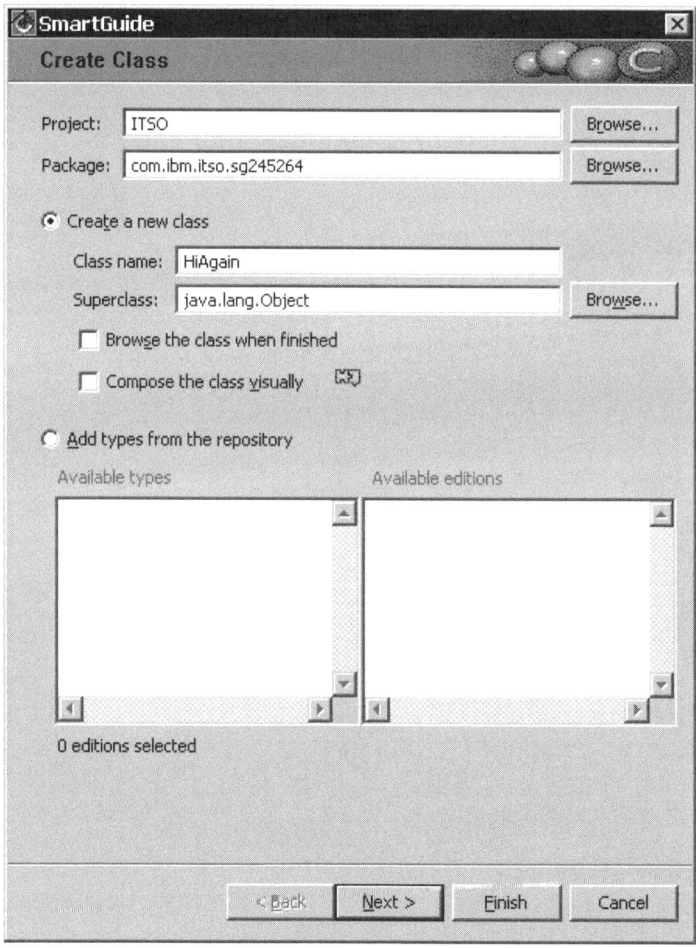

Figure 10. Creating the HiAgain Application

When you created your applet, the super class was java.applet.Applet. Now because you are creating a class that does not need a user interface and does not reuse the behavior of other objects, the super class is java.lang.Object.

Deselect the **Browse the class when finished** and **Compose the class visually** checkboxes.

Click the **Next>** button to access the second page of the SmartGuide (Figure 11), where you specify attributes of your new class.

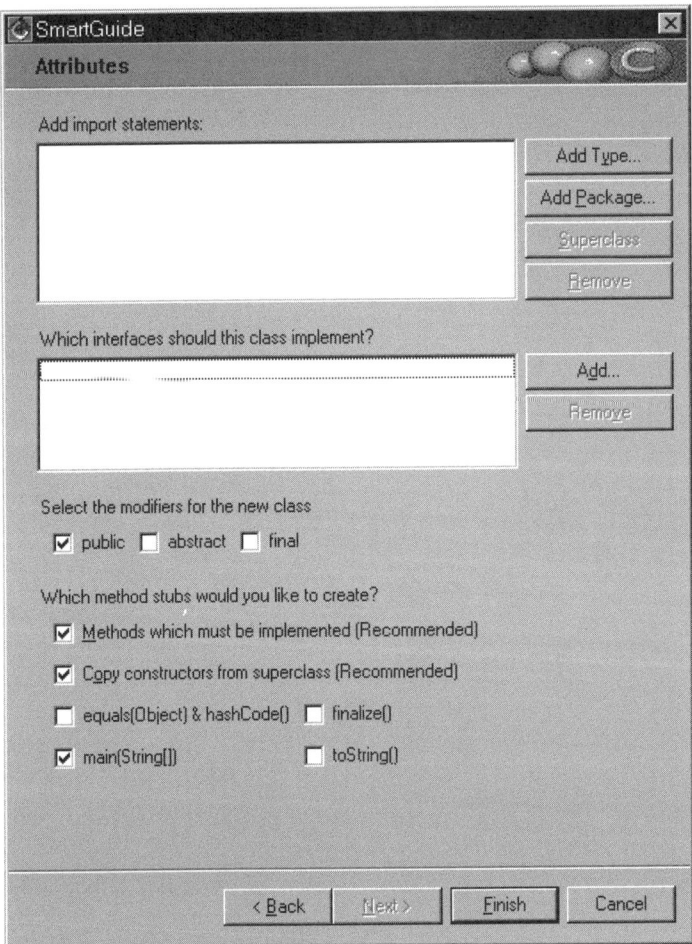

Figure 11. Application Attributes

Select the **main(String []**) checkbox under *Which method stubs would you like to create* and click the **Finish** button. VisualAge for Java creates a class declaration and constructor for `HiAgain` and a stub, or skeleton code, for the `main` method.

VisualAge for Java can automatically generate method skeletons for:

- The common methods listed on the SmartGuide
- Constructors declared in the super class
- Methods that must be implemented because of abstract inheritance or interfaces that the class implements

In the Source pane of the Workbench you can see the definition of your newly created class. In the Browse pane, expand the class by clicking the plus sign to the left of it, and you can see the *main* method. Select this method, and the Source pane shows you the method implementation. Only a stub of the method has been generated, but you can change that by adding the following code to the method body:

```
System.out.println("This is my first application!");
```

The `System.out.println()` statement prints a string to the standard output, which in turn is displayed in the VisualAge for Java Console window.

Your main method should now look like this:

```
/**
 * Starts the application.
 * @param args an array of command-line arguments
 */
public static void main(java.lang.String[] args) {
    // Insert code to start the application here.
    System.out.println("This is my first application...!");
}
```

Save the changes you made, using the menu bar (**Edit**→**Save**) or the Control-S key combination, and you are ready to see the results of your work. Select **Selected**→**Run**→**Run Main** from the menu bar. The **Console** window (Figure 12) opens to display the result. Notice that you do not have to select the class itself; the Run function knows which class you are working with and runs that class.

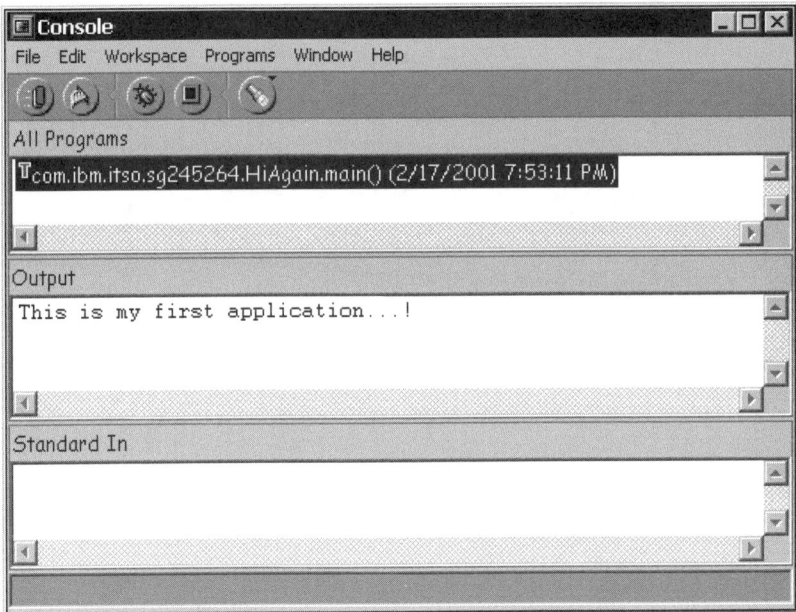

Figure 12. The VisualAge for Java Console

You have successfully created a Java application. The Console window displaying the text that your application generated is used as a standard output window for messages and for entering input through the standard input.

For each Java program that writes to or reads from the Console that you are running, the Console shows a line in the All Programs pane. To view the output or enter input for that program, select it in the All Programs pane.

Running a program as an applet and application

With VisualAge for Java, you can easily build an applet that can be run as an application: Your applet has to implement the *main* method to handle opening a window without an Applet Viewer or a Web browser.

To create this kind of applet, click the **Applet** icon in the tool bar, and the SmartGuide creates the necessary implementation for you. After providing names for the project, package, and class, select the **Next** button to access the Applet Properties SmartGuide. Select the Yes, create an **Applet which can be run by itself or in an Applet Viewer** radio button, and click the **Next** button. Click the **Next** button in the Events page. From the Code Writer page, select the **Write example** radio button and click the **Finish** button. Notice that the **Selected→Run** menu has both **Run Main** and **In Applet Viewer** options available if you select the class in the workbench.

The VisualAge for Java Source View window

The Source View window enables you to view a complete class, including all of its methods. In this view, you can see and edit the class definition and all of the methods of a class at one time. The fields and methods of the class are listed in the **Elements** pane. The Source View contains a method and field tree that is dynamically updated

Select the HiThere class in the Workbench and then select **Selected→Open Source View** from the menu bar. The window shown in Figure 13 appears.

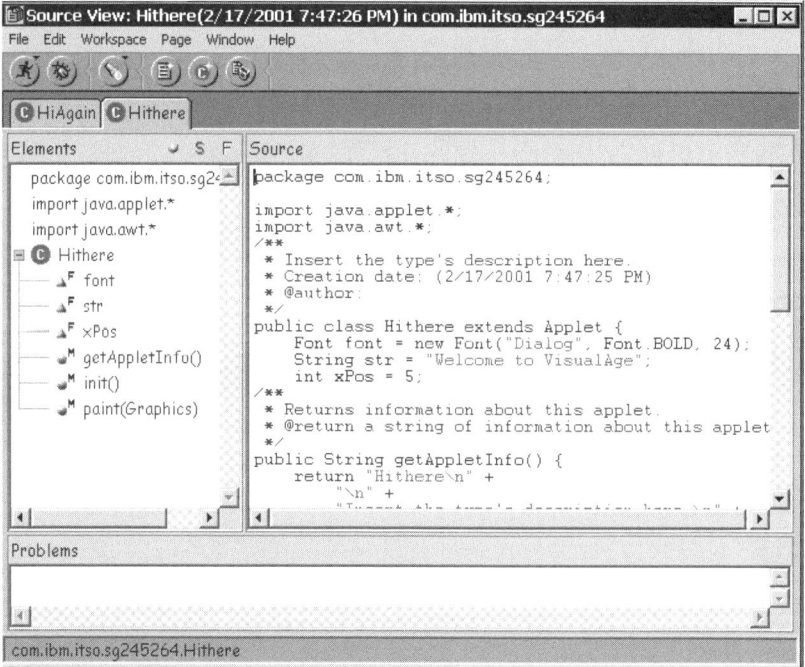

Figure 13. The Source View window

To modify the applet to show different text, double-click on the **str** field within the elements pane. The code is then highlighted in the Source pane. To change the text "Welcome to VAJ", just type over the text. The incremental compiler bring errors, if any, in the Problems pane at the bottom of the window. Save your changes by selecting **Edit→Save** from the menu bar. You can test the result by clicking the **Run** button (the left-most button with the picture of the running person).

You can work with more then one class at a time. In the Source View window, select the **Open Type** button (the one with the capital C on it) and type *hi* as **Pattern**, select *HiAgain* from the **Type names** list and select the **OK** button. From the Source View Window you can select the class you want to work with by selecting the appropriate class button (just below the menu bar buttons).

The VisualAge for Java Scrapbook

The Scrapbook enables you to evaluate Java expressions. Just type in any expression, highlight it, and execute it. The Scrapbook can have several pages. You can consider each page of the Scrapbook to be a separate JVM that compiles or runs separate code fragments. The Scrapbook can also be used to edit and import files.

Using the Scrapbook

To enter and run Java code in the Scrapbook:

From the Workbench menu bar select **Window→Scrapbook** (Figure 14) to display the Scrapbook window (Figure 15).

Type some Java code (for example, the code shown in Figure 15) into the Scrapbook and highlight the text by using the mouse or the shift and cursor keys.

From the menu bar select **Edit→Run** or click the **Run** button on the tool bar.

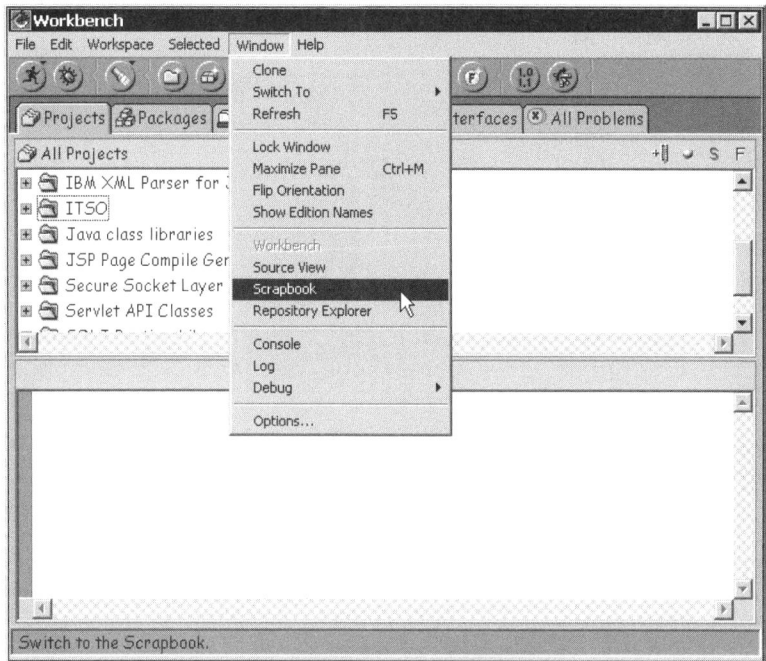

Figure 14. Launching the Scrapbook in VisualAge for Java

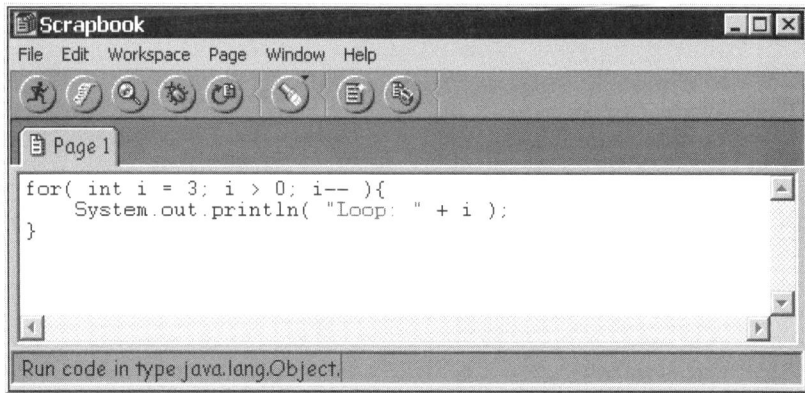

Figure 15. Evaluating Java Code in the Scrapbook

By highlighting the Java statements and selecting **Edit→Run**, you instruct the compiler to compile the statements and execute them immediately. A Console window opens, and the output of the `System.out.println("Loop number: " + i);` statement is displayed (Figure 16).

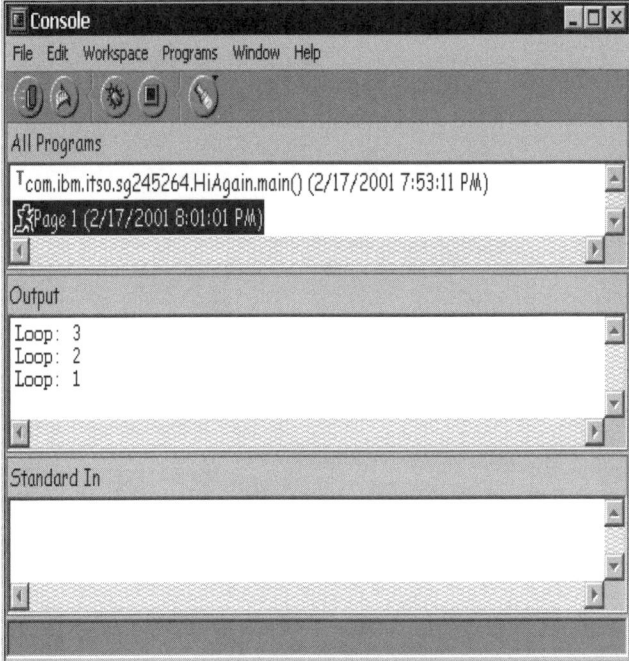

Figure 16. Console output for the loop executed in the Scrapbook

If you want to save the code you have created in the Scrapbook, select **File→Save** from the menu bar, and you can save the Java source code into a text file.

Figure 17 shows some examples of using operators in the Scrapbook.

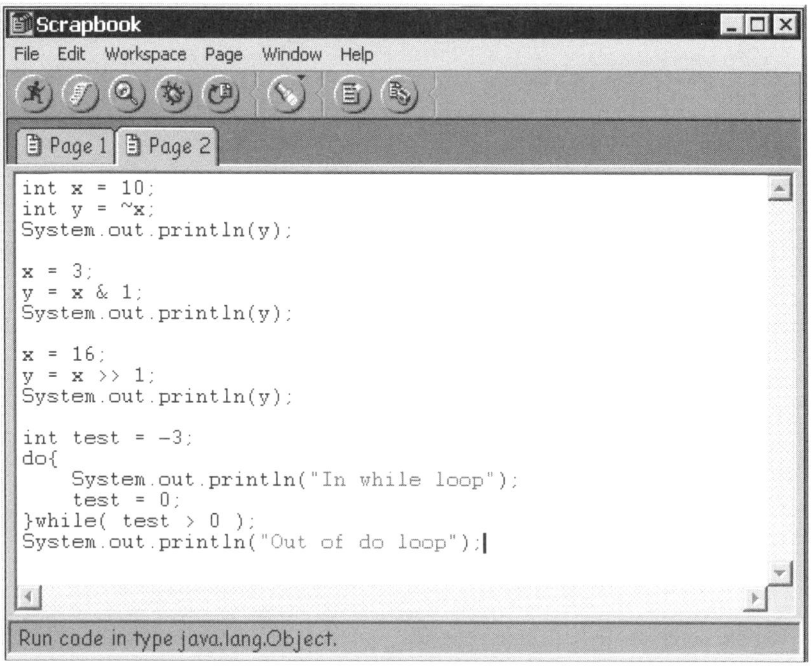
Scrapbook
File Edit Workspace Page Window Help
Page 1
Page 2
int x = 10;
int y = ~x;
System.out.println(y);
x = 3;
y = x & 1;
System.out.println(y);
x = 16;
y = x >> 1;
System.out.println(y);
int test = -3;
do{
System.out.println("In while loop");
test = 0;
}while(test > 0);
System.out.println("Out of do loop");
Run code in type java.lang.Object.

Figure 17. Using operators in the Scrapbook

Scrapbook context

When you execute code in the Scrapbook, the code runs in the context of a static method in the Object class. Select **Page→Run In** to change the context in which the code runs. By changing the context, the code in the scrapbook would be run as if it was in the (static) method main() of the selected type instead of that of Object.

You can create an instance of the type and then perform operations on it. The benefit of the **Page→Run In** selection is that you do not have to use absolute package names and you are running with private access permission on the class. Because the context is defined by the Run In function, you cannot use import statements in the Scrapbook.

Correcting errors in the Scrapbook

If you make a coding mistake, for example, you type the letter o instead of the number 0 `in the i > 0` statement, VisualAge for Java places a highlighted message where it detects the mistake (Figure 18).

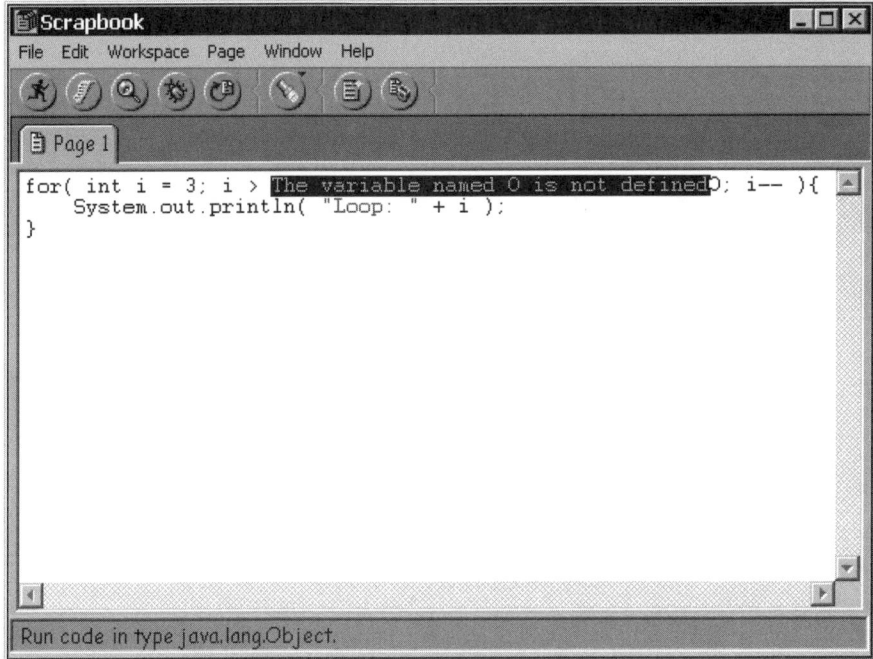

Figure 18. An error message in the Scrapbook window

In this case, four simple steps will correct the error:

1. Read the error message to determine what is wrong.
2. Press the Delete key to delete the compiler information.
3. Correct your code.
4. Run your example again.

VisualAge for Java also provides Automatic Code Completion, also known as Code Assist or Code Clue. Code Assist can help you locate the correct type, method, or field while you are coding. You can invoke it from method source, Scrapbook, Inspector windows, the event-to-code editor, the conditional breakpoint editor and the Source View. To see Code Assist in action, go to the Scrapbook window. Type `System.out`. (You can type one or more of the starting letters), hold down the Control key, and press the spacebar. A dialog appears showing all possible methods you could call in the System.out context (see Figure 19): just press Enter to paste the current selection.

When you save methods, VisualAge for Java provides you with a list of suggested corrections for errors in your code. You can select the correction, save the code as is, or cancel the save.

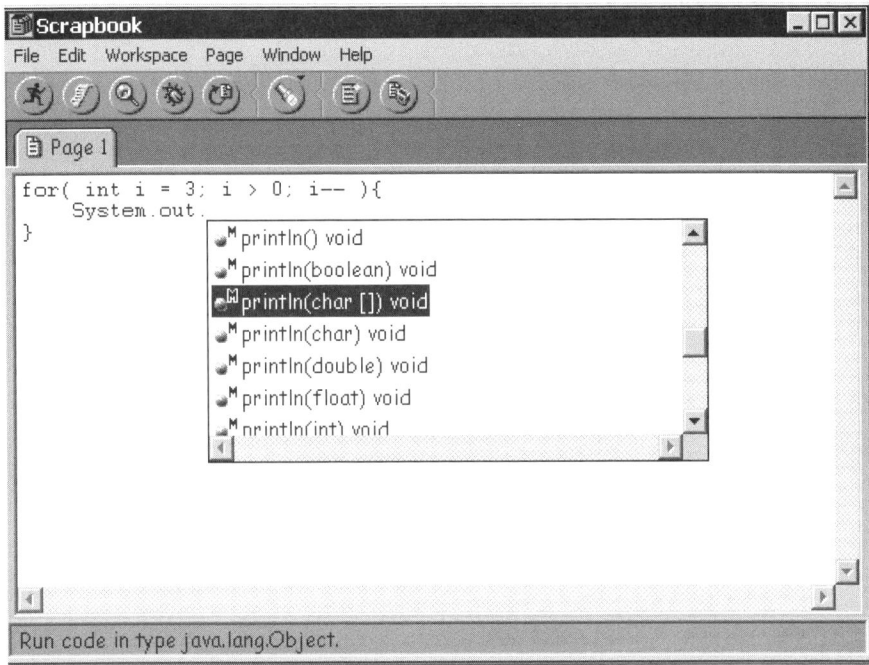

Figure 19. Using the Code Assist facility

If your Scrapbook page remains busy

Whenever a code fragment is evaluated in a Scrapbook page, that page is made inactive (busy) for the duration of the evaluation. Two visual cues indicate that a page is busy: The document icon in the tab contains a small clock icon, or the status line for the busy page contains the following text: "This page is busy running the selected code."

The page remains busy until the selected code fragment is finished running. Your page may remain busy because the code actually takes a long time to evaluate, or you are debugging a thread started from that page.

To terminate the evaluation of the code and return the page to its original state, select **Page→Restart Page** from the menu bar. Note that all threads, and therefore all windows, started from that page will be stopped and closed.

Customizing VisualAge for Java

You may have noticed by now that your windows may not look exactly like those in this book. We changed our environments to make the screen captures as readable as possible. It is possible to customize VisualAge for Java in several ways:

- Workbench Options
- Tool Integration Framework
- Palette modification

In this section you will learn about the Workbench Options. Tool Integration Framework is an API set that enables to control VisualAge tools from your Java code. Palette modification is discussed in Chapter 7, "Creating GUI applications" on page 143, "Modification of the Beans Palette" on page 147.

Workbench Options

The Workbench Options (accessed by selecting **Window→Options** from the Workbench menu bar), enable you to customize the VisualAge for Java environment in many ways (see Figure 20).

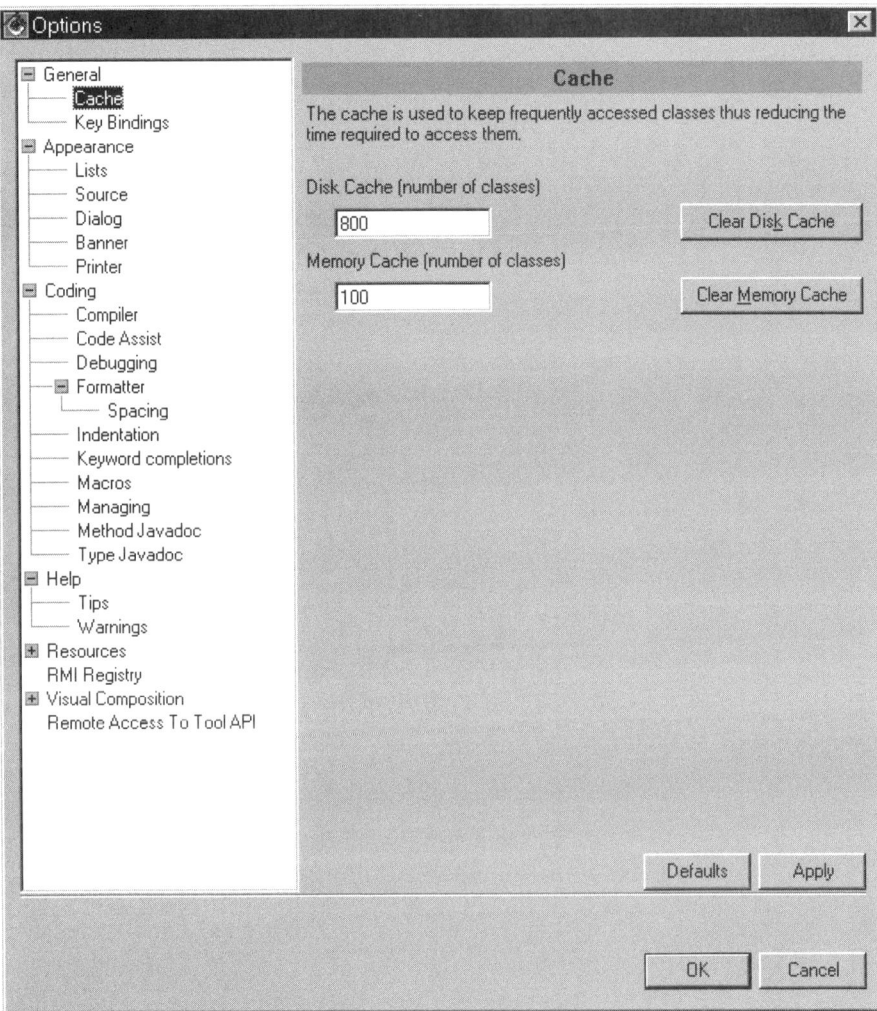

Figure 20. Workbench Options

For a complete description of the options, see the VisualAge for Java product documentation. Some of the options you may use throughout this book are:

- General
  - Cache

    The Cache feature improves the performance of the VisualAge for Java IDE considerably. You can set the number of classes cached in memory and on your hard drive.

- Appearance
  - Source

    To make your source code easy to debug, you can choose the font type, size, and foreground and background color of the source code. You can customize different colors for the default code, its comments, keywords, literals, errors and HTML Tags.
  - Printer

    This option lets you chose the default printer for VisualAge for Java.
- Coding
  - Debugging — The debugger options are discussed in Chapter 9., "Testing and debugging the Web application" on page 231.
  - Formatter — Many developers are stringent about the formatting of their code. With VisualAge for Java you can set the way your code is formatted:
    - Compound statements begin a new line
    - Opening braces begin a new line
    - Compact assignment statements
    - Keep 'else it' on the same line
    - Keep existing layout
    - Set a maximum line length
    - Spacing: You can specify if you only want one blank line in your code, or if you want to remove all blank lines. You can also modify the indentation settings.
  - Method Javadoc

    This option provides a text template for comments added when you create a method with the Add Method SmartGuide. The comment is inserted into Javadoc-style comments.
  - Type Javadoc

    This option provides a text template for comments added when you create a class or interface with the Add Class, Add Servlet or Add Interface SmartGuide. The comment is inserted into Javadoc-style comments.

- RMI Registry — With VisualAge for Java Professional, you can develop distributed Java applications that use RMI. You can:
    - Start the RMI registry on VisualAge startup
    - Use the default or another RMI port
    - Restart or stop the RMI registry

Building your first servlet

A servlet is a server-side component written in Java witch is protocol and platform independent. A servlet run inside a Java enabled server or application server, such as the WebSphere Application Server.

A servlet is invoked by a server in response to a request from a client. Typically the server is a Web server, and the client is a Web browser.

In VisualAge for Java, you can create, run, and debug servlets within the VisualAge for Java environment.

VisualAge for Java provides the Create Servlet SmartGuide, which can be use to develop servlets and their related Web resources quickly.

In this section you create a very simple HTTP servlet that accepts a request and writes a response.

Before starting to create your Servlet, you need to add new features to your workspace: the Servlet API feature and the WebSphere Test Environment feature. From the Workbench, select **File→Quick Start** from the menu bar. Then select **Features→Add feature** and select the **OK** button. From the window displayed, select the **Sun Servlet API 2.1** feature and **IBM WebSphere Test Environment 3.5** (use Ctrl + select for the second selection. The two lines selected must be highlighted) and select the **OK** button. From the Workbench window, you now can see the two new projects added named **Servlet API Classes** and **IBM WebSphere Test Environment.**

Now start creating your servlet. In the Workbench, select the package you created (com.ibm.itso.SG245264), then select **Selected→Add→Servlet** from the menu bar. The Create Servlet SmartGuide window appears. Enter *HiHttpServlet* in the *Class Name* field (see Figure 21).

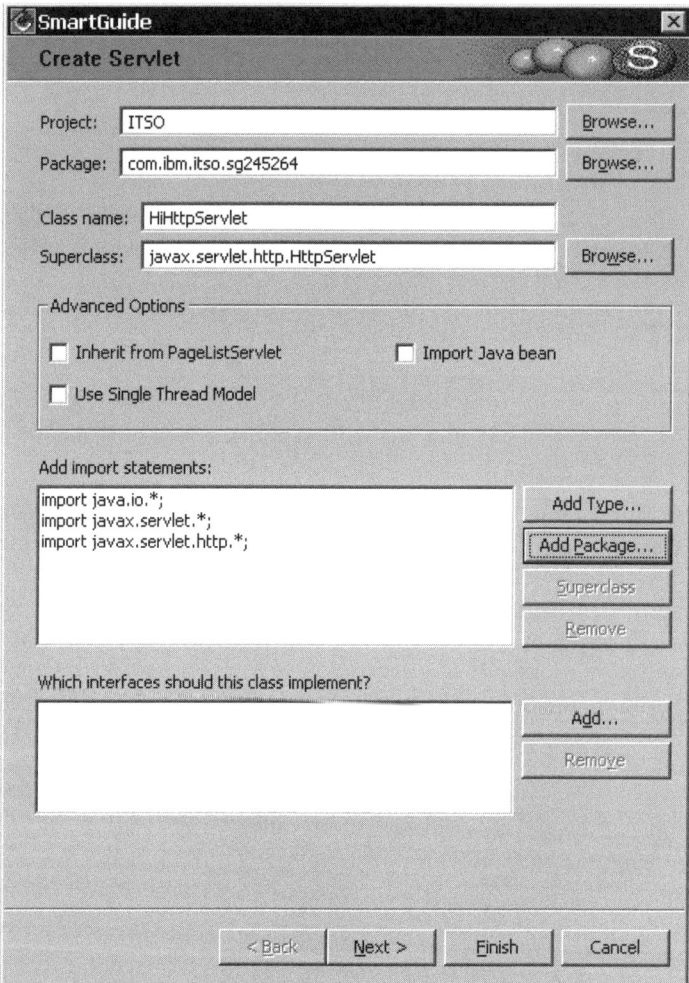

Figure 21. The Servlet SmartGuide

Select **Add Package** button to display the Import statement window (see Figure 22).

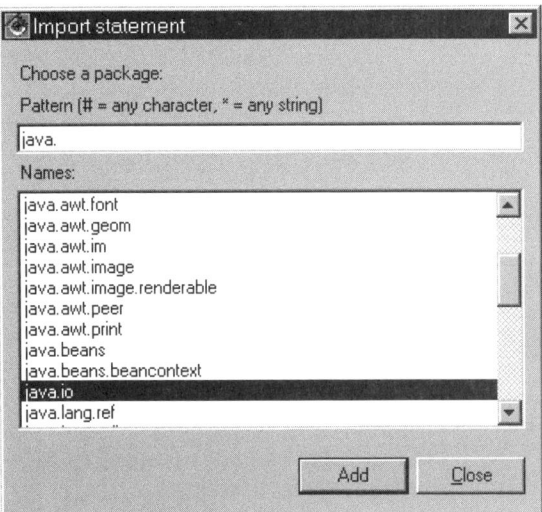

Figure 22. Servlet SmartGuide Import Statement window

Type java. as **Pattern** and select java.io from the Names list. Select the **Add** button. Use the same process to add javax.servlet and javax.servlet.http packages. Close the Import statement window by selecting the **close** button.

From the Create Servlet Window, select the **Next** button to access the SmartGuide page where you specify attributes of your new servlet.

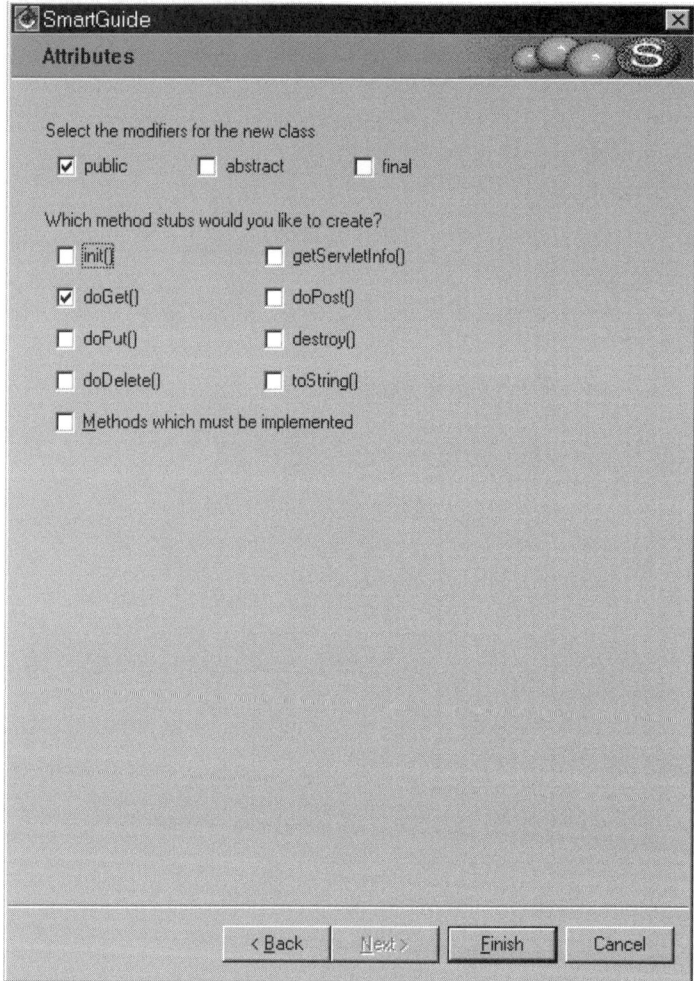

Figure 23. Servlet attributes

Select only the **doGet()** checkbox under *Which method stubs would you like to create* and click the **Finish** button to generate the Servlet,

VisualAge for Java Servlet SmartGuide will automatically generate default versions and signatures for the selected methods and add them to the class's source code.

In the Workbench you can see a new line added for your newly created class. Select this new class and select **Selected→Open Source View** to get a view of the complete class generated, including all of its methods (Figure 24).

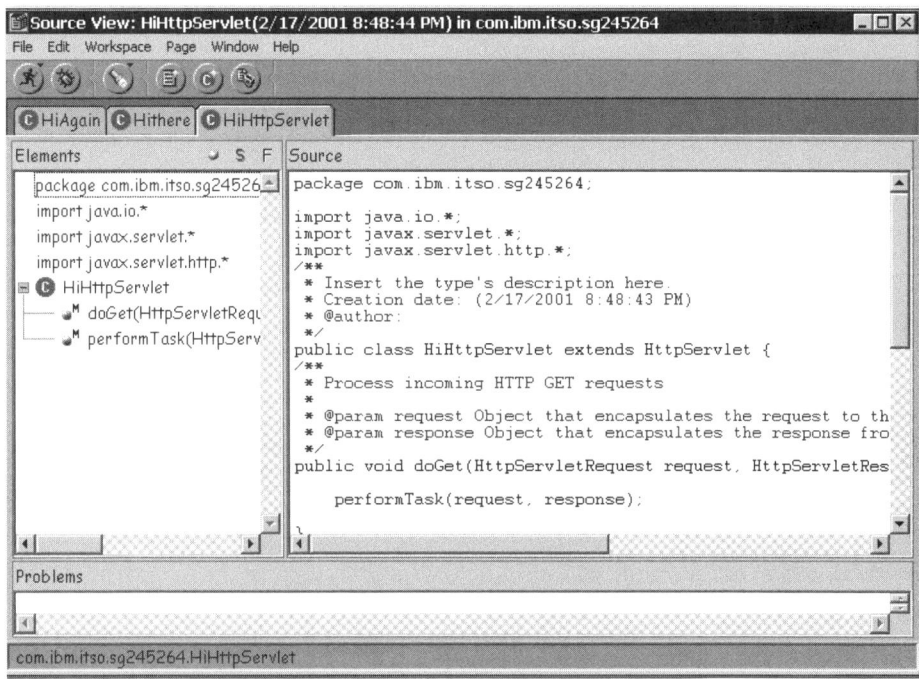

Figure 24. HiHttpServlet Source View

From the elements pane of the HiHttpServlet Source View, double-click on the performTask method. The code is then highlighted in the Source pane. You then have to add the heart of this servlet, the implementation of the performTask method for the handling of the request and response objects of the servlet (see the HiHttpServlet code below)

```
package com.ibm.itso.sg245264;

import java.io.*;
import javax.servlet.*;
import javax.servlet.http.*;
/**
* Insert the type's description here.
* Creation date: (2/17/2001 8:48:43 PM)
* @author: Administrator
*/
public class HiHttpServlet extends HttpServlet {

/**

  * Process incoming HTTP GET requests
  *
```

Chapter 1. Introduction to the environment   **35**

```java
 * @param request Object that encapsulates the request to the servlet
 * @param response Object that encapsulates the response from the servlet
 */
public void doGet(HttpServletRequest request, HttpServletResponse response)
throws ServletException, IOException {

    performTask(request, response);

}
/**
 * Process incoming requests for information
 *
 * @param request Object that encapsulates the request to the servlet
 * @param response Object that encapsulates the response from the servlet
 */
public void performTask(HttpServletRequest request, HttpServletResponse
response) {

    try

    {
        // Insert user code from here.

        response.setContentType("text/html");
        PrintWriter out = response.getWriter();
        out.println("<HTML><TITLE>HiHttpServlet</TITLE><BODY>");
        out.println("<H2>Servlet API Sample - HiHttpServlet</H2><HR>");
        out.println("<H4> This is created by VisualAge Java Servlet" +
                                            "SmartGuide!</H4>");
        out.println("</BODY><HTML>");
        out.close();

    }
    catch(Throwable theException)
    {
        // uncomment the following line when unexpected exceptions
        // are occuring to aid in debugging the problem.
        //theException.printStackTrace();
    }
}
```

In this simple servlet, you will not do anything with the request. You do some handling of the response object, which is responsible for sending your response back to the client. Your response is a formatted HTML page.

Save your changes by selecting **Edit→Save** from the menu bar. To test the result you will use the WebSphere Test Environment.

The WebSphere Test Environment (WTE) enables you to run your servlet in a controlled, simulated Web Application Server environment (Figure 25). See Chapter 9, "Testing and debugging the Web application" on page 231, for more information on the WTE.

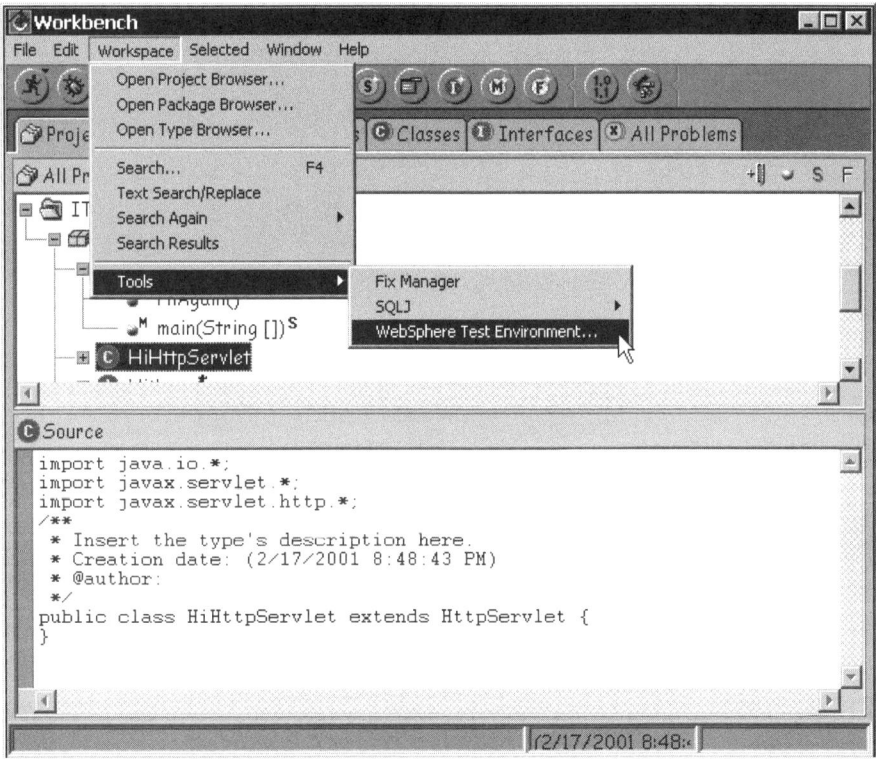

Figure 25. Starting the WebSphere Test Environment

To test your HiHttpServlet, start WTE from the Workbench window selecting **Workspace→Tools→WebSphere Test Environment.**

The **WebSphere Test Environment Control Center** opens. Select **Servlet Engine**, this displays the Servlet Engine options in the right pane (see Figure 26).

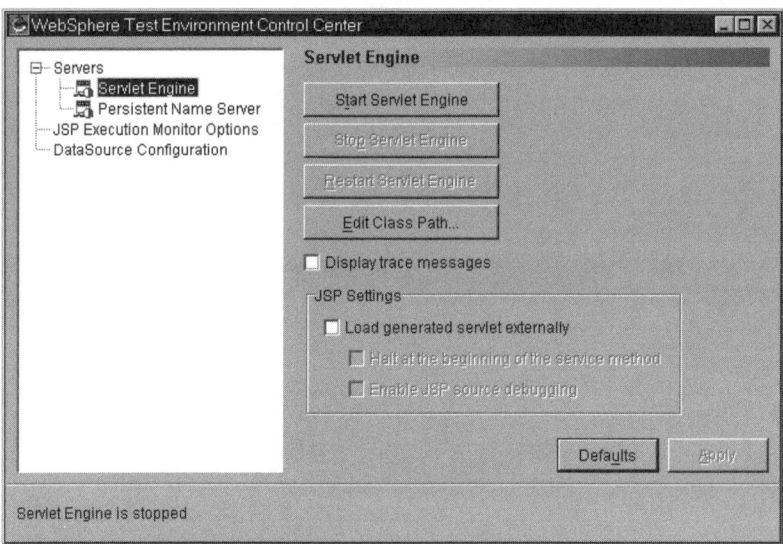

Figure 26. WebSphere Test Environment Control Center

Select **Edit Class Path...** button. Click **Select All** button. This will include your project (ITSO) on the class path. Select the **OK** button.

Then start the servlet engine by clicking the **Start Servlet Engine** button. This activates a Console window. Wait until you can see the message *****Servlet Engine is started***** (see Figure 27).

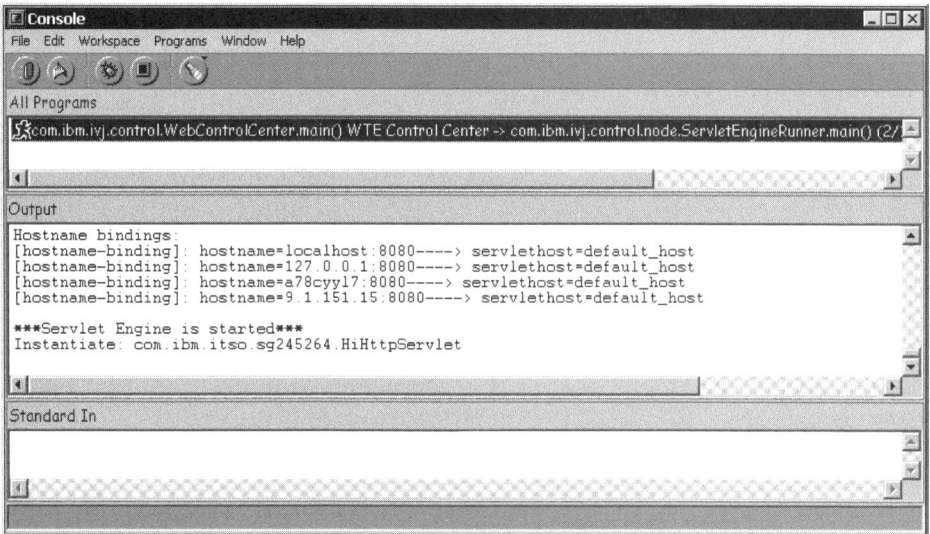

Figure 27. Console window when starting the WTE Servlet Engine

You can also see the message **Servlet Engine is started** at the bottom of the WebSphere Test Environment Control Center window.

You are now ready to launch your servlet. Open your favorite Web browser. Invoke your servlet from the browser by using the URL:

   `http://127.0.0.1:8080/servlet/com.ibm.itso.sg245264.HiHttpServlet`.

You should see the results of your servlet's execution displayed in your Web browser window. The results of your HiHttpServlet are shown in Figure 28.

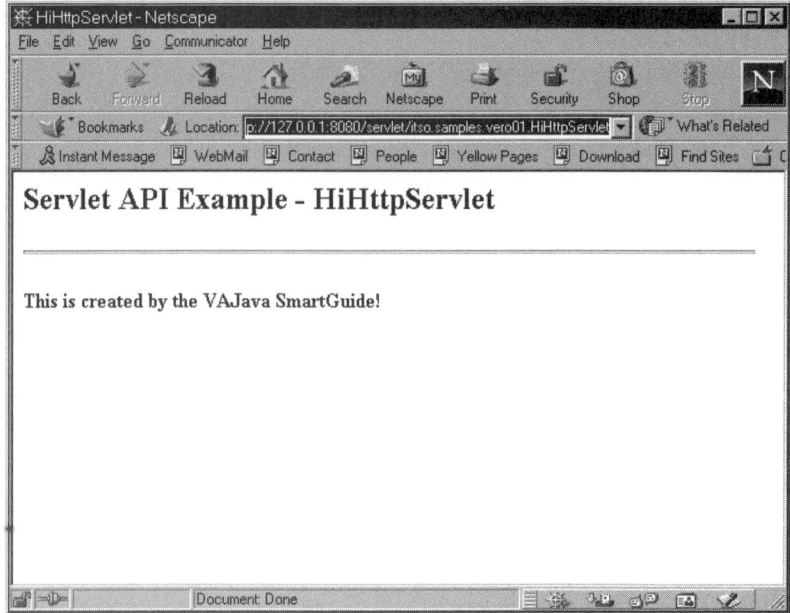

Figure 28. HiHttpServlet Output

Chapter 2. Organizing your code

With VisualAge for Java you use projects and packages to organize your work. Projects are a feature of VisualAge for Java that provide a high-level means of grouping the development efforts of a project. Packages are the standard Java scheme of organizing classes and interfaces that are intended to work together.

In this chapter you will learn to work with projects and packages in VisualAge for Java.

Visual Age for Java uses projects and packages to organize your code. Projects contain everything that is currently being worked on by a developer. Projects contain packages, which in turn contain Java classes and interfaces. Projects can also contain resources. Resources are non-Java files which are considered part of an application. Resources are covered in more detail in"The Workbench Resources page" on page 50.

In this chapter you will learn about the tools Visual Age for Java provides to help manage and maintain your work. We will also cover bringing in external Java code and resources and exporting your work.

Projects in VisualAge for Java

You have already created a project to organize all of the work you do while reading this book. Projects provide a way of organizing your Java code at the highest level. Whenever you create a new package, you must place it in a new or existing project. Projects do not have any equivalent in the Java language.

In VisualAge for Java 3.5, projects contain Java packages plus other resources. Resources are related files that are part of the Web application, such as images, multimedia, JSPs, and static HTML documents.

The first time you start VisualAge for Java and go to the Workbench, you see several projects in your workspace, all of which contain several packages. Table 2 lists these projects and their contents.

Table 2. Default VisualAge for Java projects and their contents

Project	Contents
IBM Java Implementation	com.ibm.uvm.* packages, which enable and support the VisualAge for Java VM and environment
Java Class Libraries	java.* and javax.* packages, which contain the Java Class Libraries
Sun Class Libraries PM Win32	sun.* packages, which are extensions to standard java.* packages

The code in the projects in Table 2 cannot be modified or deleted. It is required by VisualAge for Java to function correctly.

Adding features

You need to add several features to develop database applications, servlets, as so on. To add a feature, select **Quick Start** from **File** menu or press F2. Select **Features** and **Add Feature** from Quick Start dialog, then click OK button. You can choose available features from list. You need to add at least the WebSphere Test Environment, Servlet, IBM JSP samples, and Data Access Beans to execute samples in this book.

Packages in VisualAge for Java

Packages are Java containers used to group related classes and interfaces together. The package name is part of a fully-qualified class name. It is important to decide how to group various classes together.

You have a choice of using a fully qualified name or using an import statement. VisualAge for Java searches for external packages in the classpath of the workspace. The classpath can be changed by options dialog.

The Workbench

To understand how VisualAge for Java organizes projects and packages, you have to know a little more about the Workbench. The Workbench provides different views of your current development environment or workspace. The layout of the Workbench window depends on the tab selection above the pane. To switch between the Projects, Packages, Resources, Classes, Interfaces, and All Problems pages, just click on the corresponding tab. The menu bar of these pages also changes as you switch from tab to tab.

From any Workbench page you can access the menu of the currently selected item (project, package, resource, class, interface, or method) in two different ways. You can:

- Access the pop-up menu by right-clicking the selected item
- Use the menu bar

The pop-up menu of the Source pane and the Edit menu in the menu bar have the same contents. The Browse pane's pop-up menu is the same as the Selected menu in the menu bar.

The Workbench also provides a toolbar for quick access to functions. Figure 29 shows the toolbar, and Table 3 describes the icons.

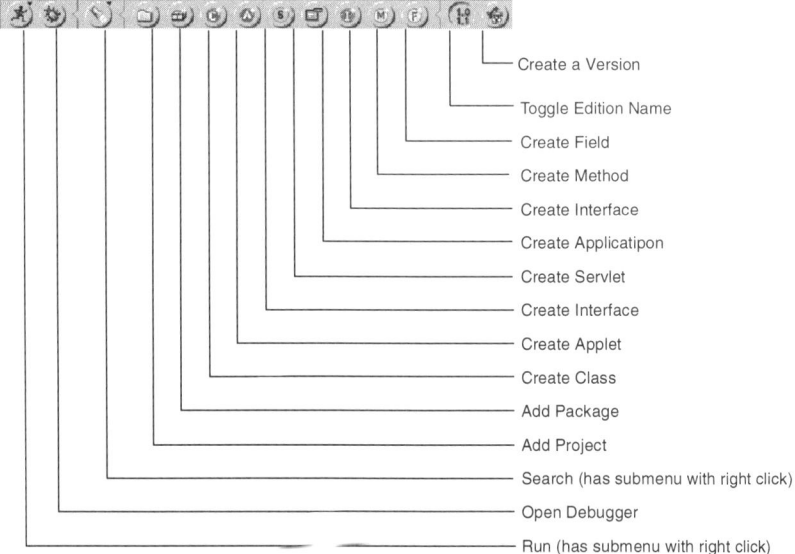

Figure 29. The Workbench toolbar

Table 3. .Toolbar icon descriptions

Icon	Description
Run	Run the selected class or a class from the selected project or package. Shows history by clicking right button.
Open Debugger	Start the debugger.
Search	Search for a reference or declaration of a field, method, or class. Shows history by clicking right button.
Add Project	Add a project to the current workspace.
Add Package	Add a package to the current selected project.
Create Class	Invoke the Create a new Class SmartGuide.
Create Applet	Invoke the Create a new Applet SmartGuide.
Create Interface	Invoke the Create a new Interface SmartGuide.
Create Servlet	Invoke the Create a new Servlet SmartGuide.
Create Application	Invoke the Create a new Application SmartGuide.
Create Method	Invoke the Create a new Method SmartGuide on an existing class.
Create Field	Invoke the Create a new Field SmartGuide on an existing class.
Toggle Edition Names	Show or hide the edition names of program elements.
Version	Make a Version.

The Workbench Projects page

The Projects page of the Workbench (Figure 30) contains two panes: a Browse pane and a Source or Comment pane.

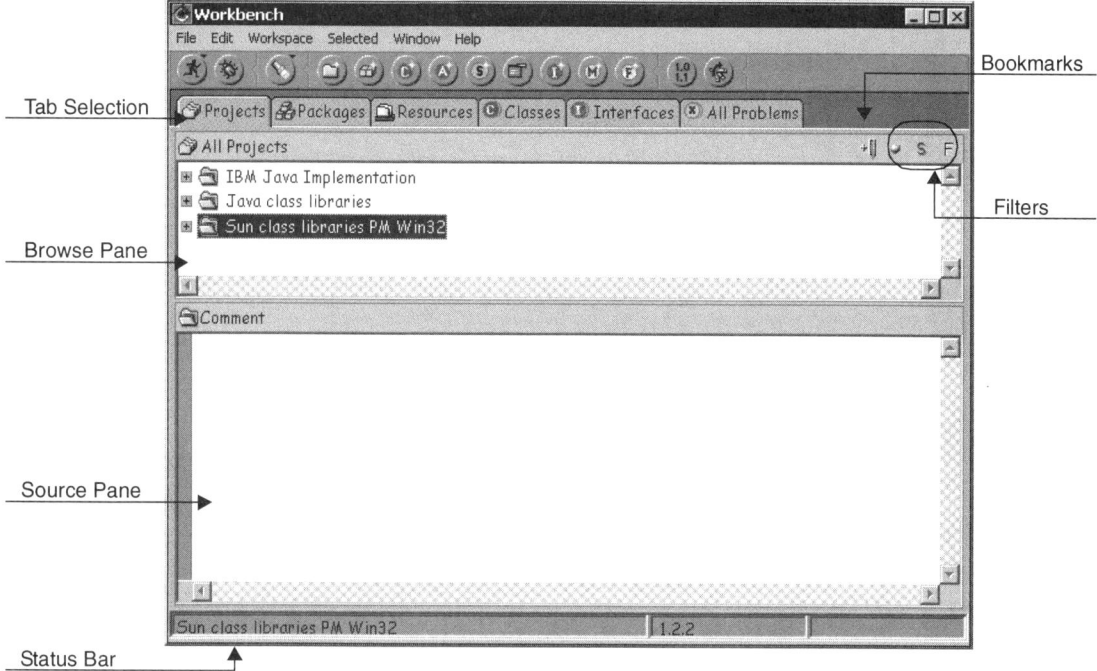

Figure 30. Workbench Projects page

The orientation of the panes is by default set to horizontal. If you want to change the orientation, you can select **Window→Flip Orientation**.

If you select a program element in the Browse pane, which contains code, such as a class, interface, or method, the other pane is labeled Source and contains source code. If you select a package or project, the other pane is labeled Comment and contains any comments you have added to the project or package.

A tree view of the projects, packages, classes, and interfaces that are currently loaded in your workspace is shown in the Browse pane when you select the Projects, Packages, Classes, or Interfaces views. The Projects view is the default view shown when you open the Workbench for the first time. To collapse or expand any item in the list, click the plus or minus sign to the left of the item (or use the plus sign and minus sign keys). To show the source code for an item in the Source pane, select the item, using your mouse.

You can create new projects by selecting **Selected→Add→Project** in any browser window.

Other features in window

VisualAge for Java provides many useful features for viewing different parts of your projects. Three of these features are:

- The Projects page enables you to set bookmarks. In the upper-right corner of the Browse pane, click on the plus sign to set a bookmark. When you want to return to a particular piece of code, click the number that appeared when you created the bookmark.

- You can use three filters to show public members only or static members only and show all fields (class variables).

- You can clone any window in VisualAge for Java. Selecting **Window→Clone** opens another window in the same context. A clone of a window can be very useful when you need two similar views, but be careful about updating the same class in two views. It is possible to overwrite changes you have made in one view with changes made in another window.

- Double-clicking on the title bar of any pane maximizes that pane within the window. Double-click again to restore the normal view. You can also select **Window→Maximize Pane/Restore Pane**

The Workbench Packages view

The Packages page of the Workbench (Figure 31) contains three Browse panes — All Packages, Types, and Methods — and one Source pane.

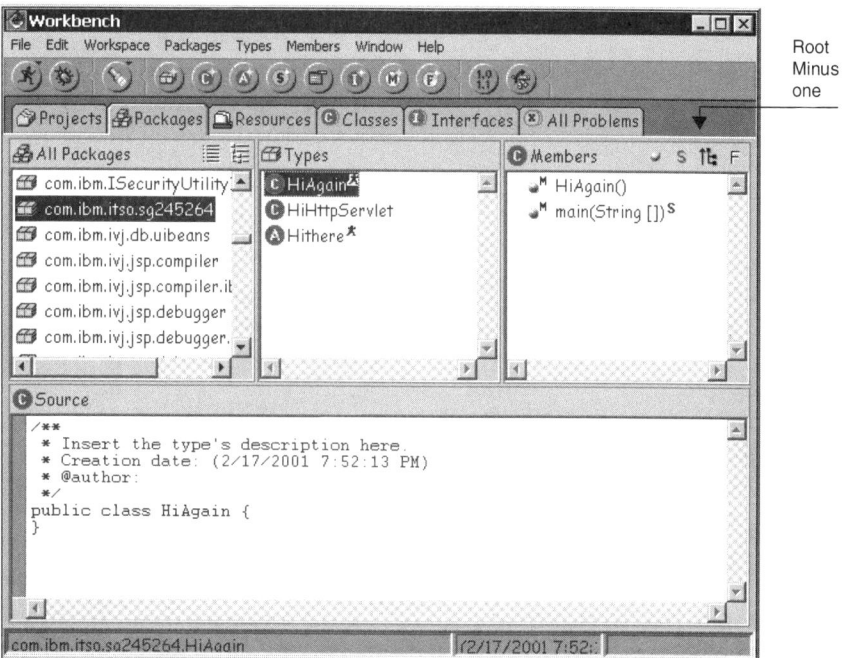

Figure 31. Workbench Packages page

You can use **Packages**→**Layout** to customize your view, and you can choose between **Tree Layout** or **List Layout**. You can access the same functionality through the layout icons at the top right of the All Packages pane.

The **Orientation** option is also available for this view under **Window**.

Creating packages

With the JDK, directories are used to organize packages on your file system, whereas in VisualAge for Java packages and classes are kept in the workspace.

The workspace contains all of the program elements with which you are currently working. Rather than creating directory structures, VisualAge for Java organizes its packages and classes internally. If you export classes, the directory structure is created on your file system. This approach makes managing packages and classes simple. Although classes of your projects are kept in the workspace, any resources of those projects are kept separately in your local file system in this directory:

```
\[vaj installed directory]\ide\project_resources\project_name
```

In Java you can declare a class to be part of a package by using the *package* keyword at the top of your Java source file:

```
package account;
public class BankAccount{
     private string accountId;
     private double balance;
}
```

In VisualAge for Java you select the package that will contain each new type that you create. If you specify a package name that does not exist, that package will be created for you. After creating new classes in a selected package, the package name is not shown in the code; it is implied in the list of classes in the package.

You can also create or import code that has been defined with the default package, the package used when no package is explicitly defined. Because you cannot access members of a default package from other packages, the use of a default package is not recommended.

You can also create new packages by selecting **Selected→Add→Package** in any browser window. To create the Automated Teller Machine (ATM) application used throughout this book, you need two packages:

```
com.ibm.itso.sg245264.atm.memory
com.ibm.itso.sg245264.atm.database
```

Create these two packages now by selecting the Programming VAJ V3.5 project and then **Selected→Add Package**. Fill in the *Create a new package named with* field with the name of the first package and click **Finish**, then repeat the process for the second package.

Root Minus One
Click Root Minus One button on the top right corner to see inherit class members.

Using types from other packages

With VisualAge for Java or the JDK environment, you have two ways of using a class from another package:

- Refer to the class by using the fully qualified name
- Use the import keyword

You can either import all types defined within a package or be more selective. Note that importing a package does not import the subpackages of that package, you have to import them separately. You can use the star notation (java.awt.*) to import all types within a package, but you have to separately import any subpackages, such as java.awt.event.

If you already know which packages you will need within your class when you are creating it, use the Attributes dialog box (which opens when you click **Next** in the Create Class or Interface SmartGuide). The Attributes dialog box enables you to specify the packages to be imported. Use the **Add Class** and **Add Package** buttons to browse and select classes and packages to import into your class (Figure 32).

You can also add the import statements manually by editing the class declaration.

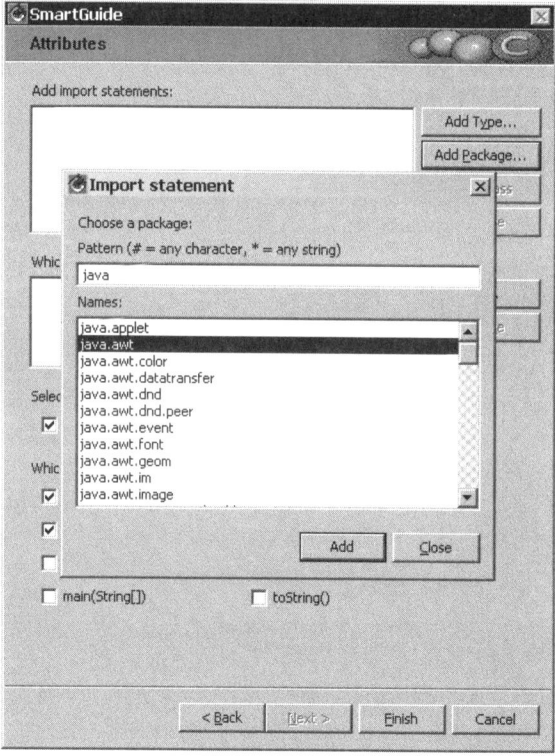

Figure 32. Create Class SmartGuide: Import statement dialog box

The Workbench Resources page

The Resources page of the Workbench (Figure 33) shows all resources contained in your project. You can add or remove the resources or directory structures that related to your project. Several JSP files and SQLJ files related to the projects are shown.

To add or remove resource files, use the popup menu and select add or delete. To edit the file, double click on the file or use open menu. VisualAge for Java opens the resource file using related application.

The resource files will be stored in the repository file when you make a version of your project. Unless you make a version, resource files are kept in the project_resources directory under the VisualAge for Java installed directory and are not copied to the repository.

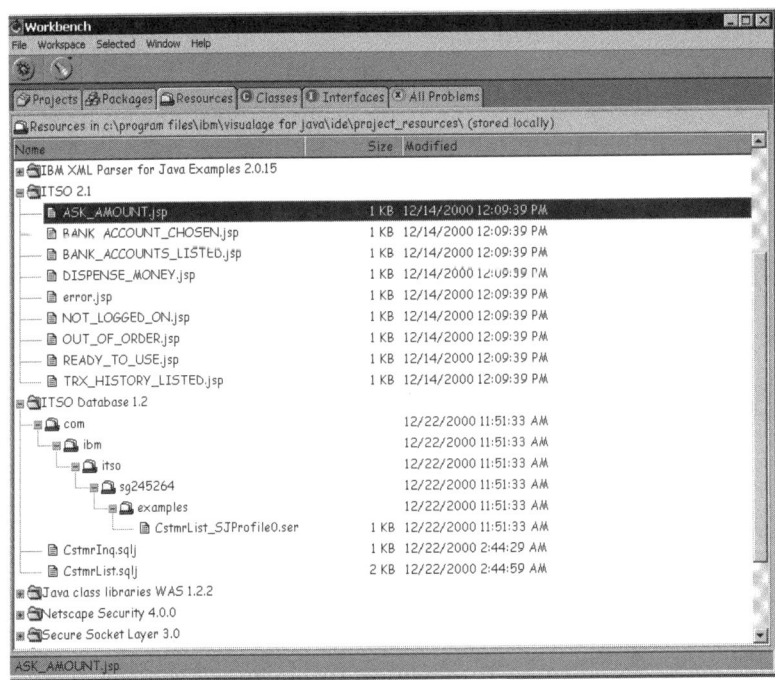

Figure 33. Workbench Resources page

The Workbench Classes page

The Classes page of the Workbench (Figure 34) contains three panes: Class Hierarchy, Methods, and Source.

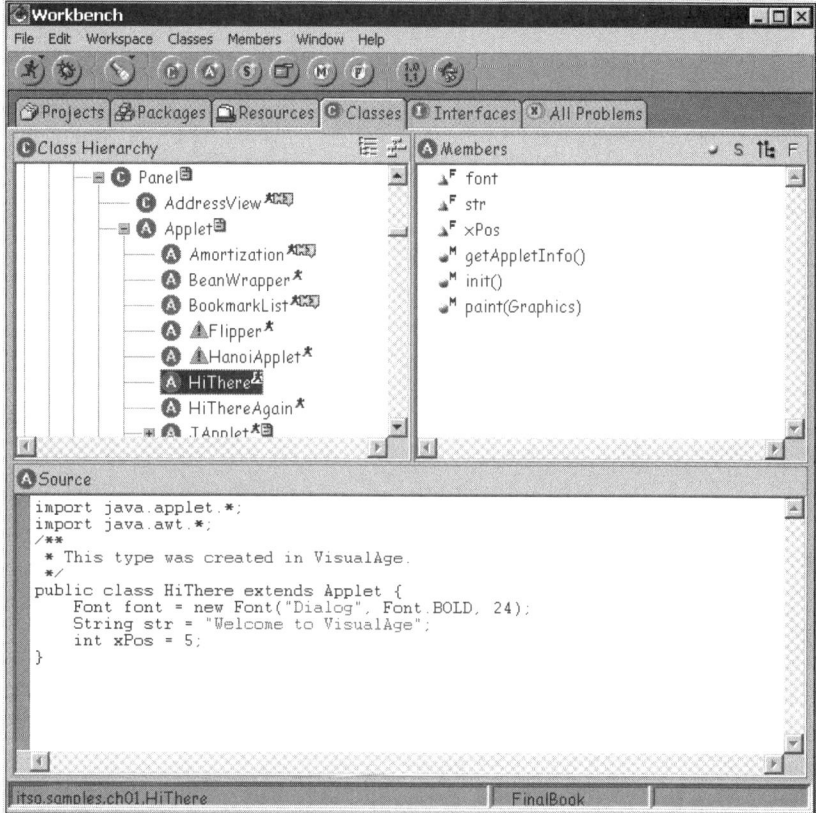

Figure 34. Workbench Classes page

You can change the layout of your classes, using **Classes→Layout** from the menu or the layout icons at the top right of the **Class Hierarchy** pane. You can also select the orientation of the Browse pane, using **Window→Flip Orientation.** Click **Root Minus One** icon at the top right of the Member pane to show inherit class members.

The Classes view is useful because it shows the class hierarchy of types, and you can quickly follow the inheritance tree of classes. In the Classes view you can quickly find a class you are interested in by selecting **Classes→Go To Class** and then typing in the class name until the complete name shows up in the list.

Navigation aids

The Go To Class function is just one of the many navigation aids in the WorkBench. Here are some other aids:

- Each window has a different **Go To** option.
- Each window has an **Open To**, which opens the selected item in a selected browser.
- Each window has a **Clone** function if you want to have two views of the same information.
- You can search for different items, using **Workspace→Search**.
- You can find all code that has references to a selected type, using **Selected→References To**.

The Workbench Interfaces page

The Interfaces page of the Workbench (Figure 35) is similar to the Classes page (Figure 34) except that it displays interfaces instead of classes. The Interfaces page consists of three panes: Interfaces, Methods, and Source.

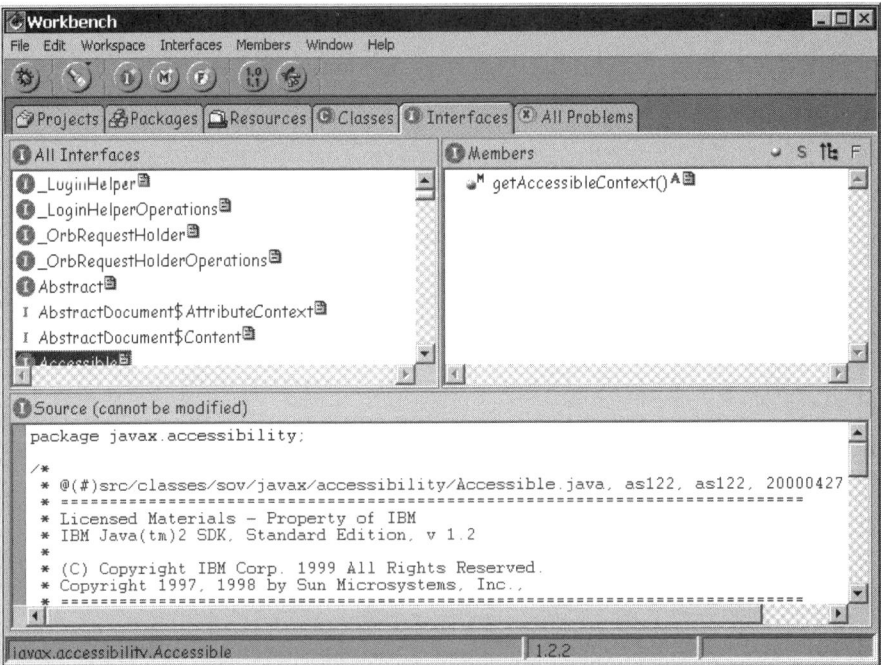

Figure 35. Workbench Interfaces page

The Workbench All Problems page

On the All Problems page you can find all incorrect code in the workspace. The incorrect code found within a method causes the method to be flagged with a red X, and the method's class will be flagged with a grey X (see Figure 36). If you have incorrect code in a class or interface declaration, the class or interface is flagged with a red X.

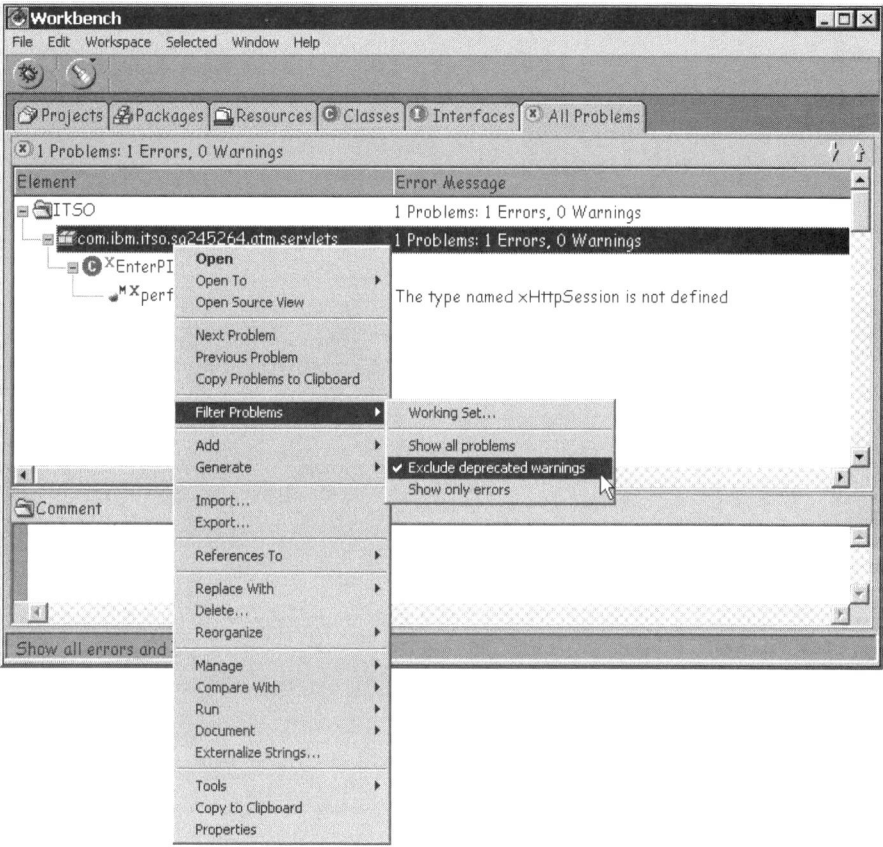

Figure 36. Workbench All Problems page

If some problems are known, you can filter them and hide certain ones. There are three ways to apply a filter:

- Select Show all problems to see all problems.
- Select Exclude deprecated warnings to hide deprecated warnings.
- Select Show only errors to hide all warnings.

You can also narrow the search range to specific projects by using working sets. To use a working set, select the projects that you would like to include in the working set dialog that appears when you click **Filter Problems →Working Set...**.

Chapter 2. Organizing your code   53

In your version of VisualAge for Java, you should not have any errors (not yet, anyway!). You can create an error to see the result:

- Select the **Projects** tab on the Workbench.
- Expand (click on the plus sign) the HiThere class and then select the main(String)[] method.
- Add the line: x=2; before the closing brace (}) and save the method (using **Edit→Save** or Control-S).

Figure 37 shows the Warning dialog box that appears when you attempt to save incorrect code. At this point you can cancel, return to the code and fix the error, or save the code with the error.

If VisualAge for Java can suggest corrections to the code, it displays them in the lower pane. You can select the entry under Suggested corrections and click the **Correct** button to correct your code.

- Click the **Save** button in the Warning dialog.

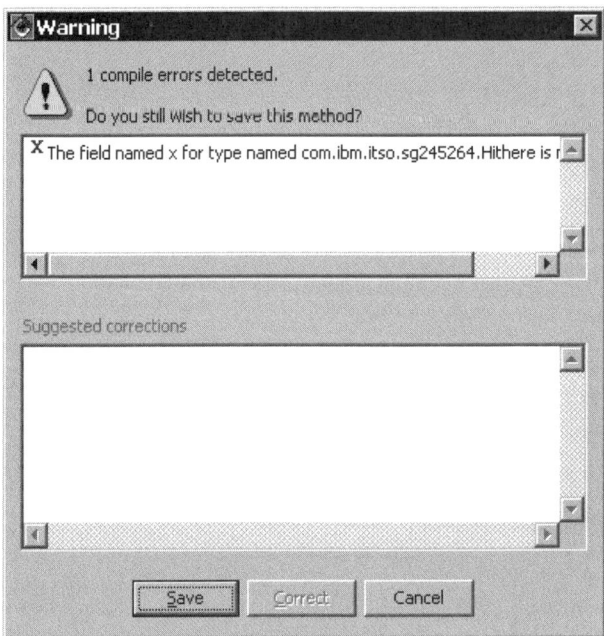

Figure 37. Warning Dialog: Undefined Variable

- Select the **All Problems** tab on the Workbench(not shown). Select the main method, delete the line x=2;, and save the method. The problem should disappear.

In most cases, when you type incorrect code, you get the Warning dialog shown in Figure 37. In some cases, when the VisualAge for Java compiler cannot parse the incorrect code, you get an Error dialog. In this case, you must return to the code and fix it before you can save it. If VisualAge for Java can suggest corrections to the code, it shows them in the lower pane.

Leaving errors in your code
It may seem a little strange to leave errors in your code. However, in VisualAge for Java there is little risk. For example, if you forget to create a variable before you reference it, you can save the code that references the variable, go the All Problems page later, and add the variables to the class declaration.

In the worst case, where you are not sure what you should fix, you can just return to an earlier version of the code.

Full source code edit

The Source View provides a full source code editing capability. For programmers that like to edit a complete class source file instead of individual methods, this facility is the answer. To use this Source View from the Workbench, use **Open Source View** menu. You can also use this full source code editing in class browser. In this case, click **Source** tab in class browser.

Source View is not part of the Workbench and is a separate window (Figure 38). The Source View browser consists of three panes: Elements, Source and Problems.

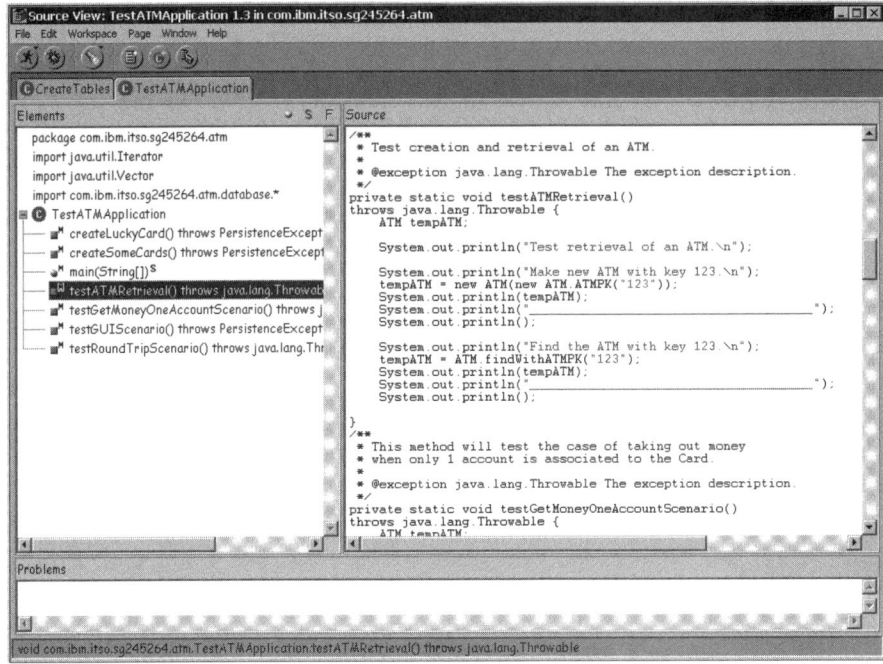

Figure 38. Source View

The Source pane shows all of your source code, and you can jump to your method or definition statement by clicking on the Elements pane. The Order of methods is preserved from the first import, or when changed in the Source View. When exporting a class, the sequence is preserved as well. VisualAge for Java does not modify the file format, and includes black lines and indentations.

There is only one window with the Source View. Each class will be a page in this view. You can edit multiple classes in one time by selecting a tab. You can also edit in parallel in Source View and in another view.

Note that the first open may take a while to fill the left-hand side of the split screen.

Code Assists

While editing your code, VisualAge for Java Code Assists can help you type. Code Assists show you a list of candidates that satisfy your incomplete typing. To show the list, press Control plus the Space key (Figure 39).

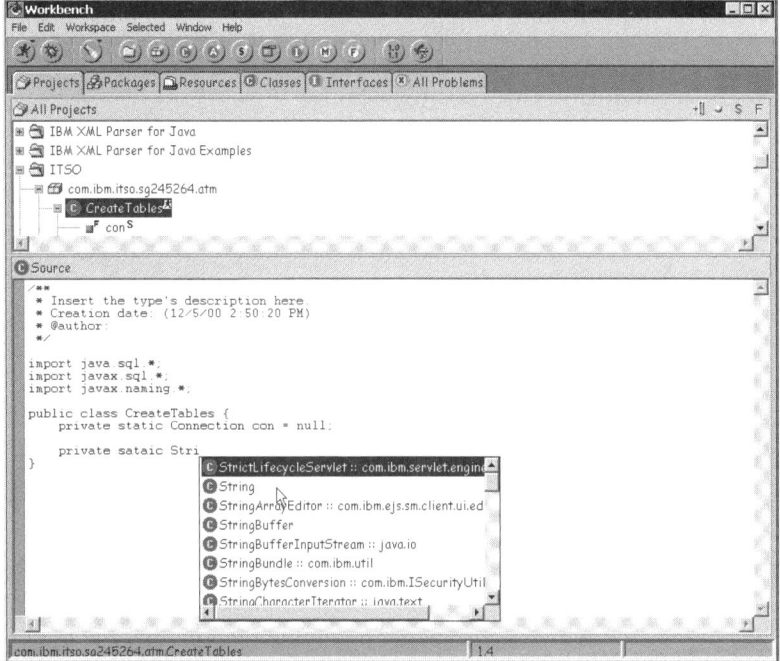

Figure 39. Code Assists

Importing and exporting with VisualAge for Java

You have already learned that VisualAge for Java Professional stores your projects in a repository, not directly in the file system. To deploy your Java projects, or to share code with other developers, you have to import and export Java classes.

You can import and export Java classes and resources to and from the VisualAge for Java environment in several formats:

- Directory

    You can import Java source code or class file from the file system. The source code is compiled as it is imported, and package hierarchies are retained. You would export Java source code when you want to share it with developers who are using a different development environment or edit it using a different editor from that provided with VisualAge for Java. If you specify the directory as the package, you can import entire packages under the specific package. This function also imports resources under the directory. To import resources, click **Details** button next to **Resource** check box and select the resources that you would like to import.

Chapter 2. Organizing your code   **57**

- JAR files

    Java archive (JAR) is a platform-independent file format that enables you to compress a Java applet and its resources (such as .class files, images, and sounds) into a single file. JAR files are a good way of distributing Java applets, applications, and their supporting resources. You can install the files on a Web server where Web browsers can access them. You can export a complete VisualAge for Java project as a JAR file.

- Repository (known as VisualAge for Java interchange files)

    Repository files are used to exchange Java classes, which are built with VisualAge for Java Professional, among different VisualAge for Java Professional environments. The files maintain version information and comments as well as visual development information.

    When you import a Repository file, it is loaded into your repository. You then have to load it into your workspace from the repository. If you would like to load to your workspace automatically, select this option on the repository import dialog. This function loads only the most recent project. Otherwise, you should load your project manually. Any program elements that you export by using a repository file must be versioned first. Versions and the repository are fully explained in "Workspace versus repository" on page 185.

Importing into VisualAge for Java

Note that importing code into the VisualAge for Java environment is not the same as using the import keyword in Java source code.

To import code into VisualAge for Java:

1. Open the Import dialog, using one of these methods:

    - **File→Import** from the menu bar on any page.
    - **Selected→Import** from the menu bar on the Projects page.
    - **Packages/Types→Import** from the menu bar on the Packages page.
    - **Classes→Import** from the menu bar on the Classes page.
    - **Interfaces→Import** from the menu bar on the Interfaces page.

    A SmartGuide prompts you for the source of import (Figure 40).

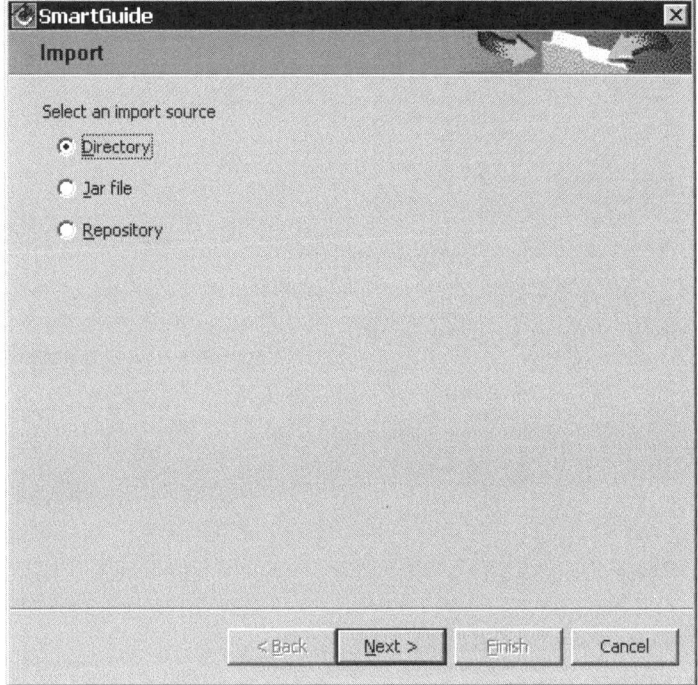

Figure 40. Importing Java Files into VisualAge for Java

2. Select the source of import:

- **Directory** — .java or .class files
- **Jar file** — .jar files
- **Repository** — repository files

For Directory and Jar file imports, select:

- The directory where the import files reside
- The specific classes (source or bytecode) and resources to be imported
- The project into which to import the classes
- Whether or not to overwrite existing resources

For Repository imports, select:

- The repository file to be imported
- The specific projects or packages to import (Figure 41)

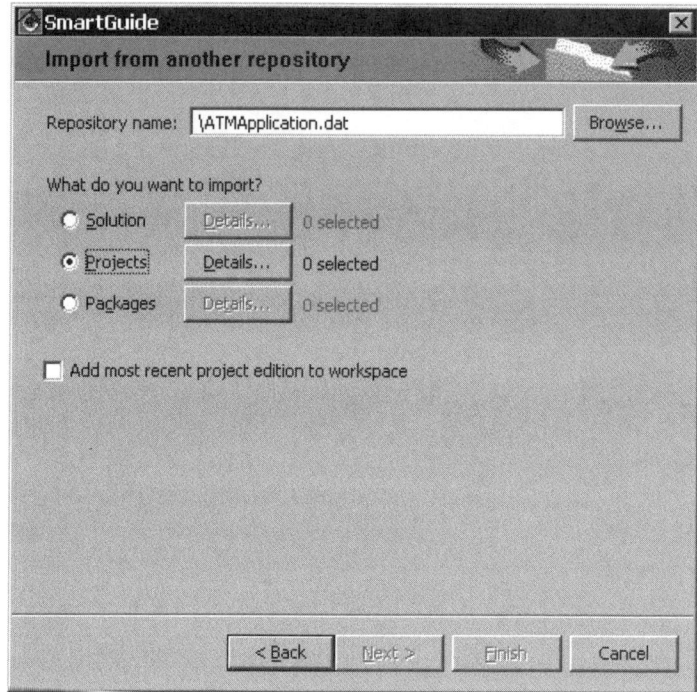

Figure 41. Importing from another repository

In addition to normal import/export options, another solution is to use a container that holds a group of projects. You can create solutions that contain related projects that you want to import or export as a group, for example a set of projects that you want to send to a particular customer. Solutions and repositories are discussed in more detail in "Import and export effects" on page 217. This chapter will focus on the import/export tool as it affects going to/from JARS and directories.

Exporting from VisualAge for Java

To export code from VisualAge for Java:

1. Optionally, select one or more projects, packages, or classes or interfaces.

    - When you select a package, all classes and interfaces in the package are exported.

    - When you select a project, all classes of all the packages within that project are exported.

2. Open the Export dialog (Figure 42), using one of these methods:
    - **File→Export** from the menu bar on any page
    - **Selected→Export** from the menu bar on the Projects page
    - **Packages/Types→Export** from the menu bar on the Packages page
    - **Classes→Export** from the menu bar on the Classes page
    - **Interfaces→Export** from the menu bar on the Interfaces page

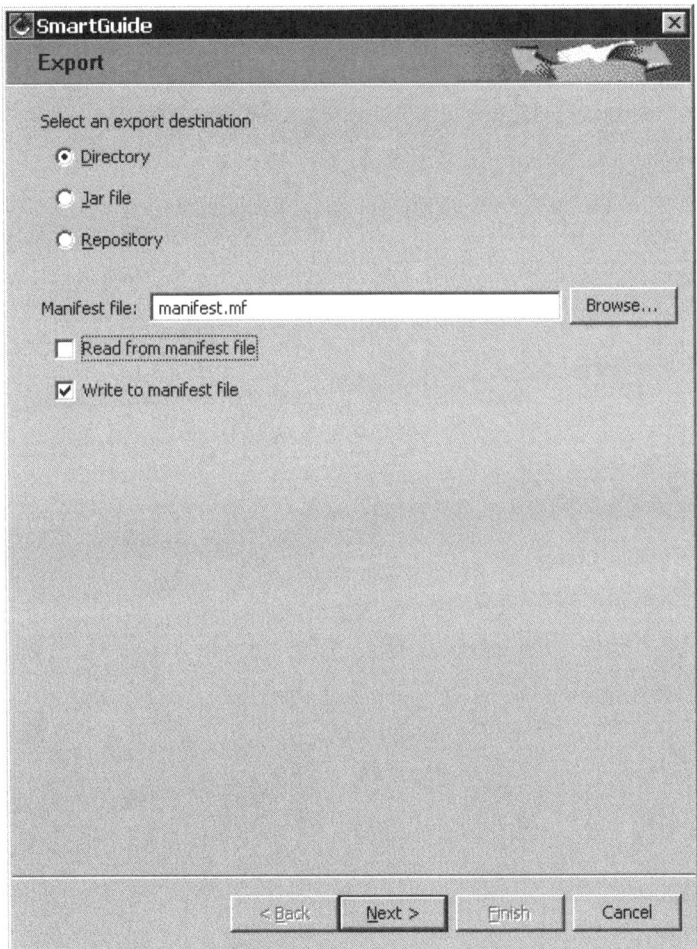

Figure 42. The Export SmartGuide

To choose a manifest file to create or update to contain your class or bean information, specify the file name of the manifest file.

3. Select the export destination:
   - **Directory** — .java or .class files
   - **Jar file** — .jar files
   - **Repository** — repository files

   For Directory exports, select:
   - The root directory where the export files will reside
   - The specific classes (source or bytecode) and resources to be exported
   - You can also set several options on the export:
     - Select referenced classes to export
     - Deselect the BeanInfo and Property Editor classes from the export
     - Whether to create HTML files to launch applets
     - Whether to overwrite existing files
     - Whether to open the created HTML files in a browser
     - Whether to seal the package

       Each packages can be specified as seal. Seal information will be written In manifest file of the JAR file.

   For Jar file exports (Figure 43), the options include those for Directory exports as well as these:
   - Selecting specific beans and classes to export
   - Whether to compress the contents of the Jar file

   For Repository exports, select:
   - The repository file to be exported
   - The specific projects or packages to export

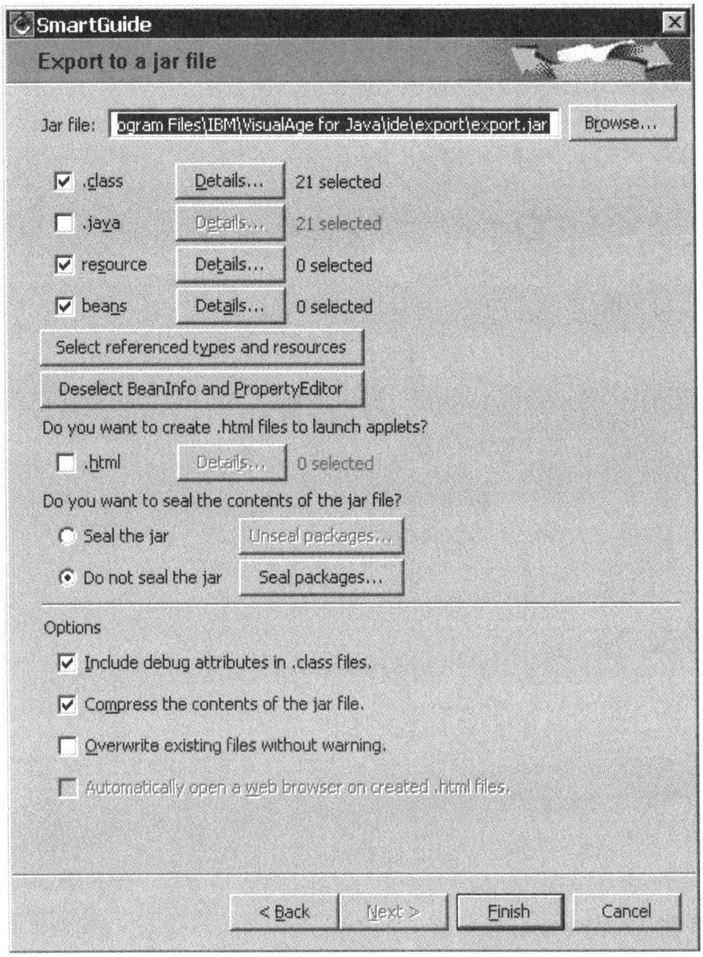

Figure 43. Exporting to a Jar file

Hints for exporting your code

VisualAge for Java has some powerful new features for exporting code. The Deployment Wizard is invoked by selecting the **Select referenced types and resources** button. The Deployment Wizard automatically includes the types your code needs. Therefore, your exported Jar files will only include the code they need.

When exporting a Jar file, you can select specific beans to export. This action forces the creation of a manifest file in your Jar file, enabling other environments to recognize the beans in your Jar file and other VisualAge for Java environments to automatically add beans from the JAR file to the palette.

If the JAR file is to be directly used in the Classpath for a Java application or applet, do not compress its contents.

You can also now export Visual Composition Editor information in Java source and class files. Select the **Generate meta data method** checkbox in the Design Time section of the Options dialog. VisualAge for Java will generate a `getBuilderdata` method that contains the Visual Builder information for the class.

Chapter 3. Migrating to Java2

VisualAge for Java Version 3.5 Professional Edition provides the full Java 2 SDK, Standard Edition, V1.2.2 support. This includes:

- JDK 1.2.2

  The IBM Developer Kit for Java code is based from Sun. The IBM requirements are: better performance, decreased time to market, improved scalability, and expertise.

  The IBM DK 1.2.2 provides enhanced functions and maintenance over the SUN reference SDK.

- Swing 1.1
- JSDK 2.1 + IBM Extension

  The JSDK 2.1 provides support to create and test Servlet 2.1 and test JSP 0.91 or 1.0 (WebSphere Application Server + FIXPACK2 supports JSP 1.1, but VisualAge for Java 3.5 + Patch 2 does not).

The Fix/Migrate SmartGuide

VisualAge Java Version 3.5 offers a tool, the Fix/Migrate SmartGuide, which provides an easy way to migrate the base Java classes and the Swing classes from JDK 1.1.x to JDK 1.2.2. It also migrates the Visual Composition information for Swing classes.

You can migrate any package or class names, for example, com.sun.java.swing.* ==>javax.swing.*

You can import code from VisualAge Java Version 2 or 3.

Do not make an open edition: The Migrate tool works on versioned editions only.

Select the class you want to migrate.

You can start the Fix/Migrate SmartGuide by selecting, from the Workbench window, **Selected→Reorganize→Fix/Migrate** (see Figure 44).

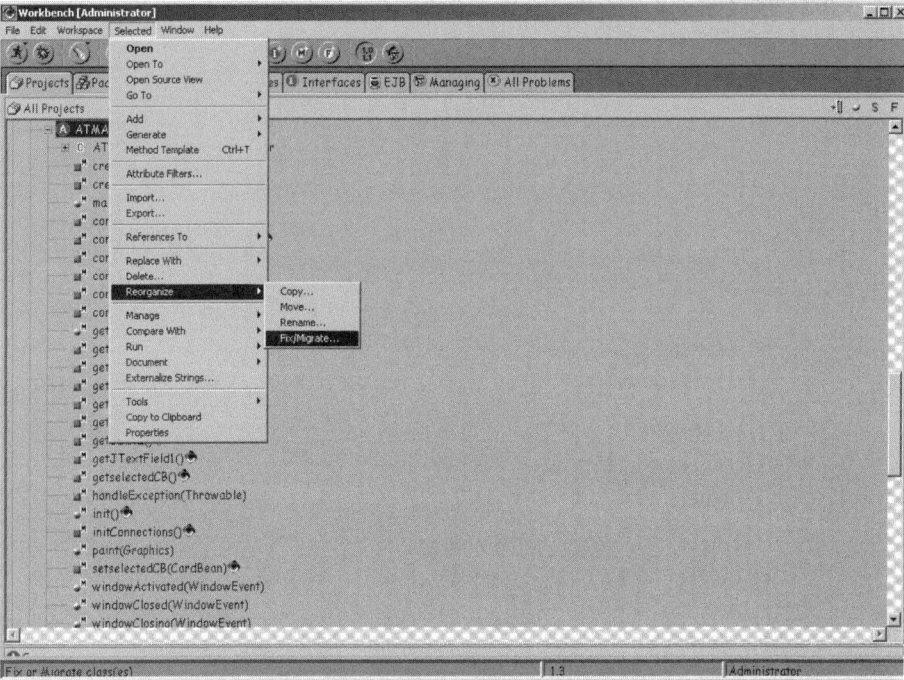

Figure 44. How to start the Fix/Migrate SmartGuide

The Fix/Migrate SmartGuide window opens. You can then indicate the From/to entries for class or package names that have changed (see Figure 45).

Select the **Include JDK1.2 renamed packages** checkbox to migrate the Swing classes in a Java application.

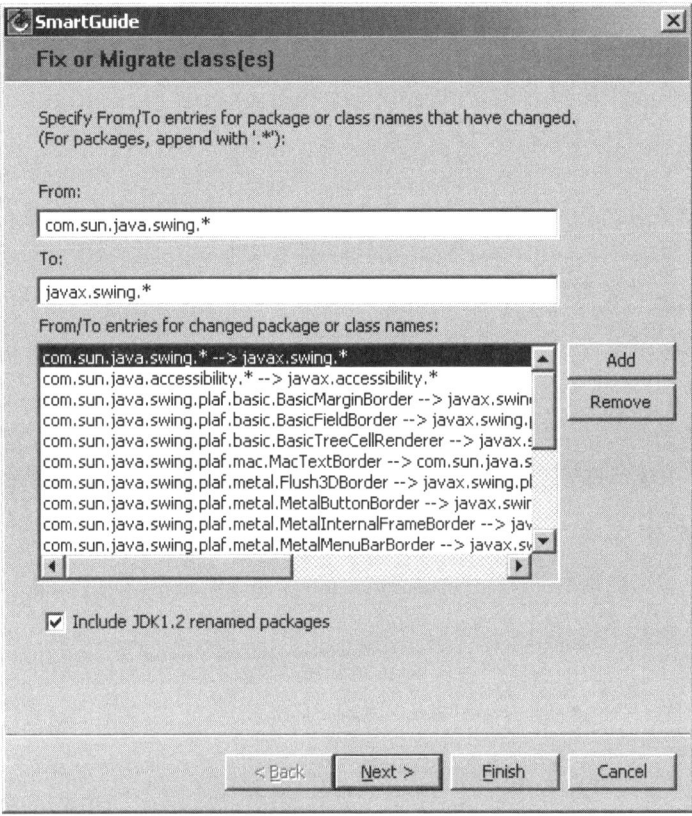

Figure 45. The Fix/Migrate SmartGuide window

Select the **Next** button.

The window from which you can specify package names to be excluded from the package name changes opens (see Figure 46).

To specify a package, append .* to the package name. For example, to repair all classes in myPackage, enter myPackage.* In the To field, enter the current name of the renamed class or package. Click **Add**.

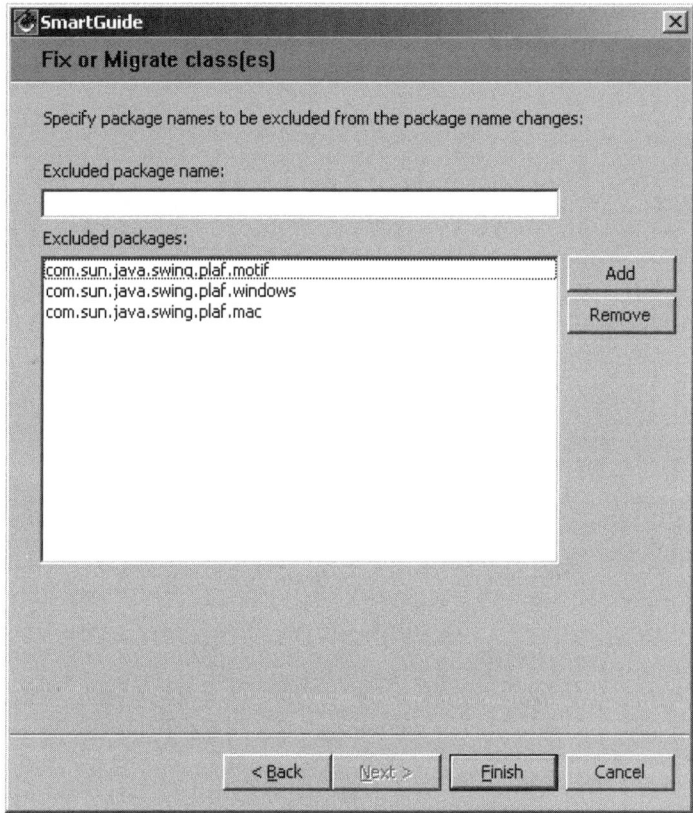

Figure 46. Fix/Migrate SmartGuide- Excluded packages-

Select the **Finish** button to run the migration.

You can then open the Visual Composition Editor and test.

The repair process

The Fix/Migrate SmartGuide can also repair broken class or package references due to migration of classes to the Java 2 SDK or the renaming of user-defined program elements. Because this sort of repair is not an exact science, follow these tips for the best results.

In the Workbench, look at the All Problems page to get a sense of what is broken. If possible, repair references at the class level. This gives you the most control over the order in which classes are repaired, minimizing transient compilation problems. If you do repair at the package or project level, VisualAge processes BeanInfo classes before their associated bean classes.

Repair referenced classes first, as necessary. Proceeding in this direction ensures that API updates for a referenced program element are available when the classes that refer to it are repaired.

If a given class has an associated BeanInfo class, repair the BeanInfo class first.

To fix errors in visual composites that remain after all classes have been repaired, open the composites in the Visual Composition Editor and regenerate code from the Bean menu.

To migrate references to the IBM Data Access libraries from Version 1.0 to Version 2.0, specify the following changes:

> COM.ibm.ivj.eab.data.* to com.ibm.ivj.eab.dab.*
>
> COM.ibm.ivj.javabeans.* to com.ibm.ivj.eab.dab.*

To migrate references to the javax.swing.preview.JFileChooser class, specify the following change:

> javax.swing.preview.* to javax.swing.*

Successful migration of class references to the Java 2 SDK does not ensure that all beans run as you expect them to.

Sun's implementation of some beans might have changed, so test migrated beans thoroughly.

You must use this tool for repairing visual composites, even if you make corrections by hand. This is because metadata must also be repaired. If you do not repair the metadata, VisualAge will probably generate incorrect code.

VisualAge can correct references to the following program elements: classes, interfaces, and packages:

- Superclass designation
- Import designations
- User-defined fields and methods
- Fields and methods that are generated for visual composites

If VisualAge detects any transient problems during the repair, an error window will appear. Make a note of the error and click **OK** to continue the process. In most cases, errors occur because of the order in which references are being repaired; these errors are usually corrected by the time that all references have been repaired. Following the repair guidelines will minimize this occurrence.

Migrating your servlet and JSPs

If you are migrating your servlet to JSDK2.1, which has been supported since WebSphere Application Server 3.0, you may update the following deprecated APIs. These APIs may be removed in the near future:

```
Sun APIs
HttpSessionContext
HttpSession.getSessionContext
HttpSession.isRequestedSessionIdFromUrl
HttpServletResponse.encodeUrl
HttpServletResponse.encodeRedirectUrl
HttpServiceRequest.setAttribute
HttpServiceResponse.callPage
ServletRequest.getRealPath
ServletContext.getServlet

IBM APIs
com.ibm.servlet.personalization.sam (removed)
com.ibm.servlet.servlets.personalization.util (removed)
com.ibm.servlet.connmgr
```

If your JSP is written in JSP 0.91, it is good time to update to JSP 1.0. You can use 0.91, but in the future, this may not be possible. To use JSP 0.91, check first to make sure that your code is not using deprecated servlet APIs.

If you are using com.sun.server.http.HttpServiceRequest or com.sun.server.http.HttpServiceResponse, you have to change the package name to javax.servlet.

Migrating JSP 0.91 to 1.0

To migrate your JSP, you have to change the tag (see Table 4).

Table 4. JSP conversion map

JSP 0.91	JSP 1.0
<SERVLET>	<jsp:include>
<BEAN>	<jsp:useBean>
<REPEAT>	<tsx:repeat>

Chapter 4. Beginning the ATM project

This chapter introduces the sample application that we will use throughout the book. It outlines the problem domain, including an object-oriented analysis, and presents the overall architecture of the solution.

This example application may seem familiar to people who read the previous version of this book, *Programming with VisualAge for Java, Version 2*, 0130212989, or to people who read the IBM Redbook, *VisualAge for Java Enterprise Version 2: Data Access Beans - Servlets - CICS Connector*, SG24-5265. Be forewarned, however, that only the problem is the same! The solution is different, as we will now focus on deploying it as a Web application where we will deal with an inherently stateless client.

Problem domain

In order to explain the various features of VisualAge for Java, we will apply the theory (explained in the following chapters), by developing one true Web application. The problem to be solved by the application is explained first.

In short, we will focus on a simulation of the interaction with an *Automated Teller Machine* (ATM), as originally used to get money "out of the wall". All around the world there are many different names for those machines, although the basic concept is essentially the same worldwide: You insert your card, type in a number, choose the amount of money, get the money, and recover your card.

Such ATM machines differ in many ways. One difference is in how or when the resulting money transaction is booked: Often it will be deducted directly from a bank account, or it might be regarded as taking a credit. The cards in these cases would then be called debit or credit cards respectively. Nowadays it is common for ATMs to accommodate both situations, but in this book, we will limit our scope to debit cards. Consequently, when we use the term *card*, you should think about a *debit card*.

There are also big differences to observe in the set of other services provided by ATM machines worldwide: They show the balance and history of the bank account, and they allow you to wire money, request cheques, put money in an electronic purse, make an appointment with a person from your bank, apply for a short term loan, and so on. Here we will talk about an ATM which is only capable of dispensing money and showing some detail on a bank account.

We continue simplifying by saying that each card has to be associated to at least one bank account. The card in our situation could be used to check the balance and get the history of transactions on the associated bank account, besides the original notion of 'distributing money'. The received money is directly deducted from the associated bank account, as in the case of a debit card.

In most countries the card can also be associated to many different bank accounts: Checking or saving accounts of somebody are normally accessible using only one card. But also, accounts owned by different persons can be manipulated using only one card. In addition, a bank account itself can be associated to many cards, as in the example of a company account where many people have the right to deduct money from one account. Those people would then only have one card giving access to both their own account and to this company shared bank account.

Our example application has no notion of the owner of an account, it will simply allow different accounts to be associated to one card and different cards to one bank account in order to incorporate all of the above cases. In our situation only the card itself has an owner.

Let us now explain what we understand by the term *transaction*. We say that a transaction is always between two accounts: The balance of the source account is deducted and the target account is augmented with the amount of money specified by the transaction. When the transaction involved collecting cash money, the target account would be a bank account associated to the ATM. A refill of an electronic purse on the other hand would have an (imaginary) bank account indicating that purse as target of the transaction. As a consequence of all this, we can assume that the amount of a transaction cannot be negative. To keep track of things, each deposit or withdraw is represented by a transaction.

We make the distinction between *checking* accounts and *savings* accounts. A checking account would have an overdraft protection up to a certain amount of money: This has the effect that money can be redrawn from the account even if there is not enough money left, up to that overdraft amount as a negative balance. Note that this is not exactly the way the US checking accounts work, although overseas checking accounts used to work like this. A savings account also has a peculiarity: There is a minimum (positive) balance to be respected at all times.With the ATM you can get money from either checking or savings accounts, an assumption which — for a change — does not match most European customs.

Another rather obvious simplification of the real world problem is to ignore the existence of different currencies and fractions: Therefore, we will talk about a certain amount of money while not specifying its currency — we will simply call it *Money*.

This example still resembles a real world application in some respects. Think about the following configuration: a "cyber" ATM (Web site on the Internet) that enables persons with an electronic purse to refill that purse via the Internet using a debit card. All you would need to accomplish this is a device to read your card and a device to update your electronic purse, both connected to a computer on the Internet.

When using SmartCard technology for both the identification of the debit card and as an implementation of the electronic purse, one could suffice with a SmartCard reader attached to the serial port of a regular computer. This configuration is already in use in some countries (for example, Belgium) where debit card and electronic purse happen to be on one and the same physical card.

Besides a Web application, we will also develop a Swing based application based on this common ATM problem description as we illustrate the usage of the graphical editor of VisualAge for Java (see Chapter 7, "Creating GUI applications" on page 143).s

Building the ATM model

The goal in building a model for the example application is one of communication and documentation: At the end of this chapter, you should be able to easily find your way in the code of the example based on the different diagrams and comments included here. If you understand everything in this chapter, you should understand everything in the test implementation that we will discuss at the end of this chapter.

When analyzing the above description of the problem domain, we directly discover the following candidates to be modelled as objects in our example application:

Card	Gives access to one or more bank accounts
Bank account	Either checking or savings accounts
Money	Represents an amount in a given currency
Transaction	A record of a money transfer between accounts
Person	The human being interacting with an ATM machine

Bank	Institution issuing the bank accounts and the cards
ATM	Machine allowing you to get cash money with a card
Electronic purse	Electronic device that can be used as a regular purse
PIN	*Personal Identification Number* protecting a card

We will keep these definitions in mind while we try to get more detailed insight by specifying the use cases.

Use cases

Here, we observe one actor: *Person*. This actor represents somebody with a card that physically fits into the card reader of the ATM machine. He or she is the only one to interact with the ATM application (which is everything behind the systems border).

The general diagram showing the interaction between Person and the system representing our *ATM application* is presented in Figure 47. We have eight use cases:

Accept Card	ATM shows a welcome message; Person can insert a card into the card reader of the ATM.
Validate Login	ATM lets Person type in the PIN for the inserted card.
Consume Card	Person tried too many times to enter a valid PIN; the card reader stores the card somewhere inside the ATM; then ATM displays a message.
List Accounts	All the accounts that the inserted card gives access to are listed, Person can select one account to work with
Show Account Detail	ATM shows the selected account and offers Person the choice of getting money or seeing the history list of transactions.
Dispense Cash	ATM asks how much money Person wants to withdraw and will give that money when the conditions (balance on account, enough money in ATM, and so on) allow it.
Show Account History	ATM lists the transactions on the current account.
Eject Card	Person wants to stop working with the ATM; the card reader gives back the current card; the ATM displays a message asking to remove the card.

A more detailed description of the use cases in the diagram can be obtained by browsing the HTML version of the model that was generated with Rational Rose. It is part of the resource package, available for download from the Redbook site or on the provided CD provided (see Appendix B, "Using the additional material" on page 363).

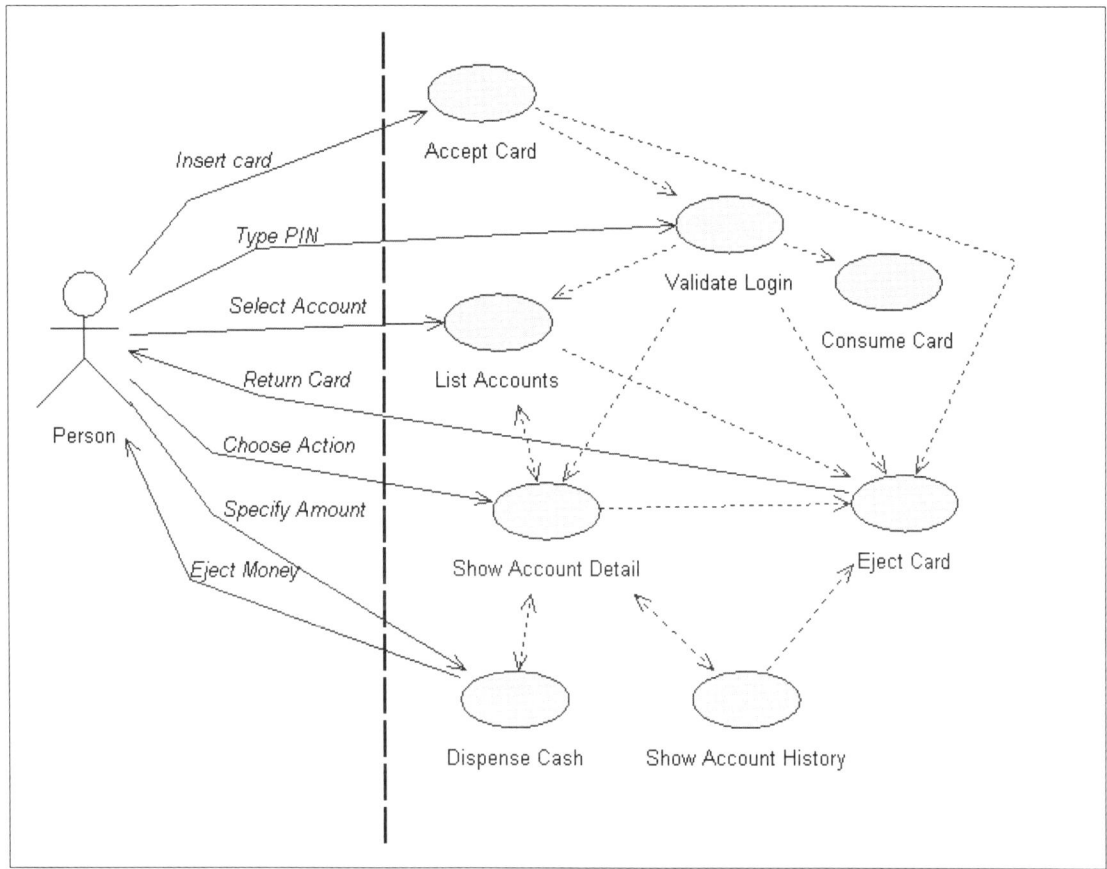

Figure 47. ATM use case diagram

You might have noticed that we have a use case called 'Dispense Cash' and no 'Refill Electronic Purse'. When elaborating the use case descriptions, we noticed that they become unnecessarily complex by trying to make a distinction between the electronic purse card and the debit card. Another observation in favor of removing this concept from our example, is that the use case 'Dispense Cash' is basically just the same. Besides, more people will recognize an ATM dispensing 'real money' then a system refilling an electronic purse.

In the beginning of this section we already came up with a first draft for a set of objects. We now see that we need to adjust this. The electronic purse would disappear but some components of the ATM are mentioned so many times by now, that we add them to our list of candidates to become objects in our example application:

- **Card reader**
- **Cash dispenser**

Another observation, when reading the use cases, is that we need to consider the state of the ATM when specifying a condition on a use case.

ATM state diagrams

The state of the ATM really says which actions are possible and which are not. In designing a Web application, it is very important to consider this. Unlike with regular client / server applications, it is possible for a client to try to execute actions which are not allowed in a certain state of the system. The reason for this is twofold.

First of all, the protocol used in the communication between both parties in a legacy client / server application is more secure (or more easily secure), so we can rely on the identity of the client. The HTTP protocol used in Web applications is prone to 'fake' clients (except for its HTTPS dialect), who can easily invoke requests 'at the wrong time'.

Secondly, there is no way the server can call back to the client to ensure that it is talking to a valid client — that is, a client which is only requesting services at the proper times. Clients expressing the behavior of taking care when to fire actions would typically implement, for themselves, a sort of state. The HTTP protocol, however, is stateless and unidirectional, so this situation cannot be attained with normal Web clients.

To document the states of a certain type, UML provides us with state diagrams. Such a diagrams show all possible states a certain type can be in, together with all the possible transitions between those states. The transitions between the states can be caused by both internal as by external actions. Not all possible actions are listed: If they have no impact on the state of a type and when they can be executed at all times (read: in all states of the type), then it is uncommon to list them at all in a state diagram.

We made two state diagrams for the ATM system because we have two big categories of states. The states where the ATM machine is used by somebody, all have common behavior: No other person can use it, the ATM can time-out because the user did not touch it for a certain time, and so on.

First we model this set of 'In Use' states as one, in order to compare it with the others, then we go into detail on the different 'sub' states of an ATM when it is being used. Figure 48 shows the general states for the ATM; Figure 49 explains the sub-states that make up the 'In Use' state in the first state diagram.

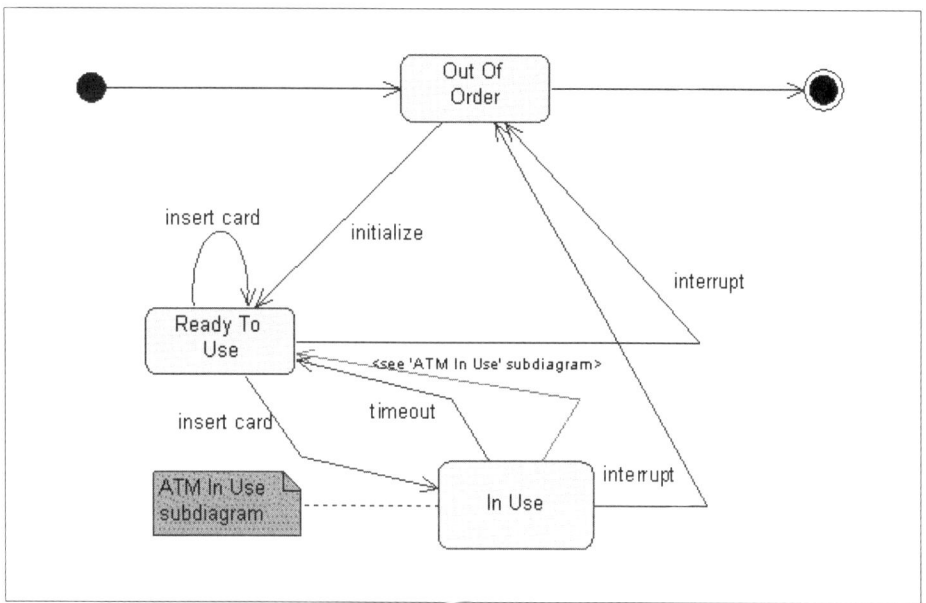

Figure 48. ATM state diagram

The 'insert card' action is mentioned twice as an action on which an ATM in the 'Ready To Use' state can react. The first transition occurs when Person enters a card which is not recognized by the card reader. The card reader will then eject that card and the ATM will stay in the 'Ready To Use' case. Only a card recognized by the card reader will be able to change the state of the ATM into 'In Use', which is represented by the second 'insert card' transition.

The 'In Use' can be abandoned not only by a time-out (when for a certain amount of time, there was no interaction between the ATM and Person), but also by one of the transitions modelled in the sub-states diagram detailing the 'In Use' state: see Figure 49.

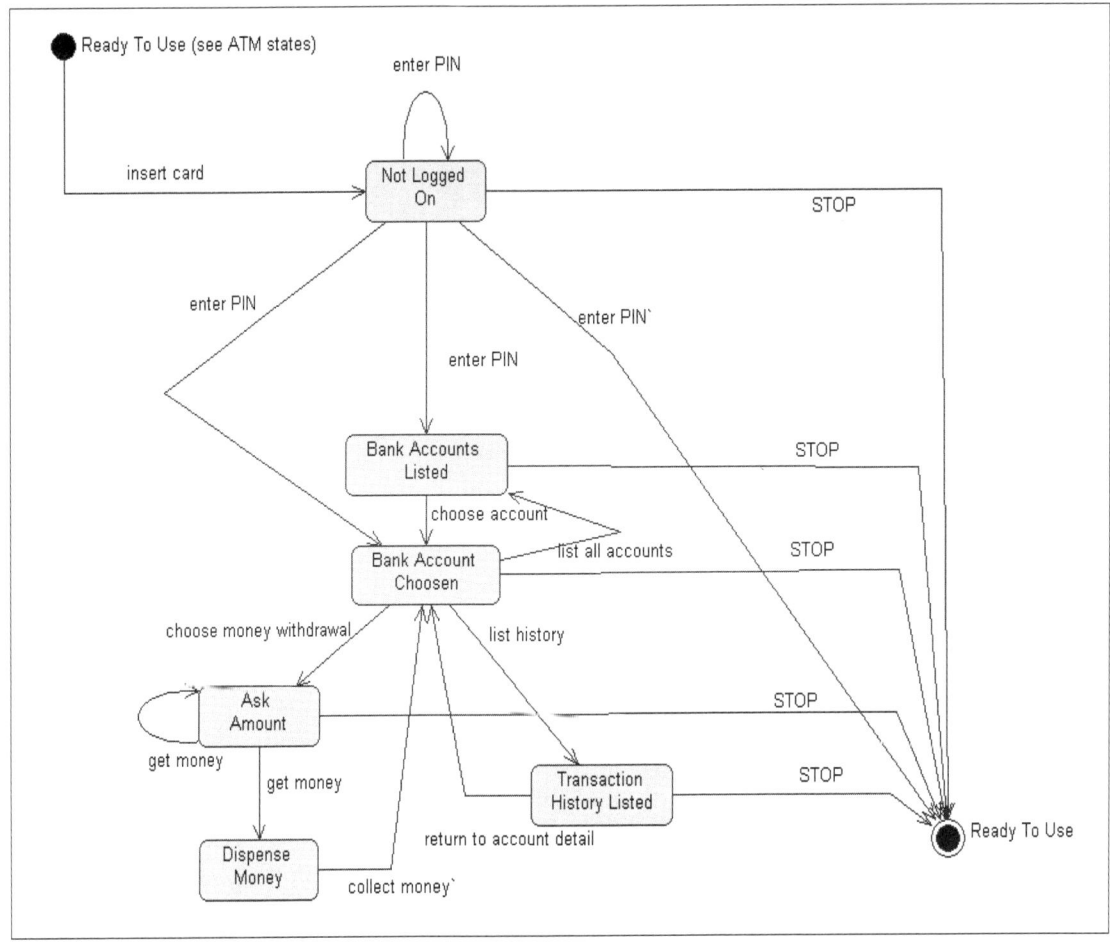

Figure 49. Sub state Diagram of ATM In Use State

The diagram shows six sub-states of the ATMs general 'In Use' case:

Not Logged On The card reader contains a card, but Person did not authenticated itself (by PIN) yet as being the owner of the card.

Bank Accounts Listed The ATM displays the list of bank accounts associated with the current card.

Bank Account Chosen Person chooses one of the bank accounts associated with the card or the card has only one bank account associated to it, in which case this account was choose implicitly.

Ask Amount   The ATM asks Person to specify the amount of money he wants to get.

Dispense Money   The cash dispenser of the ATM is searching for the requested amount of money and presents it to be taken by Person.

Transaction History Listed   The ATM presents the list of transactions for the current bank account.

Once again, we advise you to take a closer look at these diagrams by browsing the UML diagrams themselves, although some explanations are in order here.

The first thing to notice is that Person can at any time choose to stop the current session, with the exception of when the cash dispenser is giving money. The ATM will direct the card reader to eject the card and the system will return to the 'Ready To Use' state.

Another thing to notice is that there are four different transitions possible after the action of entering a PIN code:

- This is the normal case when PIN is validated and the ATM presents the list of associated bank accounts.
- This is the same as the above, but involves the case of having only one account associated to the card.
- The PIN code is incorrect; Person gets another chance to fill in the correct PIN.
- The PIN code is still incorrect, and there were too many attempts.

Two transitions on the diagram are marked with a '(dash). The 'Collect Money' action is done by Person. This would be detected by the cash dispenser in a real world application. In our implementation we simplify by saying that the ATM automatically returns to the 'Bank Account Chosen' state after a certain amount of time. This period is dependant on the amount of money to be dispensed.

This means that the 'Collect Money' action will not be implemented, the state of the machine will always make the transition by itself.

The transition between the 'Not Logged On' and the 'Ready To Use' state — which happens when too many attempts (of the action: 'enter PIN') took place — will also be skipped as a simplification.

Analysis class diagram

Let us now look back at our candidates to become types in our application. Two more proposed candidates are rejected because they do not seem to be used to solve our scope of the ATM problem:

A Bank is never mentioned anymore, so it seems that the difference between bank institutions is not more relevant to our case. We give the BankAccount type itself the responsibility of keeping track of all bank accounts. This approach uses the types ATM, Card, and Transaction, which now have to take care of their instances, together with providing the necessary behavior to search in those lists of objects.

Another type we mentioned before and that we leave out is Person. The client of a normal application can have some attributes and behavior. In a Web application, however, we cannot reach the client to retrieve those attributes or to call its methods (see also the discussion at the beginning of "ATM state diagrams" on page 78). This makes Person also superfluous.

Below is the list of classes we do retain:

ATM	Machine allowing you to get cash money with a card
Bank account	Either checking or savings accounts
Card	Gives access to one or more bank accounts
CardReader	Device in which Person inserts a card
CashDispenser	Device that can dispense cash money
Money	Represents an amount in a given currency
PIN	*Personal Identification Number* protecting a card
Transaction	A record of a money transfer between accounts

Figure 50 shows the static relationship between these types. Some methods are also listed, together with the most important attributes.

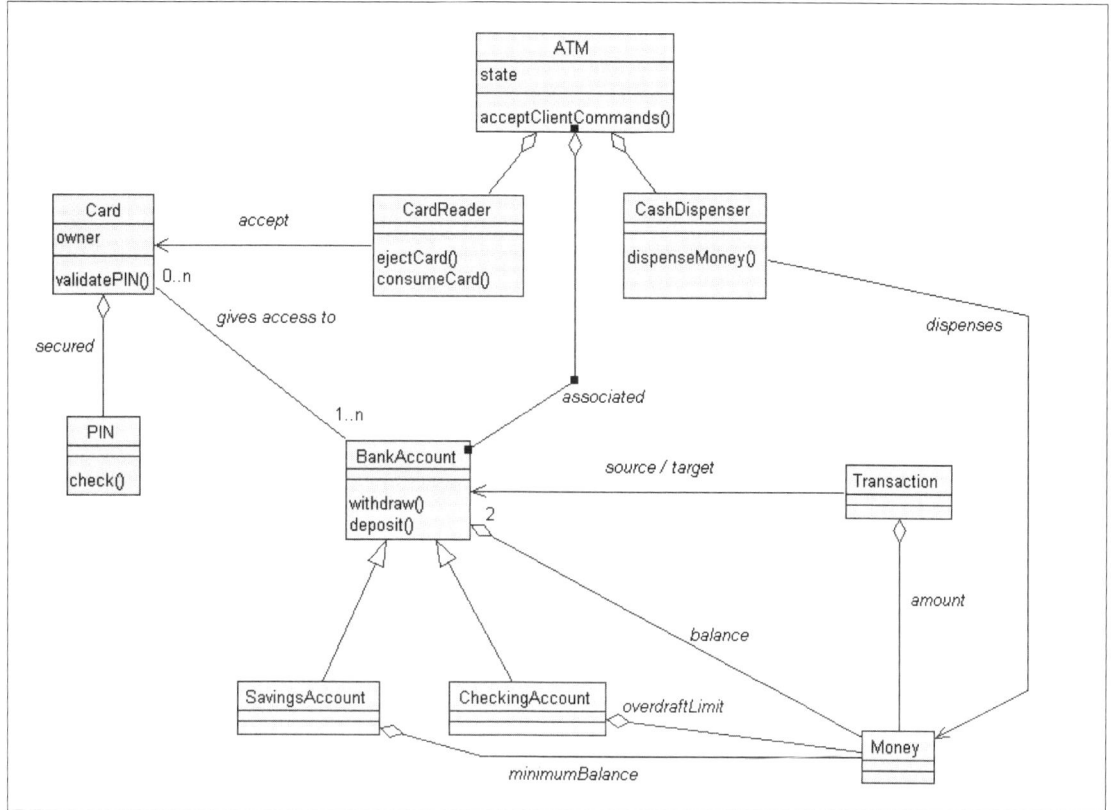

Figure 50. Analysis class diagram

Study this diagram and the associated documentation carefully in order to get a sound understanding of the requirements for our Web application.

We briefly describe the main relations here: We say that a Card is *secured* (from unauthorized usage) by a PIN; only when a correct number (checked by the PIN) is given, the ATM will allow additional actions using the card. The card reader *accepts* cards, that *give access to* — at least one, but possibly more — bank accounts.

All transactions have a *source* and a *target* account. Remember that no money can be deposited or withdrawn without a transaction: Even an ATM withdrawal is represented by a transaction. Therefore an ATM is *associated* with a (target) bank account 'receiving' all money transferred from the account the user chooses when asking for cash money from the ATM.

Each transaction also keeps track of the *amount* of Money involved. Bank accounts have a *balance*. On top of that, a CheckingAccount is protected with an *overdraftLimit*, and a SavingsAccount specifies a *minimumBalance*. Money is *dispensed* by the CashDispenser device of the ATM.

This is a model that represents the (limited) problem we want to tackle in terms of the problem domain. It is a deliverable used in *analyzing* a problem. Next we are to make some decisions that will eventually lead to a design model which is expressed in terms of concepts used to *solve* the problem.

Design class diagrams

In this section we look at how the model explained before can be turned into a system that instantiates business objects that are able to solve the stated problem: We now start the design phase. Note that we already assume using Java as the language for the implementation when taking the design decisions in this chapter. The design phase could also be split into a language independent version — and a Java version, but this would make this chapter needlessly longer.

First we look at the PIN type mentioned in the analysis (Figure 50). It models PINs that are only accessible by a Card instance. Its only responsibility is to match a given string of numbers with itself in order to authenticate the owner of the Card. Here we decide to incorporate PIN into Card: Figure 51 shows that Card gets the responsibility of validating a PIN.

The link between ATM and BankAccount in the analysis class diagram says (see the associated note) that the amount of each cash withdrawal is limited to the actual amount of cash available in the ATM. This means that the transaction — with as target the bank account associated to the ATM — can fail by this restriction. We had to decide where to implement that restriction: Make it a responsibility of the ATM or of the BankAccount. Checking if there is enough money to dispense can be compared to the restrictions on checking and savings account that restrict withdrawals based on the respective limits 'overdraft' and 'minimumBalance' which can also cause the transaction to fail.

Because of that we decided to put the implementation of checking this limitation at the side of the bank account. More specifically, we made up a new type of account: *ATMAccount*. To enable it to perform its control, an ATMAccount has an additional attribute representing the initial (or maximum) amount of cash money available to the ATM to dispense. Each time money is dispensed it is done at the same time as transferring the amount of money from the user's account to that ATMAccount, at which time it does the necessary checking.

Every dispense of money is compensated by a deposit on the associated ATMAccount, keeping the 'value' of the ATM constant over time. Compare this ATMAccount with a cashier's account used to book all money transactions a certain cashier is handling. The balance of such an account, together with the real amount of cash available in the cashier's drawer would also have to be the same at all times.

Note that we do not have to make another attribute indicating the actual amount of cash available to the dispenser, as it can be deducted from both the balance and the initial amount: It should always be the difference between the current balance and the initial amount of cash.

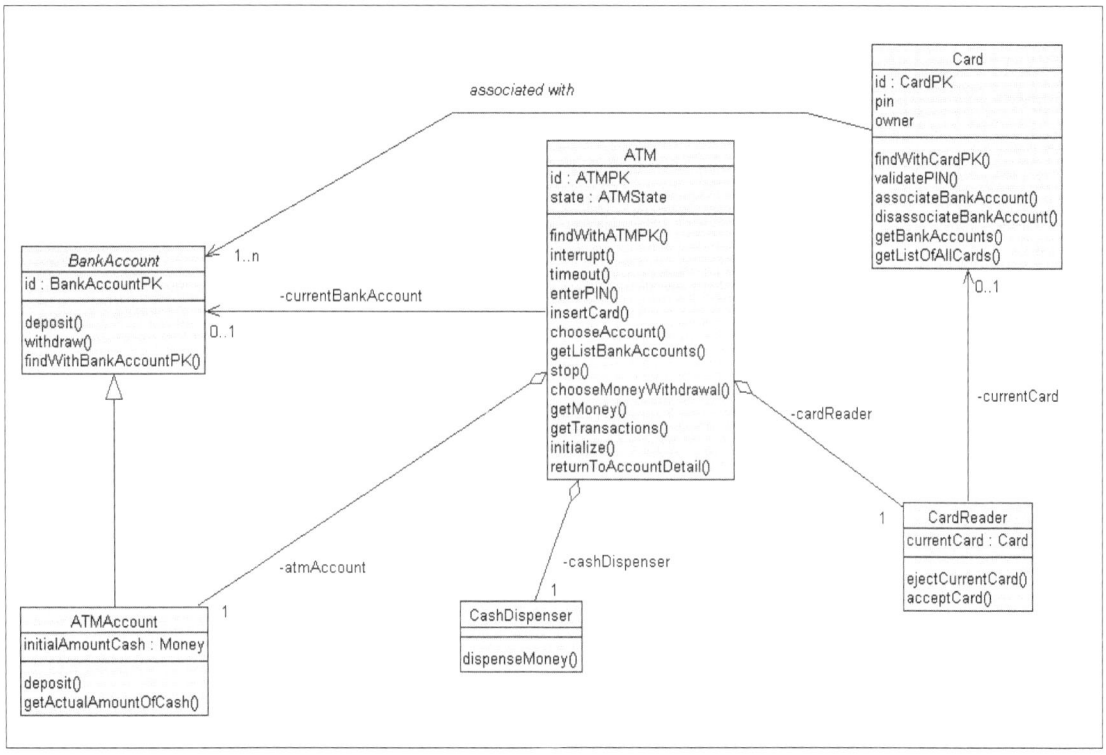

Figure 51. ATM related part of the design model

The above diagram shows that ATM also contains a CashDispenser and a CardReader besides its ATMAccount. All three subparts of the ATM are fully bound to the ATM: They are created at the same time, they cannot exist without their ATM, and they have in common that they are not viewable from the outside. The ATM uses them to implement its behavior, all requests go to the ATM which then decides whether to forward them to its parts.

Figure 51 also tells you that we gave each Card, BankAccount, ATM and Transaction an identity (attribute *id*). This will allow us to retrieve instances of this class. You can say that they are the primary key to retrieve objects of those types. We want to make sure that all these references have some common behavior (conversion to/from string, comparison, and so on.), although we also want to avoid intermixing ids pointing to different sorts of objects. Using inner classes and having them extend a common *PrimaryKey* class (see Figure 52) meets all this requirements.

Besides wanting to store primary keys in a database, we also want to include them in Web pages — thus, the need for conversion to and from the String type and constructor from a String. For convenience we provide a default constructor that generates a primary key value itself.

The hashCode() method (together with equals()) enables us to store and retrieve the business objects using the HashMap type.

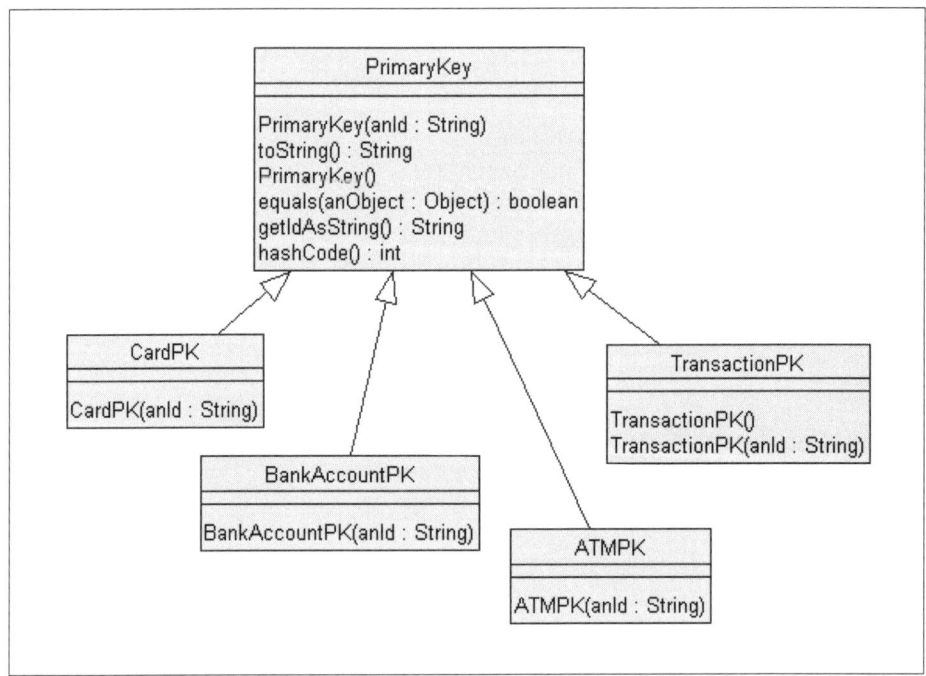

Figure 52. Design class diagram related to primary keys

The classes of all identifiable business objects — which are responsible for keeping track of all their instances — all implement a finder method: This method takes a primary of the corresponding type and looks to see if it can find an object with a matching key. If it cannot find one, we create a new object — with reasonable default state — instead. This will keep our testing code a lot simpler, because it will always work even when no testing data is supplied.

Transactions are one of these BOs that are identifiable by their own specialization of PrimaryKey. As you can see in Figure 53, the only way to create a Transaction object is by using the Transaction class method *createTrx()*. This method is responsible to ensure that no withdrawal without deposit (or no deposit without withdrawal) can take place. It will throw a *TransactionAbortedException* when it cannot create a (full) transaction and will revert all changes already done to return to the state at the start of the method.

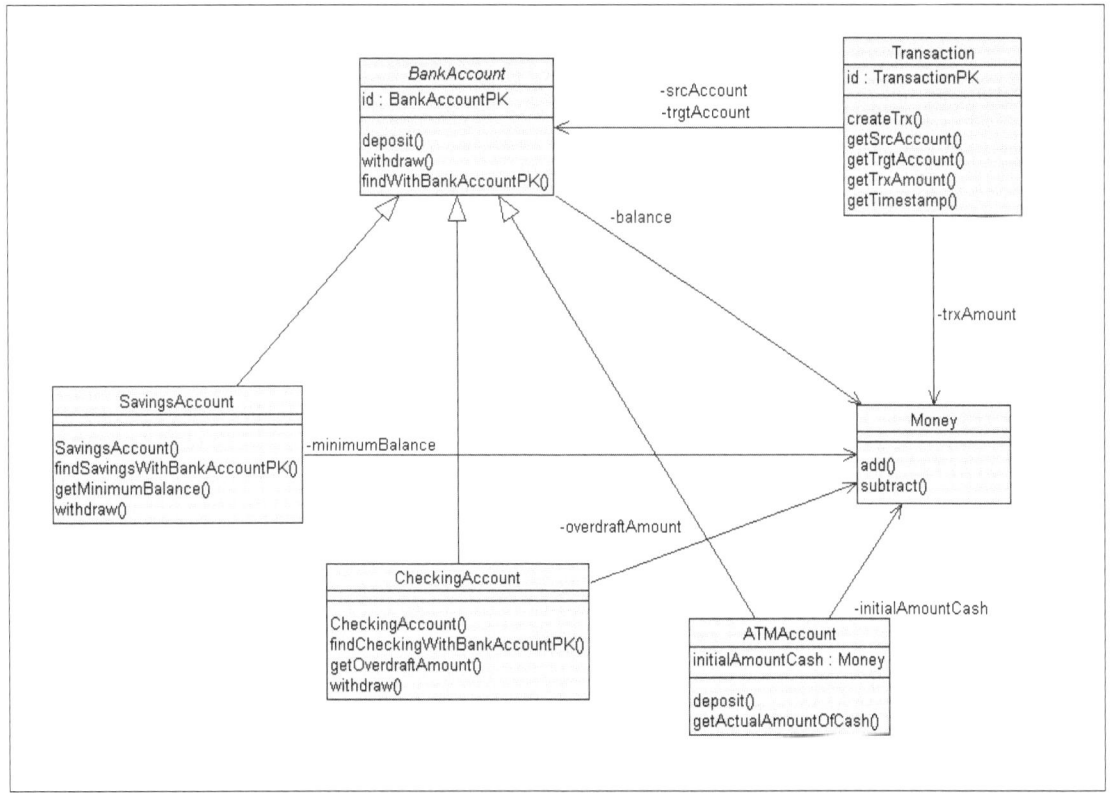

Figure 53. Transaction

Chapter 4. Beginning the ATM project **87**

This TransactionAbortedException is the parent of some other exceptions as you can see in Figure 54: A *NotEnoughCashException* is thrown by an ATMAccount when trying to do a deposit (compensating a money withdrawal) that would bring the balance above the *initialAmountCash* value: It prevents trying to dispensing more money then available to the CashDispenser of the ATM.

The other two exceptions descend from *ExceedLimitException*, which indicates that a user's account cannot cover the withdrawal. The *OverdraftLimitExceededException* signals that the current money transfer from this account would bring its balance below the overdraft limit of the CheckingAccount. *BelowMinimumBalanceException* does the same, but for SavingsAccounts that would go below their minimum balance.

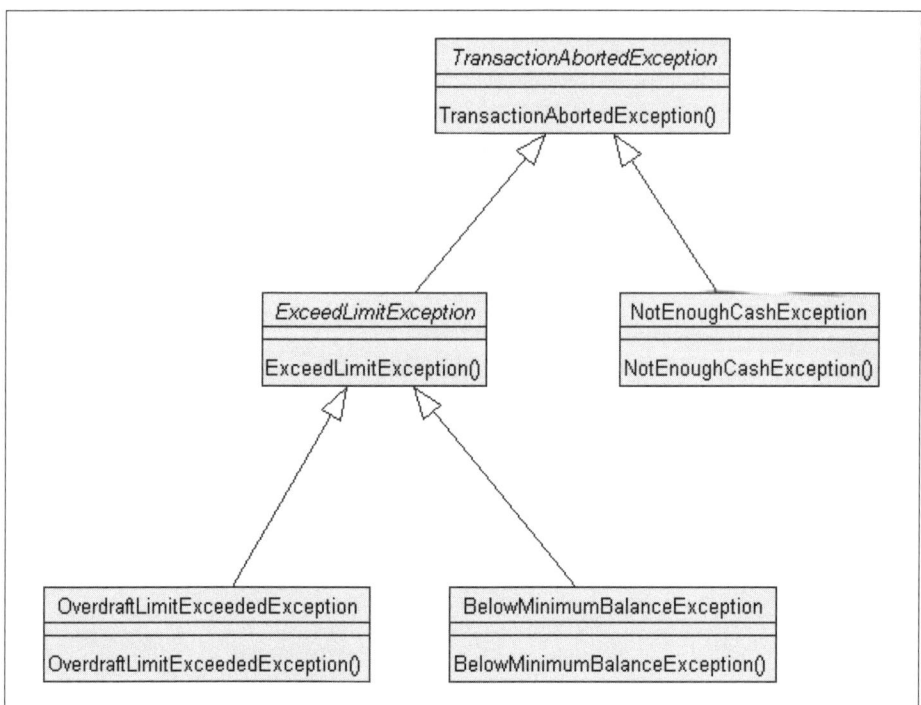

Figure 54. TransactionAbortedException diagram

This structure will prove very handy when using JSPs (Chapter 6, "Creating JSPs" on page 129) to customize the error messages of our Web application: The internal processing logic will handle (and eventually re-throw) *TransactionAbortedException*s while those JSPs can be designed in a more granular fashion (afterwards), because they can help the user find out what has happened, based on the exact subtype.

Note that all these exception types have only one constructor. The String passed describes the error message in a human readable form, suitable for debugging or testing purposes.

Another class that may seem superfluous at first sight is *Money*. We choose to model it as a separate type in order to make it easier when people want to extend this design by using a real-world version of money with currency and fractions (an argument which also holds true for the other types). Another advantage is the familiar Java type of checking: In the case of human error, it is less likely that you will accidentally misuse a method when taking a parameter of type Money, then when accepting a regular number. Also, the compiler will detect the error — even before running the program — if you are trying to pass inappropriate values.

When carefully examining the above diagrams — together with the complete design available as described in Appendix B, "Using the additional material" on page 363 — you may have noticed the fact that the identifiable BOs have no method allowing us to remove them. This is another simplification we took: Adding those methods would not bring much to our discussion, while not allowing it also relieves us from discussing synchronizing access to the HashMap we will use in the first implementation and eliminating existing references to these objects.

Interaction diagram

As an illustration of how the business objects mentioned above work together to accomplish the requested functionality, we made a sequence diagram. The scenario we choose is the most fundamental, that of getting money out:

Preconditions:

Person has entered his card in an ATM, authenticated, chosen a checking account, and asked to withdraw money: The ATM in the ASK_AMOUNT state, it asks the amount. Person wants to get 100, the chosen checking account has enough money to cover this transaction and the ATM also has the 100 in cash.

Scenario:

Person enters 100. The ATM withdraws the current (checking) account with 100 and its CashDispenser unit dispenses 100. Person takes the money. ATM returns or showing the current account.

The sequence diagram in Figure 55 shows that the actor (Person) entering 100 results in a message to the ATM: *getMoney*. The ATM then asks Transaction to create a new instance given the current (checking) account as

source, its ATMAccount as target and the amount (100): *createTrx*.
Transaction creates a *new* instance of itself and call the method *withdraw* on the checking account. This one *checks* its balance and *subtracts* the amount from it. Transaction then asks the ATMAccount the *deposit*. The ATMAccount also first *checks* before *adding* it to its balance. The transaction succeeded so Transaction *adds* its newly created instance to the list. ATM *changes its state* to DISPENSE_MONEY and asks the dispenser to *dispenseMoney*. After the CashDispenser gives the *cash*, the ATM returns to the BANK_ACCOUNT_CHOOSEN *state*.

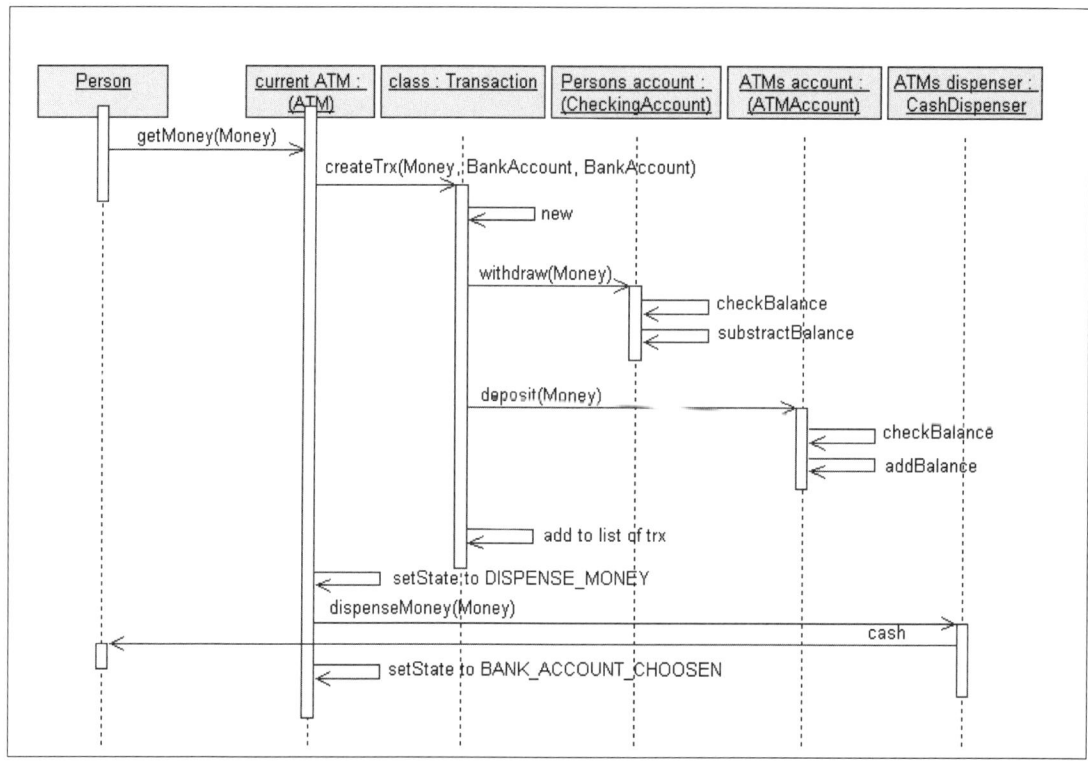

Figure 55. Sequence diagram for the 'get money' scenario

We hope that the design of our application is clear to you by now. If not, we suggest that you consult the complete model and its documentation (see Appendix B, "Using the additional material" on page 363). We can now go on discussing the infrastructure, putting all these things together with the different implementations.

Overall architecture

This section will lay out the different environments where the example will be used. The business objects designed before will form the basis of this all. They model the solution and are therefore the only ones responsible for executing the business logic.

If — at all — there happens to be any business logic present in other parts than these business objects, it will not impact the implementation of the logic in the BOs. Therefore it should only be used as an aid serving the purpose of enhancing a particular case. For example, the entered PIN number could be checked against illegal characters by using JavaScript in a HTML form asking to enter this PIN code. Although this might have been a business rule that will be checked again by the BOs, the use of JavaScript and duplicating this is generally considered a good implementation in that it avoids server round-trips: JavaScript is implemented in the user's browser which should be responsive, in contrary to a check with the BOs over the Internet which has a greater chance of being slow.

The big picture

The business objects are shown in Figure 56 as being the center of it all. The architecture throughout this book is a basic three-tiered model. The top layer represents persistent storage, while the middle layer is the implementation of the business logic (BO-layer). Everything below represents some kind of interface specific to the environment of the user of the application. This layer basically translates the input to and the output from the core implementation of the program.

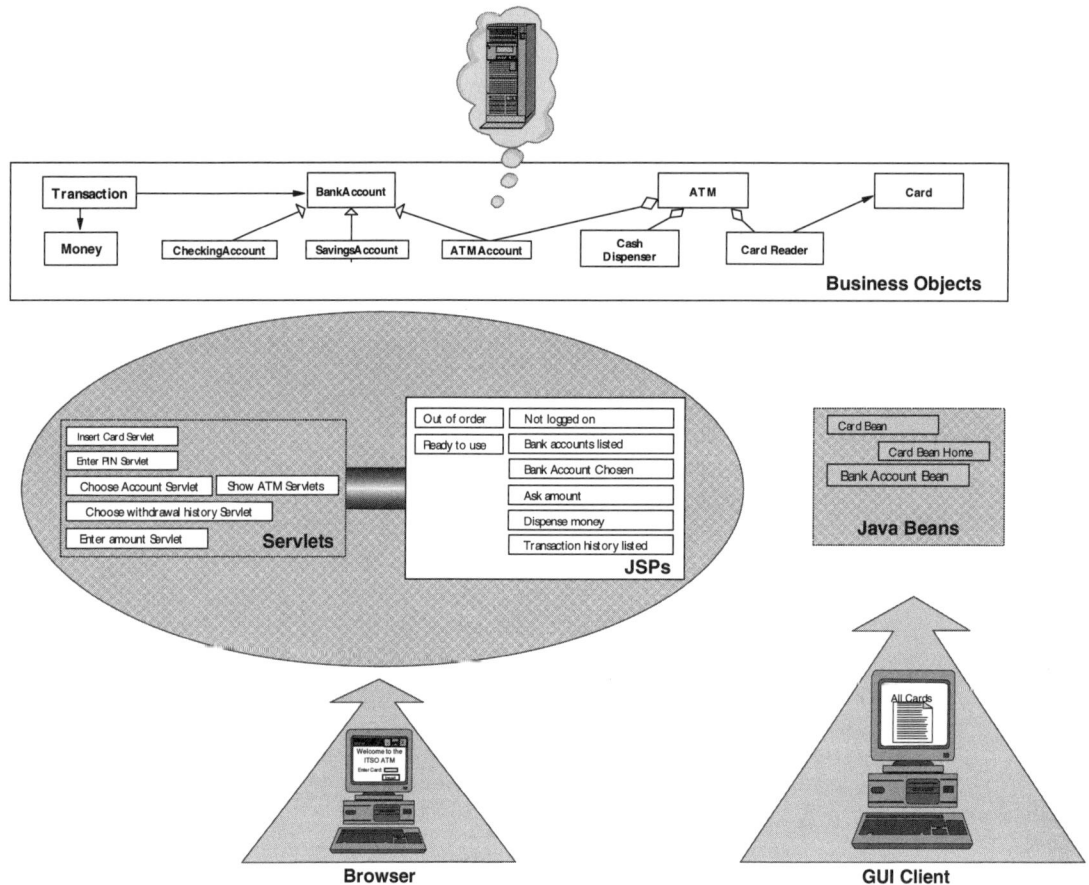

Figure 56. Architectural diagram

You can see two major implementations of the representation layer:

- GUI, traditional C/S client
- Browser, Web application

GUI client

The Graphical User Interface (GUI) version will be implemented as a Java application and as an applet. This client will illustrate the Visual Composition Editor (VCE) component of VisualAge for Java. For a change, this does not implement the ATM interaction, but instead, it provides some kind of administrative client to access the ATM system.

As you will see in Chapter 7, "Creating GUI applications" on page 143, the VCE works on JavaBeans. The block shown in Figure 56 shows some JavaBeans wrapping the business objects. A difference to note already, is that the class level responsibilities of the BOs are now separated and put in a JavaBean with the *Home* suffix: Finder methods on the Card are, for example, implemented by *CardBeanHome* which forwards its request to the corresponding Card class method.

Browser client

The Web application implementation can be seen as a convertor which converts HTTP requests to messages sent to the BOs. The results are then converted to HTML and sent back (again using the HTTP protocol) to the browser based client.

The Web application block as shown in the above figure contains two blocks:
- Servlets
- Java Server Pages

Chapter 5, "Creating servlets" on page 109 explains what servlets are and implements the example application without using JSPs. Chapter 6, "Creating JSPs" on page 129 then explains what JSPs are and make a new implementation based on a servlet-only implementation to use those JSP techniques.

In the beginning of this chapter we explained a crucial difference between traditional Client /Server applications and Web applications (clients of Web applications are inherently stateless): In short, Web applications should expect calls on all their methods at anytime, also when not appropriate considering the state of the underlying BOs. In designing this application, we have already ensured against improper use by fixing the states of the ATM.

The states of the ATM indisputably say what can be done with an ATM at any given time in its life cycle. Following this and because of the fact that you can easily discover the state of a real ATM by looking at it, we can associate the ATM states with the different representations of the ATM. Both the servlet implementation and the JSP implementation will exploit this fact. The central part in this is the *ShowATMServlet*, whose only responsibility is to return the current ATM (if it can determine any) in the state it is currently in. This servlet is the only one which will create a response to the client browser (eventually indirectly through forwarding to JSPs): Client requests on all other servlets (including JSPs) are forwarded to this ShowATMServlet. This construction insures that the access to the application (guarded by the ATM) is sound at all times.

The other servlets use the ATM to forward requests asking to take an action on the ATM. These actions (origination from the user of the system) can easily be found by examining the use case diagram (Figure 47 on page 77): Each servlet corresponds to a use case invoked by an action of Person. The mapping between the functional requirements and the implementation is made straightforward by this construction.

After analyzing and checking the HTTP request, the action servlets invoke the corresponding methods on the BOs, in this case primarily on the ATM as corresponding model representing the application. The result of these calls will either be a state change in the ATM or an error. In both cases the ATM has to be shown (eventually together with an error message), so those ATM servlets forward the request always to the ShowATMServlet to generate the response based on the current state of the ATM.

Database access

The link between the business objects layer and the database pictured at the top is, for reasons of simplicity, implemented inside another version of the business objects. A better way would be to have some intermediate persistence layer. However, this book only explains the VisualAge for Java Professional version features, which do not include the Persistence Builder Feature one would use to implement such a persistence layer more efficiently. For a discussion on how to build such a layer, you will need to consult a specialized lecture.

The implementation based on database persistence is explained in Chapter 10, "Using relational databases" on page 275. This implementation will, however, be completely compatible with the reference implementation (based on memory persistency) that we explain below: You should be able to replace the implementations for every client layer implementation without changing anything but the import statements to refer to the two corresponding packages:

com.ibm.itso.sg245264.atm.memory	This will contain the in-memory example implementation explained in the next section.
com.ibm.itso.sg245264.atm.database	This will contain the database implementation described in Chapter 10, "Using relational databases" on page 275

The database will be accessed using JDBC 2.0, so you could choose any database engine with a confirming driver on whatever platform you choose. The fact that this third tier can be put physically on a different computer, without changing the code, is one of the benefits of using JDBC. More on the database part can be found in Chapter 10, "Using relational databases" on page 275.

Example implementation

In a sense we will have three different client applications accessing the business objects, also having two different implementations. The reference implementation is explained in this section. It focusses on the business logic implementing the design model explained earlier.

A practical way to start off is by generating the skeletons of the Java classes directly from the design tool. We used a linkage tool with Rational Rose and VisualAge for Java. To use this tool, you need to download and install a patch and the Rational Rose modeling tool. Refer to Rational's Web site:

```
http://www.rational.com/support/downloadcenter/upgrades/rose.jsp
```

All the code of everything explained here and the rest of the application can be found in full in the accompanied resources; see Appendix B, "Using the additional material" on page 363. Therefore, there is no need to type all of the code yourself, although you might want to start it out yourself as an exercise and copy additional code to complete the whole sample inside your IDE. Also, there is another exercise that we would advise you to do to ensure you that you comprehend everything: Go back to the requirements section in this chapter, decide on adding or changing some functionality, then describe and implement this using the supplied code.

We start our explanation just as you should start your own project yourself, assuming that you have just installed VisualAge for Java without using any previous code generation (in contrast to the above). We begin by explaining, in detail, a good way to do this, so you can begin to feel comfortable using the tool. Be aware that there are many ways to accomplish things, so our choice of certain ways here is only meant as an introduction. Later on, you might find that you prefer some ways above others. This section will also give you some "Tips & Tricks" using VisualAge for Java.

The Workbench of VisualAge should always be your starting point, as you would normally start browsing to an existing project or create a new one.

First, we must create a project. Remember that VisualAge organizes packages into projects (see: Chapter 2, "Organizing your code" on page 41). To do this, click:

Type in the name of this project: *ATMExampleApplication.* (When we do not mention to change something else, it means that you should stick with the default values presented by the dialogs.)

Next we create two packages: One for the reference implementation itself, and one that should contain the code which is independent of the in-memory implementation (for example, the code for the test application). We open the Project browser for the newly created project, or we make sure to select this new project in the Workbench before invoking the 'Create new package' SmartGuide. Click:

Type the names of the packages we chose, following the naming conventions:

- *com.ibm.itso.sg245264.atm.memory*
- *com.ibm.itso.sg245264.atm*

Detailed steps implementing the first class

We will now start by implementing the design class Money. For the previous discussion we now that it only has to represent an amount, without fractions or any currency indication. The operations on Money are just the normal arithmetic. We chose to use the *BigInteger* type from the *java.math* package and implement Money as a child of BigInteger. To proceed, click:

Type in *Money* as name of the class and click the **Browse** button behind the entry field for the superclass. Start by typing "*big*", as shown in Figure 57.

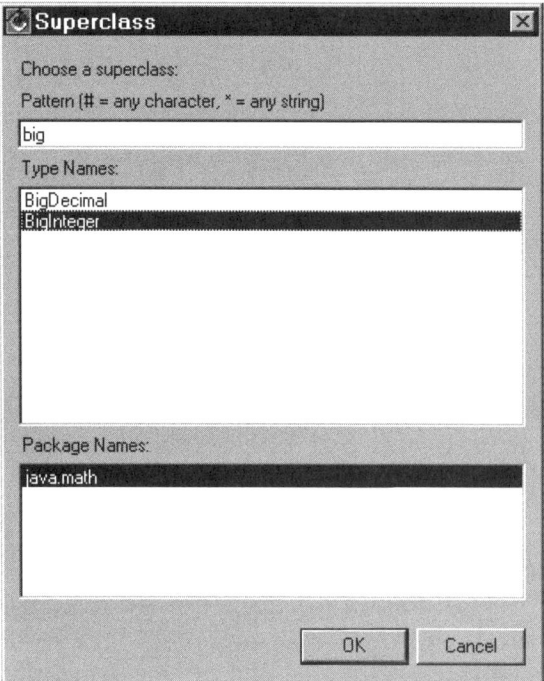

Figure 57. Specify BigInteger as superclass

The first list automatically refreshes when typing in, to match the pattern you typed in, appended with an asterisk (*). The second list will show the package names which contain the currently selected type (or the first one in the list). Such dialogs are used throughout VisualAge for Java; they give you a fast and safe way to specify a type.

On the next page of the SmartGuide, we specify that we will reference the BigInteger type in the import statement using the **Add Type...** button. Then we deselect **Copy constructors from superclass** to avoid the generation of those (because we might otherwise end up with unintended implicit castings), as shown in Figure 58.

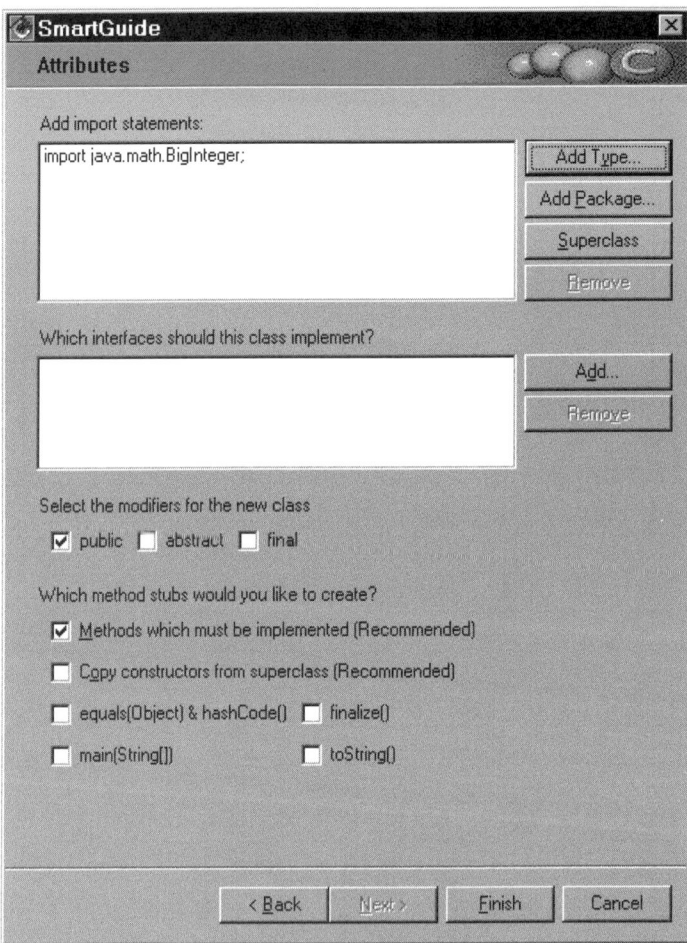

Figure 58. Second page of 'Create new class' SmartGuide for Money

When we have finished the SmartGuide, the Money class appears in our project browser. Now we have to double-click **Money** to browse the class.

We see that the class definition contains a comment block with some tags. It includes the author's name and marks it with a timestamp (to change this, go to "Customizing VisualAge for Java" on page 28 for instructions on how to use this Javadoc template).

The first thing to do is to change the comment on the class (and change some things conforming coding guidelines):

```
import java.math.BigInteger;
/**
 * Represents an amount of money.
 * The currency is not taken into account here.
 * This basically represents only a quantity, without a fraction.
 * We use BigInteger as basis for our implementation.
 *
 * Creation date: (12/15/00 6:04:18 PM)
 * @author: Frederik Haesbrouck
 */
public class Money
extends BigInteger {
}
```

We continue by creating a method which can tell us whether a Money object is positive (will be used by the ATM preventing it from dispensing negative amounts of money). The implementation is straightforward:

```
return (compareTo(ZERO) >= 0);
```

This uses the *compareTo()* method implemented at the BigInteger level to compare the current value with the BigInteger constant *ZERO*. We use the 'Create Method or Constructor' SmartGuide to create this method. Click:

This will give you a dialog where you can specify the signature of the method. Note that although you can change the return type later on, you have to specify a return type here. Enter:

```
boolean isPositive
```

Go to the next screen and change the access modifier to *public*. Click **Finish** to end up with a skeleton of the method (Figure 59).

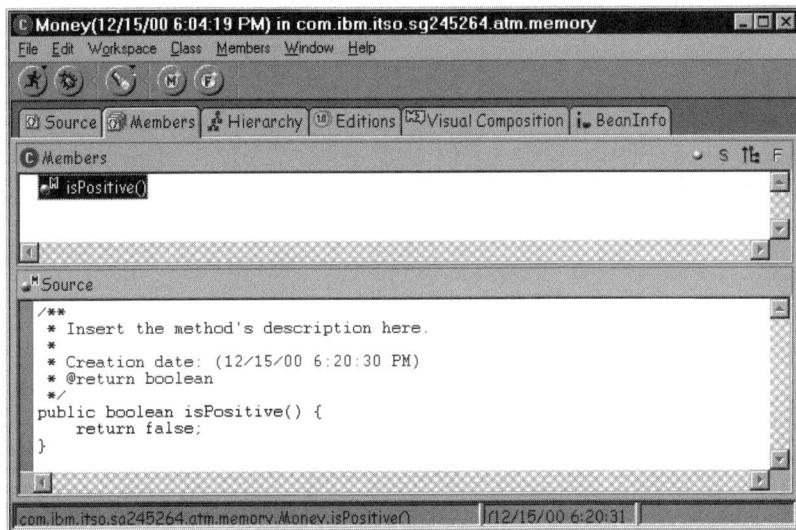

Figure 59. Skeleton method in class browser

This generated piece of code provides enough to use the method already without changing, in case you want to copy your design and gradually add the necessary logic afterwards.

Another great aspect of it is — once again — the generated Javadoc comment block: It automatically inserts the applicable Javadoc tags (@return, @param, @exception, and so on.) and marks it with a timestamp (see "Customizing VisualAge for Java" on page 28 how-to this Javadoc template).

We start by changing the text "*Insert the method's description here.*"into "*Is this instance positive (0 inclusive)?*". It is a good practice to start by explaining what you want this method to do, before implementing it. Press the shortcut *CRTL-S* to save your changes.

Replace the default implementation of returning *false* with the implementation mentioned above. This is should be the result:

```
/**
 * Is this instance positive (0 inclusive) ?
 *
 * Creation date: (12/15/00 6:20:30 PM)
 * @return boolean
 */
public boolean isPositive() {
   return (compareTo(ZERO) >= 0);
}
```

You may have already noticed a red cross in front of the Money class in the Project browser of the Workbench, indicating an error. The corresponding message shows us that our Money type is missing a constructor.

We will fix this error by making a String constructor. Invoke the class SmartGuide as described before and choose to create a constructor, add a parameter *anAmountStr* of type String. This constructor will throw an exception when it cannot convert the supplied string into an amount, so on the third page of the SmartGuide you add *NumberFormatException* to the throws list. Adjust the comment and implement this constructor to become:

```
/**
 * Create an amount of money equal to the given
 * String representation of it.
 *
 * Creation date: (12/15/00 9:36:49 PM)
 * @param anAmountStr java.lang.String
 * @exception java.lang.NumberFormatException When the parameter cannot be
                                              converted to a number
 */
public Money(String anAmountStr)
throws NumberFormatException {
   super(anAmountStr);
}
```

We want to use arithmetic functions like *add* and *subtract* directly inherited from BigInteger, but as you will see, these return BigInteger instead of Money instances. We solve this problem by making an additional constructor, called a copy constructor.

Reusing existing method to create a new method

Instead of using the SmartGuide, we create this constructor by changing the previous one and pressing Ctrl-S, which defaults into saving the code (and hence creating a new constructor) while leaving the original untouched. (See "Customizing VisualAge for Java" on page 28 to change default behavior):

```
/**
 * Copy ctor from its parent type.
 *
 * @param anAmount BigInteger
 * @exception java.lang.NumberFormatException Will never be thrown
 */
public Money(BigInteger anAmount)
throws NumberFormatException {
   super(anAmount.toString());
}
```

The implementations of the add and subtract methods now simply use this constructor to transform the result from their parents implementation into objects of the type Money:

```
/**
 * Convenience method.
 *
 * Creation date: (12/15/00 11:56:26 PM)
 * @return com.ibm.itso.sg245264.atm.memory.Money
 * @param anAmount com.ibm.itso.sg245264.atm.memory.Money
 */
public Money add(Money anAmount) {
    return new Money(super.add(anAmount));
}
/**
 * Convenience method.
 *
 * Creation date: (12/16/00 12:09:11 AM)
 * @return com.ibm.itso.sg245264.atm.memory.Money
 * @param anAmount com.ibm.itso.sg245264.atm.memory.Money
 */
public Money subtract(Money anAmount) {
    return new Money(super.subtract(anAmount));
}
```

We finish the implementation of the Money class by adding convenience field to refer to ZERO — comparable to the above methods — allowing us to use ZERO directly without having to "cast" it to Money from BigInteger.

```
public final static Money ZERO = new Money(BigInteger.ZERO);
```

We hope that you now have a better idea of how to use the VisualAge environment to enter code. The other classes will not be discussed anymore. We will only point out some peculiarities that might need more explanation.

PrimaryKey class hierarchy

The PrimaryKey class is implemented based on a String. We chose this because of two reasons: we need a string representation and because it is easier to be able to use normal names for IDs.

The field *id* contains the String, method *getIdAsString()* gives the string representation this ID. In contrary, the *toString()* method returns the ID in such a way that it is clear what it is and what its value is when browsing with the Inspector (used when debugging; see Chapter 9, "Testing and debugging the Web application" on page 231).This holds also true for the other classes we develop.

Besides the obvious String constructor we also provide a default constructor that generates a — nearly 100% unique — primary key:

```
id = Long.toString((new Date()).getTime());
```

This construction returns the current time on a millisecond precision, the change of retrieving twice the same value is very small, although existent.

In this implementation we will use HashMaps when implementing the persistency in the different classes. A *HashMap* associates a key with a value, values can be retrieved by providing the corresponding keys. The PrimaryKey objects will be used as keys for the objects to be stored in those HashMaps. The key of a hashmap must implement both *hashCode()* and *equals()*. The signature of the equals method takes a general Object as parameter, this is the way you should cope with it:

```
/**
 * Uses the equals implementation of the underlying String.
 * Needed for use in HashMap.
 *
 * Creation date: (11/28/00 4:17:42 PM)
 * @return boolean
 * @param anObject java.lang.Object
 */
public boolean equals(Object anObject) {
   try {
      return id.equals(((PrimaryKey) anObject).id);
   } catch(ClassCastException ex) {
      return false;
   }
}
```

We now show you how we implemented the *Transaction* class as an example of a class which produces 'identifiable' objects (representing 'logs of a transfer of money') and has the responsibility to keep track of all its instances.

Creating an inner class

After creating the *Transaction* class, we add a specialized version of the PrimaryKey as inner class. The way you add inner classes in VisualAge for Java is not obvious at first, so we will show you how. You have to get to the class declaration: Select the Transaction class (open it in the Class Browser or select it from the Workbench or some other browser) and make sure that there no method is selected (eventually deselect by holding the CTRL key). Then insert the code inside the class declaration like this:

```
public class Transaction
{

    public static class TransactionPK
    extends PrimaryKey
    {
       public TransactionPK()
       {
            super();
       }
       public TransactionPK(String anId)
       {
            super(anId);
       }
    }
```

The inner class *Transaction$TransactionPK* will now appear in the list with the field and methods of the enclosing class (this is new from v3.5). When you click this, it shows exactly the things you typed in just before.

The main responsibility of the Transaction class is to transfer money from one account to another as one transaction: Either such a transfer will complete, or it will roll back as if nothing happened. If it was successful, it will make a new instance that specifies the transfer with timestamp and references to the involved accounts. The *createTrx()* does just that. Consider that, although this implementation is not bullet-proof, it serves as an example:

```
./**
 * This method tries to make a transaction of the specified
 * amount of money for the given source account
 * onto the given target account.
 *
 * @param aTrxAmount
 * @param aSrcAccount
 * @param aTrgtAccount
 * @return Transaction Transaction instance indicating this transaction if successfull.
 * @exception TransactionAbortedException It will throw an exception if the transaction
           could not be completed, after it rolled back any of the already token steps.
 * @roseuid 3A1ABBA202A8
 */
public static Transaction createTrx(
                Money aTrxAmount,
                BankAccount aSrcAccount,
                BankAccount aTrgtAccount)
throws TransactionAbortedException
    {
        Transaction tempTrx = new Transaction(aTrxAmount, aSrcAccount, aTrgtAccount);

        // deduct from aSrcAccount
        try {
            aSrcAccount.withdraw(aTrxAmount);
        } catch(TransactionAbortedException ex) {
```

```
        throw ex;
    }

    // add tot aTrgtAccount
    try {
        aTrgtAccount.deposit(aTrxAmount);
    } catch(TransactionAbortedException ex) {
        // put money back on aSrcAccount
        aSrcAccount.deposit(aTrxAmount);
        // NOTE: theoretically this could also throw exception...
        throw ex;
    }

    allTransactions.put(tempTrx.getId(), tempTrx);
    aSrcAccount.addTransaction(tempTrx);
    aTrgtAccount.addTransaction(tempTrx);

    return tempTrx;
}
```

The constructor used by this method should not be accessible from outside the class, transactions should only be made by the createTrx() method, therefore it is the only constructor of Transaction and it is declared as *private*.

Persistency based on HashMaps

The Transaction class (among others) implements its persistency responsibility by using a HashMap. Each time a new transaction is created, it is added to the HashMap. The createTrx() method of Transaction (see above) contained this line that adds the newly created transaction with its primary key as key:

```
        allTransactions.put(tempTrx.getId(), tempTrx);
```

This *getListOfAllCards()* method shows how easy it is for the Card class to produce this list of all its instances:

```
/**
 * Get the list of all the Cards currently in the system.
 *
 * Creation date: (12/4/00 2:18:39 PM)
 * @return java.util.Vector
 */
public static Vector getListOfAllCards() {
    return new Vector(allCards.values());
}
```

Finder methods

The 'finder' methods described before are also implemented easily. Together with the code to create a usable new Card when the *findWithCardPK()* finder cannot find the requested Card, this results in the list:

```
/**
 * This finder will search for the Card with the given
 * primary key and return it.
 * It will create a new Card with the given primary key
 * if it didn't found an existing Card with that primary key.
 * That newly created Card will also be associated to
 * two newly created BankAccounts (one Checking and one Savings).
 *
 * Creation date: (11/22/00 5:12:16 PM)
 * @param anId CardPK Primary key
 * @return Card instance
 */
public static Card findWithCardPK(CardPK anId) {
    Card tempCard;
    Vector tempAccountsV = new Vector();

    if((tempCard = (Card) allCards.get(anId)) == null) {
        // create new one
        tempCard = new Card(anId);
        // associate checking and savings account with the same PK as base
        tempAccountsV.addElement(new CheckingAccount(
                new BankAccount.BankAccountPK(anId.getIdAsString() + 'C')));
        tempAccountsV.addElement(new SavingsAccount(
                new BankAccount.BankAccountPK(anId.getIdAsString() + 'S')));
        tempCard.setBankAccounts(tempAccountsV);
    }

    return tempCard;
}
```

We limited the scope of this example by not allowing the deletion of the object, which makes sure that we do not have to provide a method removing instances of the HashMap.

Implementations of the state diagram

ATM class implements the state diagrams — described at the beginning of this chapter — in a simple and direct way: Each of its methods (corresponding to the actions eventually inducing a state transition) works in three steps:

1. It checks if the ATM is in the correct state.

2. It does its job.

3. It changes the state of the ATM when necessary.

The states themselves are constants on the ATM class which have the ATMState type (inner class of ATM). We chose the String type as a basis for the ATMState so we can put the description on the type inside which can be practical when debugging. The fact that ATMState is a separate type makes it easier to change its implementation later and to have all of the benefits from the strong typing feature of Java.

At this point, combining the introduction of the coding with the design material from before, should enable you to finish the complete memory implementation of the ATM business objects.

Test application

The last thing to do is to make a test application that will test the whole package. (Note that the unit testing was done by implementing a *main()* method on some of the classes.) Remember that we already made a package inside the current project for this test class: *com.ibm.itso.sg245264.atm*.

This testing class is outside the package so it should also be used to tune the accessors of the different methods on the ATM classes.

As said before, the ATM business objects will be implemented again later on in Chapter 10, "Using relational databases" on page 275. This test class will ensure us of this compatibility issue.

We have four scenarios which are implemented as methods that are called from the main() of the *TestATMApplication* class:

testRoundTripScenario

RoundTripScenario will test a typical scenario for an ATM: Get money from one of the accounts and look at the transaction history afterwards.

testGUIScenario

The GUIScenario will start of with a list of all Card instances in the system. It allows choosing one of them to see its detail. The detail shows the owner of the card, the primary key and a list of associated BankAccounts. From this list BankAccounts can be added or deleted. Adding an account is accomplished by showing a list of all BankAccounts to choose from. This scenario also tests an invalid attempt to add an account twice.

testGetMoneyOneAccountScenario

This method will test the case of taking out money when only one account is associated with the Card.

testATMRetrieval

This is a test method for the creation and retrieval of an ATM from persistency.

This concludes our chapter introducing the sample application to be used subsequently. We hope it has also been helpful in familiarizing you with the VisualAge for Java environment.

Chapter 5. Creating servlets

This chapter is designed to introduce servlets both in concept and in practice. We cover the servlet API, runtime environment, and life-cycle, focusing on the portions that are utilized in building our ATM Web application. If you are already familiar with servlets, this chapter will still be of benefit because other chapters build on the concepts and the ATM Web application presented here.

There is already a great deal of electronic and printed documentation covering this technology. For complete documentation, pleas refer to `http://java.sun.com/products/servlet/`, which is the Sun Java Servlet API Specification. Other servlet references are suggested in Appendix D, "Related publications" on page 371. In order to test the servlets shown here, refer to Chapter 9, "Testing and debugging the Web application" on page 231. The ATM servlets can be deployed to any Web application server that supports servlets. For more information about deployment, see Chapter 12, "Deploying the Web application" on page 341.

Overview of Java servlets

Servlets are designed as a platform-independent way of extending any application server. In this chapter we will limit ourselves to servlets that extend a Web server. The terms used in this chapter are defined in Table 5. These terms can have different meanings in other contexts and in other books. We define the terms as they are used in this book. In order to understand how servlets work, it is important to understand in general how Web servers work and the basic nature of the HTTP protocol.

Table 5. Terms used.

Term	Definition
Web server	Any server program that implements the HTTP protocol and is able to communicate with Web browsers using HTTP.
Web application server	Any Web server that can run servlets and Java Server Pages.
Web application	A collection of related resources that are available on a Web server. This can include static HTML documents, images, multimedia, servlets and/or JSPs.

Term	Definition
Web browser	Any client program that implements the HTTP protocol and is able to communicate with Web servers using HTTP. Two examples are Netscape Navigator and Microsoft Internet Explorer.
servlet	A Java program that extends the Java class HttpServlet and runs inside a Web application server.
persistence	The ability of a program to have a state and to remember information in between requests.
request	An HTTP request which includes information such as the URL of a resource.
response	An HTTP response which could include an HTML document, or an image.

Servlets are typically used to provide dynamic Web pages and to take some action on behalf of an end-user. Servlets are run inside the Java Virtual Machine (JVM) of the server. Therefore all servlets running inside a single server can share access to resources, such as open database connections and other Java business objects. Servlets are not dependant on the resources available on the client. A servlet can interact with any Web browser, even if the Web browser does not support Java.

Servlets are similar in some ways to other technologies used to extend the function of a Web server, such as CGI programs. Servlets should not be equated with Java applets, as applets run on a client Web browser in a restricted environment. Servlets receive a request from a Web browser and dynamically build a response. The response can be based on information accessed from a database, business objects, or other sources of information. The flow of the communication is as follows:

1. The Web browser sends a request to a Web server for one particular servlet. The request includes the URL of the desired servlet.
2. The Web server receives the request and determines that the request is for a servlet.
3. The Web server passes the request to the Web application server (which is typically on the same physical machine)

4. The Web application server receives the request and passes it to the correct servlet.
5. The servlet runs and builds a response. The response is usually based on the request and other resources, such as a database and other Java business objects.
6. The servlet sends the response to the Web application server.
7. The Web application server sends the response back to the Web server.
8. The Web server sends the response back to the Web browser from step 1. Then the communication channel to the Web browser is closed.
9. The Web browser displays the response to the end-user.

The above steps are best illustrated in Figure 60.

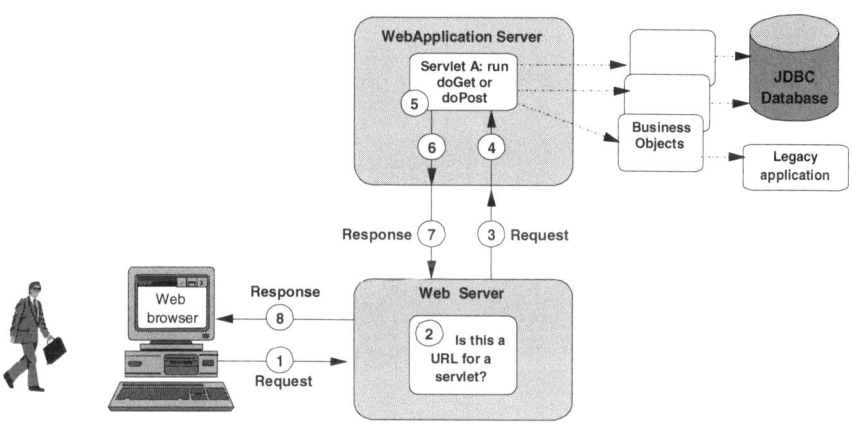

Figure 60. Overview of communication between Web browser and servlet

If the Web browser requests a new servlet (or even the same servlet) the communication process starts over from the beginning. Since the communication channel is closed after each request is answered, the any additional requests are treated identically by the Web server as the very first request. This type of communication is described as "stateless." Neither Web browser nor Web server has any knowledge of the condition of the other. The Web server has no knowledge whether it is answering many different Web browsers, or many requests from a single Web browser.

Fortunately, the Web application server provides several forms of persistence to our servlets. The following list highlights some of the many advantages of servlets over other server-side technologies such as CGI.

- **Servlets are portable and platform independent.** Servlets are Java programs so they can run on any Java Virtual Machine and on any Web application server that supports to the Java Servlet API.

- **Servlets have persistence and high performance.** The servlet is only loaded once by the Web application server and simply invoked for each request. This allows the servlet to preserve information between different requests, such as open database connections. In addition the Java Servlet API defines a session object which can be used to preserve information from a particular user. Additionally servlets are multi-threaded which means all requests are processed in a single process or job.

- **Servlets are Java programs**. This means that servlets gain all the benefits of the Java language and virtual machine, which include object-orientation, access to the full Java API, the ability to use any Java package, automatic garbage collection, etc.

Servlets need to be written as thread-safe programs. The possibility exists for one method which modifies a shared variable, to be executed simultaneously in multiple threads. For more information about threading issues and thread-safe programming in Java, refer to Appendix D, "Related publications" on page 371. For a visual illustration of multiple requests reaching the servlet at the same time, refer to Figure 61.

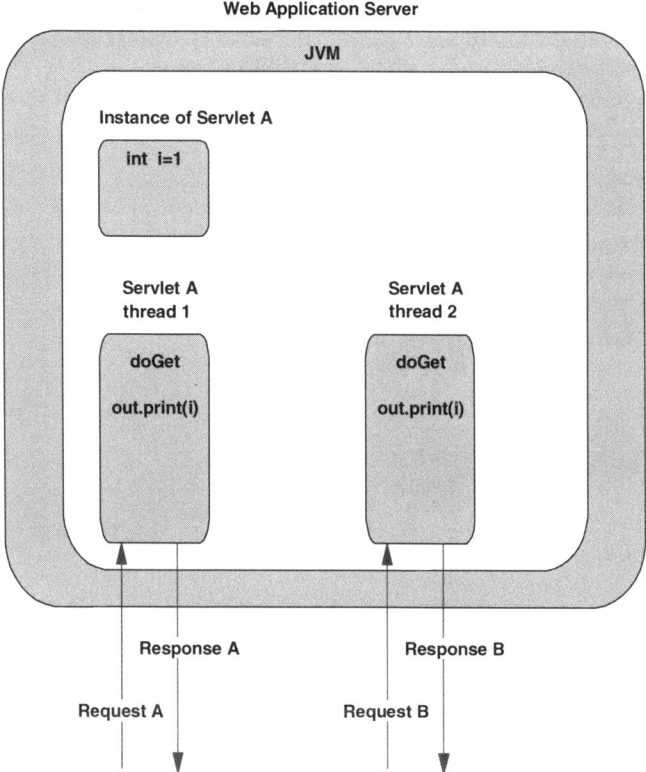

Figure 61. Multiple requests reaching the servlet

The Java Servlet API

The Java Servlet API is a group of Java classes which define a standard interface between a servlet and a Web application server. These classes allow the servlet to access the request initiated by the Web browser, any parameters that were set, and the Web application containing the servlet. The API also provides access to persistence mechanism called a session and methods for managing the life-cycle of the servlet. The life-cycle of every servlet includes the stages described in Table 6.

Table 6. The stages of the servlet life-cycle

Description of stage	Method called
The servlet is loaded into memory by the Web application server for the first time. The instance variables are initialized and stay in memory until the end of the life-cycle. This typically happens the first time a Web browser requests the servlet. The server administrator can also choose to load certain servlets whenever the server is started.	init
One or more Web browsers have requested the same servlet. A thread is created for each request. Each thread has access to the shared instances variables and to its own request.	n/a
Each thread handles its own request and generates a response. The response is send back to the Web browser.	doGet or doPost
The servlet is removed from memory by the Web application server. This typically happens when the server is shut down.	destroy

The API is contained in two Java packages:

- javax.servlet
- javax.servlet.http

These packages are part of Java 2 Platform Enterprise Edition (J2EE) and are included in all versions of Visual Age for Java 3.5. The API includes many classes for advanced servlet programming. In this section we will focus on the classes that will be used to implement the ATM application.

The *HttpServletRequest* class provides methods to access all parts of the request from the Web browser. This class provides access to any information entered into an HTML form, along with any additional information sent by the browser. The Web application server can add extra information to the request before it forwards it to a servlet.

The *HttpServletResponse* class represents the output that the Web browser is expecting to receive. The response is typically an HTML document, such as in our ATM Web application. The response could also be an XML document or any other file format.

The *HttpSession* class represents a persistent object for each user. The Web application server maintains all session objects and tracks which session is associated with each user. Servlets can ask the Web application server to create and retrieve the session object. Once the servlet has a session object, it can put objects into the session, or get existing objects out of the session. The servlet can also request to expire the session, which causes the server to remove the session from memory. The server will also expire sessions automatically if it does not receive any new requests in some set time period (that is, the session will time-out). The time period is set by the server administrator. As we have discussed earlier in this chapter, Web servers are stateless — every request is treated the same. This is still true: whenever a request is received by the server, the server checks if a session exists for this particular browser. In our ATM application we use the session to store the ATM object for each user.

The *ServletContext* class represents the Web application in which a servlet is running. The servlet can use this class to forward the request to another servlet or JSP in the same Web application. The ServletContext class can also be used to find information about the application, such as version information or the true document root within the server's file system. In our ATM application, this class is used to forward the request from one servlet to another.

The *Cookie* class represents the cookies in the HTTP header. The HTTP protocol allows a Web server to send small amounts of data to the browser along with its response. Each cookie can have an expiration date that the browser is expected to honor. Each cookie is simply a String name/value pair. The HTTP protocol also allows the Web server to retrieve a cookie it has set in the past. There are several limitations. Most Web browsers allow a user to reject cookies and to clear existing cookies. A knowledgeable user could modify the value of a cookie before it is returned to the server. In spite of these limitations, cookies are useful for storing small amounts of data for each user for long amounts of time, with virtually no cost to the server. Most Web application servers use cookies as a way of tying a session object to a particular user. If a servlet writes a cookie, it cannot be retrieved by other servlets until *after* the response has been received by the Web browser and the browser initiates a new request.

Requests for a servlet can be initiated by a user in several ways. The servlet method (doGet or doPost) reached depends on the request. The differences are summarized in Table 7.

Table 7. Methods used to request a servlet

User Action	Servlet method invoked
User directly types in a URL in their Web browser.	doGet
User clicks a **Submit** button in an HTML form that specifies GET for the method.	doGet
User clicks a bookmark in their browser.	doGet
User clicks a **Submit** button in an HTML form that specifies POST for the method.	doPost

The HTTP GET method concatenates the form data to the URL. So a GET request to a servlet would look like:

http://www.sitename.com/servlet/MyServlet?name=Sarah.

Even if HTTPS is being used, the URL is sent in plain text. Do not use the GET method if the form contains sensitive data. The method HTTP POST does not append form data to the URL. Servlets is not required to handle both doGet and doPost. Depending on the nature of the Web application, implementing both doGet and doPost may not be desired.

Building the ATM application servlets

Our ATM servlets will be part of a three-tier architecture. The first tier is the presentation layer, the second tier is the business objects, and the third tier is external sources of data, such as a database or legacy data. The presentation layer for the ATM application is comprised of HTML documents and servlets. In this chapter the HTML will be hard-coded into the servlets. This is only a temporary measure: in Chapter 6, "Creating JSPs" on page 129 the HTML will be moved into JSPs. Refer to Figure 56 on page 92 for a visual guide to the architecture. The servlets will process the data entered by the user then validate the data by calling methods on the business objects. The servlet will then forward the request to another servlet (the ShowATMServlet) which will decide which screen to show next.

We are writing eight servlets for our ATM application. There is one servlet for each possible interaction with the user, as shown in Figure 47 on page 77. There are three additional servlets for the user walking up to the ATM, the user leaving the ATM, and the user choosing a new action after looking at the transaction history. These servlets are summarized in Table 8. They build on the business objects discussed in Chapter 4, "Beginning the ATM project" on page 73. It is critical to understand the overall design of the business objects before attempting to implement the servlets.

Table 8. All servlets needed for the ATM application

Name	Purpose	When it is called
ShowATMServlet	This servlet will create (if necessary) and display the ATM object in its current state. It decides what HTML document to create based on the current state of the ATM object.	1) When the user initially walks up to the ATM, that is, they type in a URL. 2) When another servlet wants to show the current state
InsertCardServlet	To get the card that the user entered and to validate it by inserting the card into the ATM object.	When the user clicks the **Next** button after inserting their card.
EnterPINServlet	To get the PIN that the user entered and validate it by entering the PIN into the ATM object.	When the user clicks the **Next** button after typing their PIN.
ChooseAccountServlet	To get the account that the user selected and validating it by choosing that account on the ATM object.	When the user clicks the **Next** button after selecting an account.
ChooseActionServlet	To get the action that the user selected, such as withdrawal money, view transaction history, or change accounts. Then try to perform that action on the ATM object.	When the user clicks the **Next** button after selecting an action.
EnterAmountServlet	To get the amount to withdraw that the user entered. Then validate the amount by trying to withdraw that amount from the bank account.	When the user clicks the **Next** button after typing an amount.
ShowActionsServlet	To request that the ATM object show all available actions.	When the user clicks the link labeled **Choose a different action** in the transaction history screen.
StopServlet	To change the ATM object's state back to "READY_TO_USE." The user could choose to start a new interaction with the ATM object, or a new user could access the ATM object.	When the user clicks the **Restart** hyperlink on any screen

Use the Servlet SmartGuide to create all eight servlets in the ITSO project (or whatever you happened to name your project). The most important element is the package name and class names. Create all the servlets in the package named "com.ibm.itso.sg245264.atm.servlets" To learn how to use the Servlet SmartGuide, please refer to "Building your first servlet" on page 31. Make sure to select both the **doGet()** and **doPost()** check boxes under *Which method stubs would you like to create*. After all the servlet classes are created by the SmartGuide, your project tab in the workbench should match Figure 62.

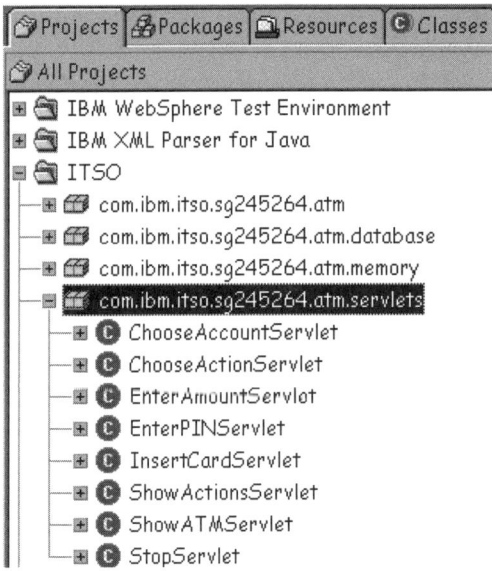

Figure 62. Workbench after creating the eight servlets

The first servlet we will enhance is the ShowATMServlet. We will open the class browser window by double-clicking the class name in the workbench. Then we will modify the performTask method. This method is called by both doGet and doPost. You will need to add the following code to the performTask method:

```
ATM userATM = createOrRetreiveUserATM(request, response);

// add the userATM object to the request, to ensure the JSPs only use the request attributes.
    request.setAttribute("userATMrq", userATM );

//Use hard-coded HTML pages
    showNextPage(request, response, userATM.getState());
```

The above code first gets the ATM that this user will interact with. If they are a returning user and already have an ATM, then that will be retrieved. If this is their first visit, then a new ATM object will be created and added to the session object. Furthermore, the key for the ATM object is stored in a cookie. This is so we can recognize a user even in the case where the session has expired. For performance reasons, most sessions are short lived. Storing a cookie on the browser does not consume any server resources.

The following code shows the implementation of the method createOrRetreiveUserATM. This is the only place in the entire ATM application that a session is created or changed. All other servlets (and later JSPs) rely on the ShowATMServlet to handle the task of recognizing new and returning users.

```
private ATM createOrRetreiveUserATM(HttpServletRequest request, HttpServletResponse
response) throws Exception {
   String         cookie_value = null;
   String          atm_key= null;
   boolean        no_ATM_cookie_found = true;

   // Get the current session object, create one if necessary
   HttpSession session = request.getSession(true);

   // Try to retieve the userATM from the session.
   ATM userATM = (ATM)session.getValue("userATM");
   if (userATM == null){
      //Check if our cookie is available in the browser.
      Cookie[] cookies = request.getCookies();
      if (cookies != null) {
         // cookies are present! loop through all the cookies looking
         // for the one we want. If we find the cookie we want,
         // assign its value to atm_key
         for(int i=0; (i < cookies.length) && no_ATM_cookie_found; i++){
            if ( cookies[i].getName().equals("ATM_KEY")){
               atm_key = cookies[i].getValue();
               no_ATM_cookie_found= false;
            }
         }
      }

      if( no_ATM_cookie_found ) {//  no ATM in session, no cookie
         // this means the user has never used the ATM application.
         userATM = new ATM();

         // put the ATM key into a cookie. That way we can recognize repeat
         // users even if they do not have a session.
         Cookie atm_key_cookie= new Cookie("ATM_KEY" , userATM.getId().getIdAsString()
);
          atm_key_cookie.setPath("/"); // this is optional. It means that any program
                                    on this server can view the cookie.
          response.addCookie(atm_key_cookie);
      }
      else{ //no ATM in session, have cookie
         // user is a returning user.
         userATM = new ATM(new ATM.ATMPK(atm_key));
      }

      if ( userATM.getState() == ATM.OUT_OF_ORDER){
```

```
            userATM.initialize();
     }
     if ( userATM.getState() == ATM.READY_TO_USE) {
         session.putValue("userATM", userATM);
     }
     else{
         throw new Exception("Error:ATM is not ready to use. The current ATM state is:"
                                                        + userATM.getState() );
     }
}

     return userATM;
}
```

It may seem confusing as to why we use both the session value and the request attribute to store the userATM. Our reasoning is based on the following assumptions and decisions:

1. We do not wish to use the session object in JSPs because it adds complexity to the architecture.
2. It is easier to track use (or misuse) of the session object in the Visual Age for Java environment in servlet code, rather than in JSPs.
3. We want servlet to JSP communication handled strictly by using the request attributes The JSP's are part of the presentation layer and should not assume anything about the architecture of the servlets and business objects.

The difference between putting objects in the session, request, and application containers is the visibility of the objects. In traditional programming languages, we can only define a variable's scope as global or local. In Java programming we can limit scope to a block, method, object, or class. In servlet programming we have even more choices! The additional Servlet choices for scope are explained in Table 9.

Table 9. Scope

Mechanism	Visibility
Request	Visible to any servlet or JSP processing the same request. Once the browser has received the response, the request object and any objects stored inside are destroyed.
Session	Visible to any servlet or JSP processing a request from the same user. Objects in the session are destroyed when the session expires.
Application	Visible to any servlet or JSP that is part of the same Web application defined by the server administrator. Objects are destroyed when the ServletContext is destroyed.

In the performTask method of the ShowATMServlet, the method showNextPage is called. The showNextPage method decides what page is shown to the user. The code for this method is shown below.

```
private void showNextPage(HttpServletRequest request, HttpServletResponse
response, ATM$ATMState curstate) throws Exception {

   if (curstate ==  ATM.OUT_OF_ORDER){
      showOUT_OF_ORDERpage(request, response);
   }
   else if (curstate ==  ATM.READY_TO_USE){
      showREADY_TO_USEpage(request, response);
   }
   else if (curstate ==  ATM.NOT_LOGGED_ON){
      showNOT_LOGGED_ONpage(request, response);
   }
   else if (curstate ==  ATM.BANK_ACCOUNTS_LISTED){
      showBANK_ACCOUNTS_LISTEDpage(request, response);
   }
   else if (curstate ==  ATM.BANK_ACCOUNT_CHOOSEN){
      showBANK_ACCOUNT_CHOSENpage(request, response);
   }
   else if (curstate ==  ATM.ASK_AMOUNT){
      showASK_AMOUNTpage(request, response);
   }
   else if (curstate ==  ATM.DISPENSE_MONEY){
      showDISPENSE_MONEYpage(request, response);
   }
   else if (curstate ==  ATM.TRX_HISTORY_LISTED){
      showTRX_HISTORY_LISTEDpage(request, response);
   }
   else{
      throw new IllegalStateException();
   }
}
```

Notice that the only criteria for deciding which page to show is based on the current state of the ATM object. This helps protect our application from allowing the user to produce errors simply by using the **Back** button in the browser or book marking a particular page. In a poorly designed Web application, it is very easy for any user to produce errors or perform an invalid action simply by using standard Web browser features, such as "back", "forward", "reload", and "add bookmark".

Here is the code from the method showREADY_TO_USEpage:

```
public void showREADY_TO_USEpage(HttpServletRequest request, HttpServletResponse
response) throws java.io.IOException {

    ATM userATM = (ATM)request.getAttribute("userATMrq");
    response.setContentType("text/html");
    PrintWriterout = response.getWriter();

    out.println("<HTML><HEAD>");
    out.println("<TITLE>" + userATM.getState() +  "</TITLE>");
    out.println("</HEAD><BODY>");
    out.println("<P>Please enter your card now. <BR>");
    out.println("If you don't have a card reader, type in your card number.<BR>");
    out.println("<FORM METHOD='POST'"
            + "ACTION='/servlet/com.ibm.itso.sg245264.atm.servlets.InsertCardServlet'>");
    out.println("card number: <INPUT TYPE=TEXT NAME='cardnum' SIZE=10>");
    out.println(" <INPUT TYPE=SUBMIT VALUE='Next'>");
    out.println("</FORM> </P>");
    out.println("<P><A HREF='/servlet/com.ibm.itso.sg245264.atm.servlets.StopServlet'>"
            + "Restart</A></P>");
    out.println("</BODY></HTML>");
}
```

This method simply sends a simple HTML page to the Web browser. The rest of the show<statename>page methods are nearly identical. The only difference is the hard-coded HTML. All of the code developed for the entire ATM application is available on the Internet as noted in Appendix B, "Using the additional material" on page 363.

To start using the ATM Web application we need to call the ShowATMServlet from a Web browser. The simplest way to do this is to type the URL for the servlet:

http://127.0.0.1:8080/servlet/com.ibm.itso.sg245264.atm.servlets.ShowATMServlet

http://127.0.0.1/servlet/com.ibm.itso.sg245264.atm.servlets.ShowATMServlet

The first URL will call the servlet in the Visual Age for Java WebSphere Test Environment, which is covered in Chapter 9, "Testing and debugging the Web application" on page 231. The second URL will call the servlet in the WebSphere Application Server, which is covered in Chapter 12, "Deploying the Web application" on page 341

After entering the URL for the ShowATMServlet, your browser should match Figure 63. After typing the URL for the servlet in the browser, the browser sends an HTTP GET request to the servlet. The doGet method receives the request from the browser and a response object to use for the reply. The doGet method then calls the performTask method, giving it the request and response objects. The performTaskmethod does all the work (by calling other private methods.) When the doGet method ends, the response is sent to the Web browser. So by the time your browser matches Figure 63, the doGet method has already finished executing and the request object has been destroyed.

The HTML that is required for the **Next** button to successfully call the next servlet (InsertCardServlet) and pass along the data the user types, is highlighted below:

```
<FORM METHOD='POST'
ACTION='/servlet/com.ibm.itso.sg245264.atm.servlets.InsertCardServlet'>
<INPUT TYPE=TEXT NAME='cardnum' SIZE=10>
<INPUT TYPE=SUBMIT VALUE='Next'>
</FORM>
```

By specifying POST for the form method, this forces the Web browser to use the HTTP POST method when sending the request. The ACTION tells the Web browser where to send the request. The name 'cardnum' in the input tag tells the browser what to name the parameter sent inside the request. When the user clicks the button identified as **type=SUBMIT**, the browser will sent the request to the InsertCardServlet.

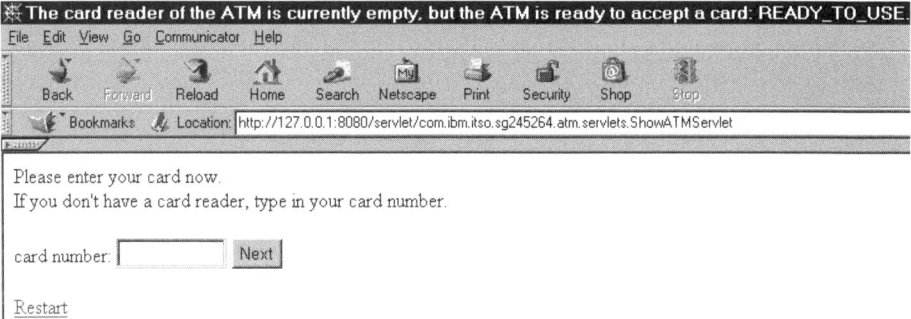

Figure 63. ShowATMServlet in the Web browser

The request is received by the doPost method of the InsertCardServlet. The implementation of this method is shown below:

```
public void doPost(HttpServletRequest request, HttpServletResponse response) throws
javax.servlet.ServletException, java.io.IOException {
    try{
        performTask(request, response);
    }catch(Exception exp){
        response.setContentType("text/html");
        PrintWriter  out = response.getWriter();
        out.println("<HTML><HEAD>");
        out.println("<TITLE>InsertCardServlet Error</TITLE>");
        out.println("</HEAD><BODY>");
        out.println("<P>Error: " +  exp.getMessage());
        out.println("</P>");
        out.println("</BODY></HTML>");
    };
```

This method simply calls the performTask method. The implementation is shown below:

```java
public void performTask(HttpServletRequest request, HttpServletResponse response) throws
Exception{

    HttpSession session = request.getSession(false);
    if (session != null ){
        ATM userATM = (ATM)session.getValue("userATM");

        if (userATM != null ){
            Card userCard;
            String cardstr= request.getParameter("cardnum");
            //validate syntax of card number. It must be numeric.
            try{
                Double cardnum = new Double(cardstr);
            }
            catch(Exception exp){
                throw new Exception(
                    "Invalid card number. Card number must be numeric.");
            }

            userCard = Card.findWithCardPK(cardstr);
            userATM.insertCard(userCard);

        }
    }

    RequestDispatcher dispatcher = getServletContext().getRequestDispatcher(
            "/servlet/com.ibm.itso.sg245264.atm.servlets.ShowATMServlet");

    dispatcher.forward(request, response);
}
```

The logic of this method can be summarized in these steps:

1. Retrieve the session object.

2. If the session exists, retrieve the userATM object

3. If the userATM object exists, get the value of the "cardnum" parameter from the HTTP request.

4. Make sure the "cardnum" parameter is numeric.

5. Retrieve instance of the business object that is returned by the method findWithCardPK. This method looks up business object by card number.

6. Insert the card instance into the ATM object. This is achieved by calling the insertCard method provided by the ATM object.

7. Show the ATM object to the user. This is achieved by forwarding the request to the ShowATMServlet.

Assuming we enter a valid card that is accepted by the ATM, then the next screen we see in the browser should match Figure 64. In our prototype application, all numbers are considered valid. Also the PIN is considered valid if it is identical to the card number. In a production application, a card would need to exist in order to be accepted, and the PIN would not match the card number.

Figure 64. InsertCardServlet in the Web browser

After typing the PIN and clicking the **Next** button, the EnterPINServlet is requested using HTTP POST. The method of the servlet called is the doPost. The implementation of the doPost method calls the performTask method, just like the InsertCardServlet implementation. The implementation of the performTask method is shown:

```
public void performTask(HttpServletRequest request, HttpServletResponse response)
    throws Exception{

        HttpSession session = request.getSession(false);
        if (session != null ){
            ATM userATM = (ATM)session.getValue("userATM");
            if (userATM != null ){
                String pinstr = request.getParameter("pin");
                if (pinstr != null ){
                    userATM.enterPIN(pinstr);
                }
            }
        }
        RequestDispatcher dispatcher = getServletContext().getRequestDispatcher(
                "/servlet/com.ibm.itso.sg245264.atm.servlets.ShowATMServlet");
        dispatcher.forward(request, response);
}
```

The logic of the EnterPINServlet is nearly identical to the InsertCardServlet. The only change is the retrieval of the parameter named "pin" and then entering the pin into the userATM object.

If the PIN is accepted by the userATM object, your browser will match Figure 65. Otherwise, it will match Figure 66.

Figure 65. EnterPINServlet in the Web browser

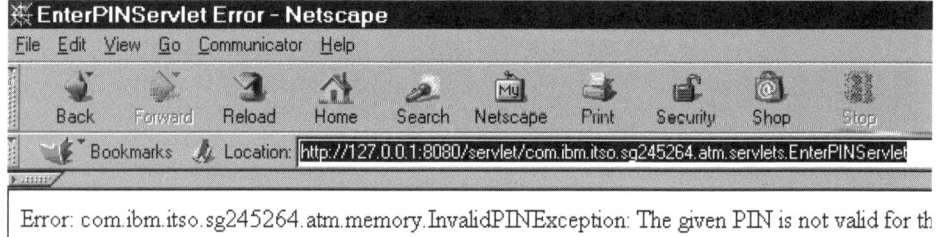

Figure 66. EnterPINServlet in the Web browser — invalid PIN

Each of the rest of the servlets follow the same design principles:

1. It retrieves the session object.
2. It retrieves the userATM object from the session.
3. It gets the request parameter(s) the user entered.
4. It performs rudimentary validation on the parameters.
5. It calls the appropriate method on the userATM object, which further validates the data and potentially causes the userATM to change states.
6. It forwards the request to the ShowATMServlet

The rest of the screens for our ATM Web application are shown in Figure 67, Figure 68, Figure 69, and Figure 70.

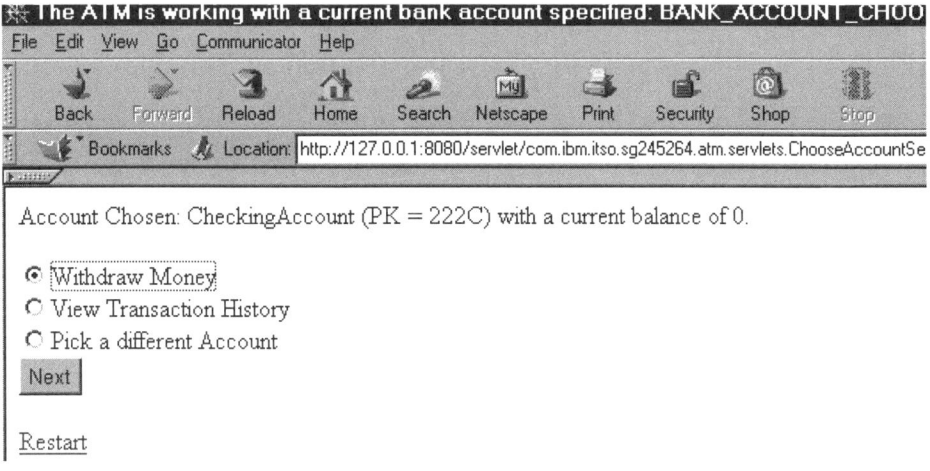

Figure 67. ChooseAccountServlet

Please enter the amount to withdraw now.

Amount: 55

Restart

Figure 68. ChooseActionServlet

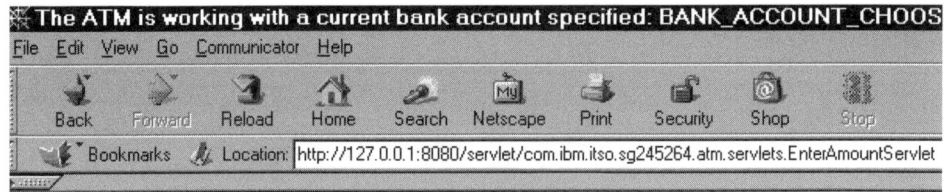

Account Chosen: CheckingAccount (PK = 222C) with a current balance of -55.

○ Withdraw Money
○ View Transaction History
○ Pick a different Account
[Next]

Restart

Figure 69. EnterAmountServlet

If you want to see the screen for the state DISPENSE_MONEY, then the EnterAmountServlet would need to be modified to call the getMoney method in a new thread. The getMoney method returns only after the dispensing action is complete. Afterwards the ATM goes to the state BANK_ACCOUNT_CHOOSEN, which is what the user sees. Normally the money would be physically spit out of the machine or added to an electronic wallet on the browser. In our ATM application, the message *"CashDispenser: Dispensing 55 ..."* is written to standard output.

Transaction History

Post Date	Post Time	Amount	Source Acct	Target Acct
Dec 22, 2000	12:14:12 AM	55	222C	977463453023

Figure 70. ChooseActionServlet — View Transaction History selected by user

Chapter 6. Creating JSPs

There are many tools to create/edit JSPs, including WebSphere studio or any text editor. VisualAge for Java allows a JSP to be included in a project as a resource. The JSP must exist in order to add it to the project. After it is added to the workspace, the first time a JSP resource is opened, VisualAge for Java will ask which external program to use for editing JSPs. This choice is saved in the workspace. It can be changed by modifying the resource associations for the workspace. In a Microsoft Windows environment, the default setting for a file association will be used if it exists. If a resource association is made in VisualAge for Java, then it will be used regardless of the Microsoft Windows setting.

Note: If you plan to use WebSphere studio to edit JSPs please refer to *Servlet and JSP Programming with IBM WebSphere Studio and VisualAge for Java*, SG24-5755 for information about synchronizing projects between the two tools.

Java Server Pages

Java Server Pages (JSPs) are similar to HTML files, but provide the ability to display dynamic content within Web pages. JSP technology was developed by Sun Microsystems to separate the development of dynamic Web page content from static HTML page design. The result of this separation means that the page design can change without the need to alter the underlying dynamic content of the page. This is useful in the development life-cycle because the Web page designers do not have to know how to create the dynamic content, but simply have to know where to place the dynamic content within the page.

To facilitate embedding of dynamic content, JSPs use a number of *tags* that enable the page designer to insert the properties of a JavaBean object and script elements into a JSP file. A number of development tools, such as the WebSphere Studio Page Designer, can be used to visually create a page containing dynamic contents based on the properties of Java beans.

Here are some of the advantages of using JSP technology over other methods of dynamic content creation:

- Separation of dynamic and static content

  This allows for the separation of application logic and Web page design, reducing the complexity of Web site development and making the site easier to maintain.

- Platform independence

  Because JSP technology is Java-based, it is platform independent. JSPs can run on any nearly any Web application server. JSPs can be developed on any platform and viewed by any browser because the output of a compiled JSP page is HTML.

- Component reuse

  Using JavaBeans and Enterprise JavaBeans, JSPs leverage the inherent reusability offered by these technologies. This enables developers to share components with other developers or their client community, which can speed up Web site development.

- Scripting and tags

  JSPs support both embedded JavaScript and tags. JavaScript is typically used to add page-level functionality to the JSP. Tags provide an easy way to embed and modify JavaBean properties and to specify other directives and actions.

How Java Server Pages work

Java Server Pages are made operable by having their contents (HTML tags, JSP tags and scripts) translated into a servlet by the application server. This process is responsible for translating both the dynamic and static elements declared within the JSP file into Java servlet code that delivers the translated contents through the Web server output stream to the browser.

Because JSPs are server-side technology, the processing of both the static and dynamic elements of the page occurs in the server. The architecture of a JSP/servlet-enabled Web site is often referred to as *thin-client* because most of the business logic is executed on the server.

The following process outlines the tasks performed on a JSP file on the *first invocation* of the file or when the underlying JSP file is changed by the developer (Figure 71):

- The Web browser makes a request to the JSP page.
- The JSP engine parses the contents of the JSP file.
- The JSP engine creates temporary servlet source code based on the contents of the JSP. The generated servlet is responsible for rendering the static elements of the JSP specified at design time in addition to creating the dynamic elements of the page.

- The servlet source code is compiled by the Java compiler into a servlet class file.

- The servlet is instantiated. The *init* and *service* methods of the servlet are called, and the servlet logic is executed.

- The combination of static HTML and graphics combined with the dynamic elements specified in the original JSP page definition are sent to the Web browser through the output stream of the servlet's response object.

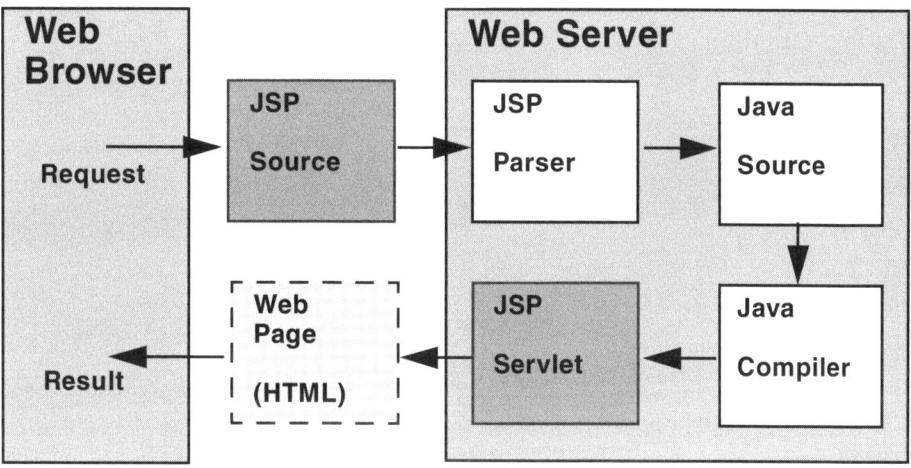

Figure 71. The JSP processing life-cycle on first-time invocation

Subsequent invocations of the JSP file will simply invoke the *service* method of the servlet created by the above process to serve the content to the Web browser. The servlet produced as a result of the above process remains in service until the application server is stopped, the servlet is manually unloaded, or a change is made to the underlying file, causing re compilation.

JSP interactions

There are a number of methods that a JSP can use to interact with the Web environment. Primarily, a JSP will use a JavaBean object to present dynamic content. However, a JSP can also invoke another JSP page by URL, by including another JSP or HTML page in the *include* directive, or by calling a servlet.

This section describes these interactions.

Invoking a JSP by URL

A JSP can be invoked by URL, from within the *<FORM>* tag of a JSP or HTML page, or from another JSP.

To invoke a JSP by URL, use the syntax:

```
http://servername/path/filename.jsp
```

For example, to invoke the Very_Simple.jsp, use this URL:

```
http://localhost/itso/Very_Simple.jsp          <== WebSphere
http://localhost:8080/itso/Very_Simple.jsp     <== VA Java
```

Calling a servlet from a JSP

You can invoke a servlet from a JSP either as an action on a form, or directly through the *jsp:include* or *jsp:forward* tags.

Form action

Typically, you want to call a servlet as a result of an action performed on a Java Server Page. For example, you may want to process some data entered by the user in an HTML form when they click the **Submit** button.

To invoke a servlet within the HTML <FORM> tag, the syntax is:

```
<FORM METHOD="POST|GET" ACTION="application_URI/JSP_URL">
    <!-- Other tags such as text boxes and buttons go here -->
</FORM>
```

For example:

```
<form method="POST"
      action="/servlet/com.ibm.itso.sg245264.atm.servlets.ShowActionsServlet">
```

JSP include tag

You can include the output of a servlet in a JSP using the jsp.include tag:

```
<jsp:include
page="/servlet/com.ibm.itso.sg245264.atm.servlets.ShowActionsServlet" />
```

Figure 72 shows a JSP that includes the servlet.

```
<HTML><BODY>
<H2> JSP to Servlet </H2>
<HR>
<jsp:include
page="servlet/com.ibm.itso.sg245264.atm.servlets.ShowActionsServlet" />
<HR>
<H2>End of servlet include</H2>
</HTML></BODY>
```

Figure 72. Sample JSP including a servlet

When you run this JSP, the output of the servlet is imbedded in the JSP output.

JSP forward tag

You can forward processing from a JSP to a servlet using the jsp.forward tag:

```
<jsp:forward
page="servlet/com.ibm.itso.sg245264.atm.servlets.ShowActionsServlet" />
```

Figure 73 shows a JSP that forwards processing.

```
<HTML><BODY>
<H2> JSP to Servlet </H2>
<HR>
<jsp:forward
page="servlet/com.ibm.itso.sg245264.atm.servlets.ShowActionsServlet" />
<HR>
<H2>End of servlet include</H2>
</HTML></BODY>
```

Figure 73. Sample JSP forwarding processing to a servlet

JSP 0.91 and 1.0

The JSP 1.0 specification contains the following changes and additions over the JSP .91 specification:

- Tags use XML formatting. For example, the JSP bean declaration tag *<BEAN>* is now declared using the syntax *<jsp:useBean ...>*. Similarly, WebSphere specific tags such as *<REPEAT>* are now declared using the syntax *<tsx:repeat>*
- Tags are case sensitive.

- Standard tags use the mixed-case convention of Java code, for example, jsp:useBean.
- Server-side includes (SSI) have been replaced with the <%@ include %> directive.
- *jsp:getProperty* and *jsp:setProperty* tags have been defined.
- *jsp:request* has been added, providing runtime forward and include functionality.
- *jsp:include* has been added to include resources from other files.
- *jsp:plugin* has been added.
- Implementation of LOOP, ITERATE, INCLUDEIF and EXCLUDEIF tags has been postponed pending enhancements to the tag extension mechanism.
- <SCRIPT> </SCRIPT> tags have been superseded with <%! ... %>

There have been other releases of the JSP specification such as .92 and .93. The additional functionality offered by these releases has not been discussed in this chapter.

Designing the JSP model

Before we implement the JSP model, let us quickly review the current servlet model. Today's most affordable implementation method is the Model-View-Controller (MVC) implementation. Our servlet model is already designed using the MVC model, and we have implemented JSP as the View component.

Model-View-Controller (MVC)

The Model-View-Controller model divides *control unit*, *business logic*, and *view* by their roles. This model allows the Web designer to design the front-end material, and the system programmer to design the business logic. In our model, and this is a major pattern, the servlet should not contain any business logic or view function. Business logic is handled by JavaBeans, and view is handled by HTML or JSP. The servlet will be a controller that invokes an appropriate business logic and view (Figure 74). Most of our servlets work as controllers, but only ShowATMServlet has both controller and view function, because we want to demonstrate how the *servlet-only* model works and how it differs from the *servlet-JSP* model.

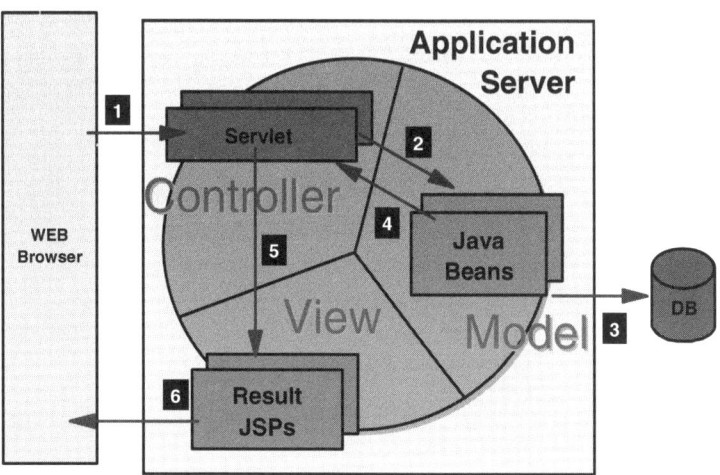

Figure 74. Model-View-Controller design

Servlet based modeling

We modified ShowATMServlet, which works as the controller and view. This version of ShowATMServlet no longer supports the view. Each servlet forwards a request to ShowATMServlet, then ShowATMServlet dispatches it to the proper JSPs.

Figure 75 is the servlet-only model. ShowATMServlet (working as controller) handles the first request (1) then uses ATM beans (models) to manipulate data and returns the returned result data through ShowATMServlet (working as view). The next requests are triggered from several forms that generated by ShowATMServlet. Then we go through each controller servlet and ATM beans, finally going back to ShowATMServlet, and that generates the resulting HTML.

Now we take away the view logic from ShowATMServlet and create JSPs as view. ShowATMServlet works as controller, and each controller servlet forwards to ShowATMServlet. However, ShowATMServlet itself does not generate the view, but forwards to JSPs, which handle the view (Figure 76).

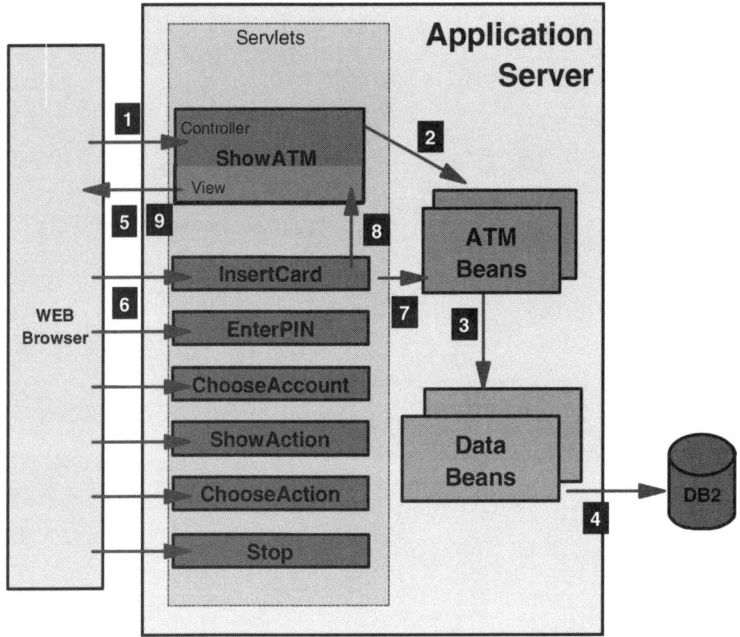

Figure 75. Servlet-only model

Here is a JSP based cash dispense flow:

1. The first request is sent from the browser to use the ATM.
2. ShowATMServlet checks availability of ATM using ATM beans.
3. ShowATM dispatches a request to READY_TO_USE.jsp to show the account number screen.
4. Account number request has been sent to InsertCardServlet.
5. InsertCardServlet checked logon status using ATM beans, then forwards it to NOT_LOGGED_ON.jsp through ShowATMServlet.
6. NOT_LOGGED_ON.jsp shows the pin number input screen.
7. The pin number request has been sent to EnterPinServlet.
8. EnterPinServlet checked that the pin number is correct using ATM beans, then forwards it to BANK_ACCOUNT_LISTED.jsp to show the account selection screen.

9. The account selection request has been sent to ChooseAccountServlet, which forwards it to BANK_ACCOUNT_CHOSEN.jsp to show the process menu which contains Withdraw, Show History and Change Account types.

10. To withdraw cash, select Withdraw.

11. The Withdraw request has been sent to ChooseActionServlet, which forwards it to ASK_AMOUNT.jsp to inquire about a withdraw amount.

12. Once the amount is entered, the withdraw process has been done through EnterAmountServlet and ATM bean (CashDispenser bean). Now we go back to the menu.

13. The Show History request from the process menu has been sent to ChooseActionServlet, which forwards it to TRX_HISTORY_LISTED.jsp after it has been processed by the ATM bean.

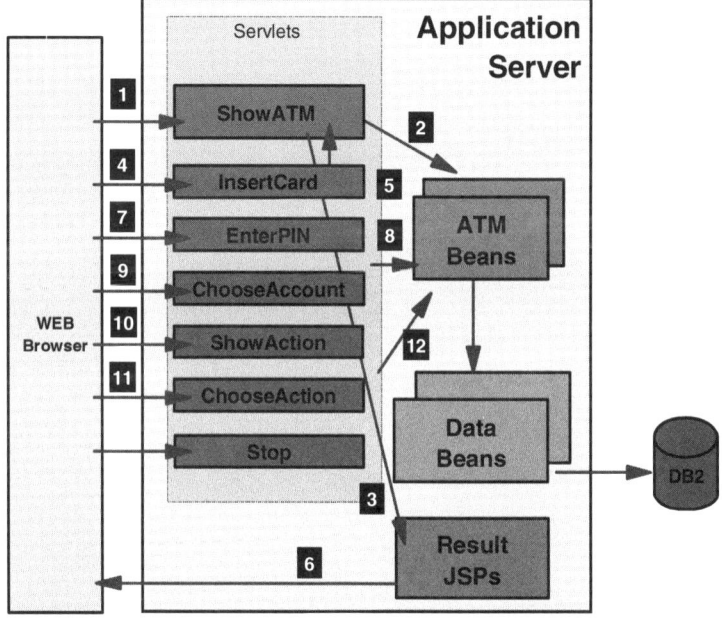

Figure 76. Servlet-JSP model

Building the ATM application

The following code listing is the performTask method of ShowATMServlet:

```java
public void performTask(HttpServletRequest request, HttpServletResponse response)
throws Exception {

    ATM userATM = createOrRetreiveUserATM(request, response);

    // add the userATM object to the request, to ensure the JSPs only use the request attributes.
    request.setAttribute("userATMrq", userATM );

    //To use hard-coded HTML pages as described in the Servlet chapter, uncomment the following line.
    //showNextPage(request, response, userATM.getState());

    // Next two lines get the JSP to show, then forward the request to the JSP. This is the
    // implementation built in the JSP chapter.
    RequestDispatcher dispatcher = determineNextPage(userATM.getState());
    dispatcher.forward(request, response);
}
```

This method uses the dispatcher.forward method instead of the showNextPage method. The showNextPage method invokes several methods that generate HTML tags directly. To determine which JSP will be used to generate the HTML tags, we create the determineNextPage method. The determineNextPage method checks current status and sets the target JSP name to the ServletContext.

```java
private RequestDispatcher determineNextPage(ATM$ATMState curstate) {
    RequestDispatcher dispatcher= null ;

    if (curstate ==  ATM.OUT_OF_ORDER){
        dispatcher = getServletContext().getRequestDispatcher("/itsojsp/OUT_OF_ORDER.jsp");
    }
    else if (curstate ==  ATM.READY_TO_USE){
        dispatcher = getServletContext().getRequestDispatcher("/itsojsp/READY_TO_USE.jsp");
    }
    else if (curstate ==  ATM.NOT_LOGGED_ON){
        dispatcher = getServletContext().getRequestDispatcher("/itsojsp/NOT_LOGGED_ON.jsp");
    }
    else if (curstate ==  ATM.BANK_ACCOUNTS_LISTED){
        dispatcher = getServletContext().getRequestDispatcher("/itsojsp/BANK_ACCOUNTS_LISTED.jsp");
    }
    else if (curstate ==  ATM.BANK_ACCOUNT_CHOOSEN){
        dispatcher = getServletContext().getRequestDispatcher("/itsojsp/BANK_ACCOUNT_CHOSEN.jsp");
    }
    else if (curstate ==  ATM.ASK_AMOUNT){
        dispatcher = getServletContext().getRequestDispatcher("/itsojsp/ASK_AMOUNT.jsp");
    }
    else if (curstate ==  ATM.DISPENSE_MONEY){
```

```
        dispatcher =
getServletContext().getRequestDispatcher("/itsojsp/DISPENSE_MONEY.jsp");
        }
    else if (curstate ==  ATM.TRX_HISTORY_LISTED){
        dispatcher =
getServletContext().getRequestDispatcher("/itsojsp/TRX_HISTORY_LISTED.jsp");
        }
    else{
        throw new IllegalStateException();
    }

    return dispatcher;
}
```

Each of the JSPs works as dynamic HTML. A title is generated by an ATM bean, and that shows current working status. Bold tags are major JSP tags (we will describe these later):

```
<jsp:root
    xmlns:jsp="http://java.sun.com/products/jsp/dtd/jsp_1_0.dtd">
<jsp:directive.page
    errorPage="/itsojsp/error.jsp"
/>
<jsp:directive.page
    import="com.ibm.itso.sg245264.atm.memory.Transaction"
/>
<jsp:directive.page
    import="java.text.DateFormat"
/>
<jsp:useBean
    id="userATMrq"
    type="com.ibm.itso.sg245264.atm.memory.ATM"
    scope="request"
/>
<jsp:declaration> Transaction curtran = null;</jsp:declaration>
<jsp:scriptlet> java.util.Vector alltrans =  userATMrq.getTransactions();
</jsp:scriptlet>

<HTML><HEAD>
<TITLE><jsp:expression> userATMrq.getState()   </jsp:expression></TITLE>

</HEAD><BODY>
<P ALIGN=CENTER>Transaction History</P>


<jsp:scriptlet>if( alltrans.capacity() > 0){</jsp:scriptlet>
<TABLE ALIGN=CENTER BORDER=1>
    <TR><TH>Post Date</TH><TH>Post Time</TH><TH>Amount</TH><TH>Source Acct</TH><TH>Target Acct</TH></TR>

<jsp:scriptlet> for (int i=0; i < alltrans.capacity(); i++){
        curtran = (Transaction)alltrans.elementAt(i);
</jsp:scriptlet>
    <TR>
        <TD>   <jsp:expression>
DateFormat.getDateInstance().format(curtran.getTimestamp())  </jsp:expression> </TD>
        <TD>   <jsp:expression>
DateFormat.getTimeInstance().format(curtran.getTimestamp())  </jsp:expression> </TD>
        <TD>   <jsp:expression> curtran.getTrxAmount()  </jsp:expression> </TD>
        <TD>   <jsp:expression> curtran.getSrcAccount().getId().getIdAsString()
</jsp:expression> </TD>
```

```
            <TD> <jsp:expression> curtran.getTrgtAccount().getId().getIdAsString()
</jsp:expression> </TD>
     </TR>
<jsp:scriptlet>}    // end for loop. </jsp:scriptlet>
</TABLE>
<jsp:scriptlet>} else {   // refers to if (alltrans.capcaity > 0 )  </jsp:scriptlet>
        <P> No Transactions found. </P>
<jsp:scriptlet>}    // refers to if (alltrans.capcaity > 0 )   </jsp:scriptlet>

<P><A HREF='/servlet/com.ibm.itso.sg245264.atm.servlets.ShowActionsServlet'>Choose a
different Action</A>
</P>
<P><A HREF='/servlet/com.ibm.itso.sg245264.atm.servlets.StopServlet'>Restart</A>
</P>
</BODY>
</HTML>
</jsp:root>
```

JSP tags

Java Server Pages are composed of standard HTML tags and JSP tags. The available JSP tags defined in the JSP 1.0 specification are categorized as follows. We used XML style JSP implementation in this case.

jsp:root

An XML document representing a JSP page has jsp:root as its root element type. The top element has an xmlns attribute that enables the use of the standard elements defined.

```
<jsp:root
    xmlns:jsp="http://java.sun.com/products/jsp/dtd/jsp_1_0.dtd">
</jsp:root>
```

jsp:useBean

The *jsp:useBean* tag is used to declare a JavaBean object that you want to use within the JSP. Before you can use the *jsp:getProperty* and *jsp:setProperty* tags, you must have first declared your JavaBean using the jsp:useBean tag. When the jsp:useBean tag is processed, the application server performs a lookup of the specified given Java object using the values specified in the *id* and *scope* attributes. If the object is not found, it will attempt to create it using the values specified in the *scope* and *class* attributes.

The syntax for inserting a JavaBean is:

```
<jsp:useBean id="beanInstanceName" scope="page|request|session|application"
         typespec>
    optional scriptlets and tags
</jsp:useBean>
```

Here, *typespec* can be declared using any of the following variations:

```
class="package.class"
type="package.class"
type="package.class" beanName="package.class"
```

You can also embed scriptlets and tags such as *jsp:getProperty* within the jsp:useBean declaration which will be executed upon creation of the bean. This is often used to modify properties of a bean immediately after it has been created.

An example of a simple form of bean instantiation is:

```
<jsp:useBean id ="userATMrq"
        class="com.ibm.itso.sg245264.atm.memory.ATM"/>
```

This example tries to locate an instance of the *ATM* bean. If no instance exists, a new instance is created. The instance can then be accessed within the JSP using the specified *id* of ATM bean.

jsp:directive.page

A JSP directive is a global definition sent to the JSP engine that remains valid regardless of any specific requests made to the JSP page. A directive always appears at the top of the JSP file, before any other JSP tags. This is due to the way the JSP parsing engine produces servlet code from the JSP file. The *page* directive defines page dependent attributes to the JSP engine.

The syntax of a directive is:

```
<jsp:directive.page>
```

The following example is defining error.jsp.

```
<jsp:directive.page
   errorPage="/itsojsp/error.jsp"
/>
```

jsp:declaration

A declaration block contains Java variables and methods that are called from an *expression* block within the JSP file. Code within a declaration block is usually written in Java, however, the WebSphere application server supports declaration blocks containing other script syntax. Code within a declaration block is often used to perform additional processing on the dynamic data generated by a JavaBean property.

The syntax of a declaration is:

```
<jsp:declaration>
```

For example:

```
<jsp:declaration> Transaction curtran = null;</jsp:declaration>
```

jsp:scriptlet

JSP supports embedding of Java code fragments within a JSP by using a *scriptlet* block. Scriptlets are used to embed small code blocks within the JSP page, rather than to declare entire methods as performed in a declarations block. The syntax for a scriptlet is:

```
<jsp:scriptlet>
```

The following example uses a scriptlet to get all transaction data as a Vector class.

```
<jsp:scriptlet> java.util.Vector alltrans = userATMrq.getTransactions();
</jsp:scriptlet>
```

jsp:expression

Expressions are scriptlet fragments whose results can be converted to String objects and subsequently fed to the output stream for display in a browser. The syntax for an expression is:

```
<jsp:expression>
```

Typically, expressions are used to execute and display the String representation of variables and methods declared within the declarations section of the JSP, or from JavaBeans that are accessed by the JSP. If the conversion of the expression result is unsuccessful, a *ClassCastException* is thrown at the time of the request.

The following example calls the *getState* method declared in the declarations block and prints the result.

```
<jsp:expression> userATMrq.getState()   </jsp:expression>
```

All primitive types such as short, int, and long can be automatically converted to Strings. Your own classes must provide a *toString* method for String conversion.

Chapter 7. Creating GUI applications

In this chapter, we will discuss about Java client-side technology. We start with AWT/JFC basics and then go through the client application of our ATM. The Graphical User Interface (GUI) version will be implemented as a Java application and as an applet. This client will illustrate the Visual Composition Editor (VCE) component of VisualAge for Java. For a change, this implements not the ATM interaction but instead provides some kind of administrative client to access the ATM system.

Abstract Windowing Toolkit and Java Foundation Classes refresher

The Java 1.0 Abstract Windowing Toolkit (AWT) programming model is awkward and non-object-oriented. The situation improved with the Java 1.1 AWT event model, which takes a much clearer, object-oriented approach, along with the addition of JavaBeans, a component programming model that is oriented toward the easy creation of visual programming environments. Java 2 finishes the transformation away from the old Java 1.0 AWT by essentially replacing everything with the Java Foundation Classes (JFC).

The JFC is also known by its code name *Swing* (derived from the music demo given at the 1997 JavaOne convention in San Francisco). The JFC component set is a new GUI toolkit that provides a rich set of windowing components, the visual components used in GUI-based programs.

With the JFC, you can develop efficient GUI components that have exactly the "look and feel" that you specify. For example, a program that uses JFC components can be designed such that it will execute without modification on any kind of computer and can always look and feel just like a program written specifically for the particular computer on which it is running.

Beans from the AWT are provided in the java.awt package (Java class libraries project). The JFC beans are provided in the javax.swing package.

Although Swing and AWT components can be mixed, it is inadvisable. For this reason, VisualAge does not allow you to drop AWT beans on Swing beans. Because you might want to add Swing beans to AWT beans that you created before Swing was available, VisualAge does allow you to drop Swing beans on AWT beans. You can morph the AWT beans to Swing beans when you are ready to convert completely to Swing (See Chapter 3, "Migrating to Java?" on page 65).

VisualAge provides its own BeanInfo classes for Swing and AWT beans. These BeanInfo classes are tailored for visual composition.

Visual Composition Editor

The Visual Composition Editor is a powerful composing tool you can use to:

- Build the user interface for your program by dropping beans.
- Construct business logic by connecting the beans.
- Edit existing beans.

The Visual Composition Editor (Figure 77) makes it easy to build applets, beans, and entire applications using the functions available on the menu bar, pop-up menus, tool bar, and the variety of reusable beans on the beans palette. A description of the functions on the tool bar or beans palette appears when the mouse pointer is positioned over the item.

The Visual Composition Editor window in Figure 77 includes several components: the beans palette along the left side, the status area along the bottom, the toolbar along the top, and the free-form surface where you lay out the beans.

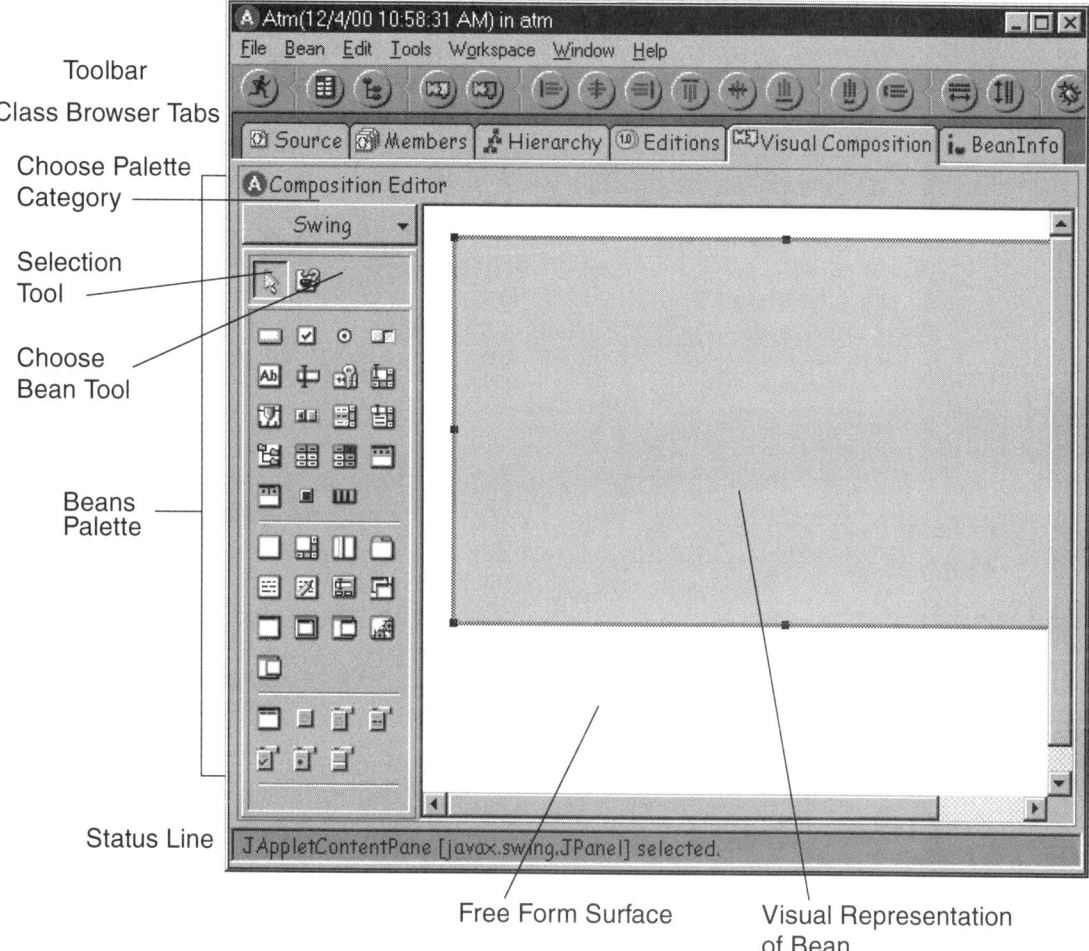

Figure 77. The Visual Composition Editor

In VisualAge for Java, beans are the components that you manipulate when you program visually. These beans are Java classes that adhere to the JavaBeans specification. In the Visual Composition Editor, you select beans from a palette, specify their characteristics, and make connections between them. Beans can contain other beans and connections to beans.

You use two types of beans within the Visual Composition Editor:

- Visual Beans, which are subclasses of the AWT Component class (which includes the JFC). Examples are List, JList, Button, JButton, and TextField. Visual beans have a visual representation at design time that is similar to their appearance at runtime. The design-time appearance of JFC beans is their default appearance using the Metal Look and Feel; at runtime they have the look and feel that your application specifies.

- Nonvisual beans usually represent the business logic in your programs, for example, a BankAccount bean. At design time nonvisual beans appear by default as a puzzle icon, or they may have a specific icon associated with them (Figure 78). They do not have a visual representation at runtime.

Figure 78. Nonvisual Bean Icons

The Beans Palette

When you first start VisualAge for Java, the Beans Palette contains all of the user interface beans in the AWT and JFC as well as some "helper" beans. There are three categories of beans originally on the palette (see Figure 79); you select them using the Choose Palette Category drop-down list. The selections are:

- **Swing**
- **AWT**
- **Other** (the helper beans)

There is also an **Available** selection on the Choose Palette Category that you use to load additional features into the workspace.

Each category is further separated into subcategories by function. For the JFC and AWT, there are three major subcategories:

- Button and data entry
- Containers
- Menus

Within each sub-category you can identify individual beans, using "over-help" (explanations that appear at the cursor when you leave the cursor over an element on the screen).

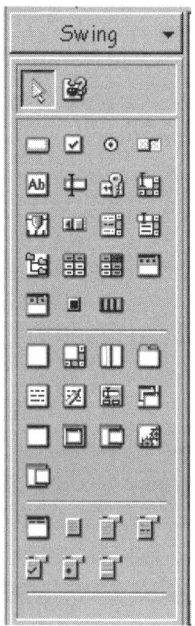 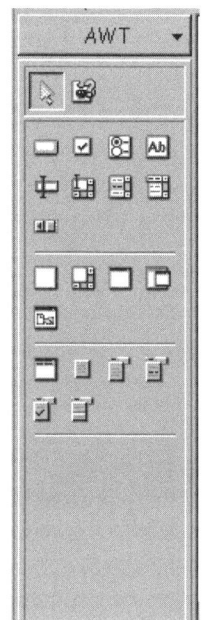 

Figure 79. The Beans Palette with Swing

Always available directly below the **Choose Palette Category** button are the **Selection** and **Choose Bean** tools:

Selection   Use the Selection tool to select and move beans and connections on the free-form surface.

Choose Bean   Use the Choose Bean tool to add beans to the free-form surface that are not on the Beans Palette.

Modification of the Beans Palette

You can modify the palette by resizing it, changing the icon size, or adding or removing categories, separators, beans you have constructed yourself, or beans supplied by a vendor.

To modify the Beans Palette, use the popup menu from the palette or select **Bean→Modify Palette** as shown in Figure 80. After you invoke the function, the Modify Palette dialog appears (Figure 81) where you can choose the bean to modify on the palette.

If you import beans from a jar file, VisualAge for Java automatically prompts you with the Modify Palette dialog.

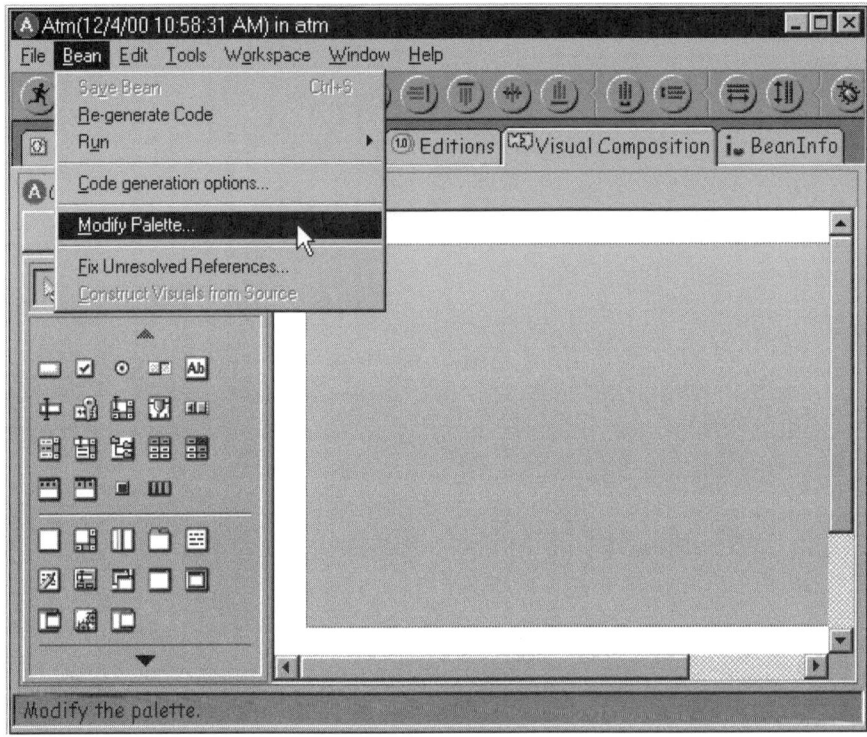

Figure 80. Modifying the Beans Palette

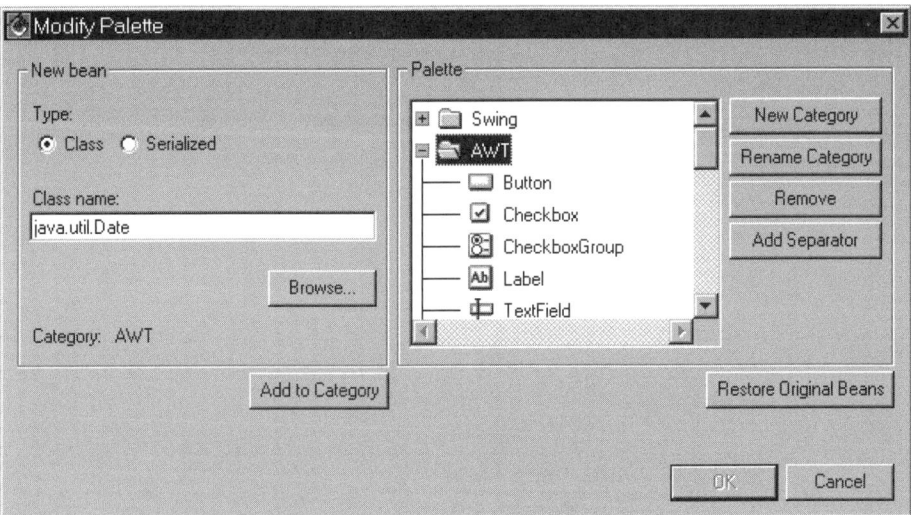

Figure 81. Modify Palette dialog box

Visual Composition Editor toolbar

The Visual Composition Editor toolbar provides you with easy access to useful shortcuts for menu actions.

By moving your mouse pointer over each icon on the toolbar, a label will appear that identifies the icon.

Most of the tools in the toolbar act on the beans that are currently selected in the free-form surface.

Using the Visual Composition Editor Alignment Tools

The toolbar has several controls to align, distribute, and size the components in the Visual Composition Editor. The controls only work with a null layout. Because using a null layout is not recommended for writing portable programs, you are better off not using the null layout and alignment tools unless you know the displays on which your programs will run or if you are creating a quick prototype.

You can also use the alignment and distribution tools to arrange the nonvisual beans on the free-form surface. Using these tools and rearranging connections can facilitate visual development.

The free-form surface

The free-form surface is where you do all of your visual programming. You select a bean from the Beans Palette or use the Choose Bean tool and then drop the bean on the free-form surface.

If the bean you are editing (the bean opened in the class browser) is a GUI bean, that is, it descends from `java.awt.Component`, it will have a visual representation (the large grey box shown in Figure 77 on page 145) on the free-form surface. This representation is where you add other GUI components to the bean. When you place beans onto any empty part of the free-form surface, you are adding them to the bean and not to the visual representation of the bean.

The empty part of the free-form surface is where you add invisible beans to the bean you are editing. For example, in the ATM application you will add buttons and text fields to the visual representation of the bean but you will add the model beans (for example, Bank and CheckingAccount) to the free-form surface outside the visual representation of the bean.

Regardless of the type of bean, every bean has a pop-up menu that contains options you can use to modify or work with that bean.

Working with beans in the Visual Composition Editor

In this section you learn how to add beans to the free-form surface and customize beans through their Property sheet.

Adding beans

The free-from surface is like a blank sheet of paper or work area where you can add, manipulate, and connect the beans that you work with to create your composite bean.

When you select a bean from the Beans Palette, the cursor is loaded with that bean and appears as a set of cross hairs. The bean can then be added to the free-from surface, the Beans List, or to an existing container bean (a bean that descends from `java.awt.Container`). When unloaded, the cursor reverts back to the Selection tool arrow (see left icon in Figure 82).

Figure 82. Selection and Choose Bean tools on the Palette

Select the **Choose bean** tool (the icon on the right in Figure 82) to retrieve a bean that is not on the palette and drop it on the Beans List, the free-form surface, or an existing container bean.

After you invoke the **Choose Bean** tool, the Choose Bean dialog (Figure 83) appears. You can type the class name of your bean in the **Class name** field (remember to use the fully qualified name) or use the **Browse** button to find the class. In the **Name** field, type the name of the bean. Finally select whether you are creating a class, a variable, or a serialized bean read from a serialization file.

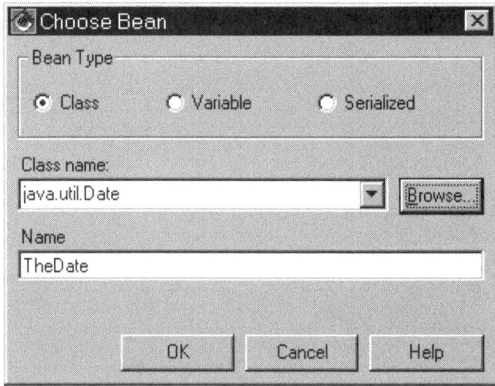

Figure 83. Choose Bean Dialog

The Sticky function

To add multiple instances of the same bean, enable the *Sticky* function by holding down the Control key while selecting the bean. Selecting a new bean or the Selection tool disables *Sticky*.

Customizing Beans

Once you have dropped a bean on the free-form surface, you can customize it by double-clicking the bean to open its Property sheet. You can also open a bean's property sheet by selecting **Properties** from the bean's pop-up menu or selecting the **Show Properties** button on the tool bar. Using the Property sheet, you can change properties exposed by the bean as well as the bean name.

You can edit the properties for a single bean or select several beans and open a Property sheet for them. When you change a property on the Property sheet for multiple selected beans, the change affects all beans selected.

Figure 84 shows the property sheet of a JTextField bean. Select the **Show expert features** checkbox to access expert properties of the bean.

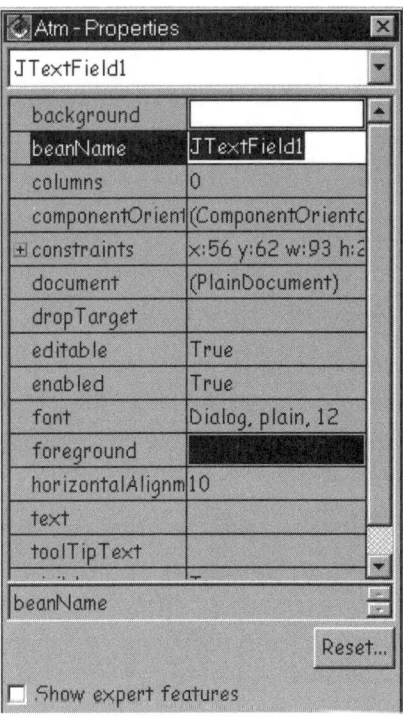

Figure 84. Property sheet of a JTextField bean

Each bean also has a pop-up menu (Figure 85) that you access by clicking the right mouse button. The pop-up menu has the following selection items:

Properties	Open the Property sheet for the bean.
Event to Code	Start an event-to-code connection from this bean.
Quick Form	Lay out a GUI panel that corresponds to the properties of a model bean. You specify the visual bean to use for each property; VisualAge drops the beans and connects them to the model bean.
Open	(Class only) — Open the bean's class in a class browser.
Promote Bean Feature	Promote a feature of the bean as a feature on the primary bean.
Change Type	(Variable or factory only) — Change the underlying type of the variable or factory.

Morph Into	Change the type of this bean or variable to another closely related type and update any conceitedness and properties. Morph Into can be used to change a class to a variable and vice versa or to change AWT components to JFC components.
Change Bean Name	Change the name of the bean in the Visual Composition Editor. The change will also affect the attribute name and the names of accessors and mutator methods.
Delete	Delete this bean from the free-form surface.
Layout	Position the bean on the free-form surface.
Connect	Start a connection from this bean.
Browse Connections	List all connections to and from this bean. You can also hide and show connections from the bean.
Reorder Connections From	Change the order in which connections from this bean are fired.
Tear-Off Property	Tear off a property from this bean so you can access it as a variable on the free-form surface.
Refresh Interface	If the BeanInfo interface has changed, use Refresh Interface to update the Visual Composition Editor environment with the changes.

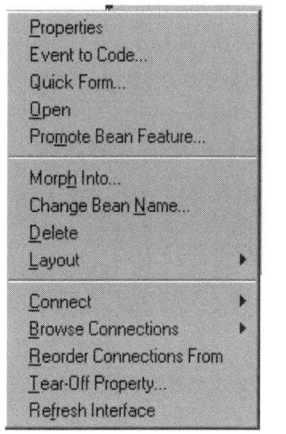 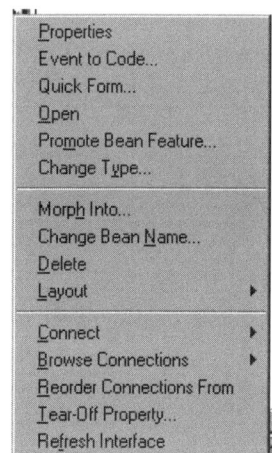

Figure 85. Bean pop-up menu for class and variable

Quick Form is a new feature of VisualAge for Java version 3.5. You can use the Quick Form SmartGuide to define and register quick forms. You can register quick forms for reuse with any property of a specific type. The Quick Form SmartGuide contains three parts:

Quick Form window You specify the properties to be included, the components to be dropped, and the location of the finished quick form. You can also register a pre-existing visual bean as a quick form from this window.

Quick Form Layout window You specify how you want VisualAge to lay the components out.

Save Quick Form window You specify how you want VisualAge to save and register your quick form for reuse.

Naming beans

The Visual Composition Editor assigns default names to distinguish beans and connections when you generate the code to build programs. It assigns bean names on the basis of the class name and the number of beans of that type on the free-form surface or the name you specify when you use the Choose Bean tool. You can give a bean a different name at any time. VisualAge for Java uses the bean name in two ways:

- The bean name is shown on the free-form surface and in the Property sheet. This name is not equivalent to the name property on objects of the Component class.

- The bean name is also used as the basis for the attribute name in the Java source and the getter and setter methods generated for the bean. The attribute name is typically ivjBeanName, where BeanName is the name of the bean.

Give beans meaningful names if they will be accessed using Java code that you write yourself. If you do not give beans meaningful names it will be extremely difficult to write code that accesses the beans. For example, if you add an Exit button to an application, VisualAge for Java gives it a name based on the number of default button names currently in use. For example, the name might be ivjButton111. It will be much easier to write code that accesses the bean if you name the button ExitButton!

Properties created in the BeanInfo page use a similar naming convention. The attribute has the prefix `field` instead of `ivj`, however.

Beans List

The Beans List is a very helpful tool. It shows all of the beans and connections on the free-form surface. From the Beans List, you can:

- Select or delete any bean
- Access the pop-up menu and Property sheet for any bean
- Move a bean to a different container or position in the container
- Select or delete any connection
- Connect beans

Factory and variable

Factory and variable are helper beans. Typically, when you add JavaBeans to the free-form surface they are instantiated when your program starts or when the bean is first accessed. In many cases, you do not want this behavior. For example:

- You may not know the specifics of a bean when the program starts.
- You may not want to use the resources when the program starts.
- You may only want a place holder or reference to an existing bean.

In these and other cases, you would use factories and variables instead of beans. Factories are visual tools that create other beans. Variables are visual place holders that reference other beans. Factories and variables are not really JavaBeans, they are helpers that cause code to be generated for you.

You can also use factories and variables to visually program the construction and manipulation of objects that are not beans, for example, objects that do not have a default constructor.

Visual Programming in action

The ATM application described in Chapter 4, "Beginning the ATM project" on page 73 is used in examples throughout this book. In this section you will use the packages you have already developed to create simples GUI applets. The first simple applet is a list of banking accounts. When selecting one of those accounts, you can see details in a second window (see Figure 86).

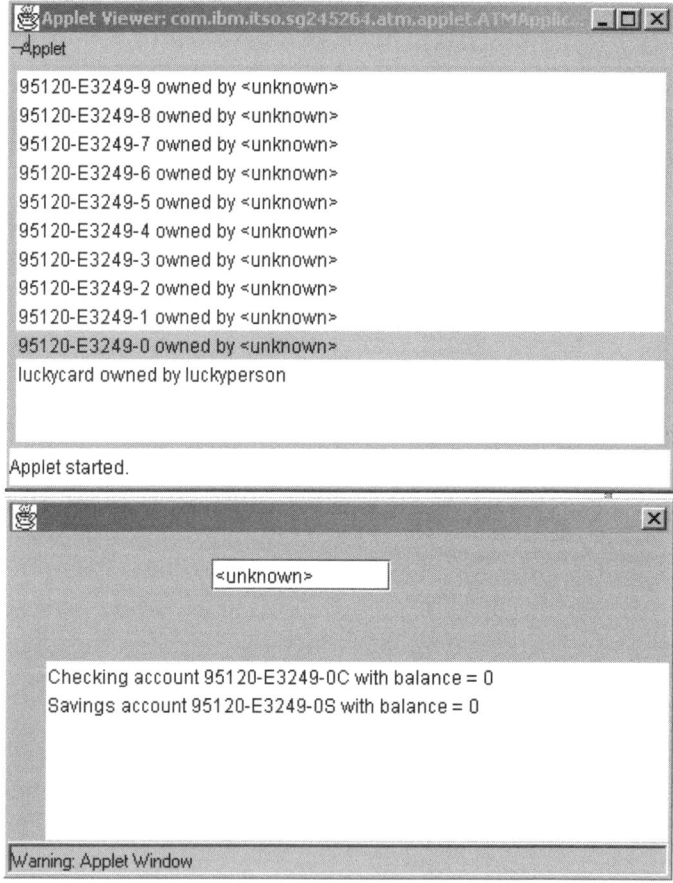

Figure 86. The finished ATM Applets

You will use the packages you have already created in the previous chapters:

- package: com.ibm.itso.sg245264.atm.memory
- package: com.ibm.itso.sg245264.atm.database

The ATM classes created

You will use the following classes already created in the previous chapters.

From package com.ibm.itso.sg245264.atm.memory: The list of classes is shown in Figure 87.

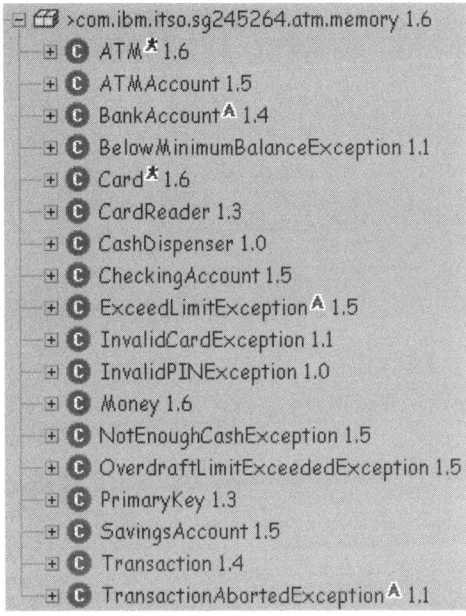

Figure 87. Classes defined in com.ibm.itso.sg245264.atm.memory package

From package com.ibm.itso.sg245264.atm.database: The list of classes is shown in Figure 88.

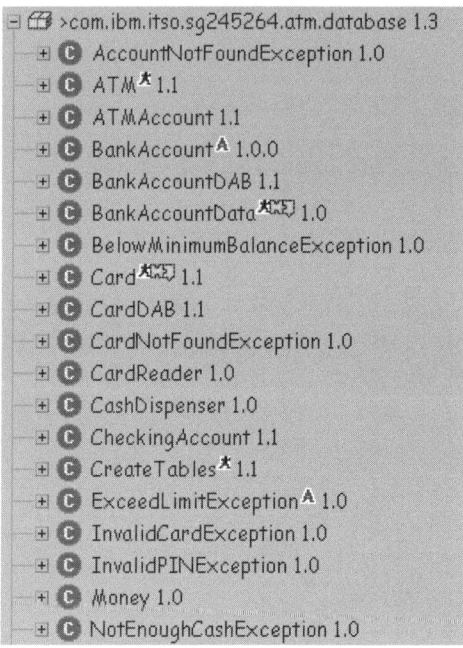

Figure 88. Classes defined in com.ibm.itso.sg245264.atm,database package

Before creating the new classes, you have to create a new package. Use the Add Package button (the fifth button in the Workbench tool bar) to start the Add Package SmartGuide. Type com.ibm.itso.atm.applet in the package field (see Figure 89).

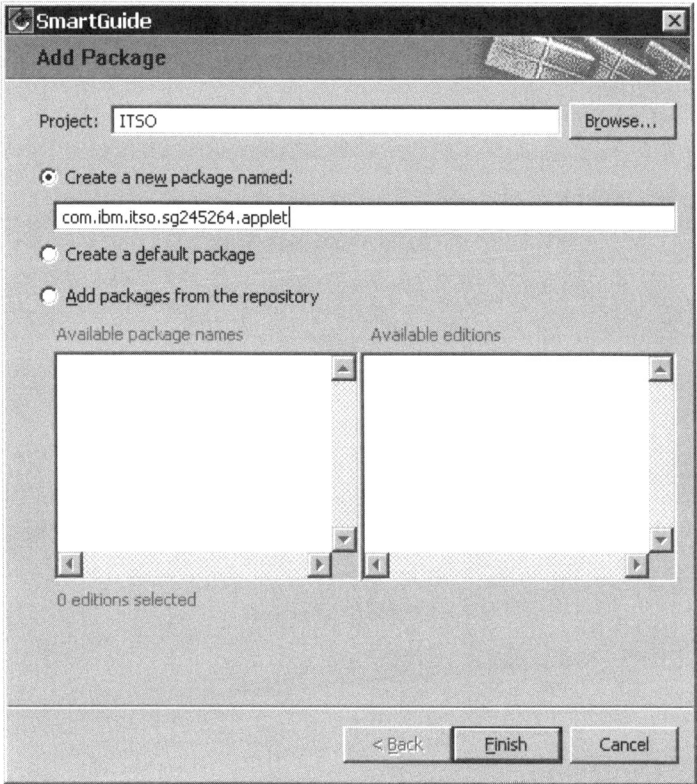

Figure 89. Add package window

To be able to work with Java Beans in your ATM GUI application and reuse the classes you have already created, you will use the wrapping technique. This will wrap the Business Objects already defined into JavaBeans. With this technique, you will be able to replace the Business Objects by another implementation.

This means that you will be able to use either the Business Objects defined in the package com.ibm.itso.sg245264.atm.memory or the Business Objects defined in the package com.ibm.itso.sg245264.atm.database just by modifying your import statements.

Building the CardBean class

With the CardBean class, you will wrap the Business Object Card into the JavaBean CardBean.

To create the CardBean class, use the Create Class SmartGuide: From the Workbench, select the **Create Class** button (the sixth button in the tool bar). Type CardBean in the **Class name** field and select the **Next** button (see Figure 90).

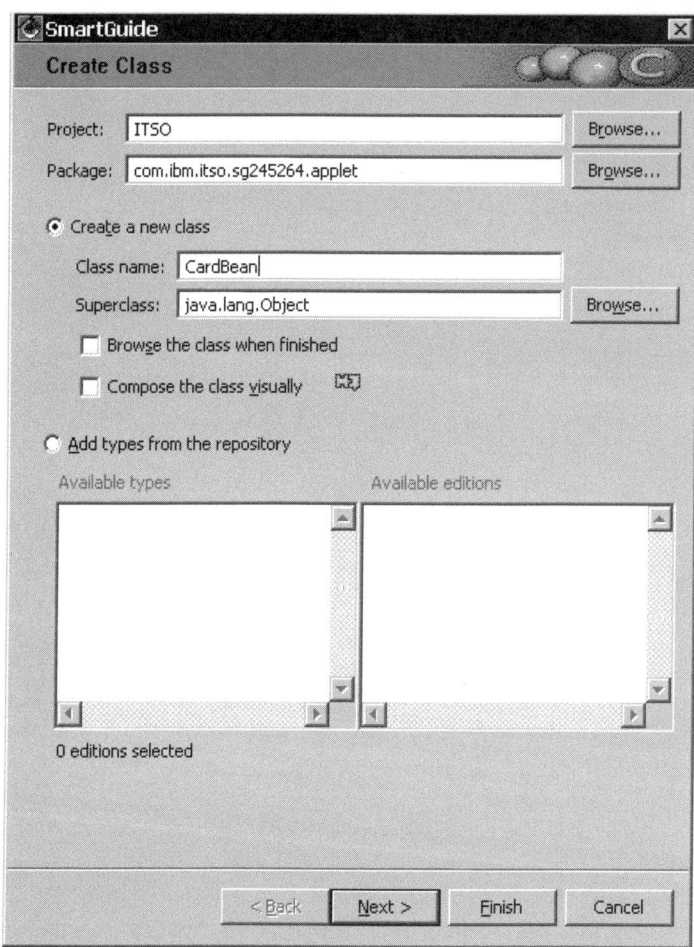

Figure 90. Create Class SmartGuide

In the Attribute Window, add the following import statements, **Add Package**: com.ibm.itso.sg245264.atm.memory and **Add Type**: Java.util.vector. In **What interface should this class implement,** select the **ADD** button and type serializable as **Pattern** (see Figure 91). Select the **Finish** button.

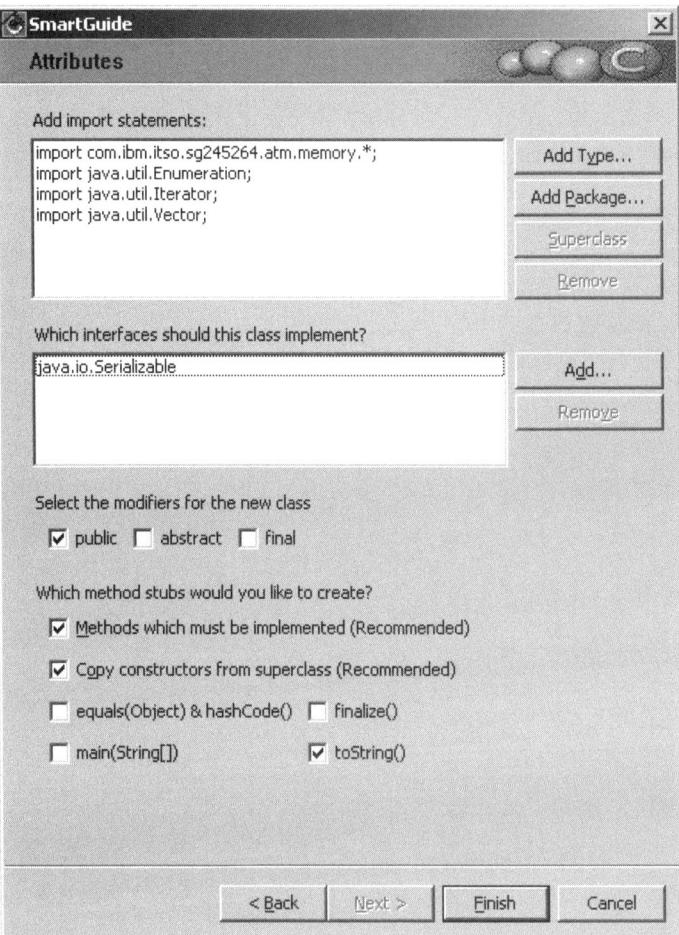

Figure 91. Create Class SmartGuide — Attributes window

From the workbench window, **Open** the new created class CardBean. Select the **BeanInfo** tag. You will add the following properties:

Name	Type	Readable	Writable	Bound
owner	String	Yes	No	No
bankAccounts	Vector	Yes	No	No
bankAccountBeans	Vector	Yes	No	No

To add the properties described, use the **Create Property Feature** button (the third button within the BeanInfo tool bar). Enter the features as described for each property.

Your BeanInfo window contains now owners, bankAccounts, and bankAccountBeans properties (see Figure 92).

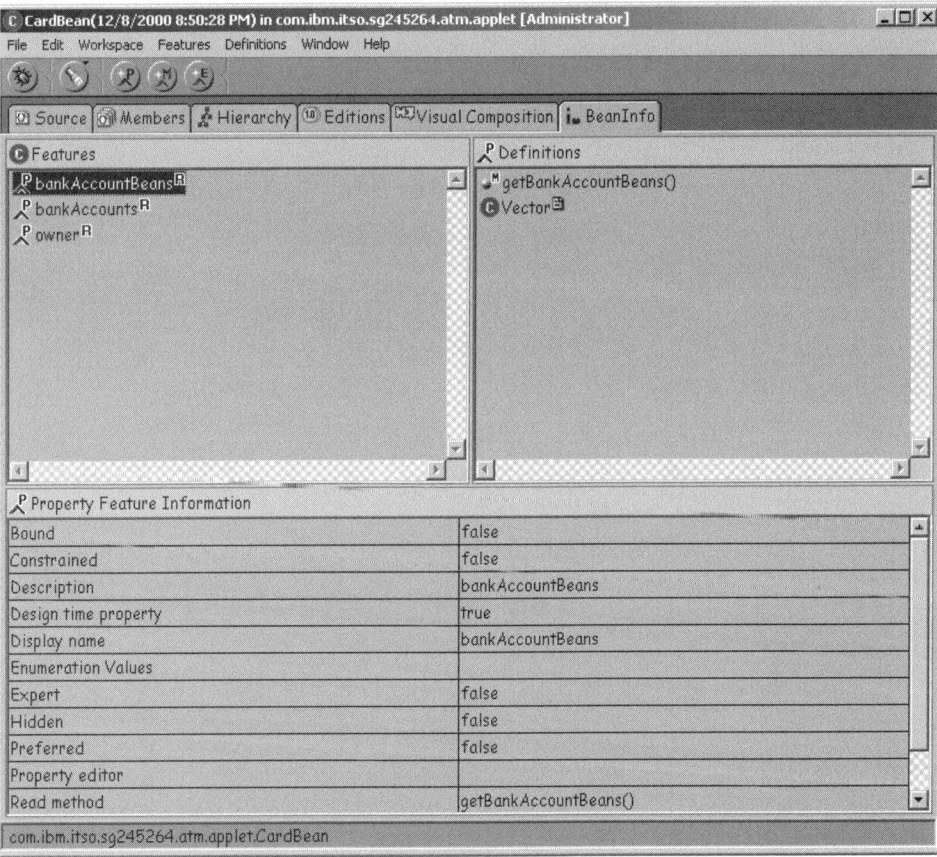

Figure 92. BeanInfo window for CardBean Class

The CardBean() constructor should match the following code:

```
/**
 * CardBean constructor comment.
 */
public CardBean() {
   cardImpl = null; // just satisfying JB
```

Add a new constructor to match the following code:

```
/**
 * CardBean constructor comment.
 */
CardBean(Card aCard) {
   cardImpl = aCard;
}
```

Edit the getOwner() method source to match the following code:

```
/**
 * Gets the owner property (java.lang.String) value.
 * @return The owner property value.
 */
public java.lang.String getOwner() {
   return cardImpl.getOwner();
   }
```

Edit the getBankAccounts() method source to match the following code:

```
public Vector getBankAccounts()
throws Exception {
   Vector tempV, newV;
   Iterator i;

   tempV = cardImpl.getBankAccounts();
   i = tempV.iterator();
   newV = new Vector(tempV.size());
   while(i.hasNext()) {
      newV.addElement(new BankAccountBean((BankAccount) i.next()));
   }
   return newV;
}
```

Edit the getBankAccountBeans() method to match the following code:

```
public Vector getBankAccountBeans()
throws Exception {
   Vector tempV, newV;
   Iterator i;

   tempV = cardImpl.getBankAccounts();
   i = tempV.iterator();
   newV = new Vector(tempV.size());
   while(i.hasNext()) {
      newV.addElement(new BankAccountBean((BankAccount) i.next()));
   }
   return newV;
```

}

Modify the toString implementation to return a variable cardImpl:

```
/**
 * Insert the method's description here.
 * Creation date: (12/6/2000 1:05:49 AM)
 * @return java.lang.String
 */
public String toString() {
   return cardImpl.toOneLineString();
}
```

Building the CardBeanHome class

Create a CardBeanHome class using the Create Class SmartGuide from your Workbench window. Type CardBeanHome in the **Class name** field and select the **Next** button. In the Attribute window, add the following import statements. **Add package**: com.ibm.itso.sg245264.atm.memory and **Add Type**: Vector and AbstractListModel. In **What interface should this class implement**, select the **Add** button and type serializable as Pattern (see Figure 93). Select the finish button.

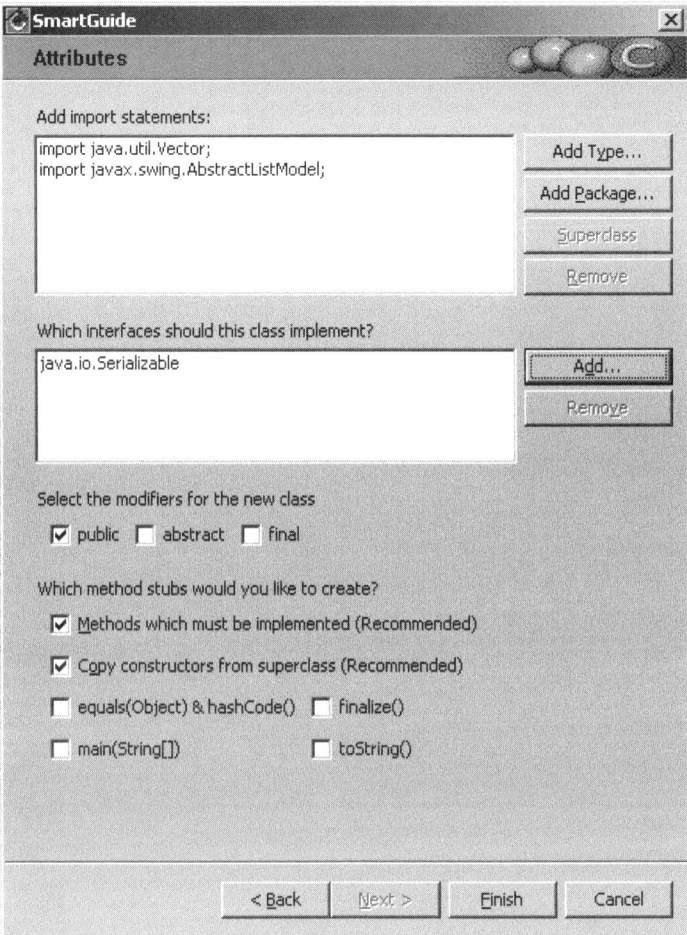

Figure 93. Create Class CardBeanHome — Attributes window

From the Workbench window, open the new created class CardBeanHome. Select the BeanInfo tag.

To find a CardBean based on a String representation of its primary key, create a new method feature using the New Method Feature SmartGuide with the following features:

Name	Return Type	Parameters	Parameter 1	BeanInfo option
findWithCardPK	CardBean	1	String primaryKeySTR	preferred

Fill in the method to match the following code:

```
/**
 * Perform the findWithCardPK method.
 * @return com.ibm.itso.sg245264.atm.applet.CardBean
 * @param primaryKeyStr  java.lang.String
 */
public CardBean findWithCardPK(String primaryKeyStr )
throws Exception {
    /* Perform the findWithCardPK method. */
    return new CardBean(Card.findWithCardPK(primaryKeyStr));
}
```

In order to get all beans of type CardBean, create a new method feature using the New Method Feature SmartGuide with the following features:

Name	Return Type	Parameters	BeanInfo option
getListOfAllCardBeans	AbstractListModelt	0	preferred

Fill in the method to match the following code:

```
public AbstractListModel getListOfAllCardBeans()
throws Exception {
    /* Perform the getListOfAllCardBeans method. */
    final Vector aV = Card.getListOfAllCards();
    return (new AbstractListModel() {
            Vector tempV = aV;
            public int getSize() { return tempV.size(); }
            public Object getElementAt(int i) { return new CardBean((Card)tempV.elementAt(i)); }
        });
}
```

Building the BankAccountBean class

To create the BankAccountBean class, use the Create Class SmartGuide: from the Workbench, select the Create Class button (the sixth button in the tool bar). Type BankAccountBean in the **Class name** field and select the **Next** button. In the Attribute window, add the following import statements. **Add Package**: com.ibm.itso.sg245264.atm.memory and Add Type: Java.util.vector. In **What interface should this class implement**, type serializable (see Figure 94).

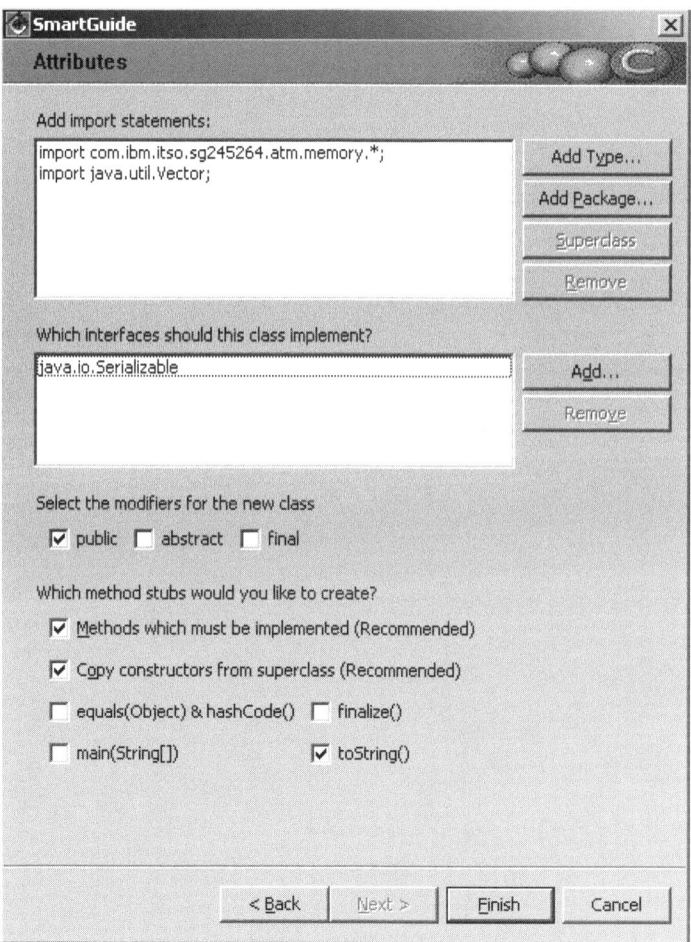

Figure 94. Create class BankAccountBean — Attributes window

Modify the BankAccountBean implementation to match the following code:

```
/**
 * BankAccountBean constructor comment.
 */
public BankAccountBean() {
    BankAccountBean = null; // because needed for JBs, does nothing !
}
```

Create BankAccountBean(BankAccount) to match the following code:

```
**
 * BankAccountBean constructor comment.
 */
BankAccountBean(BankAccount aBankAccount) {
    bankAccountImpl = aBankAccount;
}
```

Modify the toString implementation to return a bankAccountImpl variable:

```
public String toString() {
    return bankAccountImpl.toOneLineString();
}
```

Now you have a complete model!

Building the ATM application

Create a new Applet using the Create Applet SmartGuide: From the workbench window, select the **Create Applet** button from the tool bar. In the **Applet name** field type ATMApplication, select the JApplet checkbox as **Superclass**, select **Compose the class visually** (see Figure 95).

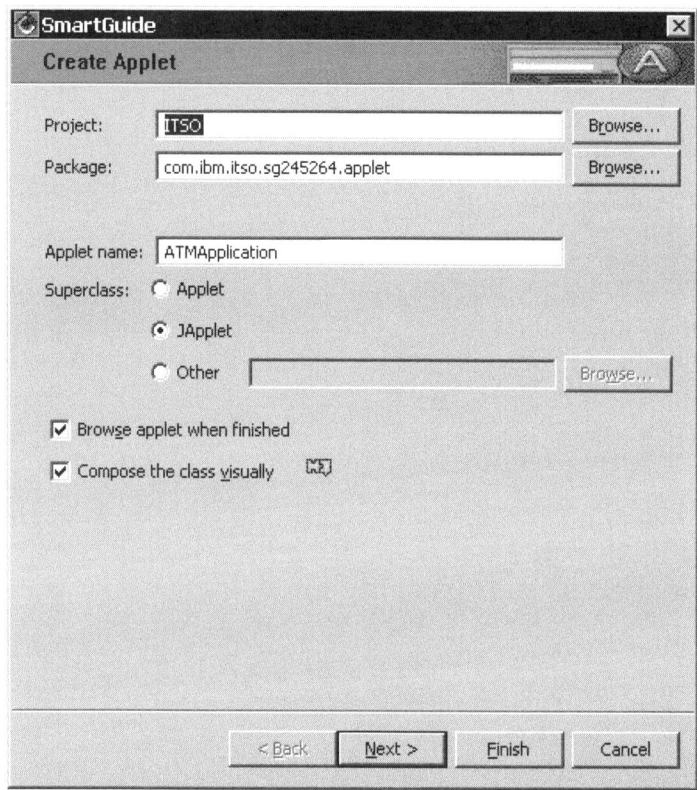

Figure 95. Create the ATMApplication Applet

Select the **Next** button. In the Applet Properties window, select **Yes, create an applet witch can be run by itself or in an applet viewer** (see Figure 96). Select the **Finish** button.

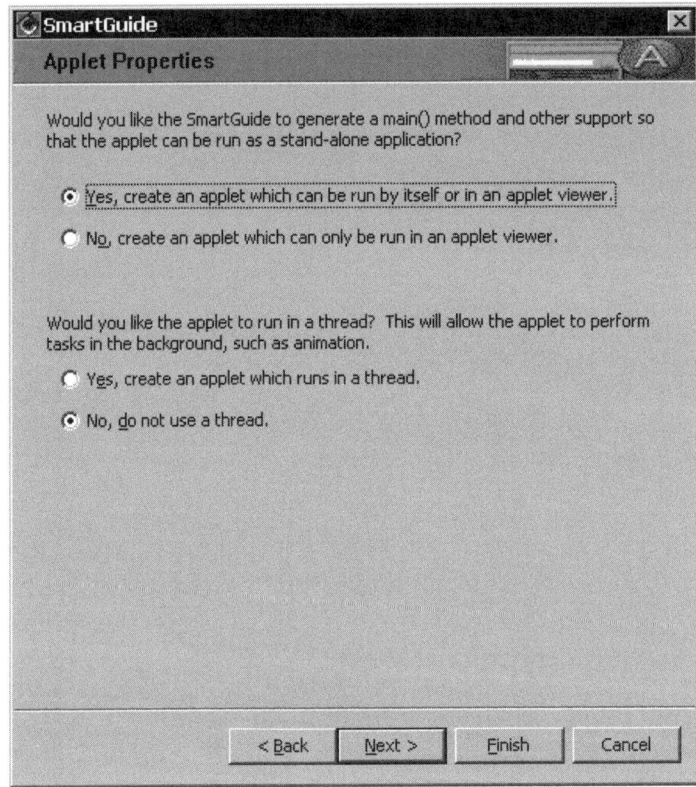

Figure 96. Create ATMApplication — Applet Properties window

The Visual Composition page of the ATMApplication class browser opens. Open the Beans List by selecting **Tools→Beans List**.

Notice that there are several beans in the list (see Figure 97). The first ATMApplication represents the complete bean you are editing and is really just a place holder. The second ATMApplication is the subtype of JApplet that you created, and the AppletContentPane is the content pane for the applet. Remember that the JFC splits the functionality of many components between a pane and the component itself.

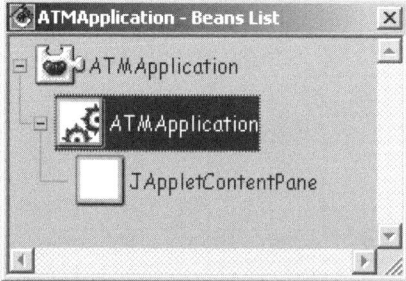

Figure 97. The Beans List

The Beans List window displays an ordered list of the beans and connections on the free-form surface. The beans are initially listed in the order in which they were dropped, which also reflects the tabbing order. If we change the order of beans that have tabbing set, the Visual Composition Editor reflects the updated tabbing order.

Keeping the Beans List visible is a good idea most of the time. It will help you:

- Locate components that are under other components.
- Move or manipulate components when layout managers are in effect.
- Quickly see the names of various components and connections.

Select JAppletContentPane. You can select it in the Beans List or by clicking anywhere within the visual representation of the applet. Open its Property sheet (see Figure 98). Notice how many more properties this component has. Set layout to GridBagLayout

It is a good idea to select the **Show expert features** checkbox now, so that you will always see all features. If you find that there are too many features and you do not use many of them, you can deselect the checkbox later.

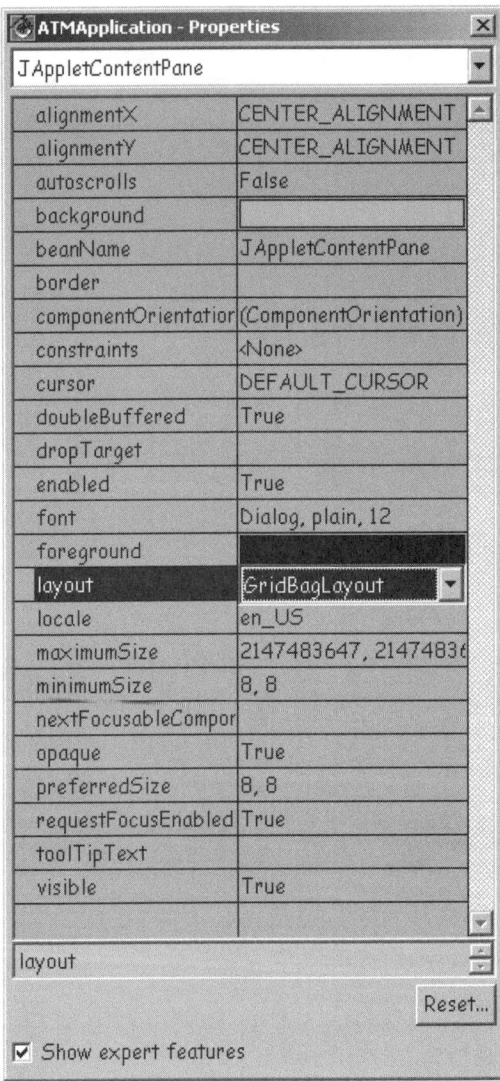

Figure 98. JAppletContentPane Property sheet

Adding the JList Bean

Now you add the JList Bean: select **JList** from the Beans Palette and drop it on the JAppletContentPane.

Adding the CardBeanHome Bean

To access the Card and to display it on the JList, you need the CardBeanHome bean.

To add the CardBeanHome Bean: select the **Choose Bean** tool. Select the **Class** radio button and click **Browse**. Select com.ibm.itso.sg245264.atm.applet.CardBeanHome from the list and click **OK**. Enter card Bean Home in the **Name** field (see Figure 99). Click **OK** again.

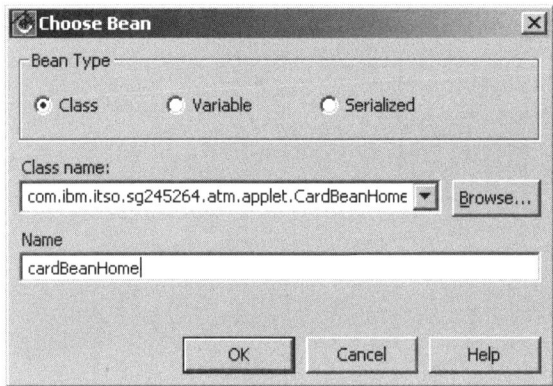

Figure 99. Choose CardBeanHome Bean

The cursor now becomes a cross-hair. Move the cursor over an empty area of the free-form surface and click the left mouse button to drop the bean.

Adding the JDialog components
To display the detail of a selected card, you add new components. Select a JDialog from the Bean Palette and drop it on the free-form surface.

Drop a JTextField in the JDialog1 and set the **beanName** property to Owner.

Drop a JList in JDialog1 set the **beanName** property to AccountsList.

Adding the CardBean Bean
To add the CardBean Bean: select the **Choose Bean** tool. Select the **Class** radio button and click **Browse**.

Select com.ibm.itso.sg245264.atm.applet.CardBean from the list and click **OK**. Enter selectedCB in the **Name** field (see Figure 100). Click **OK** again.

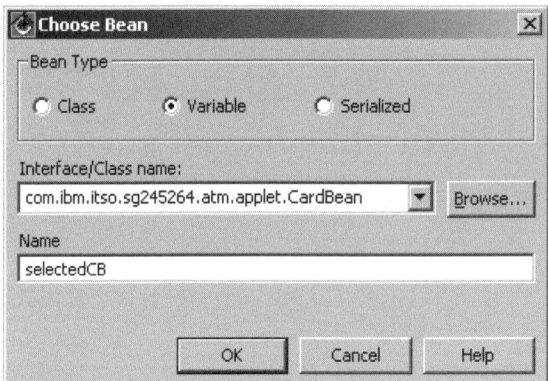

Figure 100. Choose CardBean bean

The free-form surface and the Beans List should now look similar to those in Figure 101.

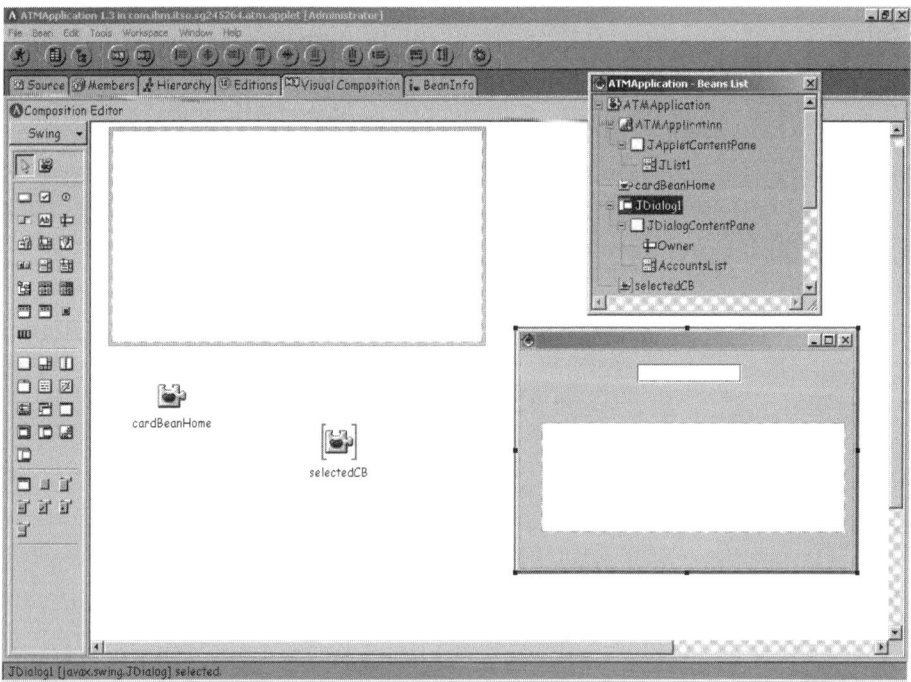

Figure 101. The ATMApplication View

Saving and generating the bean

It is a good idea to save your work frequently while visually programming, so select **Save Bean** from the Bean menu bar item. This action generates the Java code to correspond to the interface and connections you have constructed in the Visual Composition Editor. To work with the code of the beans and connections you add in the Visual Composition Editor, you must save the bean first. You cannot just switch to another view and edit code.

Connections

The Visual Composition Editor provides you with four connection types:

- Property-to-property connections
- Event-to-method connections
- Code (script) connections
- Parameter connections

Property-to-property connections:

A property-to-property connection links two JavaBean properties together. This connection causes the value of one property to reflect the other. A property-to-property connection appears as a dark blue line with dots at either end. The solid dot indicates the target, and the hollow dot indicates the source. When your bean is constructed at runtime, the target property is set to the value of the source property. These connections never take parameters.

After the initial setting of the target property, property-to-property connections require events to fire the connection. Both the source and the target can have events to fire them. If one end of the connection does not have an event, the connection is unidirectional. If neither end has an event, the connection only fires once to initialize the target. If both ends have events, the connection is bidirectional.

Property-to-property connections have a Properties dialog where you can choose the source and target properties and events and reverse the connection.

For indexed properties, VisualAge for Java generates two get-set method pairs, one for the array and one for accessing elements within the array. When you connect indexed properties, VisualAge for Java uses the accessors for the entire array. If you want to access an individual element, you must create an event-to-method or event-to-code connection to the specific accessors.

Event-to-method connections:
An event-to-method connection calls the specified method of the target object whenever the source event occurs. Often a good deal of the behavior of an application can be specified visually by causing a method of one bean to be invoked whenever an event is signaled by another bean.

If the method connected to takes parameters, you can specify them through the Connection Properties dialog box or with parameter connections. In the Connection Properties dialog box, you can also specify whether the parameter passed to the method will be the event object generated by the event.

An event-to-method connection appears as a unidirectional dark green arrow with the arrowhead pointing to the target.

Code connections:
It often happens that you want some processing to occur when an event is signaled, but none of the beans on the free-form surface exposes a method that does exactly what you want. In this case, VisualAge for Java enables you to connect to non public methods in the class you are editing. These methods of the class are called code, to distinguish them from the public methods that you may have created for your primary class and exposed as bean methods.

A code connection appears as a unidirectional dark green arrow starting from the side of the free-form surface (representing the primary class) with the arrowhead pointing to a grey box containing the name of the method.

Code connections can simplify the number of connections you need to make in your application.

Parameter connections:
A parameter connection supplies an input value to the target of a connection by passing either a property's value or the return value from a method. In a parameter-from-method connection, the connection appears as a unidirectional violet arrow with the arrowhead pointing from the parameter of the original connection to the bean containing the method providing the value. In a parameter-from-property connection, the connection appears as a violet line with the dots at either end. The solid dot indicates the target, and the hollow dot indicates the source. The original connection is always the source of a parameter connection; the source feature is the parameter itself.

You can also make parameter connections from other connections. Some connections have return values, and all connections can throw exceptions.

You can connect these return values (normalResult) and exceptions (exceptionOccurred) as parameters on other connections.

VisualAge for Java represents connections as private methods on the primary bean and names the connections on the basis of the type and number of connections using P (property/parameter), E (event), M (method), or C (code). For example, the first event-to-method connection in a bean would be named `connEtoM1`. You can change the connection names to make the code more readable.

Connection properties

Each connection type in VisualAge for Java has a different set of properties that can be accessed through the Properties dialog box. To get to the Properties Dialog box, double-click on the connection or select the connection on the free-form surface or in the Beans List and select **Properties** from the pop-up menu.

The various possibilities for the connection types are described below.

Property-to-property connections:
The following are property-to-property connections:

Source property	The source bean for the connection
Target property	The target bean for the connection
Source event	The source bean event that fires the connection to set the target bean property
Target event	The target bean event that fires the connection to set the source bean property

Event-to-method connections:
The following are event-to-method connections:

Event	The source object event that fires the connection
Method	The target object method that is invoked when the connection fires
Pass event data	If true (or checked), and if the method takes parameters, the event object associated with the event is passed as a parameter

Code connections:
The code connections are essentially event-to-method connections, so you can specify the same properties.

Parameter connections:
The parameter connection properties are the same as the property-to-property connection properties.

Creating connections

Now you can make some connections in your ATMApplicationapplet. The first time you develop a program, using visual connections can be quite a change, so make sure you read and understand the connection while you are making it. This will also help you avoid errors as you work through the examples. Once you understand why you are creating the connections in the example, you will be able to decide which connections you need in your own programs.

Event-to-method connection:

When the `ATMApplication` applet initializes, it should read the parameters with which it was supplied to build the Card list. The event that triggers this is the `init()` event. Follow these steps to connect the `init()` event to the `getall` method on the CardBeanHome:

Click with the right mouse button on an empty area of the free form surface (representing the primary class or applet). Select **Connect** from the pop-up menu. Select **Connectable Features**.

In the Start Connection from (ATMApplication) dialog select the **Event** radio button. Then select **init()** and click **OK**.

The cursor is now a spider connected to the source of the connection. Click the left mouse button over the `cardBeanHome` bean and select **getall**.

Event-to-method connection:

Click with the right mouse button on the green connection you've just created.

Select **Connect** from the pop-up menu. Select **normalResult**.

The cursor is now a spider connected to the source of the connection. Click the left mouse button over the `Jlist1` bean and select **model**.

Property-to-property connection:

Click with the right mouse button over the JList1. Select **Connect** from the pop-up menu. Select **selectedValue**.

The cursor is now a spider connected to the source of the connection. Click the left mouse button over the selectedCB bean and select **this**.

Property-to-property connection:

Click with the right mouse button over the selectedCB bean. Select **Connect** from the pop-up menu. Select **owner**.

The cursor is now a spider connected to the source of the connection. Click the left mouse button over the Owner JTextField and select **text**.

Event-to-method connection:

Click with the right mouse button over the JList1. Select **Connect** from the pop-up menu. Select **Connectable Features**.

In the Start Connection from (ATMApplication) dialog select the **Event** radio button. Then select **listSelectionEvents** and click **OK**.

The cursor is now a spider connected to the source of the connection. Click the left mouse button over the AccountsList JList and select **Connectable Features**.

In the End Connection to (ATMApplication) dialog select the **Method** radio button. Then select **setListData(Vector)** and click **OK**.

Now the connection is shown as a dotted line. The dotted line indicates that the connection (or more accurately, the method called by the connection) requires a parameter, in this case the bankAccountBeans.

Parameter-from-property connection:

Click with the right mouse button over the dotted line of the previous connection. Select **Connect** from the pop-up menu. Select **listData**.

The cursor is now a spider connected to the source of the connection. Click the left mouse button over the selectedCB bean and select **Connectable Features**.

In the End Connection to (selectedCB) dialog select the **Property** radio button. Then select **bankAccountsBeans** and click **OK**.

The last connection is the connection between the two windows:

Event-to-method connection:

Click with the right mouse button over the JList1. Select **Connect** from the pop-up menu. Select **Connectable Features**.

In the Start Connection from (JList1) dialog select the **Event** radio button. Then select **mouseClicked** and click **OK**.

The cursor is now a spider connected to the source of the connection. Click the left mouse button over the JDialog title bar and select **show()**.

In the End Connection to (ATMApplication) dialog select the **Method** radio button. Then select **setListData(Vector)** and click **OK**.

Figure 102 shows the connections of your applet.

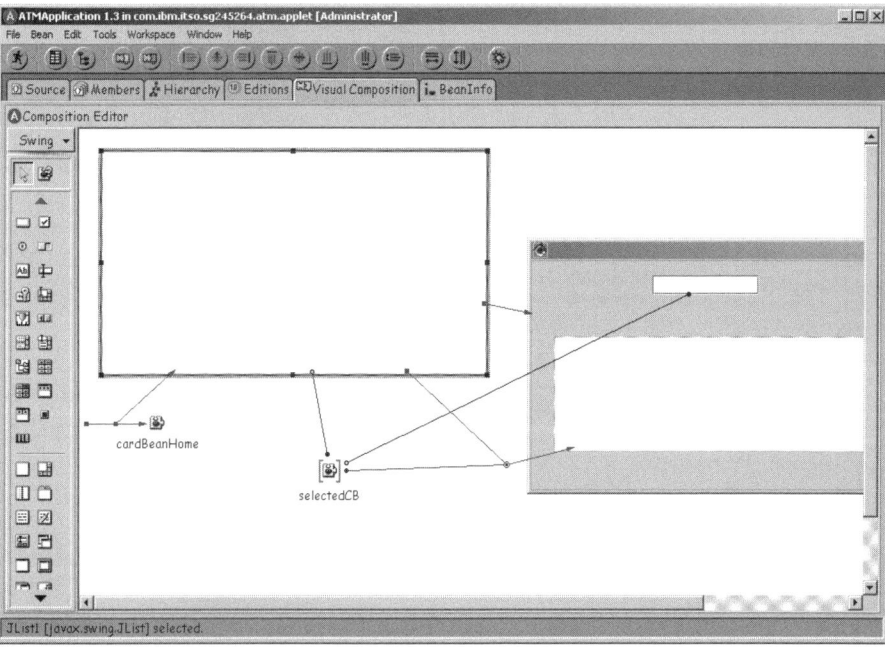

Figure 102. ATMApplication connection view

Now run the applet and ensure that it works as designed. Figure 103 shows the final result.

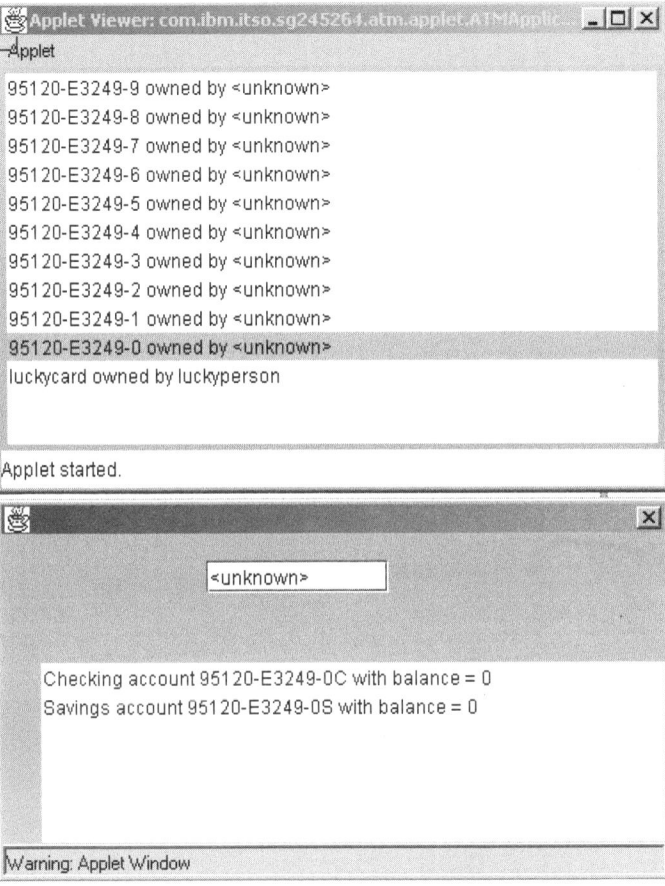

Figure 103. The ATMApplication applet view

Chapter 8. Versioning your code

This chapter discusses the versioning system incorporated into the VisualAge for Java IDE. It also explains the repository and how this relates to the workspace discussed in Chapter 2, "Organizing your code" on page 41.

We hope that this chapter will give you some feeling of the power of this system and will make it clear to you why VisualAge does not store each Java class in a separate file. Understanding this system is probably one of the most difficult tasks for a new VisualAge user. However, this same complexity is also one of the reasons that many programmers prefer the VisualAge environment above others in the long run.

Note: The versioning system explained here is only applicable to the Professional Edition of VisualAge for Java. Versioning in the Enterprise Edition is intermixed with the concepts of owners (and access control), therefore it is much more elaborate.

The VisualAge dialogs explained here are the Repository Explorer and the usage of the Edition tab appearing on many other browsers. The Comparison Result Window, which shows differences in code and enables merges, is also explained, together with some options that were skipped on other dialogs related to the repository.

introduction to versioning

Let us look at the features you normally have at your disposal when you want to undo changes in your source code:

- Using the *'Undo' function* of the editor, which may support multiple levels: This normally works on editor commands that can be reversed, and that are kept in a strict sequential order on a stack which is probably limited in size. Undoing changes in this way has no concept of classes, methods, and so on.

- Using *'Revert to saved'* will restore the last version (of the whole class) you saved on disk.

- Using a traditional *versioning system* will let you choose among all versions of classes that you checked in over time, based on the files in which they are contained.

Although this last feature gives you a lot of possibilities, it is still not flexible to use: You have to think in terms of files when you want to restore or compare to a previous version.

VisualAge is better just in that respect: It lets you reason on versions of the things you are used to working with: methods, packages, and projects, as well as classes and interfaces.

Program elements

All the things you can apply versioning to, are called *versionable program elements* for the VisualAge versioning feature: see Figure 104:

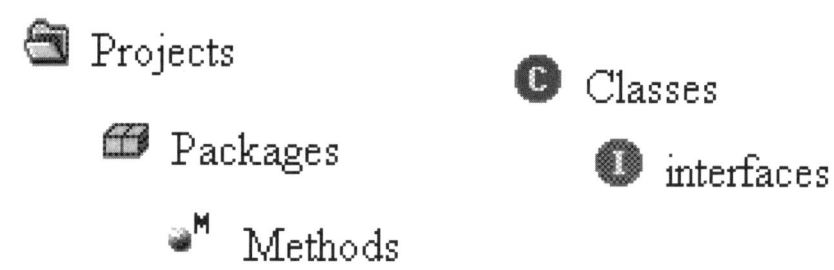

Figure 104. Versionable program elements

The subsystem of VisualAge that is responsible for versioning the program elements is called *Envy*. It is used in other VisualAge products as well (such as VisualAge for SmallTalk) and it is also available in a multi-user version (it comes with the VisualAge Enterprise edition).

Chapter 2, "Organizing your code" on page 41 has already explained briefly that we have a workspace and a repository. In those terms, the workspace contains program elements that you work on. When you revert to another version of the program element, VisualAge will get that version from the repository and put it in the workspace, replacing the previous one: The workspace is actually the "space you work in": you only work with one particular version of a program element, hence the workspace can only contain one.

The repository, on the other hand, contains every version of every program element. It adds the time dimension to program elements, much like a regular versioning system does with files. It is the database containing the master copies of every program element, in multiple versions.

Let us investigate these concepts more thoroughly.

Workspace versus repository

The repository is the database containing all (editions of) source, consider the workspace as a *cache* on the repository: It will only contain elements that are also present in the repository. When adding new program elements in the workspace (creating a new class, interface, method, package project), a copy of the element is also stored in the repository, as with a *write-through* cache.

This cache is stored in memory when using VisualAge for Java and is stored into a file to enable a quick rebuild of the cache on startup. The file in which the workspace is stored is called *ide.icx*. The repository is a file which is called *ivj.dat*. See Figure 105 for an overview:

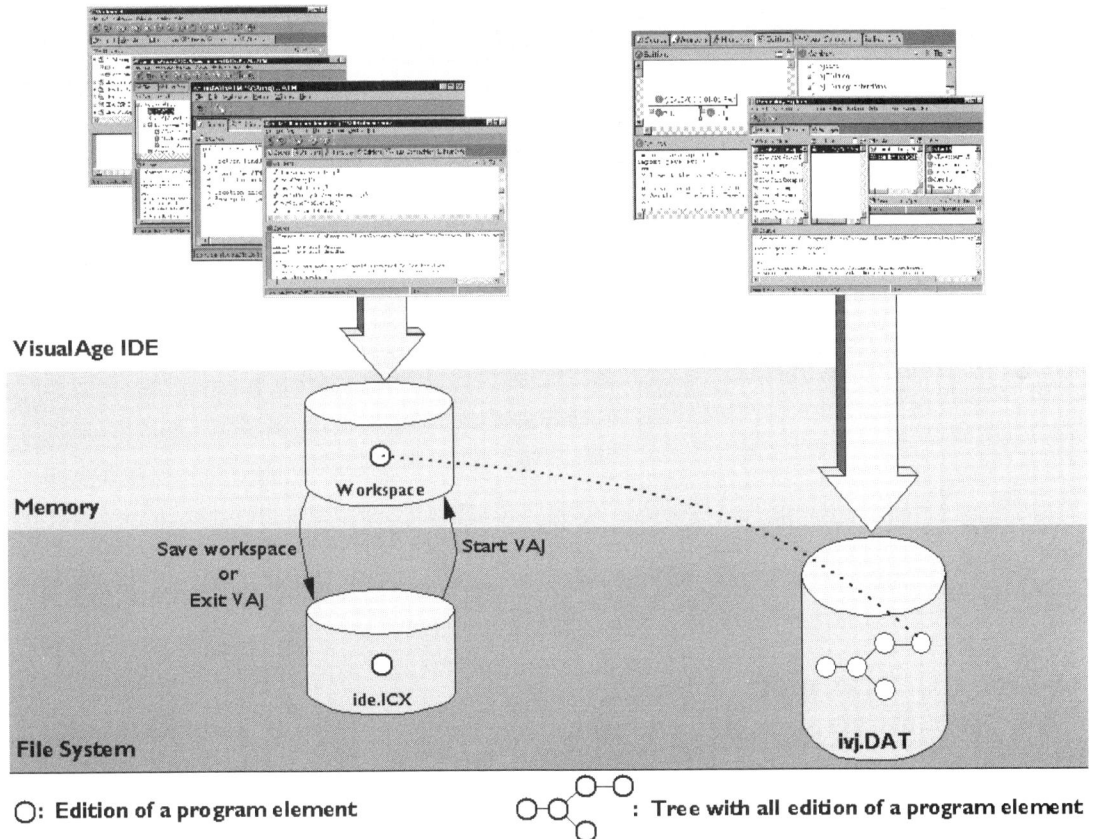

Figure 105. Interaction between IDE components, workspace, and repository

The picture shows that almost all browsers of VisualAge (all the browsers introduced to you so far in this book) only access the memory version of the workspace.

The workspace can only have one edition of a certain set of editions for a program element. This edition is also present in the repository, along with the rest of the set of editions for this element.

When you exit VisualAge for Java, the dialog window shown in Figure 106 will always pop up:

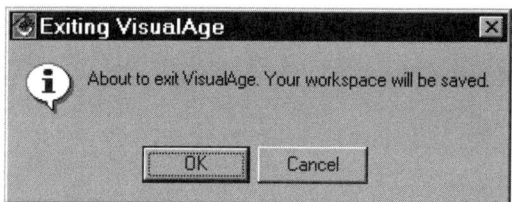

Figure 106. Exit dialog of VisualAge

You can either press **Cancel** or **OK** on this window: It forces you to save a workspace copy on the file system. You can also manually store your workspace by using the menu option on every VisualAge window: *File -> Save Workspace*.

Note that VisualAge also stores the option settings (explained in, "Customizing VisualAge for Java" on page 28) and the breakpoints (Chapter 9, "Testing and debugging the Web application" on page 231) into the workspace.

The Repository Explorer browser and the Edition tab (the two windows in the top right of Figure 105) may look unfamiliar to you. We will explain them in full detail later in this chapter. For now, just remember that these are the only browsers which show you a view on the repository.

The workspace is only a cache

As the case with normal write-through caches, no harm is done when the workspace disappears: Keep this in mind, you cannot lose your code, because it is always in the repository!

For the memory copy of the workspace, this can be the case when VisualAge was stopped without saving the workspace: The computer went out of power and the system stalled, so a hard reset was necessary.

On the next reboot, VisualAge will start from the previous stored version and will try to re-synchronize with the repository: it will say something like "Checking inconsistencies". If this has happened, check the latest things you worked on: If you see an old version of your code, make sure that you load the last changes back into the workspace (we explain how to do this later).

If you also lost your workspace file (these things may happen with a total system crash), you are still all right! Basically, you have only lost a cache.

The section below explains how to back up and restore a workspace. Here is a list of what you can lose when losing a workspace file:

- Program elements or the last editions of them may not be loaded in the workspace automatically after restoring a workspace: Later on we will explain how to browse the repository in order to find and load (the correct edition of) elements
- Options settings of the VisualAge IDE
- Unsaved pages from the Scrapbook
- Breakpoints settings
- Contents of the Log and Console windows

These are very few, so never panic when you have problems with your workspace, remember it is basically just a cache.

Backup or restore the workspace

A workspace file (.icx) always has an associated text configuration file (.ini) with the same name. Besides information about the corresponding repository, this file also contains some user settings. You should keep those files together at all times.

With a standard Windows installation, these files are:

```
C:\Program Files\IBM\VisualAge for Java\ide\program\ide.icx
C:\Program Files\IBM\VisualAge for Java\ide\program\ide.ini
```

You make a backup of these files when they are not being written to by a running copy the IDE. A regular file copy will do, for example from a command line (assuming T: is a network drive that is automatically backed up):

```
copy C:\Program Files\IBM\VisualAge for Java\ide\program\ide.i*
T:\vajbu\ws\
```

To restore a workspace, shut down VisualAge for Java and replace the existing copies of these files with their backup version:

```
copy T:\vajbu\ws\ide.i* C:\Program Files\IBM\VisualAge for
Java\ide\program\
```

After restarting VisualAge, you will only see the program elements from the time you made the backup, in the editions from that time. You only need to add the additional program elements (and restore newer versions of the existing: see below) to be back on track.

The size of the workspace file depends on how much code it contains. A big environment will eventually hurt the performance of VisualAge. After working some months with VisualAge, people tend to end up with a lot of code in their workspace that is not used anymore. A common solution to this is to restore a 'clean' copy of the workspace and gradually add the elements until you have everything you need.

There are two things which can help you prevent from running into such a situation in the first place:

- Put code that you do not change often (for example, common libraries) outside the workspace in a JAR or class files and reconfigure your project to use the code from there (see Chapter 9, "Testing and debugging the Web application" on page 231).
- Have a separate workspace for each project you work on (see "Multiple workspaces on one repository" on page 189).

We will first come back on the "clean" workspace copy before going into the details of using multiple workspaces.

Clean workspace copy

The documentation of VisualAge for Java tells you to take a backup of the initial workspace just after installation and use this when you experience problems with your workspace. It also explains that the VisualAge for Java installation program is also able to restore the initial workspace.

Of course, a fresh copy from just after the installation will work. The downside of this, however, is that you lose your settings (and some other things listed above). Instead, we suggest that you start once from an installation workspace and adjust all the option settings as you usually set them. Delete projects you do not need, and add some other projects you will always need.

Then save this workspace as your own "clean'" copy. This will take a while, but it will save you much time (and frustration) when you have to replace your workspace in the middle of a project.

Remember to copy the pair (the .icx and the .ini file) together at all times.

Multiple workspaces on one repository

Multiple workspaces can connect to one repository (just think of the copies you make as a backup). You can make different workspaces for each project you work on, which all use the same source' storage. An unsupported feature of VisualAge for Java lets you specify which workspace to use as a command line option: The command-line argument -i takes a filename as an argument:

```
ide.exe -i MyWorkspace.icx
```

Note: As you can see, you only have to specify the .icx file; VisualAge for Java assumes that it will find a corresponding file with the .ini extension.

Wrapping up: At the beginning of each project you should duplicate your clean workspace copy and rename it to reflect your project. Then add a shortcut for starting VisualAge for Java with these newly created files.

When VisualAge for Java does not want to start (to diagnose: the process stops after the splash screen), it is probably due to a corrupt workspace. In this case, you can easily restore another workspace. Take a copy of the existing workspace and restore the clean copy. Try to start the VisualAge IDE once again.

Backup or restore the repository

From the above discussion it is clear that the repository is the critical point for failure, rather then the workspace. Let us reassure you, the chances to end up with a corrupt repository are very small!

The Envy back-end has been around for a long time (longer than Java itself) and has a very good track record on this. Make sure to contact the support team or the news groups (see "VisualAge for Java product family" on page 1), when you think you have a corruption problem: This may help you determine if it is really the case.

However, this does not exclude possible hardware failure. Unfortunately, hard disk crashes still happen every now and then!

To protect you against this, the same measures as with normal file based IDE systems or versioning systems suffice: Take backups regularly!

The only file needed to back up all your Java sources is *ivj.dat* located in a standard Windows installation:

```
C:\Program Files\IBM\VisualAge for Java\ide\repository\ivj.dat
```

Shut down VisualAge for Java before taking a backup, to make sure this file does not change while copying. Simple copy commands to back up and restore also suffice here:

```
copy C:\Program Files\IBM\VisualAge for Java\ide\repository\ivj.dat
T:\vajbu\repos\

copy T:\vajbu\repos\ivj.dat C:\Program Files\IBM\VisualAge for
Java\ide\repository\
```

You can also decide to use a repository server (which comes with additional management tools) instead of a local file. Such a repository server is IP based and consists of multi-platform software. It comes with the Enterprise edition of VisualAge for Java. We refer you to the literature on the Enterprise version for more information: see Appendix D, "Related publications" on page 371.

Later on in this chapter, we will also talk about *resource files*. As we will see, they are not stored in the repository, so remember to make a backup from those too!

Workspace versus repository continued

Because Java is an interpreted language (after compilation into bytecode) and does not need linkage, the environment can easily recompile parts of the whole system without bringing down a running program (a feature that greatly expands the debugging capabilities, as will be explained in more detail in, "VAJ Debugger" on page 231).

You may also know by now that VisualAge will alert you if some piece of code contains errors when you ask it to save. So, it will probably not surprise you to learn that VisualAge actually compiles each piece of code upon saving it.

The bytecode obtained is kept inside the system to enable fast execution of code: No need to compile anything anymore when you run a program. Now just think of it: What bytecode should be kept inside the system? Everything you work on at the moment, in the version currently loaded, probably. So, again, it should come as no surprise when we tell you that this bytecode is actually stored in the workspace!

No bytecode is stored in the repository, but everything that enters the workspace is compiled first. This explains why it takes a while to add the WebSphere Test Environment, for example, although it was in the repository all the time. This may also be a reason the create your own clean copy of the workspace discussed above.

To summarize this section on workspace and repository, we give you a list of differences (which should be easy to understand by now):

Table 10. Differences between workspace and repository

Workspace	Repository
Workspace contains Java bytecode	The repository contains the source
Only one edition of currently used program elements	Contains every edition of every program element that you ever developed
Used from Workbench and all browsers	Only used from the Repository Explorer and when browsing the editions of a program element (see below)
Changes are not saved to the file version of the workspace until you choose to save it explicitly or you exit VAJ	Every code change you save is immediately stored in the repository, the ivj.dat file on disk
Elements can be deleted, removed from the workspace	Editions of program elements can only be removed after a two phased process discussed below
Will grow initially, but can shrink again later	Will grow in time
Can be lost or become corrupt without loosing code	Contains all the code, should not be lost, and will probably never corrupt

Version control

We go back to our program elements concept at the beginning of this chapter. The lifetime of these objects is key to understanding the whole versioning system.

Editions and versions

Up till now we used the terms *edition* and *version* interchangeably. In VisualAge the term *edition* has a broader meaning then version. Editions are the basis of our discussion, so we will explain the meaning of the term *version* in VisualAge shortly.

As we mentioned, the repository can only contain editions of program elements: a program element does not exist when there is no edition of it in the repository.

An edition of a program element can have two different states:

Open   Think of this as the read/write state: This edition of the program element can be changed.

Versioned   This is a read-only state: The program element cannot change.

The latter state can be considered (for now) as the final state: An edition of a program element cannot go back to the Open (Read/Write) state once it is "versioned" in VisualAge. The former state is used for work in progress. Figure 107 shows this simple state machine:

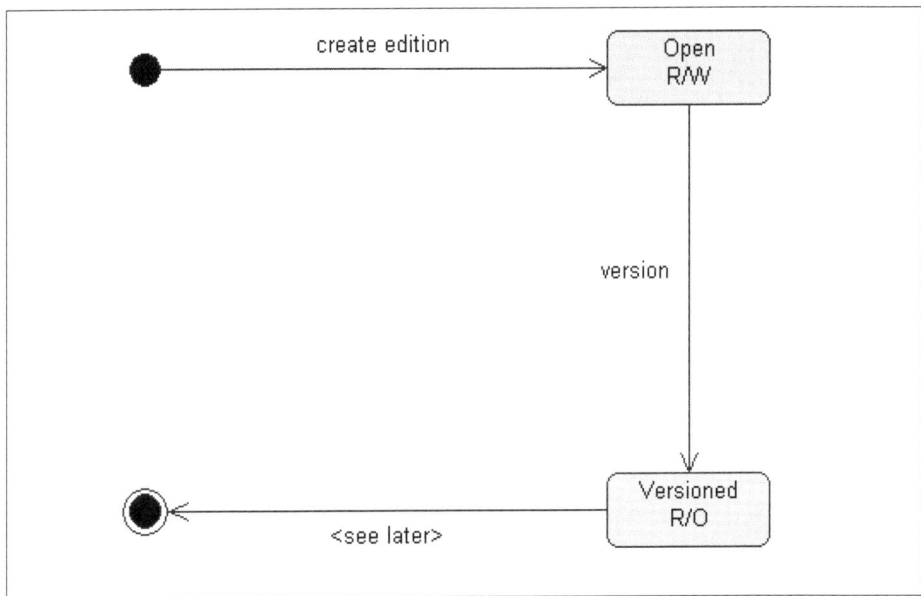

Figure 107. Basic state diagram for editions

A 'version' is an abbreviation for 'versioned edition'. When referring to 'edition' some VisualAge documentation uses it as an abbreviation of 'open edition'. We will try to keep the clear distinction in this chapter between the general term 'edition' and the more specific terms 'open edition' and 'version'.

Editions can be created in many different ways, depending on the type of the program element. We will explain this in more depth later on; for now, we will only focus on the fact that they can be created.

Versions can be labelled, usually by a number (and a fraction) but other names like "Deployed at the customer's on 12/3/2000" are also allowed. VisualAge will always propose to you a version name which starts with 1.0 and which continues from a previous version by adding 1 to the last digit of it: The next time you version a program element which used to be in version "v0.26", VisualAge will suggest that you make it "v0.27".

The key thing to remember about versions is that they always represent the same state of the program element, which makes sense when you want to refer to them using their label afterwards.

Open editions, on the other hand, cannot be labelled. VisualAge attaches a timestamp to them at the time they are created:

```
TransactionAbortedException(11/21/00 7:20:38 PM)
```

Here is one question you might ask: *What happens when a program element is versioned; you cannot change it; what if you need to change something?*

The answer is that VisualAge will automatically create an open edition of a versioned program element when you change something about it. You then have a new edition for that program element, with a life cycle of its own. Note that — besides the action of creating a new program element — we now have two ways to make a new edition. Later on, we will explain this in more detail.

Consequences of versioning

Here is another question: *The program elements (projects, packages, types and methods) are hierarchical structured (one is contained inside the other). What happens with the elements in the tree 'below' and 'above' the versioned element?*

This answer will be more involved. Until now, things were very simple:

- You have editions as the basic blocks.
- They can be in only two states.
- They are called open editions or versions depending on their state.
- There is only one possible transition (by the action of versioning).

The effect upon the environment of the program element being versioned will add some complexity to the system, although it will seem straightforward enough once you grasp the concept.

Consider the following two things:

- When you want to fix a package by versioning it, you want it to remain completely the same, including all its classes with their respective methods. The reason for versioning something is to be able to revert to the exact same state later on, with the exact same state of the sub elements.

- Changing one of the sub elements of the package (for example, a method) also changes the package in a way: it is not anymore in the exact same state as when you versioned it.

As a result, we have two basic rules of the versioning system:

1. When versioning a program element, all its sub-elements are versioned when necessary (which means that they are versioned when they are in an open edition).

2. Changing one of the sub-elements of a versioned element will result in creating an open edition for that parent element (as well).

How to version elements with VisualAge for Java

That is enough theory for the moment — let us see how to version elements in VisualAge for Java. As with most actions on displayed objects in the IDE, there are many ways to invoke the versioning action.

We first see how to version using the normal menus from the menu bar. The different browsers have menus with the name of the types of program elements they can show in their different lists. The Workbench has only one menu called 'Selected' which will change upon the current selection: The content can resemble each of the menus described below. When elements of different types are selected, this menu will only show a subset of the intersection between them.

The names of the menus are either *Project*, *Packages*, *Types*, or *Members*. *Type* means both Class and Interface; *Members* are Fields, Methods, or Inner classes.

The Project Browser has the full range of menus: The Project menu and the three others, because of its three cascading lists that show packages, types, (in the selected package) and members (from the selected type).

Figure 108 shows the menu bar of a project browser:

Figure 108. Project browser menu bar

All of these menus will have an option 'Manage' that expands to 'Version...'. When the selected items in the Workbench are of the same type, there will be a **Selected->Manage>Version...** menu option.

The other menus in Figure 108 are present on all VisualAge for Java windows: *File*, *Edit*, *Workspace*, *Window*, and *Help*. Their content is also always the same (which must give some kind of relief to a new VAJ user), although the menu items that are not applicable are greyed out.

Another — and perhaps more intuitive — way to version program elements (which is valid in any of the windows) is to invoke their popup menu (normally by pressing the right mouse button while pointing to a program element): Figure 109 shows the popup menu for a package:

Figure 109. Popup menu for a package expanded on the Manage option

Chapter 8. Versioning your code   **195**

Choosing the 'Version...' menu item will bring up the window in Figure 110.

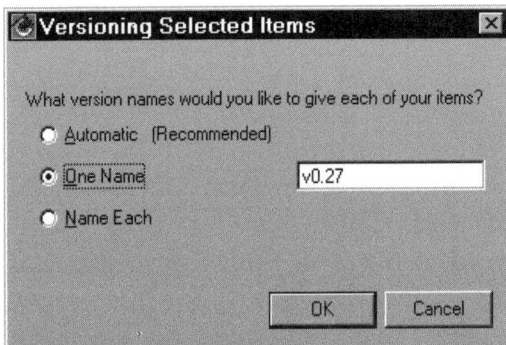

Figure 110. Versioning dialog window

This window always looks like this even when you only selected one item. The reason is that the program element to be versioned might be the parent of other program elements, which also have to be versioned.

The window will preselect the **One Name** radio button and suggest a version name (as explained before). Choosing **Automatic** will version all sub-elements by incrementing the last digit of the name of the previous version (or replacing the last character with the next in the alphabet, restarting at 'A' after reaching 'z'). **Name Each** will bring up the following dialog in Figure 111.

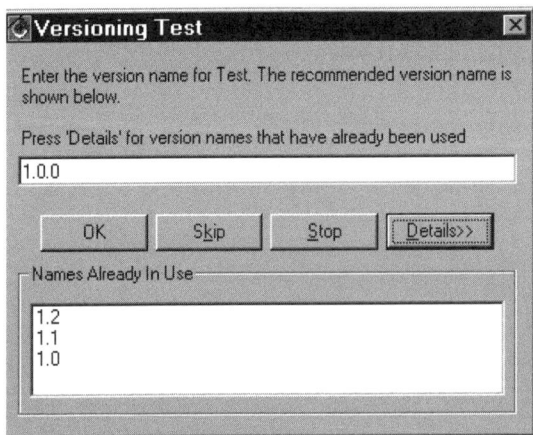

Figure 111. Dialog to specify the name of each sub-element

From Figure 111 you can see that — when you press the **Details>>** button — VisualAge will display the list of the version names already in use.

Apply this to the ATM application

Let us reconsider the example application. We assume that you created a project with the com.ibm.itso.sg245264.atm.memory package and implemented all classes that make up the core of our application. You probably did not version before, so the project with all its sub-elements are still in their initial open edition state.

Tip: When enabling the "Show edition names" toggle (see Figure 112), the VisualAge IDE will put the label of the versioned editions after the name of the program elements in lists or in the title bar of the corresponding browsers. The program elements that are in open edition are appended with the timestamp from the time they were created.

Figure 112. 'Show edition names' — toggle

Take the test to see if you understand the basic rules mentioned before: Version that initial package and look at the tree starting from the project: The project will still be in an open edition; the package and all the sub-elements will have the name you choose. Look what happens when you change (and save) something (even a Javadoc comment) on one of the classes or methods: The package (and the class in the case of changing a method) will again be in an open edition. Other classes are not affected, as nothing on them changed. The project was changed, but as it is still in its initial open edition, it can stay without changing the state of the edition: The label still shows the date and time you created it.

Methods, a special case

Now we come to the first odd fact about using terms in VisualAge: The documentation says that methods cannot be versioned, something you may already notice by now. Also consider these excerpts from the documentation:

"*A new open edition is created every time you save changes to the method*" and "*Methods are automatically versioned when the containing class is versioned.*"

Methods are special indeed in the way they are treated with respect to the versioning. But we think it is easier to understand what happens by saying that an edition of a method is never in the open state. When saved, VisualAge puts the method directly in the versioned state, giving it the timestamp of when it was created (saved) as the version label.

This means that every save of a method creates a new version, in other words: You will never lose your (method) code, you will only lose subsequent changes in class declarations and in the organization of your code.

This interpretation of the versioning process applied to methods is consistent with our basic rules about the versioning: Versioning a class will never version a method because it is always versioned. Changing a method is considered as changing a part of the class, so it results in creating an open edition of a versioned class.

This also explains why you can find back every change you made on a method, where this is not true for other program elements: Subsequent changes are only stored when you version the affected elements.

Importance of versioning your code regularly

This last observation is, in its turn, another reason we advise you to:

Version your code on a regular basis.

For example, you can version your code when you reach project milestones, or when you need to exchange code with a colleague, and — on a more fixed basis — you could do your versioning regularly at the end of each work week.

Some arguments offered for not versioning code are based on the idea that you would only be losing some minor information:

- You may believe that class declarations are not so complicated that you need to keep their state at certain points in time.
- Knowing which types or what version of the types were included in a package at a certain point may not seem relevant to you.
- You may not care about which packages (and versions of them) were included in your project at a given time.

All those things maybe true, but versioning is a small effort which will enable you to have that information at a moment's notice, whenever needed.

We realize that it may seem useless to version your code when it is not finished, or worse yet, if it is source that cannot compile. However, suppose that someone asks you about a change you made weeks ago — a change that is now causing problems in a colleague's code. Your only resort to track this change will be the versioned methods. You will have to remember which package, class, and even which methods might affect the change. You will have to sequentially browse through all versions, which were made each time you pressed Ctrl-S.

Shortly, we will also explain how you can easily browse through your editions, at the different levels of the program elements, and compare the code changes between editions. But for now, the main thing you need to remember is this: **Version your code regularly!**

Fields and inner classes

You may have noticed that we did not talk about fields and inner classes before. As Figure 104 on page 184 shows, these are not versionable program elements.

Rather, they are considered as being part of the class declaration. Subsequent changes to them are only persisted when the containing class is versioned, as is the case with every non-method program element.

Versioning resource files

A new feature from VisualAge for Java version 3.5 onwards allows you to version files that are external to VisualAge (especially non-Java files) together with the project they reside in.

In Chapter 2, "Organizing your code" on page 41 you saw that you can associate files that you use in your current project. You can add them to a project which puts them in a special directory, so they will appear in the Resource tab of the Project browser. Some additional features include using the import and export features of VisualAge to respectively import them from within VisualAge into your project and combine them with the regular deployment of your project as a whole (see Chapter 12, "Deploying the Web application" on page 341).

However, these files are not to be seen as a new sort of program element: The only support is based on the idea of being able to restore another version of a project as a whole, including the items listed in the Resource tab.

Hence, it is not surprising that these files are not put in the repository (which only contains Java code).

Originally the files are only in that special directory, but when versioning resources (by versioning the project), VisualAge creates a new directory underneath the repository directory (the directory that contains the ivj.dat file, see the foregoing discussion). The directory *ivj.dat.pr* contains subdirectories for all projects of that exist, much like the subdirectories underneath *project-resources*. The directory created upon versioning is named with the timestamp of the open edition of the project before it was versioned.

The 'versioned resources' directories for the ATMApplication project could be:

`C:\Program Files\IBM\VisualAge for Java\ide\repository\ivj.dat.pr\ATMExampleApplication\20001215.133214`

`C:\Program Files\IBM\VisualAge for Java\ide\repository\ivj.dat.pr\ATMExampleApplication\20001220.103052`

`C:\Program Files\IBM\VisualAge for Java\ide\repository\ivj.dat.pr\ATMExampleApplication\20001220.104220`

VisualAge will only make a new subdirectory to archive (all) the resources when at least one of them is changed (and the change is reflected in the project index file, see note). This can save you some disk space when working with a huge set of resource files that will remains the same during your Java development.

Note 1: Be careful when changing resource files outside VisualAge for Java. VisualAge might not have noticed that they are changed, in which case it will not make that a special directory, and will copy no files, meaning that you will lose your subsequent changes on these resource files! This is only the case for external changes not known to VisualAge, so you should be safe when changing the files and their associated program from VisualAge. You can see if VisualAge notices the change in one of the resource files, by checking if the resource index file (.idx file) associated to the project is updated.

Note 2: When the resources are the only thing you changed in a versioned project — even when this change is recorded in the resource index file — no new edition of the project is created. Therefore, you will not be able to version the project. One possible workaround is to change something in the comment of the project to force the creation of a new edition for that project.

Because the resources are separately stored from the Java code, you have to take care to include both the repository and these project directories in the your backups.

Using editions

By now, we suppose that you understood what editions are and how to version them in VisualAge. But what can you do with all those editions?

Next, we will explain how you can see the history of editions for each versionable program element.

Method edition tab

You can view the editions of a method from the edition tab of the method browser: Simply click on the tab icon to bring the tab on top when you are already in the method browser:

Because you will normally not be working in the method browser, but rather in a class browser, you could also directly go to this tab by using the popup menu on the method and choose 'to open it for viewing its editions': see Figure 113.

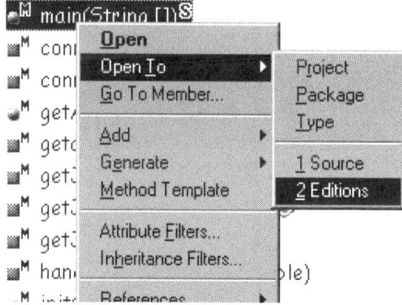

Figure 113. Using the popup menu on a method to go directly to its edition tab

The simplest edition tab is the one for methods. By default, it gives you a list of the editions that are present (and not purged, see later) in the repository. This list is shown in the upper part of the window. Clicking on one of the editions shows you the method code in that edition in the lower pane: see Figure 114.

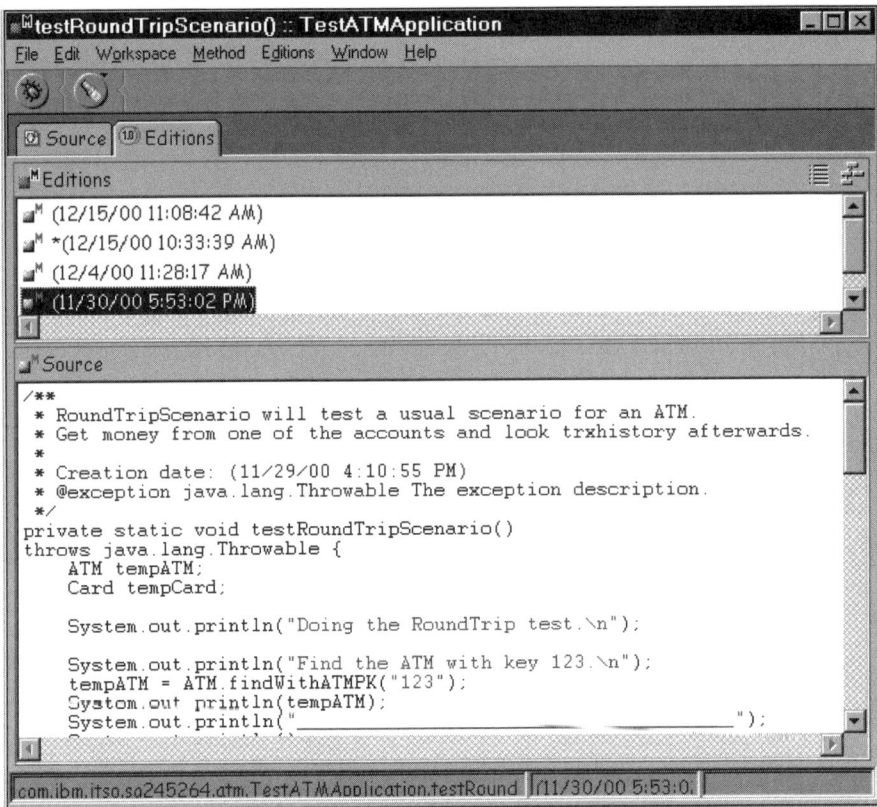

Figure 114. Edition tab in method browser showing a list view of available editions

Because methods are automatically versioned by VisualAge with the timestamp as a label, this list shows only timestamps. But remember that none of the editions shown is an open edition. The edition that is currently loaded in the workspace (the edition you are working on) is marked with a '*'.

In Figure 114, we selected the version of two 'saves' ago: VisualAge actually contacts the repository to show you this directly, without loading it in the workspace. When you want to replace the loaded edition with the another you choose: **Editions -> 'Add to workspace'** from the menu bar or — more intuitively — you can use the menu option on the popup menu of the edition.

The upper pane of this edition tab has two little icons in the upper right. You can compare them with the different icons we already discussed in Chapter 2, "Organizing your code" on page 41 when discussing the different browser windows and the workbench: They change the way the list in the upper pane is shown:

Those icons work like a toggle. By default the first one (the list) is selected, when you click on the second, the upper pane of your edition tab will show the structure of the editions in a tree view: Figure 115.

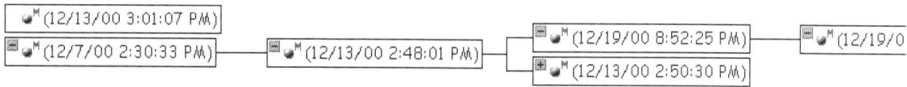

Figure 115. Hierarchical view of the editions on the edition tab

A parent connection in this hierarchical representation means that an edition was created from the other. Figure 115 shows that it is possible to have multiple roots on an edition tree. This happens when VisualAge has no idea which version you used to make the new edition you want to save. This can be the case when creating a new edition when you import code (see later).

The figure also shows that you can collapse or expand parts of the tree by clicking the '-' or the '+' sign respectively. When this window comes up, the whole tree is expanded. When searching for an edition, you could collapse the sub-tree that you already investigated so you will not try to investigate it later on.

This representation shows much more information than the list view. It can be especially useful when, for example, you have to figure out why you have seemingly lost subsequent changes of a method: This usually turns out to be caused by importing an old version or accidentally replacing an edition.

Comparison result window

Another tool that can you fix such problems is the comparison tool. We will explain this tool directly for comparing any kind of program element, not only for methods, since the differences are minor.

The comparison tool will help you in merging the differences between two editions into one. When selecting two editions, the popup menu of an edition will enable the menu option 'Compare'. This will bring up a window like the one you can see in Figure 116.

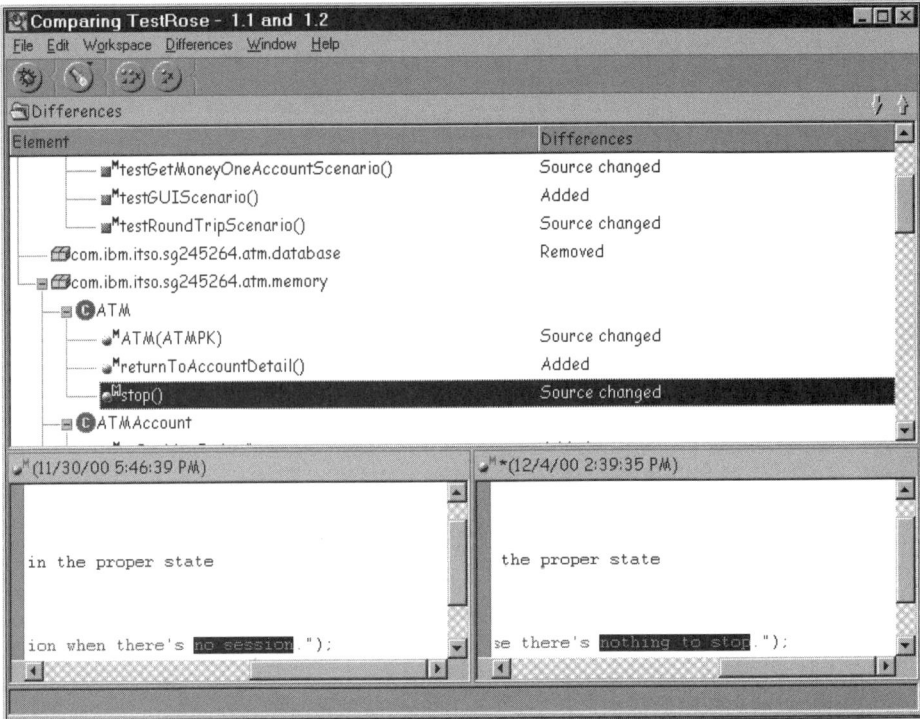

Figure 116. Comparison result window in action

The top list (*Differences pane*) is comparable to lists shown in the workbench: It contains all sorts of program elements hierarchically structured. Depending on the type of the program elements you compare editions from, it will contain everything from packages to members. At each node where a difference was detected, the second column specifies what kind of differences were found.

The source panes below show the two sources for the currently selected program element. When you select an element in the list, it will highlight the first difference found in the source panes. You can navigate through the list of difference by clicking on the arrows in the upper right part of the window (comparable with the arrows problems tab enabling browsing through the set of problems):

You can also navigate the differences by pressing CTRL-N (Next) or CTRL-P (Previous) or by using the menus. When browsing through the list of differences, the Differences pane will update its selected line with the program element containing the showed differences.

Much like the collapsing of sub trees in the graphical edition view, this window features functionality to hide all covered differences in a program element. Use the button shown below:

If you click this button when a hidden program element is selected, it will become 'visible' again.

To see the complete list again, include the hidden program elements, you click change the toggle:

When this toggle is active, the hidden program elements in the list will be shown with their names between parenthesis.

Merging compared elements

You can merge the source into one window stepping over each difference and choosing the 'Replace with Alternative' in the popup menu of the source pane to be used for the merge. This will replace the highlighted area with the one from the other source pane (see Figure 117).

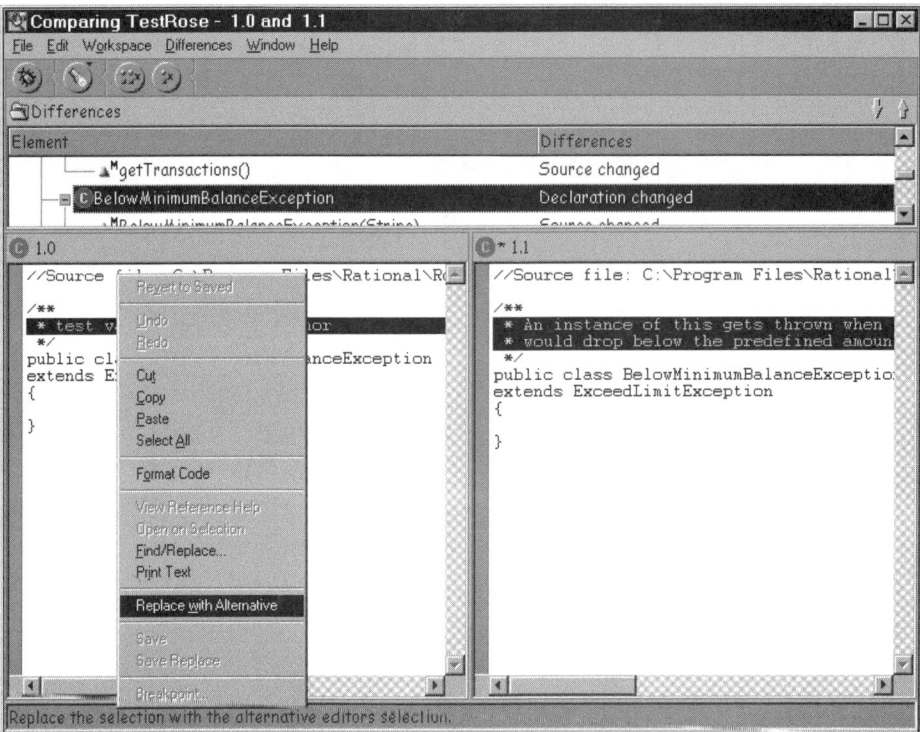

Figure 117. Replace with Alternative option to merge source

If you want to exchange the code show in the left source pane with the source in the right (to replace *all* differences by the alternative at once), choose 'Load Right' from the program element popup or from the menu bar: **Differences → Load Right**.

You would choose the **Load Left** when you want to replace the code in the right pane with the one on the left side.

When one of the panes is empty, replacing the other with this one means deleting it.

You cannot change source code in an edition that is not loaded in the workspace. Although VisualAge will let you merge code into a source pane that corresponds to an edition currently not present in the workspace, it will alert you of this when you try to save the changes or when you leave the window by clicking on something else with the dialog window shown in Figure 118.

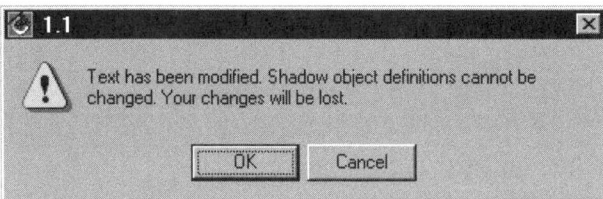

Figure 118. Shadow objects are unchangeable warning

Therefore you should always be careful to merge into the source pane that contains the loaded edition if you want to save the changes afterwards, which is normally the case anyway.

Note: You are not limited to comparing different editions of the same program element. You can also compare two different program elements together, provided that they are from the same sort (compare between packages, projects, types and members) and that they are both loaded in the workspace.

In general, you can compare each program element to another edition from the repository or to another program element by the same type everywhere within VisualAge by using the 'Compare With' popup menu submenu. It comes in two versions, depending on whether you selected one or two elements: Figure 119.

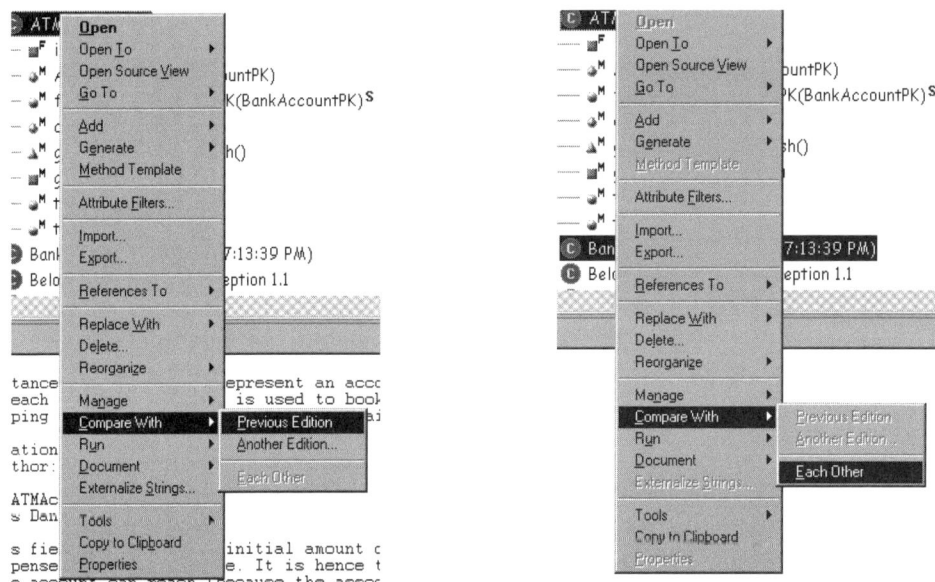

Figure 119. The two versions of the 'Compare With' popup menu submenu

We will now show you the other edition tabs specific to types, packages, and projects. From there, you can also start the comparison.

Types edition tab

The edition tab for classes and interfaces is a little more complicated than the one for methods. You access it either by using the '*Open To -> Editions*' option from the popup or by clicking on the tab icon in the Class browser. It contains three panes (see Figure 120).

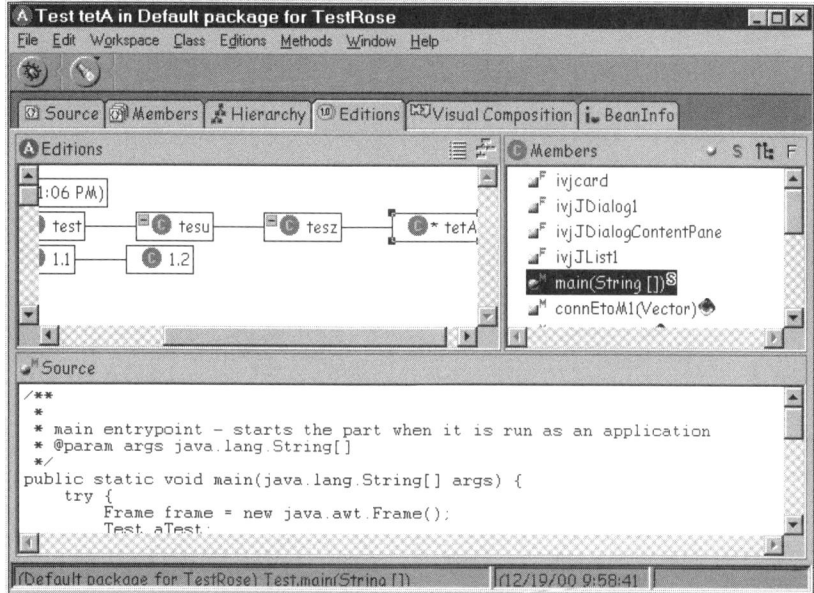

Figure 120. Edition tab in class browser

The left upper pane is similar to the one we discussed with the method browser. Notice, however, that we now have a mix of version labels and timestamps of open editions as labels to the nodes.

The right upper pane will show all fields and methods that were included in the class for the edition selected at the left. This list has similar filtering functions as described for the normal browsers.

One other difference stands out: The icons for the elements are grey. VisualAge uses this visual indication to remind you that these elements are not currently loaded. They are shadow objects; see the discussion above.

The methods from the list are listed in the edition that were in at the time the class was versioned, or in their last available edition within the open edition of the class. You can, however, easily browse the other editions for the individual methods by using the popup menu to open them in their edition tab.

The lower pane will show the class or interface declaration when no member was selected, or the code of the selected member (in the version it was in). When no edition is selected in the Editions pane, both other panes are blank.

From this window it should be clear to you that editions of types both contain code as "organizational" information: The class declaration is bound to the class edition, the version of the methods included in the class can be regarded as a set of references to method versions.

Packages edition tab

This view adds another pane that contains a list, combining them to act like cascading lists (see Figure 121).

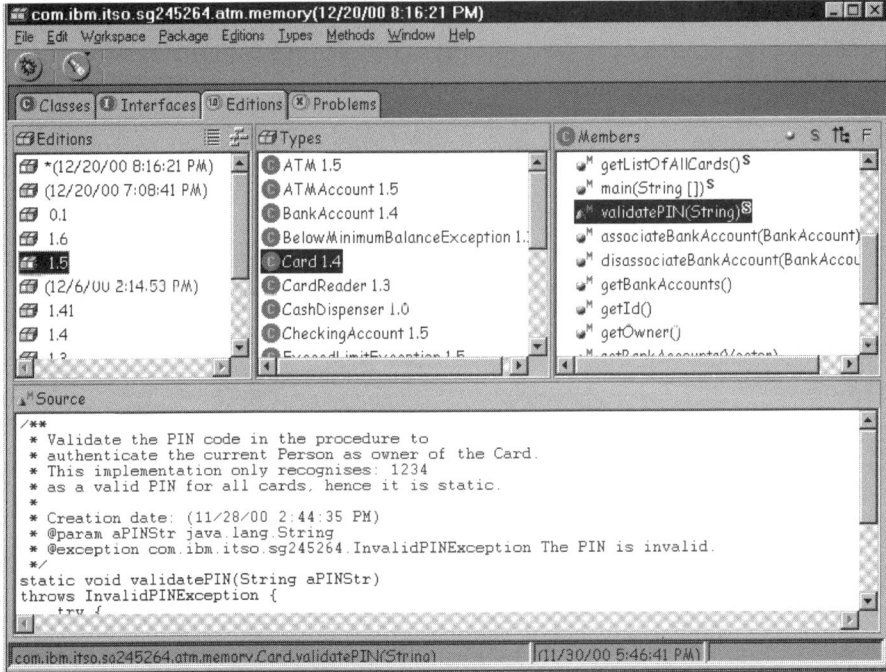

Figure 121. Edition tab in Package Browser

On this level we no longer talk about code. The information stored in an edition of a package is mainly concerned with which versions of program elements were present when that package was in that state. The lowest pane will now show the documentation associated to that package in the selected edition when a selection is only made in the first pane.

Notice that VisualAge will try to act "conveniently" when browsing cascading lists: When you selected a certain version of a package, a particular class within that package, and a method within that class. Changing the edition will in most cases result in showing the same method, but in the edition it was in when the package was versioned.

Of course, this will not work when one of the elements are missing in the newly selected edition. This makes it possible to browse editions of program elements based on the versions of their ancestor elements!

Projects edition tab

Projects have the characteristic that they can contain the exact same package (if only they are not loaded at the same time: See Chapter 2, "Organizing your code" on page 41). This browser will therefore be of great help when, for example, you want to track the impact on a set of projects (possibly corresponding to real life customer projects) of a bug that was introduced by in a particular version of a package.

Besides the additional pane that shows which packages in which version were used by a specific version of a project, this version of the edition tab also includes a resource section. This resource pane shows the names of the resource files and their timestamps. You cannot open the resources from here, or copy them; you will have to restore the complete project if you want to manipulate them.

Notice that the Project Browser showing the Edition tab has the most extensive menu bar of all VisualAge windows: It includes both the menus for all the types of program elements as the Edition and a Selected menu. The Selected menu will unify the possible actions that are available for all the selected elements across the six panes (see Figure 122).

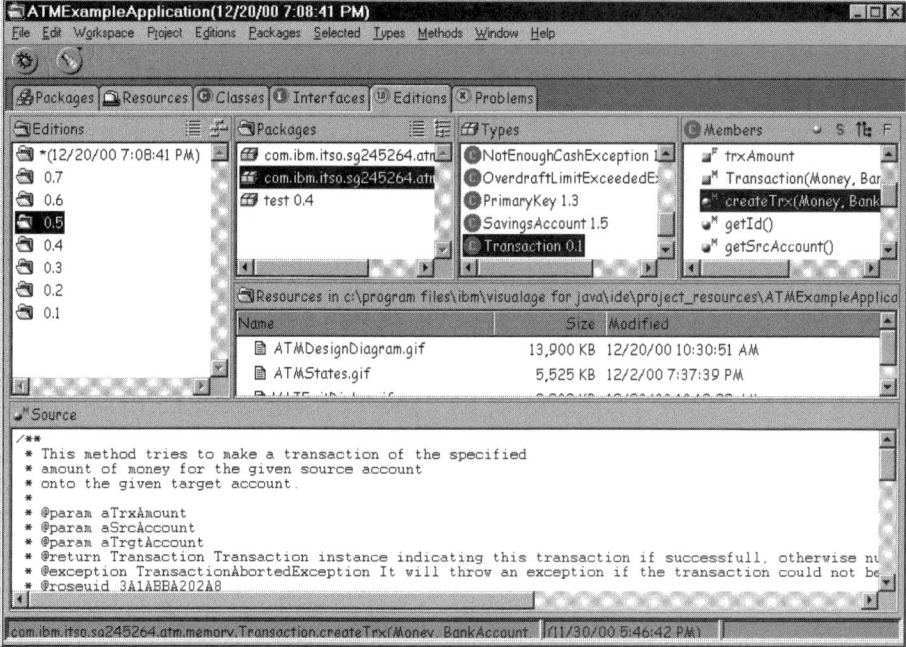

Figure 122. Edition tab in project browser

We would also like to point out that the nice feature of showing packages in the tree structure (rather than the flat sequential list) is available in the project tab. The project browser and the workbench windows discussed in Chapter 2, "Organizing your code" on page 41 also feature that functionality, review the discussion over there for more information.

Replacing current edition

There is another option in the popup menu of each program element (besides the 'Compare With') which has to do with versioning: '*Replace With*'. It has two options: '*Previous Edition*' and '*Another Edition...*' (see Figure 123).

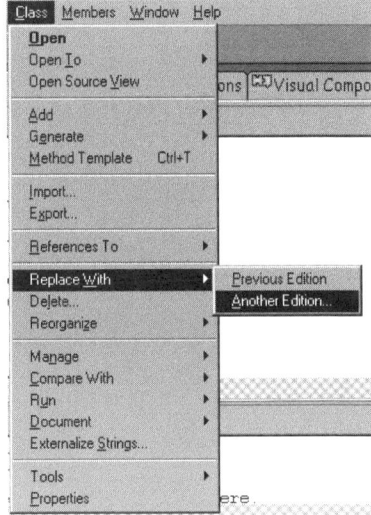

Figure 123. 'Replace Wtih' submenu available from many places

This submenu is also available from all the type menus (also see "How to version elements with VisualAge for Java" on page 194).

It will replace the current edition (version or open edition) with the previous edition or with an edition you chose from a Replacement Dialog listing all editions (only) in a list (see Figure 124).

The fact of replacing an edition in the workspace with another edition from the repository is generally referred to as *loading an edition from the repository*.

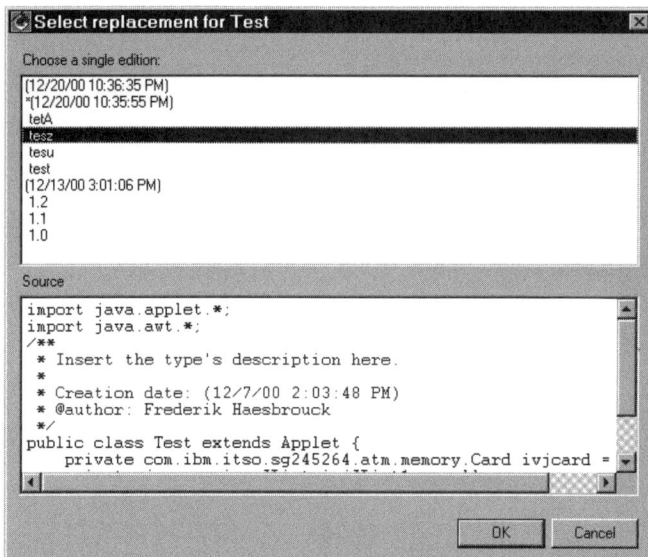

Figure 124. Replacement dialog for a class element

The edition from before is left in the repository, in the state it was in: open or versioned. If the edition you chose to load is versioned, then any change to its definition or to its subparts will result in a newly created open edition. If you choose to load an open edition, changes will be made in that same open edition. The standard rule of creating a new open edition only when changing an existing version, still stands.

Note that this can lead to multiple open editions for a specific program element: Each time you go back to a version of a program element to change something without first versioning the previously present edition, you create a new open edition leaving the other as it was.

The resource files also have a 'Replace With' submenu in their popup, although the menu for the resource files only contains the 'Another Edition...' option (see Figure 125).

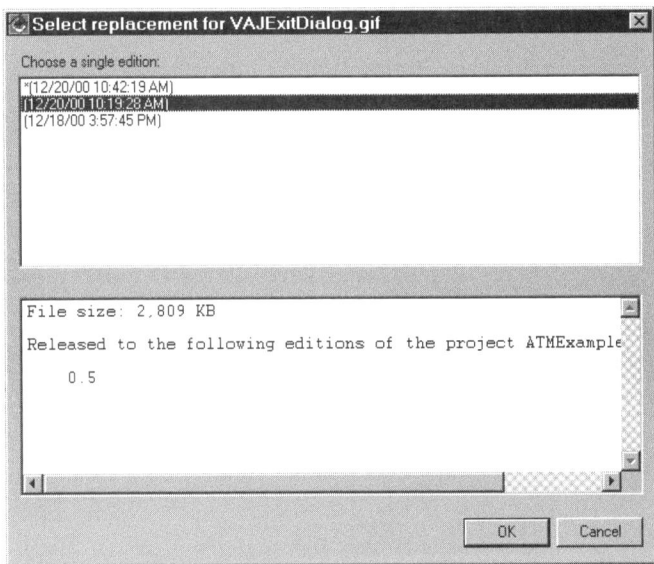

Figure 125. Replacement Dialog for resource files

From Figure 125, you can see that VisualAge generates a comment that it attaches to the edition of the file in order to recognize it later on.

The '*Add to Workspace*' popup menu option on items in the edition tab of the browsers has the same effect as 'Replace with': It loads the selected edition into the workspace. Because the replacement dialog only lists the editions sequentially, it may be handier to select **Open To -> Editions**, browse the hierarchical representation of the editions, and select **Add to Workspace** to load it (see Figure 126).

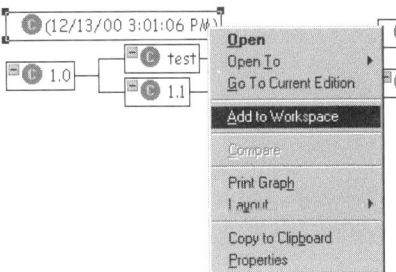

Figure 126. Add To Workspace from the edition popup menu

Here is one last piece of advice: Always compare the edition you want to load with the currently present edition by invoking **Compare To** on the two editions!

Tip: To select a second edition in the hierarchical view of the editions you must select the first one, press and hold Ctrl and right-click to obtain the popup menu. A right-click in this view will cause the selection to change to this element, so it is not feasible in the normal way.

An alternative for the 'Add To Workspace' option for program elements that are not currently in you workspace is using the respective SmartGuides for creating the different type of program elements discussed in Chapter 2, "Organizing your code" on page 41. All the SmartGuides creating versionable program elements have a '*Add <program element type> from the repository*' as the last option for the radio button on their first page (Figure 127):

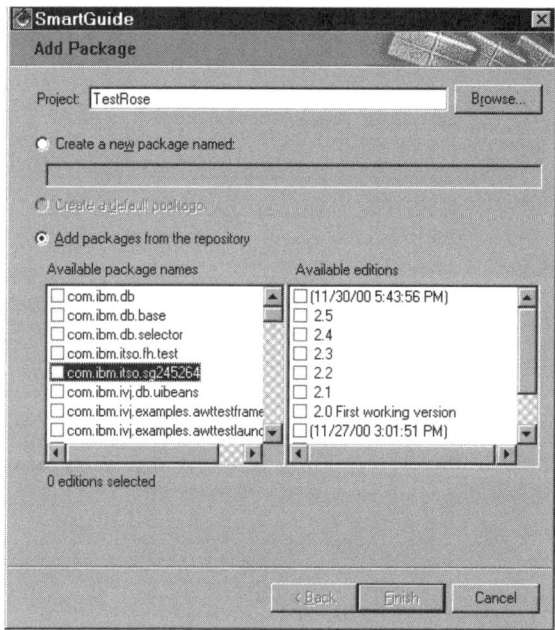

Figure 127. Create package SmartGuide

External versioning systems

To finalize this section, we offer a few words on the usage of other (external) versioning systems in combination with VisualAge for Java.

By now, it must be clear to you that a major advantage of VisualAge is the fact that versioning is centered around program elements, in addition to the granularity gained by using these program elements when applying versioning.

You can use external SCM systems, but they are file based. Because they essentially communicate by importing and exporting code from VisualAge (see the discussion of consequences below), this kind of integration has its limits.

Possibly the best combination is to use the VisualAge versioning system, and only export your code to include it in another versioning system. In this way you will be compliant with the rest of your company in case they are storing all their documents in another versioning system.

Import and export effects

This section will consider what the effects of importing and exporting code are on the versioning system and its various parts. There is a big distinction in behavior between using regular .java, .class, .jar, or .zip files, as opposed to using another storage format which we will explain shortly.

Import and export with Java files

Chapter 2, "Organizing your code" on page 41 explains how to import and export code within VisualAge for Java from or to .java, .class, .jar, or .zip files.

Importing code is treated as just another way to create an open edition. But, even when the current program element is in the open state, a new open edition will be created!

VisualAge considers that everything inside a tree is 'made from a parent node' (to which it will be linked). The import will create a *new root*, because it is not possible to know what the exact predecessor was for imported code.

Finally, we now have all the cases in which a new edition (in the open state, except with methods) of a program element is created:

1. When a new program element is created in the IDE.
2. When something is changed on a versioned edition of a program element, or on its sub-elements.
3. When importing code from a .java, .class, or .jar file that replaces the current edition of a program element.

Import and export with repository files

In this chapter we already saw that the VisualAge for Java IDE uses a repository called ivj.dat to store all editions of all program elements. The *export to repository* creates and updates similar files as this; they are called *repository files* and should have a *.dat* extension.

These repository files can also contain more then one version of your code. Just like the main repository of VisualAge, they store editions of program elements. When the parent of imported edition is also available in the repository (of the IDE that imports the element), it will be placed in the correct place inside the existing edition tree, otherwise it will still create a new (edition) root.

Where the regular import and export can only be invoked on packages or types, the export to a repository file is only supported for packages, projects and — as we will explain shortly — for solutions (see Figure 128).

Another limitation is that you can only export versioned editions of program elements. This makes sense: How would you otherwise be able to know what version of the sub elements would be in an exported open edition (where this is not fixed)? Two exports of a same open edition would potentially be different when allowing this.

Export
We will first explain the option in the export dialog (discussed in Chapter 2, "Organizing your code" on page 41) to export to 'Repository', which will use repository files.

When exporting to a repository file, you have to specify the repository file and choose which versions you want to export, see Figure 128. You can export multiple editions of an element, not only the current version, but also versions that are in the repository.

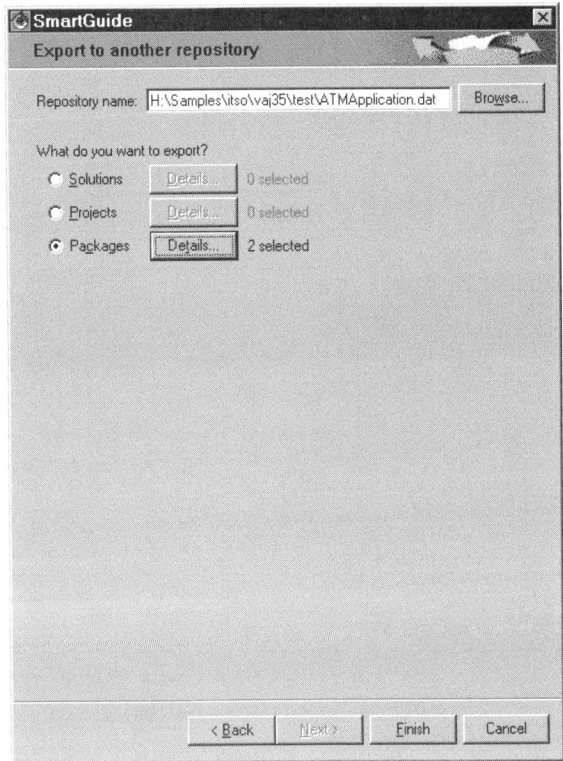

Figure 128. Export to a repository file, second page of SmartGuide

If you specify a file that does not exist, VisualAge will create a new repository file. Reusing an existing repository file, on the other hand, will add the editions you chose; they will be added to the existing editions.

Select the type of program elements you want to export and specify the editions you want by pressing **Details**. The dialog (Figure 129) that pops up will list every program element of the selected type that you can export. If you choose one, the list at the right will show the available editions.

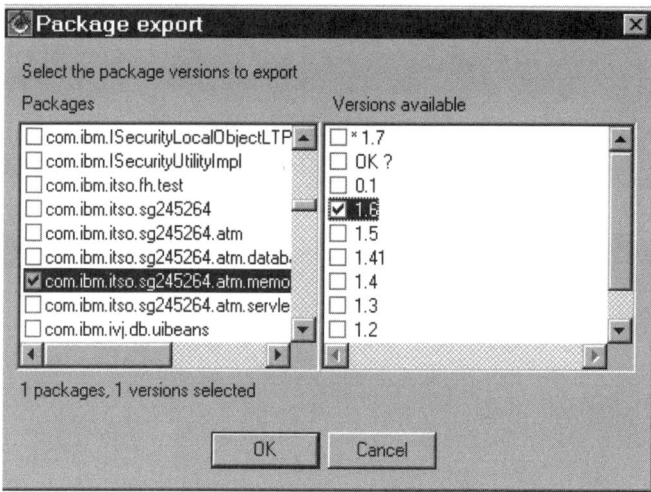

Figure 129. Specify the packages and the editions to export

When you select something in the first list, all editions of that element are shown in the right list. When you select the first edition of a program element that was not selected in the first list, it will automatically check the box in front of that element.Below the lists you see how many program elements (in this figure how many packages) you currently selected and how many selected versions of those elements you currently have.

The program elements exported to repository files will keep everything VisualAge adds to them; the Visual Composition Editor information (see Chapter 7, "Creating GUI applications" on page 143), the comments on program elements (see Chapter 2, "Organizing your code" on page 41), and the edition information (explained before in this chapter). This is in contrary to the export to traditional Java files which have no concepts of editions.

Therefore exporting to repository files is the preferred way to share code. As an alternative to the team version of the versioning system (which is supplied with the VisualAge Enterprise edition), you can use a common repository file: Everybody releases their new versions into one common .dat file. You can then chose individually what changes of other team members you import, when to import them and still revert to previous editions if those changes do not suit you.

When you export projects and packages, your corresponding project resource files are also exported when exporting to a repository file (unlike exporting to a .jar file or directory where you have the choice to export them or not). VisualAge will make a directory (at the same place and) with the same name as your repository file appended with '.pr'.

Let us assume our example code is in a project with the name "ATMExampleApplication", which contains the JSPs (developed in Chapter 6, "Creating JSPs" on page 129) as resource files. If you are exporting this project to a repository file named "D:\data\temp\test.dat"; then the following path will be created as well, containing the corresponding versions of your resources:

```
D:\data\temp\test.dat.pr\ATMExampleApplication\20001220.104220
```

Import

Unlike when importing from Java files, the import from repository file dialog looks very much the same as its exporting counterpart: Compare Figure 128 on page 219 and Figure 130 below. They are the same, except for the checkbox with '*Add most recent project edition to workspace*' which you could check when importing projects from the repository file. This will automatically load the most recent edition of all projects you selected to import.

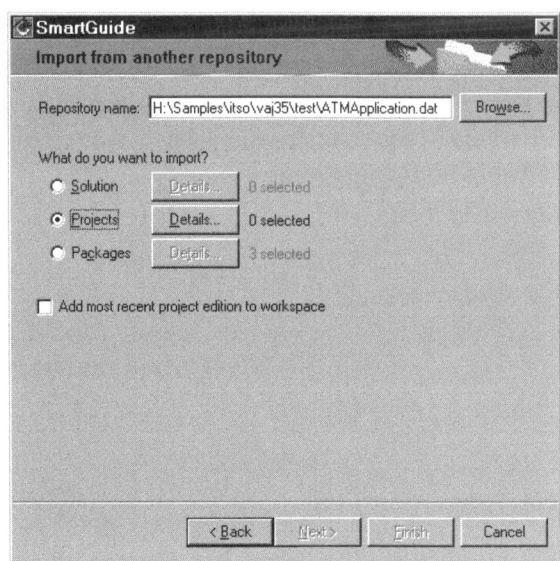

Figure 130. Import from resource file dialog

In the details dialog — which is exactly the same as the one used for exporting code in Figure 129 — you can also specify multiple elements and multiple versions of elements to be imported into the repository.

After importing code from a repository file, VisualAge will not load an edition of that code to your workspace (except when checking the toggle mentioned above for projects). This results in not seeing your code in the workbench, which may confuse new users of VisualAge, who may think that the import did not work!

There is a big difference in importing from Java files and repository files. Importing from a .class, .java, .jar or .zip file will import the code in the workspace (and as a side effect also in the repository). Where the import from .dat files will import into the repository.

Tip: Think of this importing and exporting tools for resource files, as if it was just one tool: a *repository copying tool* that is used to transfer editions of elements from one repository to another (from an external .dat file to ivj.dat or the other way around). This also explains why the respective import and export dialogs are similar.

Repository Explorer

The Repository Explorer is a window that shows what editions of all sorts of program elements are present in the current repository (only the ivj.dat file is browsable). The way to explore this is by browsing from either a package edition, a project edition, or a solution edition to the program element you want to look at. Using the technique of the cascading list, you can navigate down to the level of detail you want.

Figure 131 shows the Repository Explorer on its *Package* tab.

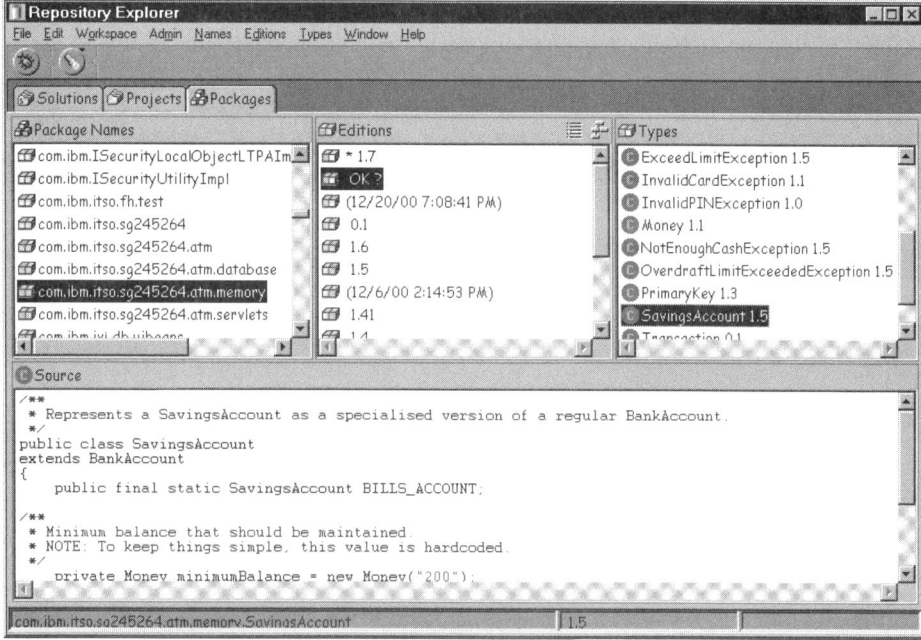

Figure 131. Repository Explorer e on package tab

This display starts with a list of all available packages in the current repository in the 'Names Pane'. This list is probably much longer than the list on the package tab of the workbench, showing all the packages available in the workspace.

All functions explained before, when discussing the different Edition tabs on the browser windows, are also applicable . here.

Here is a short recapitulation of the functions you would need in the major usage scenarios:

- The items displayed in the Repository Explorer are all shadow objects; you can see and change the source of elements, but you cannot save your changes.
- The currently loaded edition of a program element is indicated with a '*', you can use the popup menu to add the selected edition to the workspace (to become the currently loaded element).
- You can compare between editions of the same program element or between elements of the same type.

- To see the edition history of the other elements (besides the solutions, project and packages) browse them in the edition tab using the **Open To -> Editions** menu option.

Editions of packages, projects and solutions can be listed sequentially or as a graph in the second pane on the respective tabs of the Repository Explorer in the 'Editions Pane'.

The *Project* tab closely resembles the edition tab of the project browser shown in Figure 122 on page 212, and is discussed above in the section on editions. Figure 132 below shows that it is different only in that it adds the additional pane with the list of all existing projects as the beginning of the cascading lists.

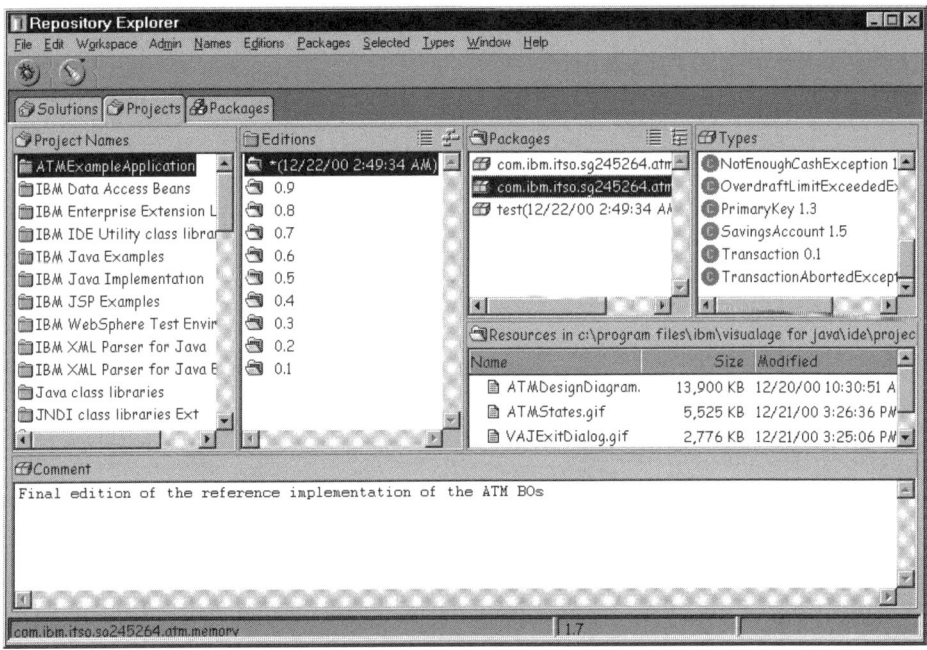

Figure 132. Repository Explorer showing the available projects

Another view that might look completely new to you is the Repository Explorer showing the *Solution* tab. This tab will be discussed shortly in the section on solutions.

Purging and restoring elements

One of the VisualAge actions on program elements that is only available from the Repository Explorer is purging and restoring program elements.

Purging elements means that you mark elements to be deleted later on (when compacting). They will not show up anymore in VisualAge. But you can still get them back by using the *restore* function. Remember that you essentially do not lose code by purging elements accidentally, until you compact the repository, it can be restored.

You can only purge editions of elements that are not present in the (current) workspace, VisualAge will generate an error if it detects an element that is still in the workspace.

Before you purge anything VisualAge asks for a confirmation (Figure 133).

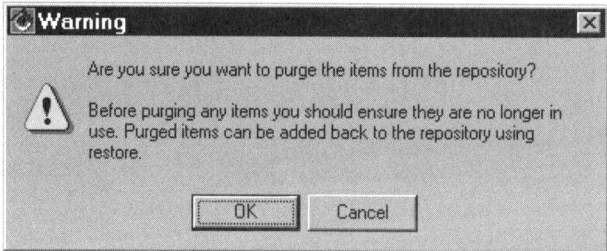

Figure 133. Confirmation before purging elements

You can only purge solutions, projects and packages. The other program elements all link to editions of packages, they are purged when (all the editions of) the packages they belong to are purged. More specifically, when there is still a reference to a type (and its methods) present in the repository (even only by an old version of the package) the full edition tree of the type (and its methods) is preserved!

In other words: On the class, interface or method level, you either have the full tree of editions, or you have nothing left of it (after compacting the repository, of course).

Purging solutions or projects will only purge the organizational information: What editions of packages were in a certain edition of a project and what editions of projects were in a certain edition of a solution. Even when all projects that ever contained a certain package are all purged, the package itself will not be purged, it will remain in the repository even after compacting it!

You can select to purge or restore an element from the edition of the element (in the second list from the left) or you can purge or restore all editions of it by starting these actions from the first program elements list.

Restoring elements is the act of undoing a previous purging of them. You can always restore everything you purged up to the moment that you compact the repository.

Figure 134 shows a list that will be presented when you want to restore a package. This dialog looks the same whether you want to restore either one of the tree types of elements you can purge.

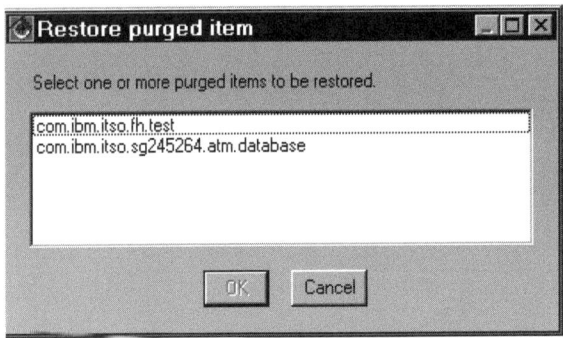

Figure 134. Restore purged items

In fact the action of purging elements can be compared to marking it for deletion for the compacting process. Restoring an element is only removing that marking.

Compacting a repository

The compacting process will effectively remove all items marked for deletion (by purging them). It will also remove any open editions of program elements.

The menu option to start compacting the repository can be found in the menu bar: '**Admin -> Compact Repository...**'.

You can only compact the repository when no copies of the elements that would be deleted are present in the workspace. For purged elements VisualAge already alerted us to first remove the edition you want to purge from the workspace. For the open editions that the compacting process will remove, the warning is shown at this time (see Figure 135).

Figure 135. Cannot compact the repository while there are open editions

Note that no open editions of program elements that you would be using can get lost because you cannot start compacting until all elements in the workspace are versioned!

Because you tend to end up with a lot of versions after a period of intense development (remember: version regularly!), the repository may become too large. Purging all the versions up till the one that you are finished with will probably reduce your repository dramatically, as all deleted code will now be removed from the repository.

Before compacting a repository, VisualAge will first make a copy of the current one in *ivj.bak*. You can always revert the compacting process by replacing ivj.dat by that backup file (after closing VisualAge).

You are reminded about these things by a dialog just before starting to compact the repository (Figure 136).

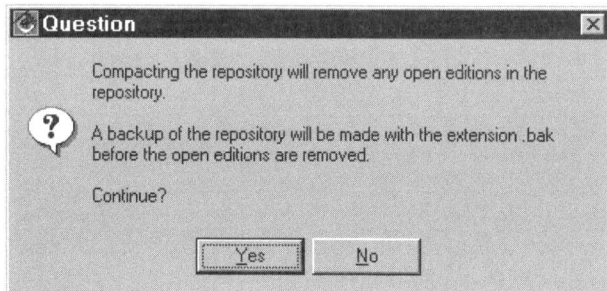

Figure 136. Compacting will remove open editions and will create a backup

Note: Types that are included an open edition of a package (for example, the automatically generated Default packages) are — even if they are themselves versioned — deleted if they do not exist in a versioned edition of that package! All open editions are deleted, and trees of editions of types and methods are deleted if everything that once contained them is deleted.

Chapter 8. Versioning your code   **227**

Note: The possibility that you might "lose" your code is, by now, reduced to the chance that you might accidentally purge all editions of the package in which your code resides, and you have also compacted the repository and removed the created backup file of the repository.

Go To tools

In the different tabs of the Repository Explorer you have a searching tool at your disposal in order to find a particular item in the names pane. Much like the dialogs used by the different SmartGuides to look up classes, this dialog will allow you to use patterns to specify what your searching for (see Figure 137). You can access it from the popup menu of the Names pane or from the menu bar: '**Names** → **Go To** *<typename>*'.

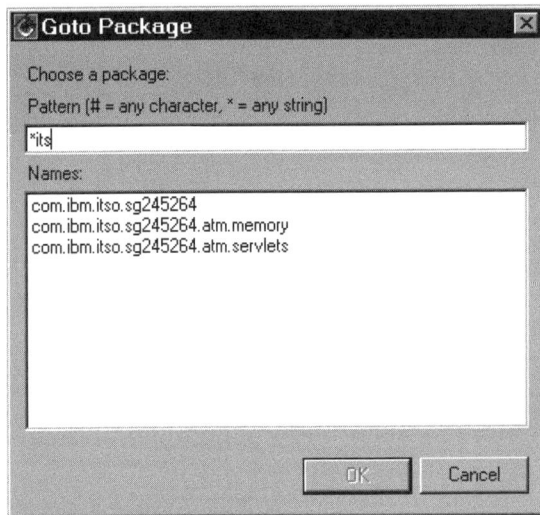

Figure 137. Go To dialog

The list showing the results will automatically update after each keystroke. When you click **OK** the Names list is positioned to the result from the Go To dialog.

We will now explain the concept of solutions in more detail.

Solutions

Solutions provide a simple sort of configuration management across multiple projects. They are very well suited to act as deployment units for real world projects that may be incorporating multiple VisualAge projects.

Solutions are groups of projects. You can assemble relating projects in one solution which could be a convenience for importing and exporting. As you might already notice in the export dialogs (Figure 128 on page 219) or on the import dialogs (Figure 130 on page 221) for repository files, solutions are listed as another program element to base exports and imports on. They are not visible elsewhere in the workbench or type browsers.

The way to view all solutions (in the repository) is by using the Repository Explorer. The *Solution* tab will let you view, create, and delete solutions (see Figure 138):

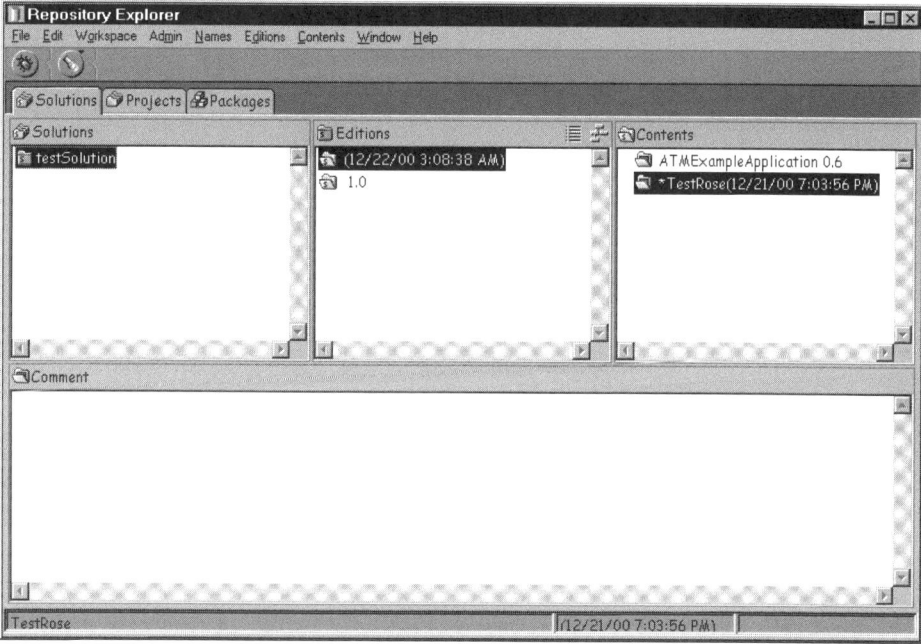

Figure 138. Solutions are manipulated in the Repository Explorer

You can add solutions by using the 'Solutions' menu in the menu bar or by using the popup menu of the list showing the solutions (Figure 139):

Figure 139. Popup menu for solution list

Solutions are also versionable program elements: Whenever you change a solution by adding a (new edition) of a project, an open edition will be created. The popup menu of that open edition will contain the '**Version...**' menu option.

External repository files can also contain solutions. The import and export dialogs for repository files have an option to use solutions as organizational elements (see Figure 140).

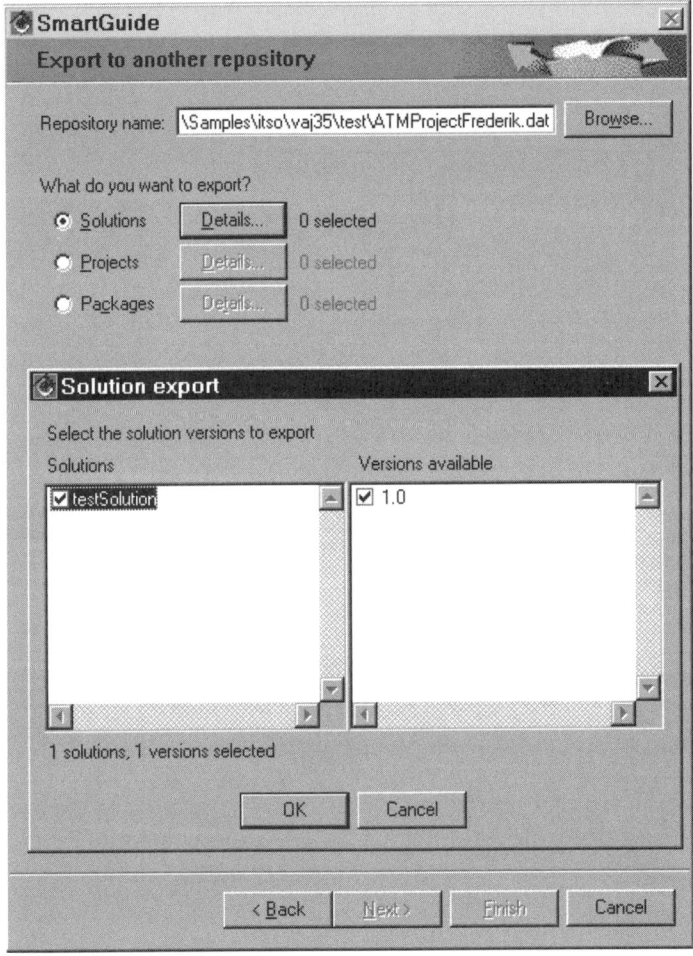

Figure 140. Solution export dialogs

Chapter 9. Testing and debugging the Web application

In this chapter we will be taking you through one of the nicest features of VisualAge for Java: the integrated debugger. Besides showing you all the important features you should use regularly, our goal is also to help you appreciate the debugger. We want you to understand why you cannot exchange implementations of the Java Virtual Machine in the VisualAge IDE (even though this is a common practice with competing integrated development environments).

The browsers explained here are the three tabs on the Debugger window and the Inspector that is used to browse inside the virtual machine.

VAJ Debugger

If you are looking for reasons why you might want to use an IDE at all, this one should be at the top of your list: Because it eases the (unit) testing and debugging of your programming code. VisualAge (in our opinion) does an especially good job of this: It gives you intuitive access to the whole system that constitutes your program. As you will see later, it even allows you to change everything on the fly.

The debugger

You use the debugger to step through and fix your Java code. As with the Inspectors, you can also inspect and change the state of objects. Because the debugger is tightly integrated with the VisualAge for Java IDE, you can make changes to code in the debugger, and these changes are reflected in your workspace.

The debugger display consists of two pages: the Debug Page and the Breakpoints Page.

The Debug Page

The Debug Page toolbar (Figure 141) provides easy access to common debug functions.

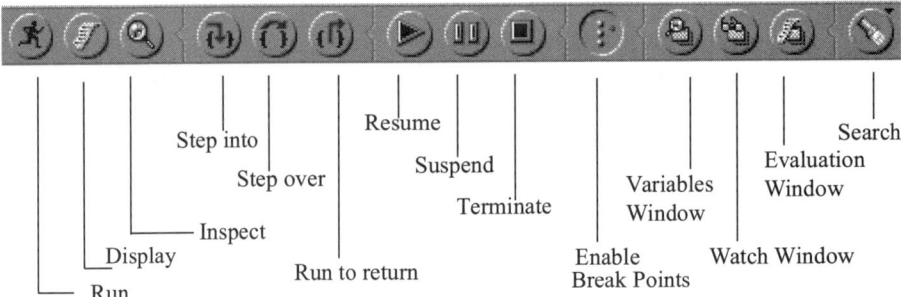

Figure 141. Debug Page Toolbar

The Debug page shows all currently running threads, grouped by program in the All Programs/Threads pane. The running programs can be of three types (Figure 143 on page 234):

System programs

If you have selected the **Show system programs in debugger and console** option (Figure 142), system programs, including any open Visual Composition Editor sessions will be displayed. A Visual Composition Editor session can be identified in the list of running programs by the format of the program name:
classname (VCE) (System) time.
For example:
HiThere (VCE) (System) (2/6/2001 2:29:21 PM)
Visual Composition Editor programs have two threads: the common AWT event queue and a timer queue. Displaying these programs in the debugger is useful for debugging code, such as property editors or customizers, that is invoked by the Visual Composition Editor.

Scrapbook sessions

Scrapbook sessions are shown in the All Programs/Threads pane with the name of the Scrapbook page as the title in the form:
page (time).
For example:
Page 1(2/7/2001 2:54:58 PM)
Simple Scrapbook programs have one thread named main.

Applets and applications

Applets and applications are shown in the All Programs/Threads pane in the form:
Applet classname (time) for applets

classname.main() (time) for applications.
For example:
Applet com.ibm.itso.sg245264.HithereAppletVCE (2/6/2001 2:29:21 PM)
Applets and applications have at least three threads: the AWT event queue, a timer queue, and the other threads of the applet or application. When a program is suspended because of a breakpoint, the AWT event queue thread shows the call stack of your applet or application. If the program is suspended because of an exception, the call stack shows up in the thread that threw the exception.

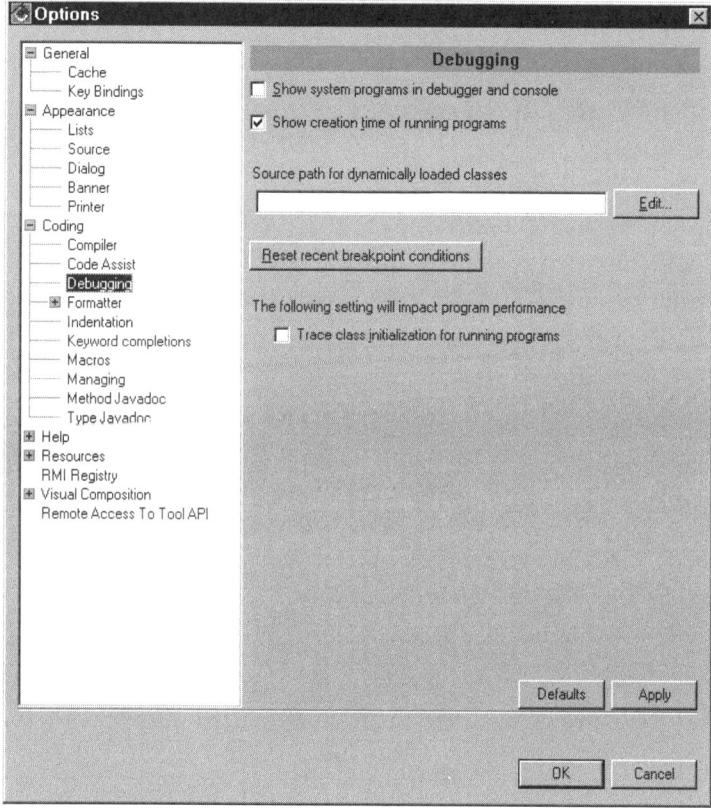

Figure 142. Debugger option

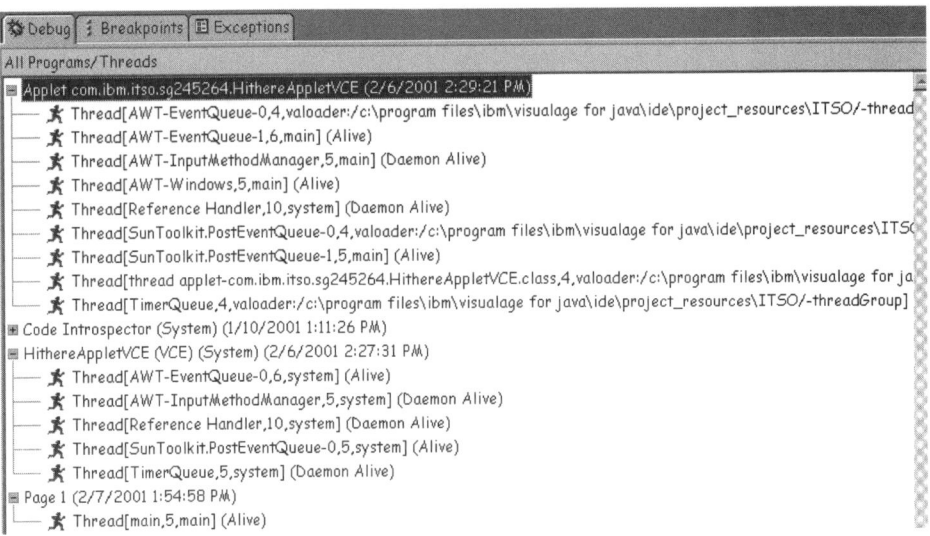

Figure 143. Running programs in the Debugger

When a program is expanded, the threads in the program are shown. When a suspended thread is expanded, the execution or call stack is shown. The execution stack shows the methods entered leading up to the method that was executing when the thread was suspended.

Another pane is the Source pane, which shows the source code of the method that is suspended.

The other panes on the Debug page show code relating to a selected suspended thread:

Visible Variables   Shows the visible variables in the thread.

Value   Shows the value of the selected variable.

Source   Shows the source of the method that is suspended.

The Visible Variables and Value panes can be separate windows. Click the Visible Variable button on the toolbar to externalize this pane.

The Watches window

The Watches window provides a place to watch the value of any expression as you step through a program that you are debugging. To open the Watches window, click the **Watches** button on toolbar. The Watches window has two columns: Expression and Value (see Figure 144). Before you start debugging a program, enter the expressions you want to evaluate in the Expression column by double-clicking an expression field. Each time the debugger suspends execution, the expressions listed in the Watches window are evaluated and their values (or an error message if no value can be determined) are shown in the Value column.

By right-clicking on a particular row, you can do the following actions on an expression:

- Edit the expression.
- Delete the row from the Watches window.
- Open an Inspector on the expression.
- Open a class browser for the associated type.
- Refresh the value.

Figure 144. Watches window

Evaluation

You can evaluate any expression in the source code to see what its value is. To evaluate an expression, you can copy an expression into the Evaluation window and evaluate it (see Figure 145).

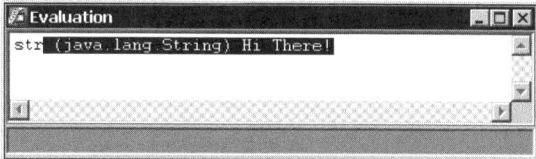

Figure 145. Evaluation window

To open the Evaluation window, click the Evaluation Area toolbar button. Copy in the expression from the debugger source pane to the Evaluation window. Select it and right-click.

From the pop-up menu, select one of the following options:

- **Run** to run the selected code.
- **Display** to display the results of running the selected code in the window.
- **Inspect** to open an Inspector on the results of running the selected code.

The Breakpoints Page

The Breakpoints page shows:

- All methods in the workspace that have breakpoints set in them
- The source code for the methods

The Breakpoints page toolbar (Figure 146) provides buttons for manipulating breakpoints.

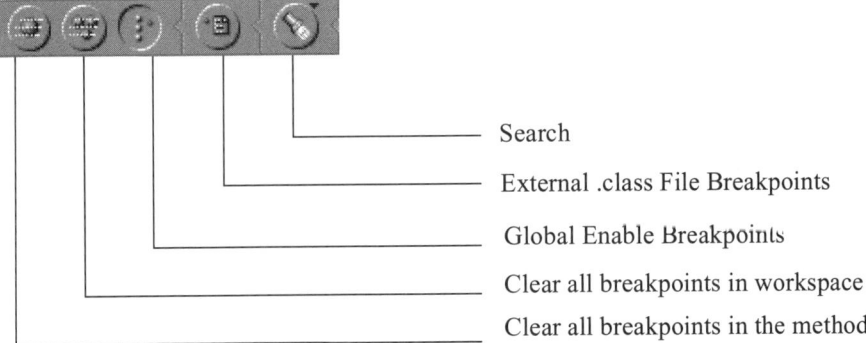

Figure 146. Breakpoints Page toolbar

Adding breakpoints

Breakpoints can be set on any instruction in source code in the workspace. The code must be saved and error free. You can set breakpoints only on instructions, not on all statements in your code. For example, you cannot set breakpoints:

- In class declarations
- In inner classes
- On try or catch statements
- On else or case statements
- On comments

VisualAge for Java does not let you set a breakpoint in a class declaration. If you try to set a breakpoint on an invalid statement in a method, the breakpoint will be set on the next valid statement.

Breakpoints can be set at any time, including while code is being debugged; that is, you can add a breakpoint to a method in a suspended thread's stack without the execution of the program being reset to the beginning of the method.

Follow these steps to set a breakpoint in the paint method of the HiThere applet (see , "Building your first applet" on page 5):

1. Go to the Workbench and select the com.ibm.itso.sg245264 package and then the paint method of the HiThere applet.

2. Double-click margin of the line containing g.drawString(str, xPos, 50).

   You can also place the cursor in the line of code and set a breakpoint by selecting **Breakpoint** from the **Edit** menu, typing Ctrl-B, or selecting **Breakpoint** from the pop-up menu.

A breakpoint symbol appears in the margin of the Source pane next to the line in which you set the breakpoint (Figure 147).

Figure 147. Breakpoint in the Paint Method

Alternative way to open the Debugger

An alternative way of halting your program and opening the debugger is to insert the halt method in your Java code. Like the inspect method, the halt method is useful if you have a difficult-to-debug program that should not be interrupted with breakpoints. However, it is most useful in debugging inner classes where you cannot set breakpoints. To halt your program and open the debugger insert the following code in your program:

```
com.ibm.uvm.tools.DebugSupport.halt();
```

Removing breakpoints

Once a breakpoint is set, you can remove it at any time, including while you are debugging the code that contains the breakpoint. If you remove a breakpoint from a method while the thread it is in is suspended, the debugger does not drop to the top of the method.

To remove a breakpoint in source code, double-click its symbol in the margin of the pane. You can remove breakpoints from any Source pane (not just the Source pane in the Breakpoints page in the debugger).

If you are in the Breakpoints page, you can also use the clear toolbar buttons to clear breakpoints.

Disabling breakpoints

Suppose you want to run a program that has breakpoints set throughout its code, but you do not want the debugger to open during this execution of the program. You can disable the breakpoints by clicking the **Enable Breakpoints** toolbar button so that it is in the "up" position. The IDE ignores all breakpoints it encounters (although the debugger may still launch for other reasons, such as an uncaught exception). All debugger symbols in the margin of Source panes change color from blue to grey.

To re-enable all breakpoints in the workspace, click the **Enable Breakpoints** button so that it is in the "down" position.

Conditional breakpoints

Conditional breakpoints are breakpoints that suspend code and open the debugger only when certain conditions are met. For example, you can set a breakpoint to suspend code only if a variable's value falls within a particular range of values.

To set conditions on the breakpoint in the paint method, click mouse button 2 on the breakpoint symbol, and select **Modify** from the pop-up menu. Select on Expression checkbox and enter xPos == 50 and click **OK** (Figure 148). The debugger opens on this breakpoint only if the xPos variable is equal to 50.

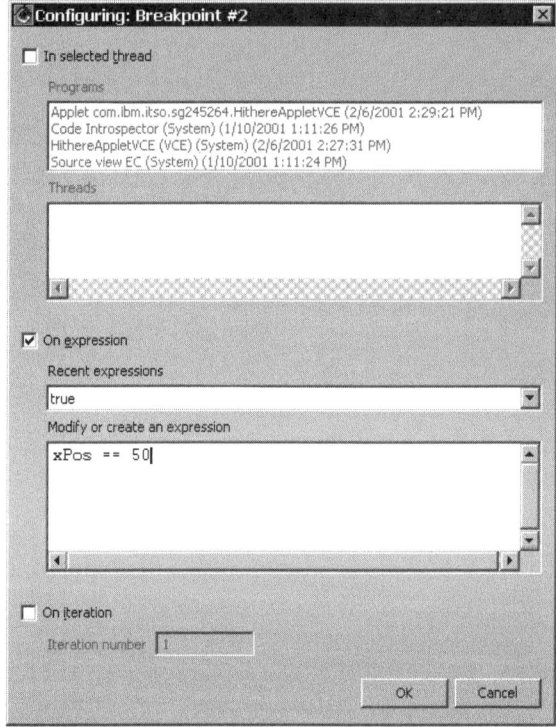

Figure 148. Conditional Breakpoint Configuring Dialog Box

In the Configuring dialog box (Figure 148), you can select a condition, or you can type in your own condition. The dialog box contains up to 10 conditions you have previously set on breakpoints. If the condition is evaluated to a boolean value of true, VisualAge for Java suspends the code and opens the debugger.

To narrow the timing, you can configure a breakpoint to specific thread or iteration number.

You can also configure a breakpoint to run a Java statement and then return true or false. For example, when the IDE encounters the breakpoint, you can have it output a message and then evaluate to false and not suspend the code (Figure 149).

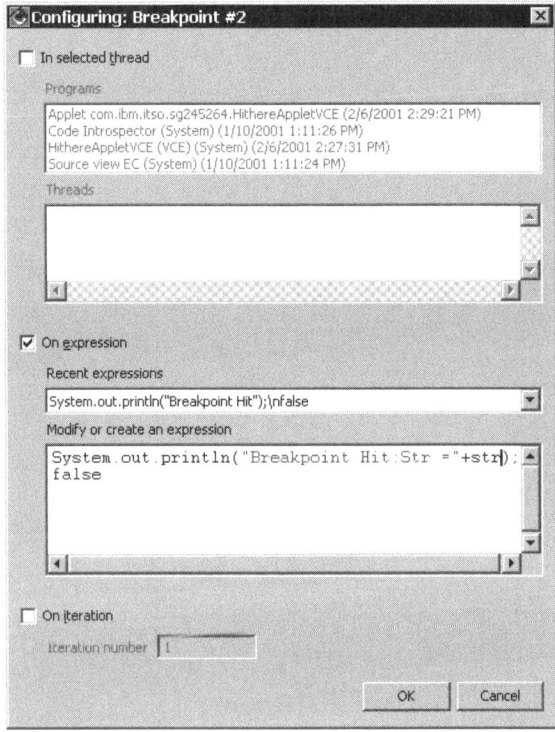

Figure 149. Breakpoint Configuring Dialog Box: Printing Diagnostics

The Exceptions Page

If an exception is thrown while a program is running in the IDE, and the program does not catch it, usually the IDE debugger opens and the offending thread is suspended. However, if the program catches the exception, the debugger will not open, and the program will continue. Even if the program outputs the stack trace when it catches the exception, you might not be able to determine the exception's origin.

To facilitate debugging, the IDE debugger lets you effectively set breakpoints on types of exceptions. Therefore any time an exception of a certain type or a subtype of that exception is thrown, the JVM suspends the thread that threw the exception and opens the debugger. The suspended thread will be of the form className (Exception Caught) exceptionclassname.

Follow these steps to select a type of exception to be caught by the debugger:

1. Select **Debug→Caught Exceptions** from the **Window** menu or click the **Caught Exceptions** tab in the debugger.
2. From the list of available exception types (Figure 150), enable the checkboxes of the types of exceptions on which you want to set breakpoints. Remember that all subtypes of an exception are caught, so if you select `java.lang.Exception`, all exceptions thrown will cause the program to suspend.
3. Click **OK**.

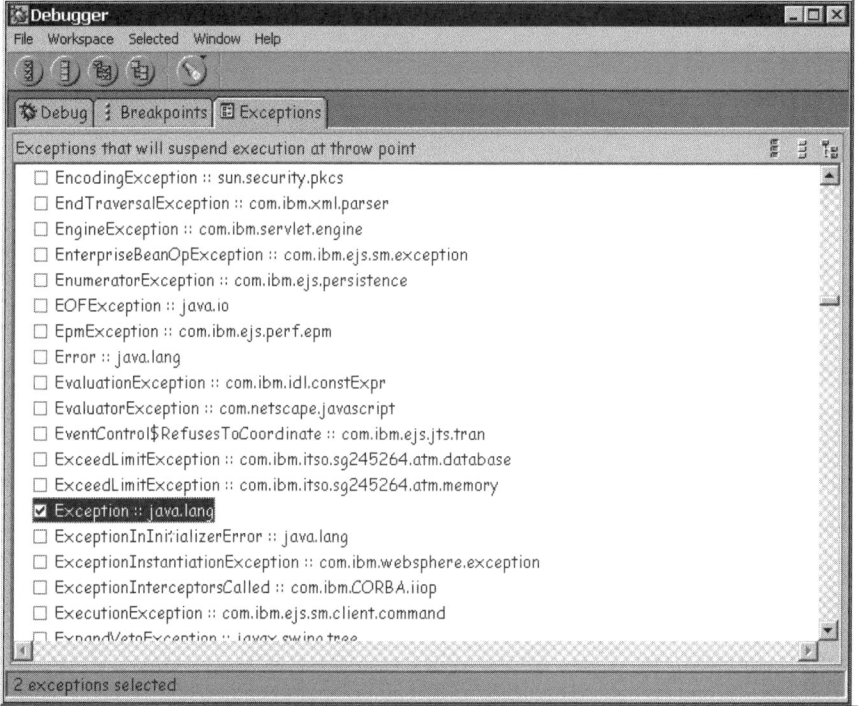

Figure 150. Exceptions

Now when you run a program that throws an exception (of the types you selected), the thread is suspended and the debugger browser opens, regardless of whether the program catches the exception.

The handleException Method

When VisualAge generates the code in the Visual Composition Editor, it generates a `handleException` method for each class. This method is called when any generated code throws an exception. By default the body of this method is commented out, and you will not see exceptions being thrown.

By removing the comment symbols from the lines in `handleException`, you can see the message and stack trace for each exception that causes `handleException` to be run. Thus it is easy to spot problems during development, although many exceptions may be displayed, especially if you have many property-to-property connections where one side of the connection is not initialized when the program starts. It is possible to catch these exceptions within the user code section of the connection itself.

External Debug

VisualAge for Java Version 3.5 can run programs that dynamically load and run external classes. External classes are classes that have not been imported into the workspace, but rather reside in a class, Zip, or JAR file on the file system. The path to the file must be part of the class path for the program or the workspace.

If you want to debug such a program, you have the option of setting breakpoints on methods in the external classes. Follow these steps:

1. Select breakpoints tab from the Debugger Window, and click the **External Breakpoints** toolbar button in the debugger browser.
2. The Add External Methods dialog looks into .class, .zip, and .jar files and lets you select methods of class3es within those files to add to the list of methods available for setting breakpoints. To access methods in a .jar file:
   a. Click **File in directory**.
   b. Click **Browse** button next to **File name**.
   c. Browse through the file system to the directory that contains the .class files in which you want to set breakpoints.

   To access methods in a .class file that has been archived:
   a. Click **File in jar/zip Archive.**
   b. Click **Browse** button next to **Archive name** and select **Zip Files** (*.zip) or **Jar Files** (*.jar).
   c. Browse to the archive file that contains the .class files in which you want to set breakpoints.

   The dialog lists all of the class files in the selected directory or archive. Select a file to see the list of methods available for setting breakpoints.

3. You can add a break point on your source code on your archive file or entry of your class method. Click the **Details** button.

4. To set a breakpoint on one of these methods, enable its checkbox.

5. Click **OK** to exit the dialog.

Figure 151 shows the dialogs used to set external breakpoints, which are set at the method level, not on individual statements. To see the source for the external file in the debugger, the Java code must be available and included in the *Source path for dynamically loaded classes* setting in the Debugging section of the Options dialog. Once the breakpoint is set, any thread that calls it will be suspended when the method is entered. External breakpoints cannot be conditional and do not display the breakpoint symbol in the Source pane margin.

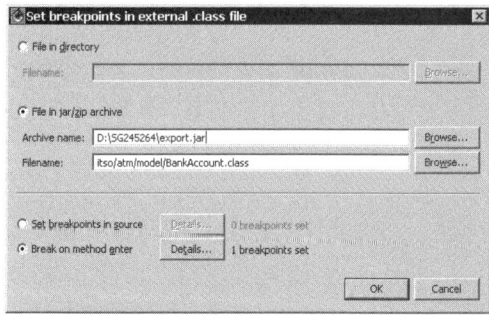

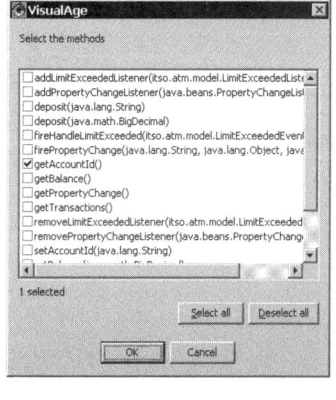
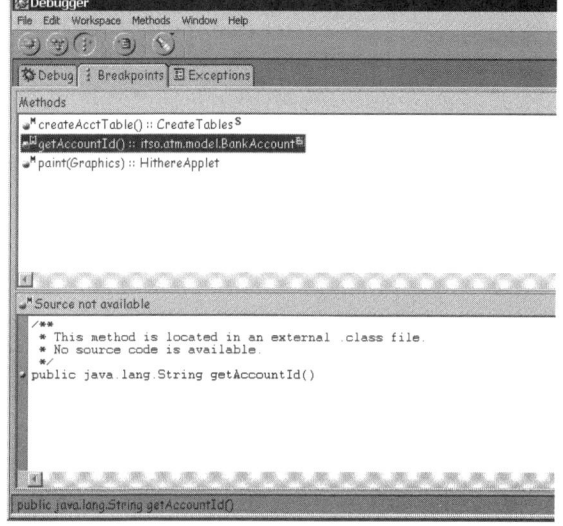

Figure 151. External method breakpoint dialogs

Removing external debug breakpoints

To remove a breakpoint from an external method, clear its checkbox in the External Method Breakpoints dialog. You can leave the method on the list so that it is easily accessible if you want to set the breakpoint again later. If you want to remove the method from the list, however, select it and click **Remove**.

Generating a Class Trace

The debugger generates a trace of class loading and initialization if you enable the Class Trace option. The Class Trace is useful for determining which classes your program uses and can help in debugging. To see the trace, select the program (not a thread) in the All Programs/Threads pane of the debugger. The trace is shown in the Source pane.

The trace is enabled through the **Trace class initialization for running programs** option in the Debugging section of the Options dialog.

Performance and the Class Trace option

When the Class Trace option is enabled, some processing time is required to compute and store the trace. As a result, the program may run significantly more slowly.

Inspectors

You can use Inspectors to view and change the state of objects in your programs. For example, if you are working in the Scrapbook, you can open an Inspector by following these steps.

1. Open the Scrapbook and type the following code:

    ```
    new java.awt.Point(1,2);
    ```

2. Highlight the code, and from the menu bar, select **Edit→Inspect**.

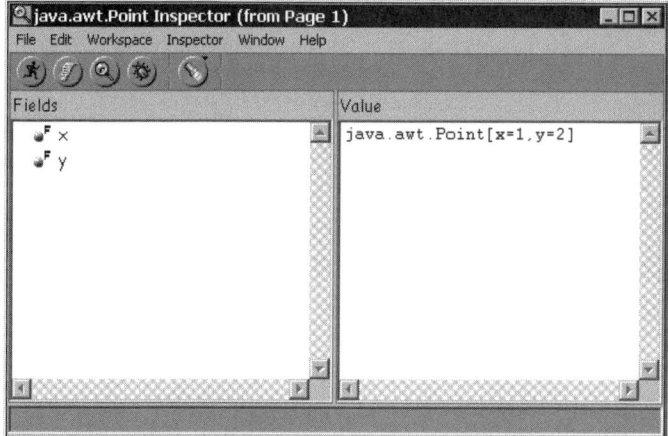

Figure 152. An Inspector window

You can also open an Inspector by highlighting the code and then pressing the accelerator key, **Ctrl-Q**, choosing **Inspect** from the pop-up menu, or clicking the **Inspect** navigation button (the magnifying glass).

Inspectors are most useful when you are using the debugger. You can open an Inspector on each object in which you are interested. As you step through the program, you can see the state of all inspected objects at once.

Alternative way to open an Inspector window

An alternative way of opening an Inspector is to insert an instruction in your Java code to inspect a specific object. This is a useful method if you have a difficult-to-debug program that should not be interrupted with breakpoints. In the Scrapbook type the following code:

```
String[] numbers = {"one", "two", "three"};
com.ibm.uvm.tools.DebugSupport.inspect(numbers);
```

Highlight the code and from the menu bar select **Edit→Run**
(or press **Ctrl-E** or click the **Run** navigation button). The following instruction: `com.ibm.uvm.tools.DebugSupport.inspect(anObject)` advises the JVM to open an Inspector on the specified object.

The Inspector window

The title bar of an Inspector window displays the type of the displayed class and the context in which you have opened the Inspector. In the example in Figure 152, the class is *java.awt.Point*, and the context is *Page 1*. There are two panes in the Inspector window:

Fields   Shows the fields of the object.

Value   Displays the values of the fields of an object.

The Fields pane displays items in hierarchical order with the inherited fields first. Therefore, when you inspect a more complex object, the fields that you have declared in your object are at the bottom of the Fields pane.

Changing the value of a field
In the Value pane of the Inspector window you can manipulate the values of the object's fields (Figure 153). Select the int x field and change 1 to 100, then select **Edit→Save** (or use the accelerator key, **Ctrl-S**, or **Save** from the Value pane's pop-up menu). VisualAge for Java also prompts you to save the field when you access another field.

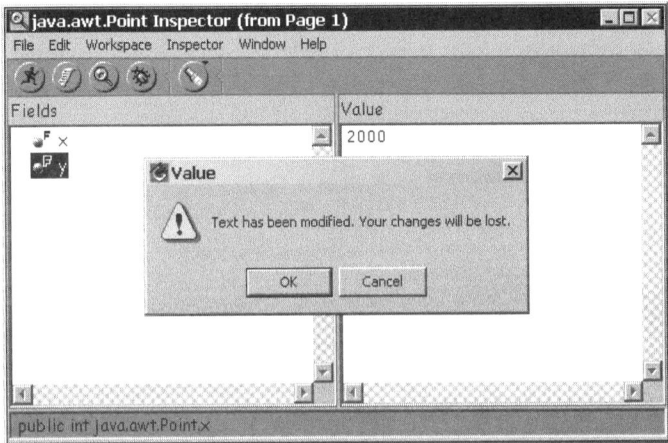

Figure 153. Changing the Value of a Field

When stepping through your code with the debugger, you also can change a field value on the fly and resume the execution of your program with the changed field value.

Navigating to other fields or objects
If you have a more complex object, say, an aggregation of several objects, it is easy to open an Inspector on the other objects. Just select the other object in the Fields pane and choose **Inspector→Inspect**. In this way you can inspect very complex data structures by accessing their different layers, just like peeling an onion.

The String class

Because the String class represents immutable strings, you cannot change the characters of a String object in an Inspector window. However, you can change the characters of a StringBuffer. In this case, you must enclose the new character in single quotes.

Controlling the display of fields

When an Inspector first appears, all public, protected, and private fields of the inspected class and the inherited classes are displayed. You can modify the fields that are displayed, using any of these Inspector menu bar items:

- Field Names Only
- Public Fields Only
- Hide Static Fields
- Show Fields In
    - Actual Type
    - Declared Type

Evaluating code in the context of an object

If you open an Inspector on a particular object, you can apply methods to that object and inspect the results. In Figure 154, for example, the getLocation method is invoked on a Point object.

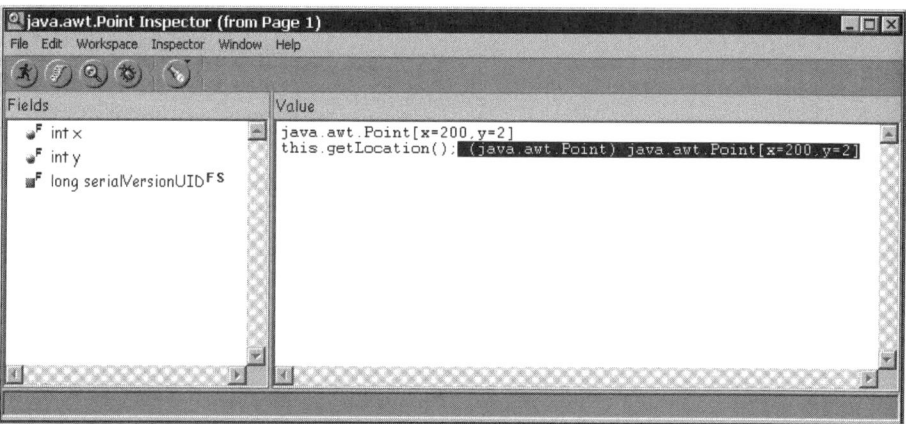

Figure 154. Evaluating Code in the Context of an Object

To evaluate an expression and display its result, type in the expression in the Value pane, highlight it, and select **Display** from the menu bar or from the Value pane pop-up menu.

WebSphere Test Environment (WTE)

VisualAge for Java integrates much of the WebSphere Application Server runtime so that debugging servlets and JSPs is possible in a highly integrated development environment. The WebSphere Test Environment (WTE) in VisualAge for Java actually encompasses the servlet and JSP runtime and test environments.

The WTE enables us to run our servlet examples in a controlled, simulated Web application server environment. Typically, one consequence of the servlet life-cycle is that you must normally stop and restart the Web application or reload the class file to apply your updated code changes. This can become tedious during development, when you are making many changes (see Figure 155).

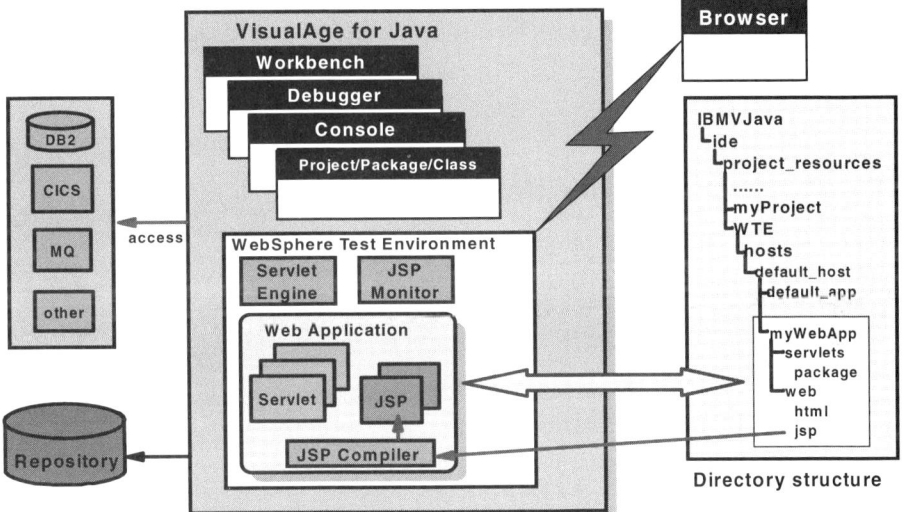

Figure 155. WebSphere Test Environment

Fortunately, WTE offers a much more productive way to develop and test servlets (and JSPs) for WebSphere. When you change a method in the servlet, VisualAge for Java incrementally compiles only this modified method of the class, not the entire class, and hot-links it into the running program. This type of incremental compilation is an important productivity boost, because you do not have to stop and restart the WTE in programs that you are debugging to execute your updated code, and rebuild program state.

To configure and run the WebSphere Test Environment, you use WebSphere Test Environment project and WebSphere Test Environment Control Center.

The WebSphere Test Environment is a feature that has to be loaded into the Workbench. Before starting, configuration of the class path is required.

We describe how to configure, run, and test our *SimpleHttpServlet* using the WTE within the VisualAge for Java tool.

Start the WebSphere Test Environment

To start WebSphere Test Environment, select Tool menu Workspace and click on the WebSphere Test Environment.

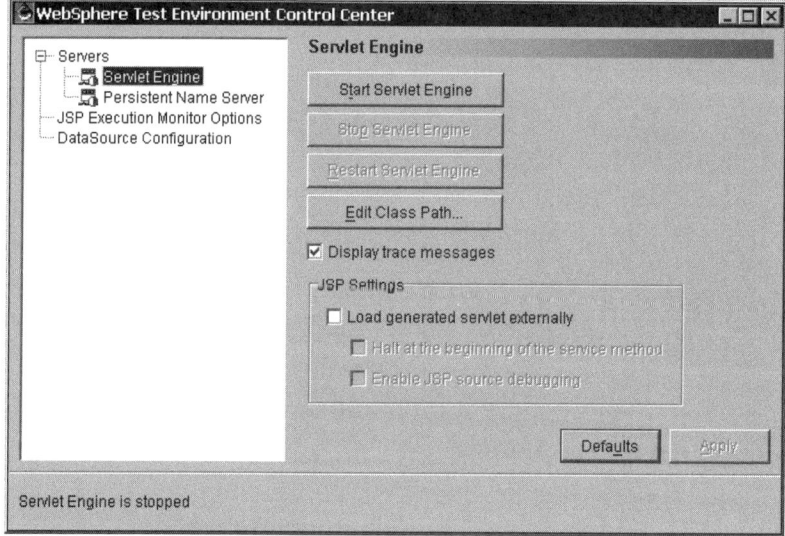

Figure 156. WebSphere Test Environment Control Center

Before start your Servlet Engine, ensure that your projects and classes are in the class path by clicking the **Edit Class Path** button (see Figure 157).

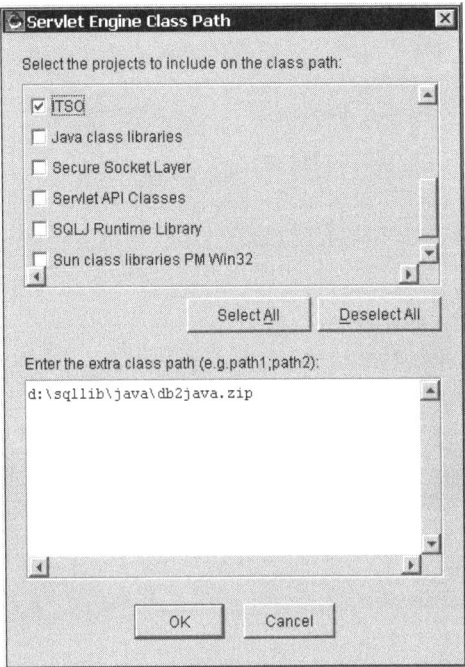

Figure 157. WebSphere Test Environment Class Path

Now we want to run the *HiHttpServlet* example in the WebSphere Test Environment. Click **Start Servlet Engine** button on the WTE Control Center (Figure 156). Check that your Servlet Engine icon goes to blue and console window (see Figure 158). If your servlet process requires any classes (jar files) that are not part of the VisualAge for Java workspace (for instance, external API or DB2 jars, such as `d:\SQLLIB\java\db2java.zip`), you have to add in the Options Dialog.

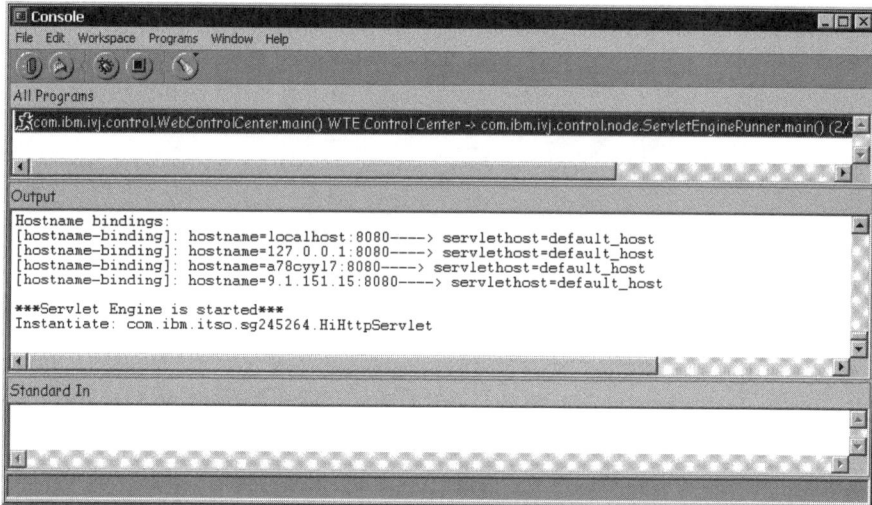

Figure 158. Servlet Engine Console Status

Once started, you invoke the servlet from a Web browser by entering the appropriate URL of the servlet, for example:

    http://localhost:8080/servlet/com.ibm.itso.sg245264.HiHttpServlet

Stopping/restarting the Servlet Engine
You can stop or restart the *Servlet Engine* from the WebSphere Test Environment Control Center. This will gracefully shut down the Web server and call the destroy methods for any loaded servlets. One of the nice things about this test environment, however, is that if you change your underlying class, you most likely do not have to restart *Servlet Engine* allowing for incremental development and debugging within the VisualAge for Java environment.

One situation where you may have to restart the *Servlet Engine* is if you change the *init* method of the class. Because the *init* is processed only once within a servlet's life-cycle, changes to this method (such as the changing of initialization parameters), do not take effect until *Servlet Engine* is restarted.

Console window
The VisualAge for Java Console window displays the status of the *Servlet Engine*, and any servlets that you launch. The Console window basically displays the standard output and standard error of the Java program's execution. If there were problems starting up the environment, they would be display here. The messages that you see on successful start-up of the *Servlet Engine* are shown in Figure 158.

We mentioned that the status of any of our servlets is also displayed in this window. The HiHttpServlet servlet has started successfully if the line: `Instantiate: com.ibm.itso.sg255264.HiHttpServlet` appears in the Console window (Figure 158).

Launching the browser
If you launched your servlet through the Servlet Launcher method, you should see the results of your servlet's execution displayed in your Web browser window. The results of the *HiHttpServlet* are shown in Figure 159.

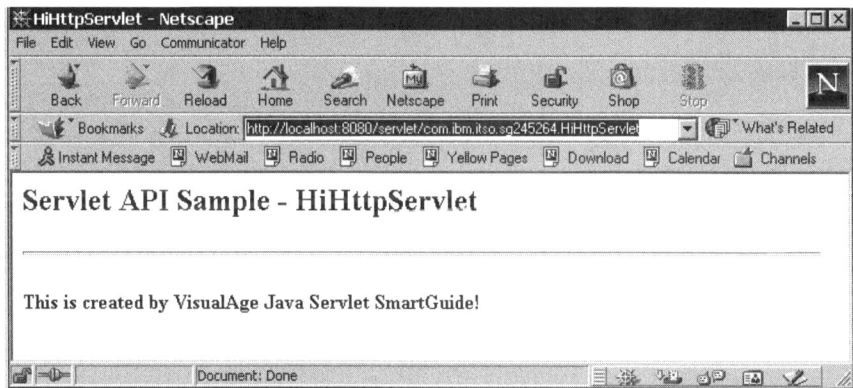

Figure 159. HiHttpServlet output

Web host path
Notice that the servlet is invoked with `http://127.0.0.1:8080` (or `http://localhost:8080`). There may be variations here based upon your TCP/IP settings, and any special configuration that you may do under WTE.

Servlet root path
The servlet Web path is `/servlet/com.ibm.itso.sg245264.HiHttpServlet`. The */servlet/* path is the default for servlets running in the default application environment in the WebSphere Test Environment. This corresponds to the default_app Web application in the Web Application Server environment.

Fully qualified class name

The fully qualified class name, com.ibm.itso.sg245264.HiHttpServlet, contains the package name, *com.ibm.itso.sg245264*.

In our true WebSphere Application Server environment, we most likely would not invoke our servlets directly by their fully qualified name, because we would want to hide this implementation detail from the user. We do this by creating aliases for Web invocation. Because this is how servlets are invoked by default in the WTE, you have to keep this in mind when designing your programs, and use relative paths in your code when appropriate.

VisualAge for Java provides the facility to use multiple Web applications and servlet aliases. See , "Configuring multiple Web applications" on page 271 for more information.

Testing JSPs under WebSphere Test Environment

This section describes how to run JSPs under the VisualAge for Java environment, and how to have those JSPs interact with other servlets and/or JavaBeans.

VisualAge for Java configuration for JSPs

You have to make sure that the WebSphere test environment features under VisualAge for Java have been successfully installed and configured.

Visual Age for Java version 3.5 supports both JSP .91 and JSP 1.0 versions, and defaults to JSP 1.0. To change the version of the JSP support used by the Visual Age Test Environment, perform these steps:

- Open the configuration file of the default application:

    ```
    d:IBMVJava\ide\project_resources\IBM WebSphere Test Environment
        \hosts\default_host\default_app\servlets\default_app.webapp
    ```

- Find the JSP compiler servlet (Figure 160):

```
<servlet>
    <name>jsp</name>
    <description>JSP support servlet</description>

    <!--
    <code>com.ibm.ivj.jsp.debugger.pagecompile.IBMPageCompile
Servlet</code>
    -->

    <code>com.ibm.ivj.jsp.runtime.JspDebugServlet</code>
    <init-parameter>
    ...
```

Figure 160. The default_app.webapp: JSP 1.0 configuration

- Change the text for the <code> tag (Figure 161):

```
<servlet>
    <name>jsp</name>
    <description>JSP support servlet</description>

    <!--
    <code>com.ibm.ivj.jsp.runtime.JspDebugServlet</code>
    -->
    <code>com.ibm.ivj.jsp.debugger.pagecompile.IBMPageCompile
Servlet</code>
    <init-parameter>
    ...
```

Figure 161. The default_app.webapp: JSP 0.91 configuration

Running a simple JSP

JSPs in VisualAge for Java run in the same WebSphere Test Environment that servlets do. (After all, JSPs actually become servlets once they are page compiled.) Because we cannot create JSP files directly in the VisualAge tool, we have to make sure that *Servlet Engine* can find the JSP files in the file system.

Location of JSP files

The default location for HTML and JSP files is:

```
D:\\IBMVJava\\ide\\project_resources\\IBM WebSphere Test Environment
\\hosts\\default_host\\default_app\\web
```

Running a simple JSP

VisualAge for Java ships with a couple of sample JSPs that we can use to test out our configuration, and see that JSPs have been enabled. Follow these steps to run the *very_ simple.jsp* example:

- Start the *Servlet Engine* and wait until it is ready.
- Enter the following URL in a Web browser:
  http://127.0.0.1:8080/very_simple.jsp

Figure 162 shows a successful JSP response.

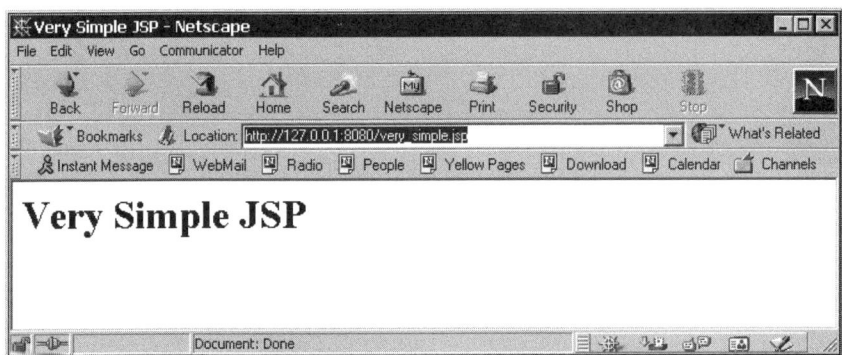

Figure 162. Very simple JSP response

As the message indicates, this is a *VERY* simple JSP. In fact, the only tags it uses are HTML tags (Figure 163). It is essentially an HTML file saved with a .jsp extension.

```
<html><head><title>Very Simple JSP</title></head>
<body>
<h1>Very Simple JSP</h1>
</body>
</html>
```

Figure 163. Very simple JSP source

How do we know it ran as a JSP?
This file is still very much a JSP. This example does not have any advanced JSP tags, so how do we know that *ServletEngine* really ran it as a JSP and not as a regular HTML file? You can tell because of the .jsp file extension.

When *WTE* (and the WebSphere Application Server) receives a request for a .jsp file, it compiles this JSP into a servlet. This happens only the first time the JSP is requested; subsequent requests use the already compiled JSP.

So where is the compiled JSP stored? The JSP is translated into a servlet Java source file, and imported into VisualAge for Java (*JSP Page Compile Generated Code* project). The intermediate .java files, however, can be found in the file system, in the WebSphere Test Environment \temp\ directory:

```
<IBMVJava>\ide\project_resources\IBM WebSphere Test Environment
\temp\Jsp1_0\default_app\_very__simple_xjsp.java
```

Debugging servlets and JSPs

This section describes how we can debug our servlets and JSPs within the VisualAge for Java environment.

Debugging a servlet

Now we will walk through the debugger by debugging and stepping through one of our servlet examples.

Set a breakpoint
Set a breakpoint at the **response.setContentType("text/html");** statement in the **performTask** method.

Run the servlet
Start the *Servlet Engine* and launch the servlet. The browser window will be launched, but will be waiting for the response from the servlet. You should see the code stop at your breakpoint in the Debugger window (Figure 164). Your request is captured by the class of Servlet Engine which is ServletEngineRunner. Now you can debug your servlet just like your applications.

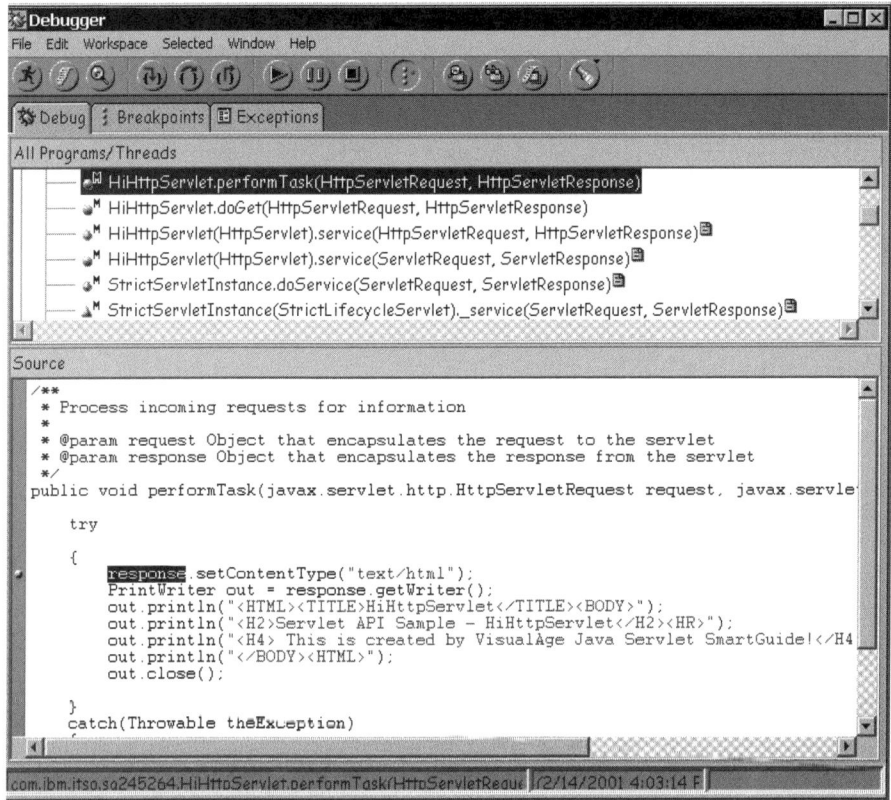

Figure 164. Debugging the HiHttpServlet

Working with servlet threads

In the All Program/Threads window pane of the debugger, you can see that there are multiple threads of execution. Many of these threads have to do with the running of the *ServletEngineRunner* class. In addition, you will see a Thread for each servlet that is running. In the example below, we have triggered *HiHttpServlet* from two browser windows. We can see that both threads are running, and have stopped at the breakpoint (Figure 165).

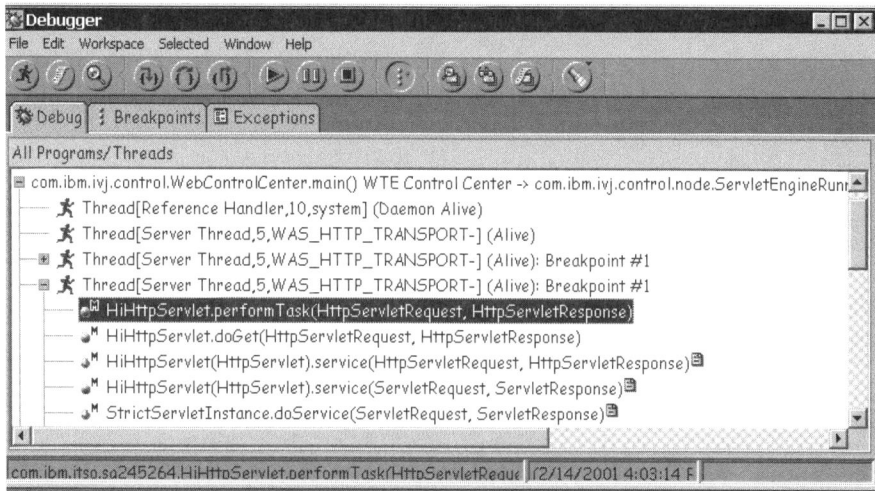

Figure 165. ServletEngineRunner threads

This is a useful technique to show thread interaction among servlets.

JSP Execution Monitor

The JSP Execution Monitor enables you to monitor the execution of JSP source, the JSP-generated Java source, and the HTML output. With the JSP Execution Monitor, you can efficiently monitor JSP run-time errors. The JSP Execution Monitor displays the mapping between the JSP and its associated Java source code, and enables you to insert breakpoints in the JSP source.

If you find an error in a JSP page, you can also modify the JSP source in a text editor, and then run the JSP source in the JSP Execution Monitor. To load the updated version of the JSP source into the JSP Execution Monitor, you simply have to refresh from the Web browser.

The JSP Execution Monitor highlights the location of syntax errors in both the JSP and JSP-generated Java source.

Launching the JSP Execution Monitor

To launch the JSP Execution Monitor, perform these steps:

- From the WebSphere Test Environment Control Center, select *JSP Execution Monitor Options.* The JSP Execution Monitor Option opens (Figure 166). (The default internal port number for the use of the JSP Execution Monitor is 8082. If port number 8082 is already in use, change the port number in the JSP Execution Monitor internal port number field.)

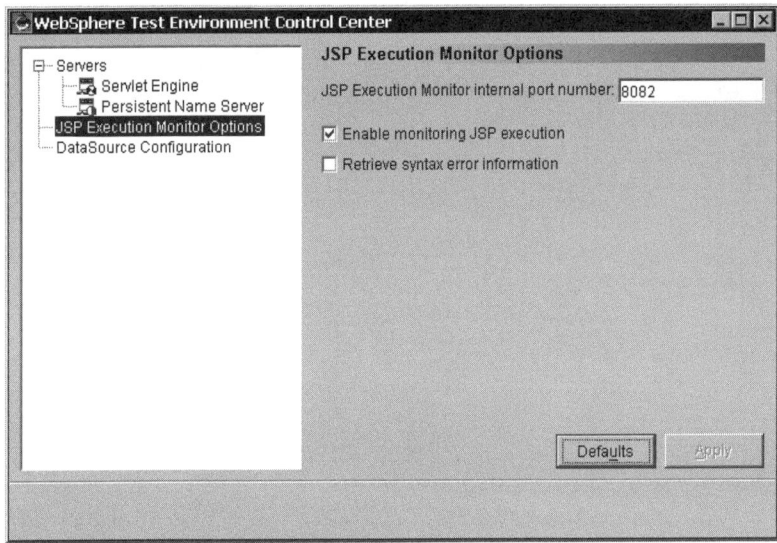

Figure 166. JSP Execution Monitor options

- By default, the JSP Execution Monitor mode is disabled. You must select *Enable monitoring JSP Execution* to activate monitoring when a JSP file gets loaded.

- By default, the *Load generated servlet externally* option is disabled. Selecting this option from Servlet Engine (Figure 156 on page 250) enables you to load a generated servlet, so that the servlet does not get imported into the IDE. We usually recommend leaving this unchecked because you do not get the class path options that were configured in the WebSphere Test Environment, and your JSPs might not load properly.

Stepping through the JSP

Follow these steps to run the *Very Simple* JSP example, and test its result:

- Start the *Servlet Engine*.
- Enable the JSP Execution Monitor.
- Enter the following browser command:
  http://127.0.0.1:8080/very_simple.jsp

The JSP Execution Monitor window appears and displays the current status of the JSP (Figure 167).

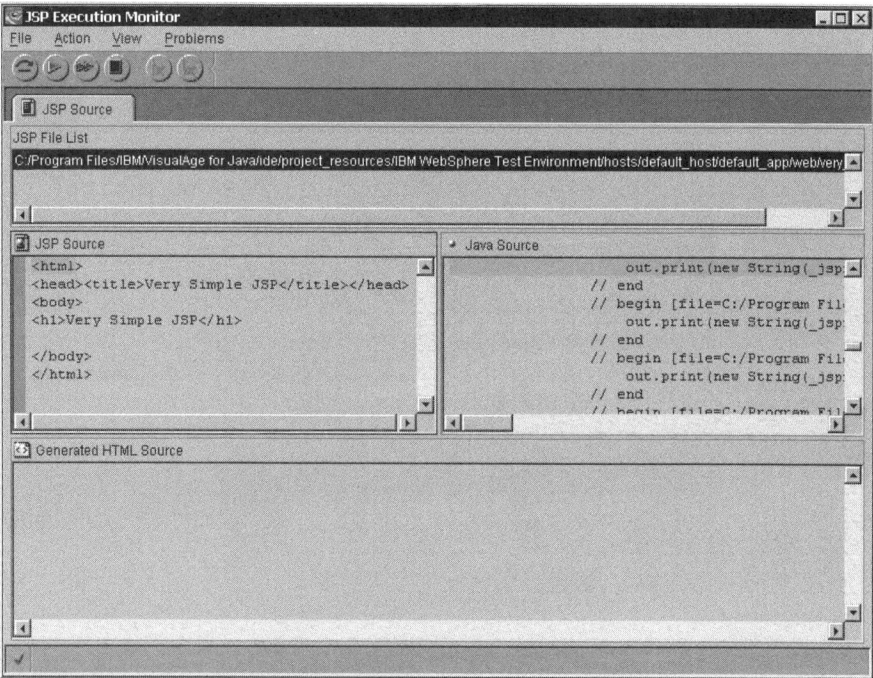

Figure 167. JSP Execution Monitor window

Similar to the debugger window for our servlets, you can step through this code, or run to completion. We can also fast-forward and terminate. Using the JSP source and Java source panes, you can see the JSP that was invoked, and the corresponding Java source file that was compiled, and walk through them simultaneously. The HTML output pane shows the JSP response that is generated.

Debugging JSP generated source code

We mentioned earlier that the compiled .java files for JSPs are stored in the file system (WebSphere Test Environment\temp). These files are also imported into the workspace, in the project *JSP Page Compile Generated Code*, and a package named after the \web subdirectory.

JSP compilation occurs when a JSP is invoked the first time (each time after starting the WebSphere Test Environment), or when the underlying JSP file is changed.

Because these servlets exist in the workspace, they are candidates for interactive debugging. You can set breakpoints in the JSP generated source servlets, and debug these servlets in the same way as you debugged the servlet. You can also step through the code using the JSP Execution Monitor, but this does not give you the ability to interactively change the variable values, or inspect the call stack or threads.

Debugging JSP without importing

As we mentioned, you can debug JSPs without importing the source code. You can select the option (Figure 168) that the debugger starts when the JSP's service method is invoked. You can also debug the JSP from its source code, instead of the generated Java source code. Debugging from the file system without import keeps the repository free from all the versions of JSPs.

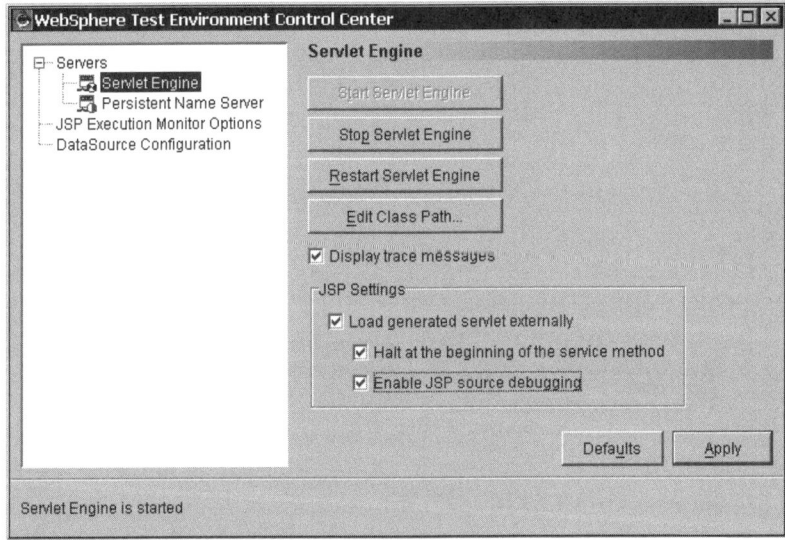

Figure 168. JSP settings

Persistent Name Server

The Persistent Name Server used to be associated with the application which uses JDBC 2.0 data source function. As we mentioned, one of the features of JDBC 2.0 is the ability to use a DataSource object to get a connection. A DataSource is an alias to a database. Using the DataSource object allows the Java program to request a connection to a database using the alias. To configure the DataSource definitions, select Persistent Name Server from WebSphere Test Environment Control Center (Figure 169).

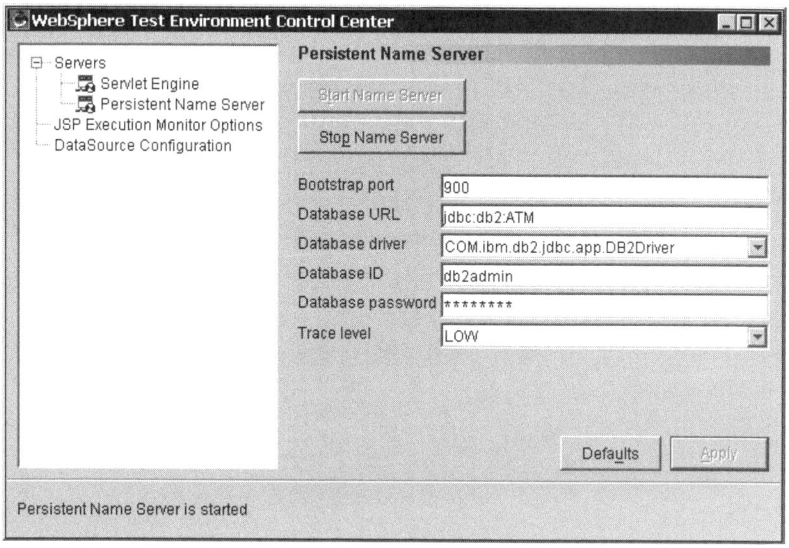

Figure 169. Persistence Name Server settings

The Persistent Name Server can store definitions in the InstantDB or in a relational database (DB2, Oracle, Sybase). To test your ATM Servlet which uses the datasource, you must start Persistent Name Server with URL jdbc:db2:ATM (ATM is database name, as we mentioned in the database chapter). Click the **Start Name Server** button and wait for the blue status indicator. Also look at the console window to see what is going on (Figure 170).

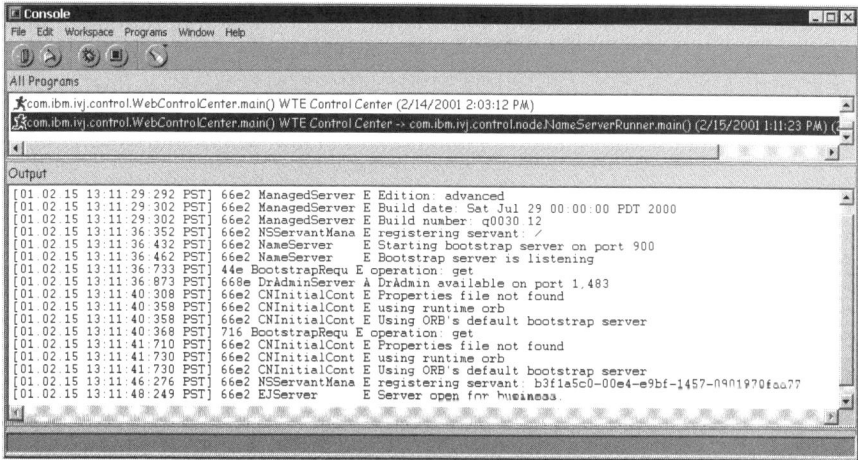

Figure 170. Persistence Name Server console

Specifying your data source

You need to configure your data source to use with your Web application. Once you configured your data source, the persistent name server handles the lookup request from the application and returns the DataSource object.

```
// Use JNDI to lookup the Data Source named "SampleDB"
    Context ctx = new InitialContext();
    DataSource ds = (DataSource)ctx.lookup("jdbc/ATM");
// Retrieve an open connection from the DataSource object.
    Connection con = ds.getConnection("db2admin", "db2admin");
```

Context is the reference to Persistent Name Server. And lookup method is the request to retrieve the data source. Once you received the data source object, you can get the connection through the data source.

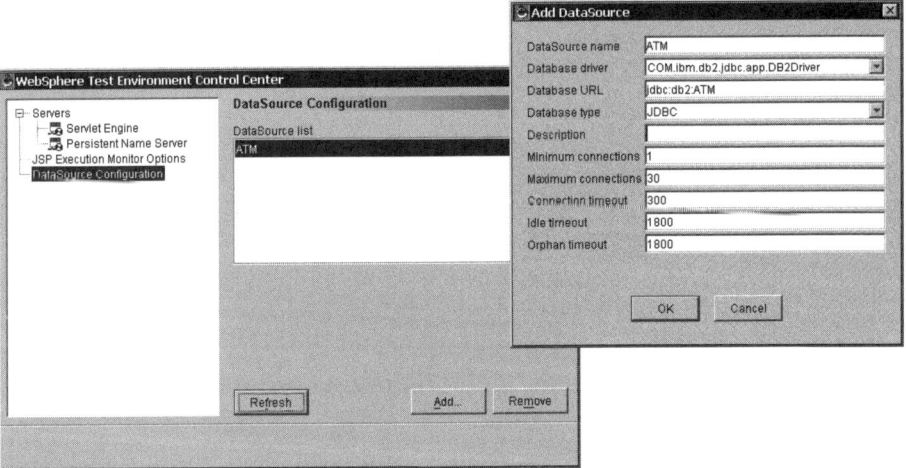

Figure 171. DataSource configuration

To configure the DataSource, the Persistent Name Server must be running. Click **Data Source Configuration**. You can see the current DataSource Configurations. To add a new configuration, click the **Add** button and set up the DataSource name to use with the lookup method, driver type, and actual URL (Figure 171).This facility allows testing of Web applications using the same code as is used in WebSphere Application Server. You cannot start the Persistent Name Server on port 900 if WebSphere Application Server is running on the same machine.

WebSphere Test Environment — advanced configuration

In the VisualAge for Java *WebSphere Test E*nvironment, all servlets and JSPs, by default, belong to the same default Web application. Thus, they share a common *ServletContext*, and can share resources even if we have defined them in different VisualAge projects.

In this section, we describe the WTE default configuration, as well as how and where to locate, build, and/or change servlet resources that your Web application might need. Being part of the same Web application, all servlets and JSPs that are launched through *WTE* share this same configuration. Keep this in mind when configuring the test environment.

Later, in "Configuring multiple Web applications" on page 271, we describe how to set up additional Web application environments in VisualAge for Java.

Types of resources

Servlets may require additional resources as part of a Web application. These could include active server resources, such as other servlets and JSPs, or passive resources, such as HTML files. Additionally, servlets may require access to servlet configuration files.

Resource locations

In this section, we use <IBMVJava> to describe the root path where VisualAge for Java is installed on your system, and <IBMVJavaWTE> for the resource directory of the IBM WebSphere Test Environment, for example:

```
<IBMVJava>:     d:\IBMVJava
<IBMVJavaWTE>:  d:\IBMVJava\ide\project_resources\IBM WebSphere Test Environment
```

WebSphere Test Environment root locations

These describe the default root locations for the server process:

- *Server root:* `<IBMVJava>\ide\project_resources\IBM WebSphere Test Environment`: This is the server root from which all paths are derived.

- *Default file root:* `<IBMVJava>\ide\project_resources\IBM Servlet IDE Utility class libraries\filename`. When running servlets that perform I/O and you do not specify a path, files will be created here, for example, SaveStats.ser, for a serialized file.

WebSphere Test Environment default application locations

By default, the WTE uses the following directory locations:

- *Document root:* `<IBMVJavaWTE>\hosts\default_host\default_app\web`, is the root directory for HTML and JSP files. For example, `index.html` and `very_simple.jsp` are found here, and are invoked through `http://localhost:8080/very_simple.jsp`.

- *Document root folders:* You can create additional folders under the document root for specific configurations, for example, `itsoservjsp`.

    The URL path for a JSP in this folder would be:
    `http://localhost:8080/itsoservjsp/myjsp.jsp`.

- *Compiled JSP:* `<IBMVJavaWTE>\temp\Jsp1_0\default_app\filename`. (For JSP 0.91 the directory is `\temp\default_app\pagecompile\filename`.) This is useful if you want to see the compiled JSP's servlet code.

- *Class path for servlets:* `<IBMVJavaWTE>\hosts\default_host\default_app\servlets`. This is where the default_app.webapp configuration file can be found.

Configuring project resources

If a servlet requires a configuration file (for example, `impleInitServlet.servlet`, which is an XML servlet configuration file), or a property file, you can place this file anywhere in the class path. However, we suggest using the following conventions in order to keep your various project resources separate:

- *Build project specific resource directory root:* `<IBMVJava>\ide\project_resources\ITSO`, is the ITSO VisualAge for Java 3.5 Redbook project resources root. This assumes that the ITSO Project has been added to the ServletEngine class path.

- *Build package directories:* You have to create fully qualified directories that match the servlet's package name.

Keep in mind that you can also manage your resource files in the workspace.

The key configuration files

The following three files are the primary files used to configure the WebSphere Test Environment. The configuration matches very closely the configuration in the WebSphere Application Server environment.

Servlet Engine

Location: `<IBMVJavaWTE>\properties\default.servlet_engine`

The default.servlet_engine file contains the definitions of Web applications and mime-types. By default, only one Web application, the default_app, is configured. We will see later how to configure additional Web applications.

```xml
<?xml version="1.0"?>
<websphere-servlet-engine name="servletEngine">
   <active-transport>http</active-transport>
   <transport>
      <name>http</name>
      <code>com.ibm.servlet.engine.http_transport.HttpTransport</code>
      <arg name="port" value="8080"/>
      <arg name="maxConcurrency" value="50"/>
      <arg name="server_root" value="$server_root$"/>
   </transport>

   <websphere-servlet-host name="default_host">
    <websphere-webgroup name="default_app">
       <description>Default WebGroup</description>
       <document-root>$approot$/web</document-root>
       <classpath>$approot$/servlets$psep$$server_root$/servlets</classpath>
       <root-uri>/</root-uri>
       <auto-reload enabled="true" polling-interval="3000"/>
       <shared-context>false</shared-context>
    </websphere-webgroup>
    <mime> ....</mime>
   </websphere-servlet-host>
   <hostname-binding hostname="localhost:8080" servlethost="default_host"/>
   <hostname-binding hostname="127.0.0.1:8080" servlethost="default_host"/>
</websphere-servlet-engine>
```

This is an XML formatted file. It is the main configuration file for the servlet engine. The key parameters are:

- *Virtual host:* `<websphere-servlet-host name="default_host">`. This tag defines the virtual host in the servlet engine.

- *webgroup tag:* `<websphere-webgroup name="default_app">`. This tag defines the Web application deployment bindings within the servlet engine.

- *Hostname bindings:* `<hostname-binding hostname="localhost" servlethost="default_host">`. This tag is for binding a DNS name to a virtual host.

- *MIME types:* This tag defines a mime type mapping for the virtual host.

default_app.webapp

Location: `<IBMVJavaWTE>\hosts\default_host\default_app\servlets\default_app.webapp`

The default_app.webapp file contains the specifications of the default Web application. This file is in the hosts\default_host\default_app\servlets subdirectory.

It is configured with 4 utility servlets:

```xml
<?xml version="1.0"?>
<webapp>
   <name>default</name>
   <description>default application</description>
   <error-page>/ErrorReporter</error-page>

   <servlet>
      <name>ErrorReporter</name>
      <description>Default error reporter servlet</description>
      <code>com.ibm.servlet.engine.webapp.DefaultErrorReporter</code>
      <servlet-path>/ErrorReporter</servlet-path>
      <autostart>true</autostart>
   </servlet>

   <servlet>
      <name>invoker</name>
      <description>Auto-registration servlet</description>
      <code>com.ibm.servlet.engine.webapp.InvokerServlet</code>
      <servlet-path>/servlet</servlet-path>
      <autostart>true</autostart>
   </servlet>

   <servlet>
      <name>jsp</name>
      <description>JSP support servlet</description>

      <!--
      <code>com.ibm.ivj.jsp.debugger.pagecompile.IBMPageCompileServlet</code>
      -->
      <code>com.ibm.ivj.jsp.runtime.JspDebugServlet</code>

      <init-parameter>
         <name>workingDir</name>
         <value>$server_root$/temp/default_app</value>
      </init-parameter>
      <init-parameter>
         <name>jspemEnabled</name>
         <value>true</value>
      </init-parameter>
      <init-parameter>
         <name>scratchdir</name>
         <value>$server_root$/temp/JSP1_0/default_app</value>
      </init-parameter>
      <init-parameter>
         <name>keepgenerated</name>
         <value>true</value>
      </init-parameter>
      <autostart>true</autostart>
      <servlet-path>*.jsp</servlet-path>
   </servlet>

   <servlet>
      <name>file</name>
      <description>File serving servlet</description>
      <code>com.ibm.servlet.engine.webapp.SimpleFileServlet</code>
      <servlet-path>/</servlet-path>
      <init-parameter>
         <name></name>
         <value></value>
      </init-parameter>
      <autostart>true</autostart>
   </servlet>
</webapp>
```

The key parameters are:

- *Error page:* `<error-page>/ErrorReporter/</error-page>`, the URI page that is called in response to an error during the processing of a servlet; it can be a customized servlet, JSP, or HTML file.

- *Servlet properties:* `<servlet> <name>myser</name> <code>MyServlet</code> <init-parameter> <name>key</name> <value>123</value> <servlet-path>/servlet</servlet-path> <autostart>true</autostart> ... </servlet>`, defines a servlet within a Web application. There can be many servlets defined in this file. A user defined servlet in our application does not have to be defined here (by default, it will be invoked by its class name), but we can use this to specify some additional servlet properties, such as the name (alias) that we use in the browser, and configuration parameters. This defintion is necessary for call by short name and for servlet chaining.

- *Invoker servlet:* `<servlet> <name>invoker</name> <servlet-path>/servlet </servlet-path> ... </servlet>`, is a special servlet that allows us to load a class by name. The servlet-path value of */servlet* specifies the URL prefix used to invoke servlets in the browser.

- *JSP:* `<servlet> <name>jsp</name> <code>...</code> </servlet>`, is a special servlet that is used to compile JSPs. The init parameter of *jspemEnable* allows us to enable or disable JSP Execution Monitor support. The class specified in the `<code>` tag specifies the level of JSP support:

    - `com.ibm.ivj.jsp.runtime.JspDebugServlet` (JSP 1.0)
    - `com.ibm.ivj.jsp.debugger.pagecompile.IBMPageCompileServlet` (JSP 0.91)

    By default JSP 1.0 is enabled and you have to change the class name of the servlet to use JSP 0.91. This is the configuration file for the default Web application.

- *Error Reporter:* `<servlet> <name>ErrorReporter</name> ...< /servlet>`, is a special servlet that handles the error reporting in our application.

session.xml

Location: `<IBMVJavaWTE>\properties\session.xml`

This controls the WebSphere Session Management functions in the servlet engine.

```
<?xml version="1.0" ?>
- <session>
  <sessions-enabled>true</sessions-enabled>
  <session-manager-name>Session Manager</session-manager-name>
- <session-data>
  <url-rewriting-enabled>false</url-rewriting-enabled>
  <protocol-switch-rewrite-enabled>false</protocol-switch-rewrite-enabled>
```

```xml
- <cookie-data>
  <enabled>true</enabled>
  <name>sesessionid</name>
  <comment>WebSphere Session Support</comment>
  <domain />
  <maximum />
  <path>/</path>
  <secure>false</secure>
  </cookie-data>
  <timeout>1800</timeout>
  <size>1000</size>
  <enable-overflow>true</enable-overflow>
  <enable-measurements>true</enable-measurements>
  </session-data>
- <session-store>
  <persistent-store>false</persistent-store>
  <persistence-type>directodb</persistence-type>
  <persistence-database>db2</persistence-database>
  <persistence-multirowschema>false</persistence-multirowschema>
  <persistence-cache>true</persistence-cache>
  <persistence-asyncupdate>false</persistence-asyncupdate>
  <persistence-connectionsize>50</persistence-connectionsize>
  <persistence-datasource-name>jdbc/db2/sample</persistence-datasource-name>
  </session-store>
- <db2-info>
  <driver>COM.ibm.db2.jdbc.app.DB2Driver</driver>
  <tablename>sessions</tablename>
  <url>jdbc:db2:was</url>
  <owner />
  <userid />
  <password />
  <native-access>false</native-access>
  </db2-info>
- <oracle-info>
  <driver>oracle.jdbc.driver.OracleDriver</driver>
  <tablename>sessions</tablename>
  <url>jdbc:oracle:oci8:@</url>
  <owner>scott</owner>
  <userid>scott</userid>
  <password>tiger</password>
  </oracle-info>
- <mssql-info>
  <driver>COM.ibm.db2.jdbc.app.DB2Driver</driver>
  <tablename>sessions</tablename>
  <url>jdbc:db2:sessions</url>
  <owner>none</owner>
  <userid>none</userid>
  <password>none</password>
  </mssql-info>
  </session>
```

The session.xml file controls if sessions and URL rewriting are enabled.

WebSphere Test Environment — multiple Web applications

The WebSphere Test Environment can be configured to have multiple Web applications. Web applications are specified in the default.servlet_engine file, where you can add additional <websphere-webgroup> tags. For each Web application you have to create the directory structure:

```
<IBMVJavaWTE>\hosts\default_host\..webapp..\servlet
<IBMVJavaWTE>\hosts\default_host\..webapp..\web
```

This configuration gives you the following control over your Web application environment:

- You can run multiple Web applications with their own document root configurations
- You can set the servlet class path individually for each Web application
- You can define individual Web application servlet contexts

The following section describes how to configure the environment for a tailored Web application, in addition to the default application.

Configuring multiple Web applications

In this section, we build a new Web application, *itso*, to run our examples. The following sections walk us through the steps to configure the *ServletEngine* for two Web applications.

Create new directories

Create the following directories under the WTE root directory
`<IBMVJava>\ide\project_resources\IBM WebSphere Test Environment`:

- `\hosts\default_host\itso\servlet` — class path for servlets, and location of the .webapp file
- `\hosts\default_host\itso\web` — document root (for testing, we suggest you include an index.html document in this directory)
- `\temp\JSP1_0\itso` — scratch directory for compiled JSPs

You have to create these three directories for each Web application that you define.

Modify default.servlet_engine

Edit the `<IBMVJavaWTE>\default.servlet_engine` file to set up the itsoservjsp Web application. We suggest that you back up this file first prior to making any changes. Add a <websphere-webgroup> for itso below the websphere-servlet-host:

```
<websphere-servlet-host name="default_host">
<websphere-webgroup name="itso">
   <description>ITSO Redbook</description>
   <document-root>$approot$/web</document-root>
```

```
<classpath>$approot$/servlets$psep$$server_root$/servlets</classpath>
   <root-uri>/itso</root-uri>
   <auto-reload enabled="true" polling-interval="3000"/>
   <shared-context>false</shared-context>
</websphere-webgroup>
```

In this definition, we set the `<root-uri>` to `/itso`, so that servlets are invoked with `http://localhost:8080/itso/servletname`.

With this configuration, we should be able to call HTML files, servlets, and JSP for the itsoservjsp Web application as:

```
http://localhost:8080/itso/index.html
http://localhost:8080/itso/myPackage.myServletClass
http://localhost:8080/itso/myJSP.jsp
```

Create a new itso.webapp file

We use the `default_app.webapp` file as our initial template. Copy the file into the new servlets directory (`<IBMVJavaWTE>\hosts\itso\servlets`) and rename it as `itso.webapp`. This provides us with some basic support, such as the ErrorReporter, Invoker, and JSP servlets.

Customize the `itso.webapp` file as follows:

- Provide a tailored name and a description for the application:

```
<webapp>
   <name>itso</name>
   <description>ITSO Redbook</description>
```

- Change the JSP servlet to use JSP 1.0 and point to the correct directories for compiled JSPs:

```
<servlet>
   <name>jsp</name><description>JSP support servlet</description>
   <code>com.ibm.ivj.jsp.runtime.JspDebugServlet</code>
   <init-parameter>  <name>workingDir</name>
      <value>$server_root$/temp/itso</value>  </init-parameter>
   ...

   <init-parameter>  <name>scratchdir</name>
      <value>$server_root$/temp/JSP1_0/itso</value>  </init...>
   ...
</servlet>
```

- Configure one servlet for this application to demonstrate how to specify specific servlet parameters and an alias:

```
<servlet>
    <name>HiHttpServlet</name>
    <description>Hi Http Servlet</description>
    <code>com.ibm.itso.sg245264.HiHttpServlet</code>
    <servlet-path>/simple</servlet-path>
    <init-parameter>
        <name>xxxxxxxx</name>  <value>yyyyyyyy</value>
    </init-parameter>
    <autostart>true</autostart>
</servlet>
```

You can later configure additional servlets.

Using the ServletEngineConfigDumper servlet

The *ServletEngineConfigDumper* servlet is a servlet provided in IBM JSP Samples project.

```
com.ibm.ivj.wte.samples.servletconfig.ServletEngineConfigDumper
```

Running the servlet

To run this servlet, enter the following URL:

```
http://localhost:8080/servlet/com.ibm.ivj.wte.samples.servletconfig.ServletEngineConfigDumper
```

You need add IBM JSP Samples project to the class path before run. Figure 172 shows a partial display of the servlet output that is generated.

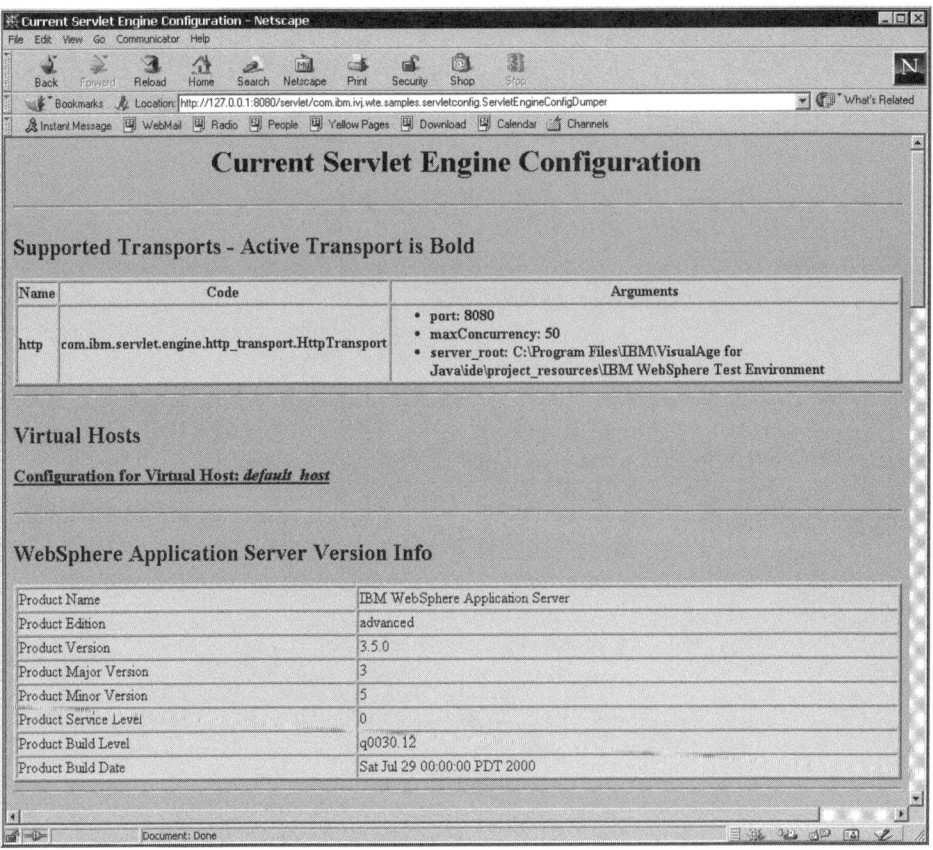

Figure 172. Servlet engine configuration

Chapter 10. Using relational databases

Java can be used to access relational databases without using vendor-specific or platform-specific APIs. Two standard techniques exist for accessing relational databases in Java, JDBC, and SQLJ. In addition, Visual Age for Java offers Data Access Beans. The JDBC API is a dynamic SQL API for Java. It can be used to build dynamic queries, perform updates, call stored procedures, and create tables.

The JDBC API is the most common way to access the database from Java. SQLJ is an ANSI standard for embedding static SQL statements in Java and creating stored procedures. Both SQLJ and JDBC can be used in the same program. It is possible to query a database using JDBC then process the results using SQLJ. The reverse is also possible. The data access beans provided by VisualAge for Java allow us to visually create queries, updates and call stored procedures, without having to know SQL or write code (see Table 11).

Table 11. Accessing relational data in Java

Name	Description
JDBC	This is a dynamic SQL API for Java, which should be used if explicit control is needed. The SQL is not validated against the database.
SQLJ	This is a way to embed static SQL statements into Java code. SQL variables can be used. The SQL is validated against the database and an access path is generated. Can be used if a programmer is more comfortable with SQL than JDBC. SQLJ code must be translated into Java code then compiled into a Java class.
Data Access Beans	This is a set of Java beans that allow database access to be built visually. This should be used for rapid prototyping or whenever manual coding is not desired. Knowledge of SQL is not required.

JDBC 2.0

JDBC 2.0 is implemented with the packages java.sql and javax.sql. A JDBC application gets a connection to the database using a JDBC driver. The driver hides the details of connecting to a particular database. Once the application has a connection, it can then submit queries, submit updates, call stored procedures and modify the database. When the application is finished accessing the database, it closes the connection.

One of the features of JDBC 2.0 is the ability to use a DataSource object to get a connection. A DataSource is an alias to a database. Using the DataSource object allows the Java program to request a connection to a database using the alias. The alias is resolved by JNDI to the real database URL and JDBC driver. The program does not need to know which JDBC driver is used, nor the URL to the database. The following code snippet shows establishing a connection to the DataSource "SampleDB", running a query, then closing the connection:

```java
import java.sql.*;
import javax.sql.*;
import javax.naming.*;
public class testJDBCclass
{
// Use JNDI to lookup the Data Source named "SampleDB"
    Context ctx = new InitialContext();
    DataSource ds = (DataSource)ctx.lookup("jdbc/SampleDB");
// Retrieve an open connection from the DataSource object.
    Connection con = ds.getConnection("username", "password");

//Create and run a query. The cursor can be moved forward or backward.
    PreparedStatement stmt = con.prepareStatement("Select * from SALES",
ResultSet.TYPE_SCROLL_INSENSITIVE, ResultSet.CONCUR_READ_ONLY);
    ResultSet rs = stmt.executeQuery();
// process the result set 'rs'
// ....
    con.close(); //close the connection
}
```

In order to use a DataSource in our ATM application, it must be added to the WebSphere Test Environment for testing and to the WebSphere Application Server for deployment. Refer to the section "Specifying your data source" on page 264.

Visual Age for Java also supports the older JDBC 1.1 method of getting a connection using the DriverManager. To use this method, the programmer must provide the JDBC driver class name and the URL to the desired database. These two pieces of information can be externalized using parameters or a properties file, but typically they end up hard-coded in an application.

The following code sample shows how to use the DriverManager to get a connection:

```
import java.sql.*;

public class testoldJDBCclass
{
//Declare the class name of the JDBC driver.
Class.forName("COM.ibm.db2.jdbc.app.DB2Driver");
//Get an open connection from the DriverManager by supplying the URL
// to the database, the user name, and password.
      Connection con  = DriverManager.getConnection("jdbc:db2:SAMPLE",
"username", "password");

//Create and run a query.
      PreparedStatement stmt = con.prepareStatement("Select * from
OSAMURS2.SALES");
      ResultSet rs = stmt.executeQuery();

// process the result set 'rs'
....
con.close();//close the connection
}
```

In order for these two Java programs to work, the location of the JDBC driver must be added to the classpath of both the VisualAge for Java workspace and the WebSphere Test Environment. Figure 173 demonstrates adding the DB2 JDBC driver to the workspace classpath. The Options window can be reached under the Window menu.

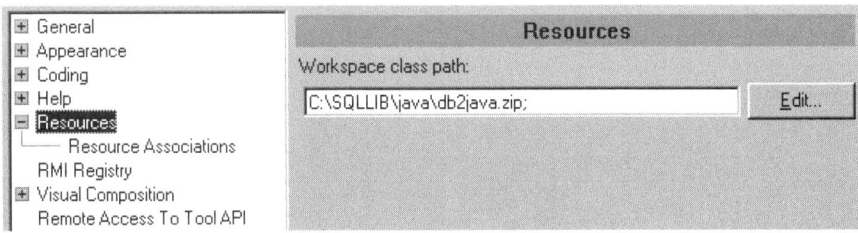

Figure 173. Add a JDBC driver to the workspace classpath

The exact name of the JDBC driver class and the URL are provided by the driver vendor. The URL for a JDBC database always uses the following syntax: jdbc:<subprotocol>:<subname> The URL is in the code sample is "jdbc:db2:SAMPLE" which connects to a DB2 database named SAMPLE:

- jdbc is the name of the protocol.
- <subprotocol> is the protocol used within a JDBC driver. This is usually the name of the driver.
- <subname> is a mechanism to identify the database. This is usually the database name.

DataSource versus DriverManager

Using a DataSource object is the recommended method for getting a connection. This approach allows the application to take advantage of connection pooling and distributed transactions. Another advantage is that the connection details can be maintained outside of the application. The only limitation is that the JDBC driver must support JDBC 2.0 in order to use the DataSource object. No matter which method is used, the JDBC driver must be in the classpath.

Queries and result sets

The JDBC package contains several classes that act as containers for sending SQL statements to the database. The class names are Statement and PreparedStatement, which is a child of Statement. These classes have methods for executing queries and retrieving the results of the query. The result of a query is kept in a class called ResultSet. The result set contains methods to access all the rows and columns retrieved. It is similar in some ways to an SQL cursor. The result set methods "previous" and "next" changes the current row position. The following code snippet shows the execution of a query and printing each row returned. Note: The con variable refers to an open database connection.

```
String name = "GOUNOT";
PreparedStatement stmt = con.prepareStatement("Select * from
OSAMURS2.SALES WHERE SALES_PERSON = '" + name + "'");

ResultSet rs = stmt.executeQuery();
while(rs.next()){
   out.println( rs.getString("SALES_PERSON") + " " +
rs.getString("REGION"));
}
stmt.close();
```

Stored procedures

Most relational database systems support writing and calling stored procedures. A stored procedure is similar to a static method in Java — it cannot access any class variables. It does a predefined task based on the parameters. Typically stored procedures are a collection of SQL statements written in a database-specific language. Fortunately they can now be written in Java, using JDBC and SQLJ. One of the advantages of writing a stored procedure in Java is that it can be called by any language that supports calling stored procedures. The calling program does not need to know that the procedure is written in Java. For more information about authoring stored procedures in Java read "JDBC API Tutorial and Reference, Second Edition"

In this chapter, we will focus on calling an existing stored procedure. The JDBC class CallableStatement is used to define and call a stored procedure. The CallableStatement class is a child of the PreparedStatement class. The following code sample calls an existing stored procedure named "SALESPROC" which is part of the database schema named "ITSO". This procedure accepts two input parameters which are set to the values of "LEE" and 15.

```
CallableStatement stmt = con.prepareCall("{call ITSO.SALESPROC(?, ?)}");
stmt.setString(1, "LEE");
stmt.setInt(2, 15);
ResultSet rs = stmt.executeQuery();
```

In the above code sample, the ? symbol acts as a place-holder for the input parameters. The setter method used (that is, set String, setFloat, setInt) depends on what type of parameter the procedure is expecting. The procedure named "SALESPROC" expects a string and an integer. The executeQuery method calls the stored procedure and returns a ResultSet object to the variable, rs. The result set in rs is used to access the results from the stored procedure, as shown in the section, "Queries and result sets" on page 278.

Updating the database

JDBC allows us to manipulate the database by inserting, updating, and deleting tables and rows. The JDBC classes that allow database modifications are the Statement and PreparedStatement classes, that were introduced in Chapter , "Queries and result sets" on page 278 The statement class provides a method named ExecuteUpdate which takes a String as a parameter. The parameter string is the SQL that will change the database.

The following code shows the insertion of one row into the "CARDS" table.

```
String insertstr = "INSERT INTO CARDS (CARD_NUM, OWNER, PIN )" +"VALUES
    ('124', 'Mitchell Gladstone', '124')";
Statement stmt = con.createStatement();
stmt.executeUpdate(insertstr);
stmt.close();
```

Using SQLJ inside Visual Age for Java

The SQLJ ANSI X3.135.10-1998 Standard can be found at:

http://www.sqlj.org/

When importing SQLJ into the project, use the "resource" tab in the workbench for adding SQLJ files. These can handle adding an entire directory of files at one time.

During translation, the dialog in Figure 174 is displayed:

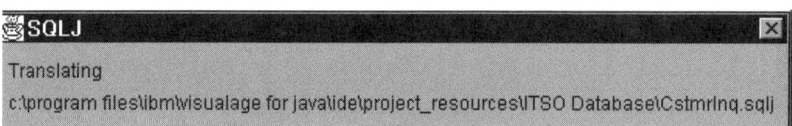

Figure 174. dialog during translation process.

The following code sample shows output in the Visual Age console:

```
[Translating 1 files.]
[Reading file CstmrInq]
[Translating file CstmrInq]
C:\Program Files\IBM\VisualAge for
Java\ide\program\..\..\ivjtools\temp\Temp414\CstmrInq.sqlj:50.2-50.93:
Info: [Registered JDBC drivers: COM.ibm.db2.jdbc.app.DB2Driver]
C:\Program Files\IBM\VisualAge for
Java\ide\program\..\..\ivjtools\temp\Temp414\CstmrInq.sqlj:50.2-50.93:
Info: [Connecting to user db2admin at jdbc:db2:SAMPLE]
C:\Program Files\IBM\VisualAge for
Java\ide\program\..\..\ivjtools\temp\Temp414\CstmrInq.sqlj:50.2-50.93:
Info: [Querying database with "select FIRSTNME    from OSAMURS2.EMPLOYEE
where ( EMPNO = ?  ) "]
```

Figure 175 and Figure 176, respectively, show the workspace SQLJ menu and the SQLJ Properties window.

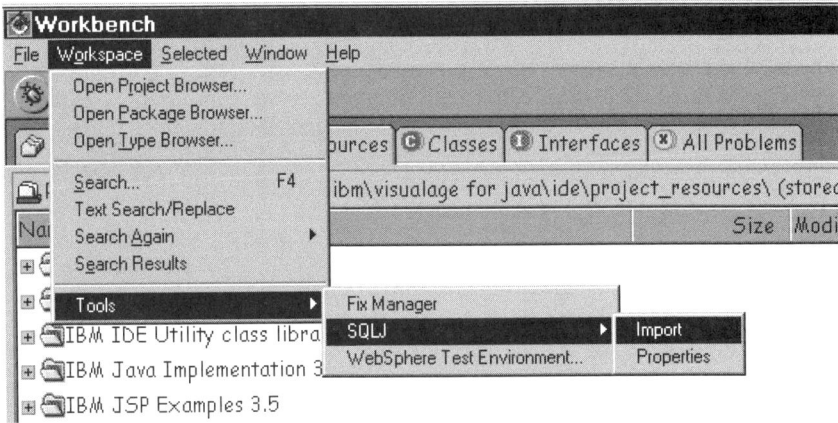

Figure 175. Workspace SQLJ menu

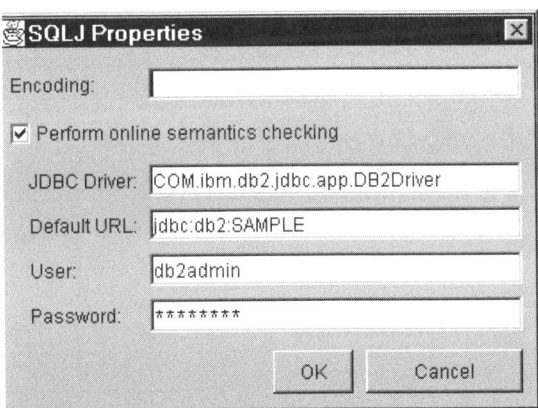

Figure 176. SQLJ Properties window

Data access beans

Visual Age for Java 3.5 allows us to write JDBC code by hand, as illustrated in the previous sections. VisualAge for Java also provides Data Access Beans which will generate the code for us. Before using the Data Access Beans, this feature must be added to the workspace. To add this feature go to **File->Quick Start**. Then choose **Feature-> Add Feature->Data Access Beans 3.5**.

Table 12 summarizes characteristics of the data access beans.

Table 12. Summary of data access beans

Bean name	Description	Visual or non-visual
Select	Used to query a database. Can be used as a table model	non-visual
Modify	Used to insert, change, or delete records.	non-visual
Procedure Call	Used to call an existing stored procedure. Can be used as a Swing table model	non-visual
Navigation	Used to run or navigate the output of a Select or Procedure Call bean. It can also be used to commit or rollback changes.	visual — This is a Swing component
CellSelector	Provides access to a single cell from a query or stored procedure call.	non-visual
CellRangeSelector	Provides access to a subset of the results of a query or stored procedure call.	non-visual
ColumnSelector	Provided access to a single column of data from a query or stored procedure call.	non-visual
RowSelector	Provides access to a single row of data from a query or stored procedure call.	non-visual

To use the Select, Modify, and Procedure Call beans in a Java class, you need to follow these general steps:

1. Open the Class Browser window and go to the "Visual Composition" tab.
2. Change the pull-down menu in the left portion of the window to "Database" as shown in Figure 179 on page 287.
3. Click and drag the Select, Modify, or Procedure Call bean onto the free-form surface as shown in Figure 180 on page 287.
4. Double-click the new bean instance from the free-form surface in order to view the Properties window. The default name for the new bean is "<beanname>1".

5. Bring up the Properties window for the bean added in step 4. For a Select bean change the "query" property. For a Modify bean change the "action" property. For a ProcedureCall bean change the "procedure" property. This opens up the Query SmartGuide window. The Properties window for a Select bean is shown in Figure 181 on page 288.

6. Use the Query SmartGuide to specify a database access class and connection to use. You can use an existing database access class or create a new one. In addition you can use an existing connection or create a new one. In a simple query application that only accesses one database, only a single database access class and a single connection is needed. At runtime, each connection corresponds to one physical connection to the database.

7. Click on the SQL tab to name and specify the SQL. You can specify the SQL manually or use the SQL Smart Assist Guide. The SQL Smart Assist Guide will allow the SQL to be built visually. It will also test the SQL against the database.

8. After clicking **OK** on the Query SmartGuide window, the Properties window should show "sql name:connection name" for the property that was set.

9. If you need to modify the generated code in the database access class, then look in the workbench for the database access class. It show part of the project and package selected when the bean was created. The data access bean will contain one static method for each connection and for each SQL statement created in the Query SmartGuide.

Refer to Figure 177 for an illustration of the relationship between the data access bean, queries, connections, and select beans.

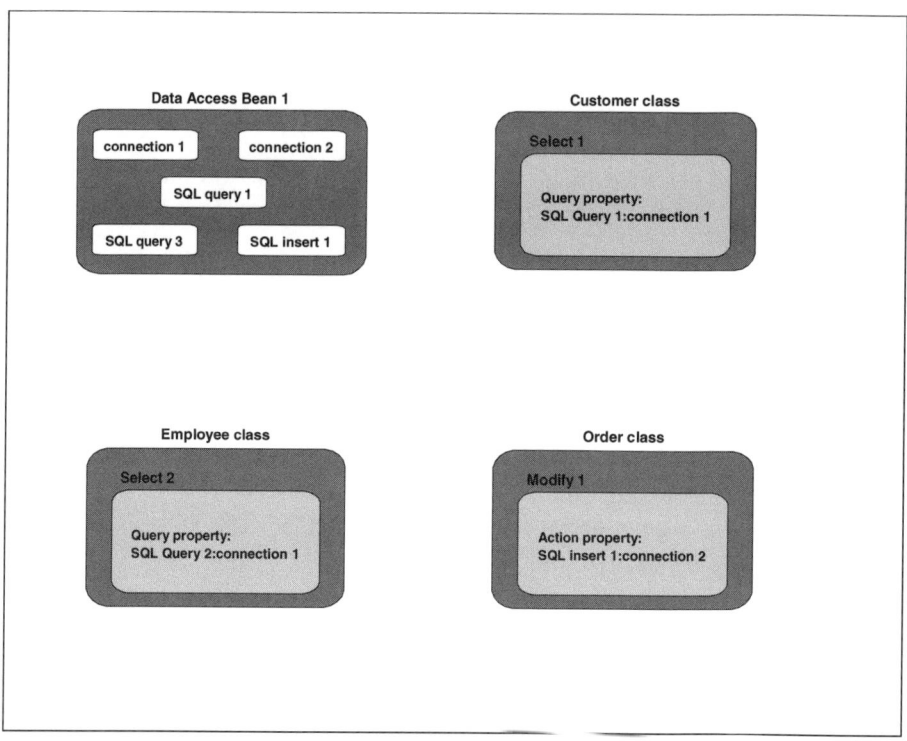

Figure 177. Relationship between the select and modify objects

When creating a new data access bean, it can be placed in any package. If a different package than the current package is used, then one of the following steps must be done:

a. The package containing the data access bean is added to the current project.

OR

b. The package containing the data access bean is added to the classpath.

Making the ATM persistent

In Chapter 4, "Beginning the ATM project" on page 73, many classes were developed, but none are persistent. Whenever the applications shut down, all data is lost. To make our ATM application more robust, we would like to store all cards issued, all accounts, the relationship of particular cards with particular accounts, and transactions that have been completed. For our ATM application, we are going to store all this information in a relational database named ATM. In this chapter we will make the Card class persistent. In the sample code included with this book, the account class and transaction class are also persistent. They were made persistent with the same technique that is shown here for the card class.

Prerequisites

To complete this example and to run the complete ATM application, you will need a relational database and a JDBC 2.0 driver for the database. You will also need to create a database named "ATM" The ATM application we develop uses DB2 Universal Database 7.0 running on Windows NT. This chapter also assumes that DB2 and TCP/IP are successfully running on your machine. Since we are using the data access beans, the jar containing these beans will need to be in the classpath for deployment. The jar can be found root\eab\runtime30\ivjdab.jar where root is the directory where Visual Age for Java is installed. Also, the database access beans feature must be added to the workspace.

Creating tables

Before you create the sample programs, you will need to run the com.ibm.itso.sg245264.atm.CreateTables class (Figure 178). This creates the tables and adds some sample data they require to run the sample programs. To run this class, you need to create ATM database, because the create database function is not supported by any JDBC APIs.

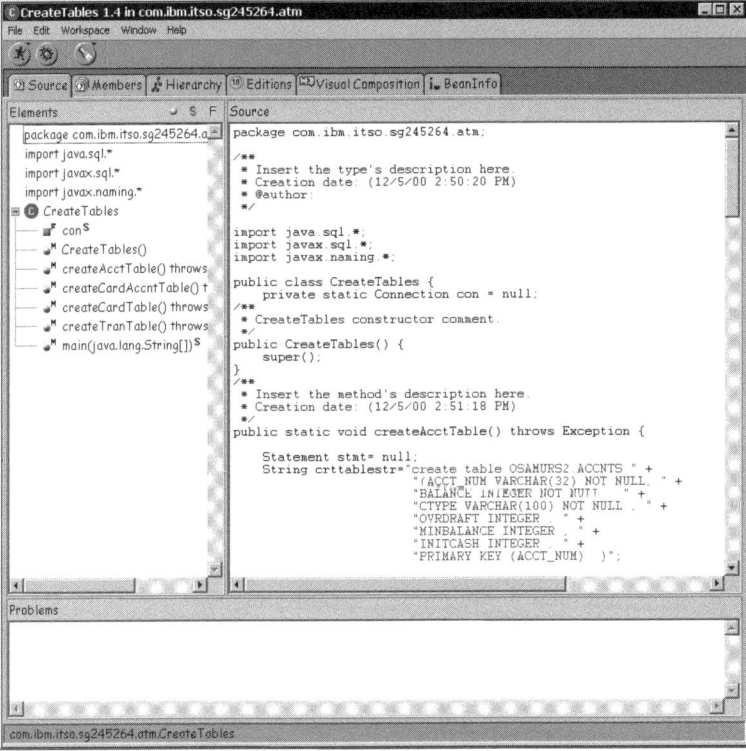

Figure 178. CreateTable class

Making the card class persistent

The first step in making the card class persistent is to open the class browser Visual Composition tab. Then change the bean palette to Database as shown in Figure 179. Then add the Select bean to the free form surface as shown in Figure 180.

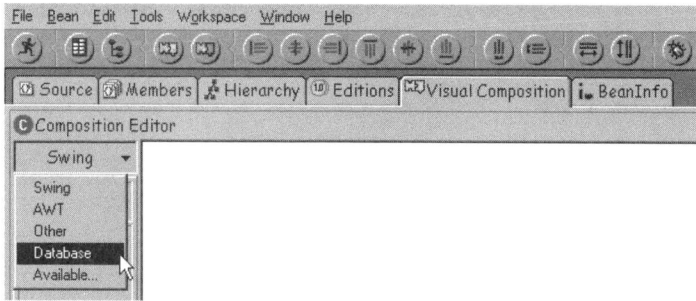

Figure 179. Change the VCE palette to the data access beans

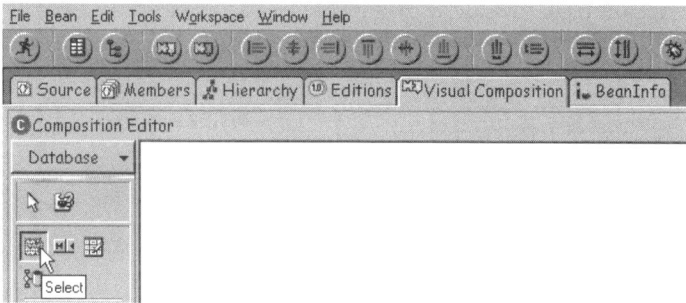

Figure 180. Choose the Select data access bean

Creating the Select beans

Now we will create three Select beans:

- CardSelect bean

  Return a card class related to specified card number.

- CardSelectAll bean

  Return all card classes.

- CardAcctSelect bean

  Return an account number related to specified card number.

Card Select bean

Now we would like to define an unique card selection method in Card class. First of all, we create a new database access class which contains a database connection and each SQL statement that requires in card class.

Creating a new database access class

Open the property dialog of the Select bean and open the query definition dialog by clicking a button located on the right of the query field (Figure 181).

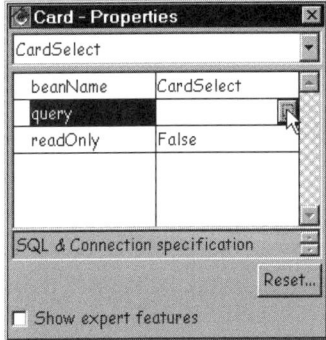

Figure 181. Properties window for the Select bean

We need to have a new class to access the ATM database. Click the **New** button on the Query dialog and name it to **CardDAB**, then click **OK** to close (Figure 182).

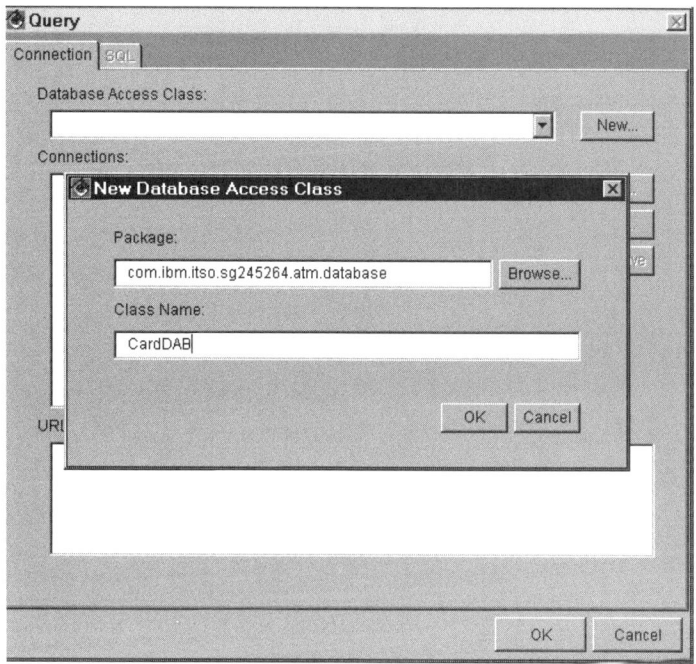

Figure 182. New database access class

Connection Alias Definition

We need to have a connection to the ATM database. Click **add...** button on the Query dialog and define the database connection. Set conn1 as the connection name. This will be a method of CardDAB class and returns database connection handle for Data Access Bean. Select Driver Manager instead of Data Source at this time and set URL as jdbc:db2:ATM. We used type 2 driver **COM.ibm.db2.app.DB2Driver** to access to DB2 because we do not assume this class will be used at remote location such as an applet.

Auto commit is the default in the JDBC environment and we leave it as the default, but we suggest not to use auto commit in a real complex transaction environment. The application should have responsibility to commit after all update/inserts has done well. Set a userid and password which can access to your database ATM. If you do not set them, default windows userid/password will be used. Or click **Prompt for logon ID and password before connecting** to ask user to input those.

Figure 183 shows a sample connection definition.

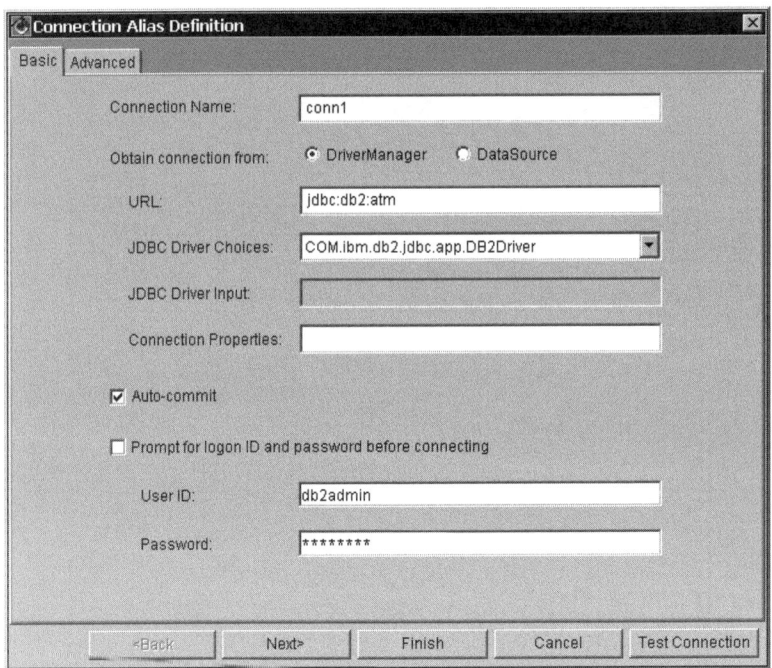

Figure 183. Connection Alias Definition

Once you have defined your connection, click the **Test Connection** button to test that your definition is correct. You will see a message "The connection is successful", if your definition has no problem. Click the **Finish** button to save your definition. You can see the code that was generated by the Connection Alias Definition. To see the code, go to the Workbench and see the conn1 method on com.ibm.itso.sg245264.atm.database.CardDAB class:

```
public static com.ibm.db.DatabaseConnection conn1() throws java.lang.Throwable,
com.ibm.db.DataException {
  com.ibm.db.DatabaseConnection connection = null;
  try{
    connection = new com.ibm.db.DatabaseConnection();
    connection.setConnectionAlias("com.ibm.itso.sg245264.atm.database.CardDAB.conn1");
    connection.setDriverName("COM.ibm.db2.jdbc.app.DB2Driver");
    connection.setDataSourceName("jdbc:db2:atm");
    connection.setUserID("db2admin");
    connection.setPromptUID(false);
    connection.setAutoCommit(true);
    connection.setPassword("acedg0574g0864623261646d696e", true);
  }
  catch(com.ibm.db.DataException e){throw e;}
  catch(java.lang.Throwable e){throw e;}
  return connection;
}
```

Create a new SQL specification

Now we will define an SQL statement that select a unique card record by card number from the card database. Click the SQL tab to show the SQL view (the SQL tab is not selectable unless you define the database connection. Use the **CardDAB** class as the container of our SQLs and then click the **Add** button to create a new SQL statement using **SQL Assist SmartGuide**. Type **CardSelectSQL** as the name of SQL, then click **OK** (Figure 184).

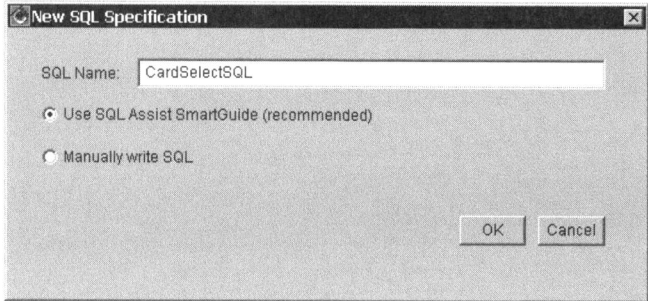

Figure 184. New SQL Specification

Define an SQL specification

You can construct your SQL using the SQL Assist SmartGuide.
To create an SQL statement to get a unique card-by-card number, select **DB2ADMIN.CARDS** as the select table and choose **Select Unique** as the statement type (Figure 185).

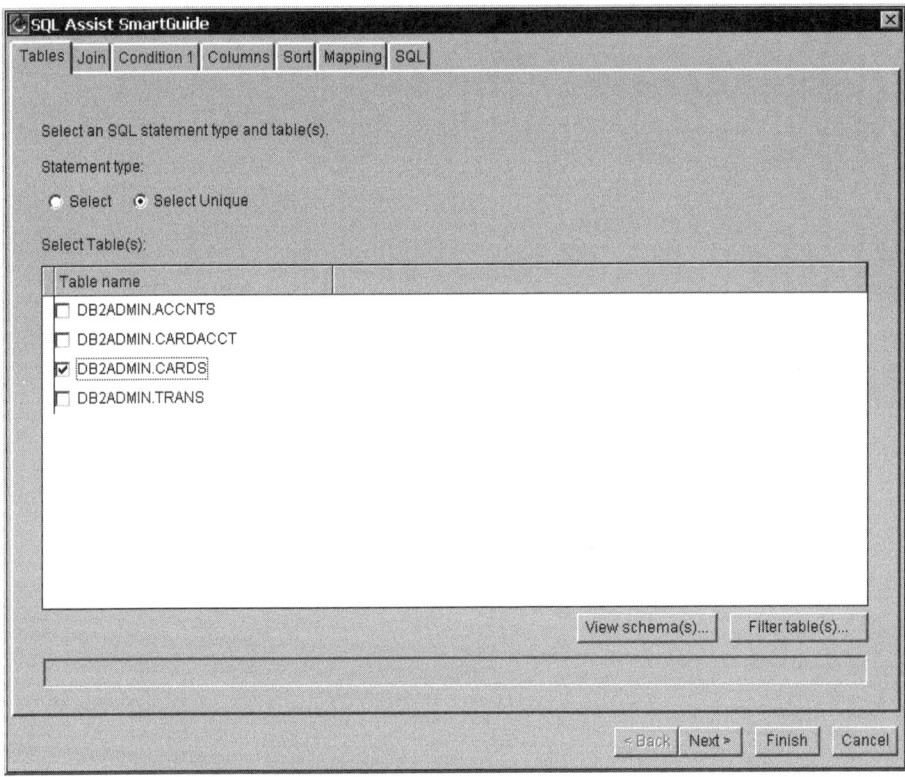

Figure 185. SQL Assist SmartGuide — Tables

Specifying a "where" statement

To select an unique card, you must have a "where" statement. Click condition1 tab to specify a condition (Figure 186). Select CARD_NUM as table columns and select **is exactly equal to** as operator. Then type **:CARDNUM** as values. These selection represents the statement "*WHERE CARD_NUM = :CARDNUM*".

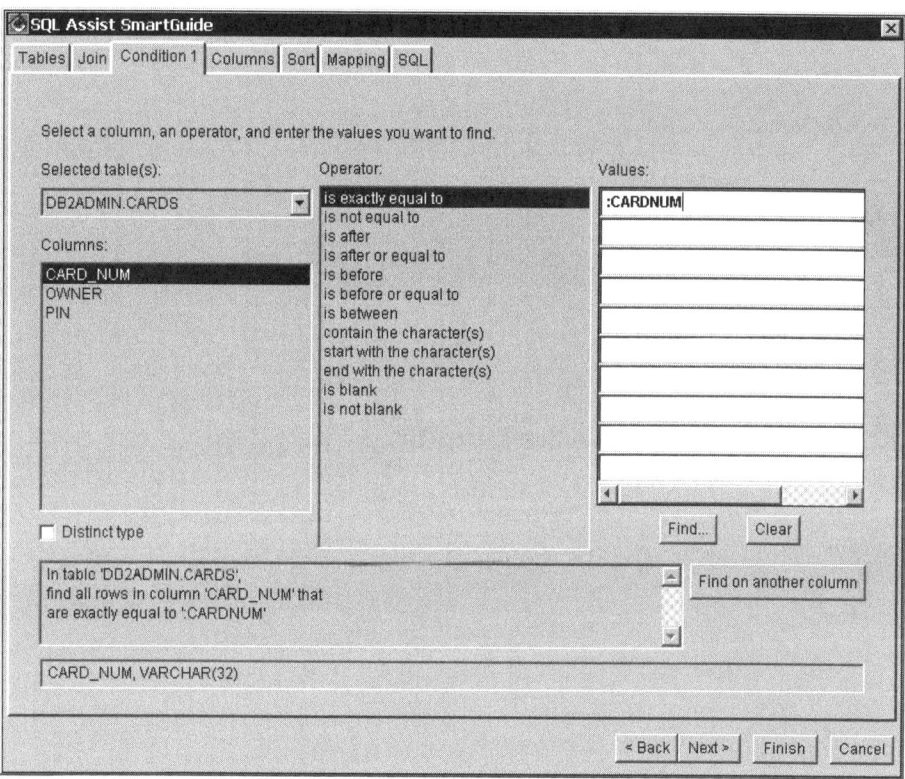

Figure 186. SQL Assist SmartGuide — Condition 1

Column selection

Now you need to specify which columns are required to your SQL. Click **Next** button or **Columns** tab, then select columns and click **Add>>** button to add to your SQL statement. In this case, we select all columns by clicking **SelectAll** and **Add>>** button (Figure 187). This means "SELECT CARDS.CARD_NUM, CARDS.OWNER, CARDS.PIN" or "SELECT *".

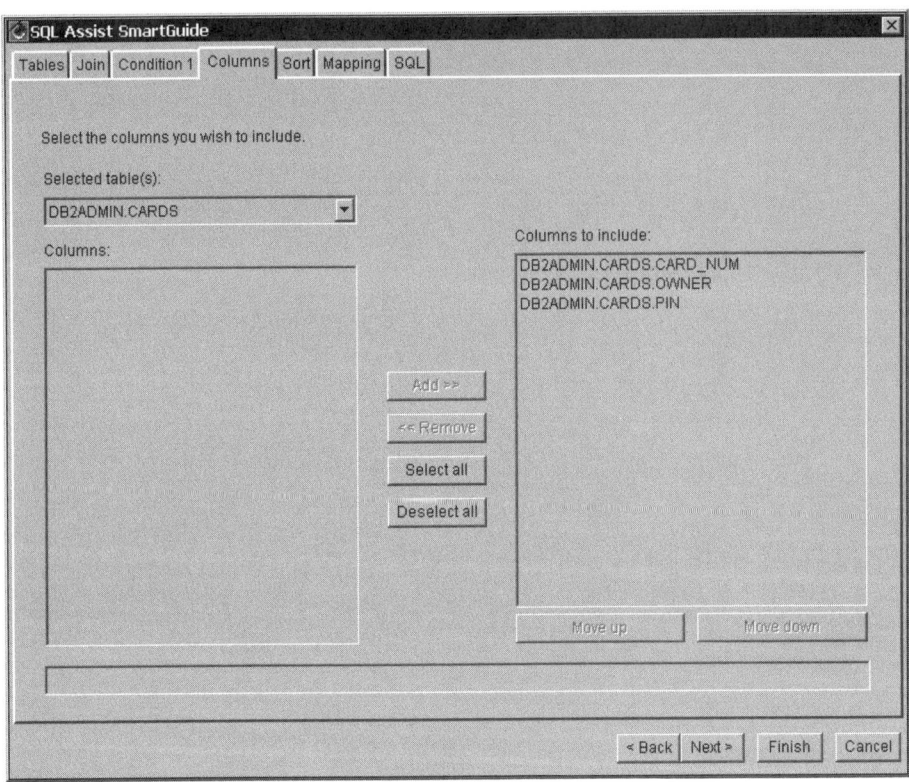

Figure 187. SQL Assist SmartGuide — Columns

Testing your SQL

Now, you are almost done creating your SQL. Click the SQL tab and see your generated SQL statement (Figure 188). Click **Schema qualified names** to remove the schema names from your SQL to keep the portability of your SQL. If the statement does not match your requirements, you can go back to each tab at any time. If it seems satisfactory to you, click the **Run SQL...** button to test it. Then you need to specify a parameter on the next dialog to test your SQL, because your SQL has a "where" statement (Figure 189). Type "123" as the card number and click **Run SQL...** button again. Then you will see the window which contains the result set of your SQL (Figure 190).

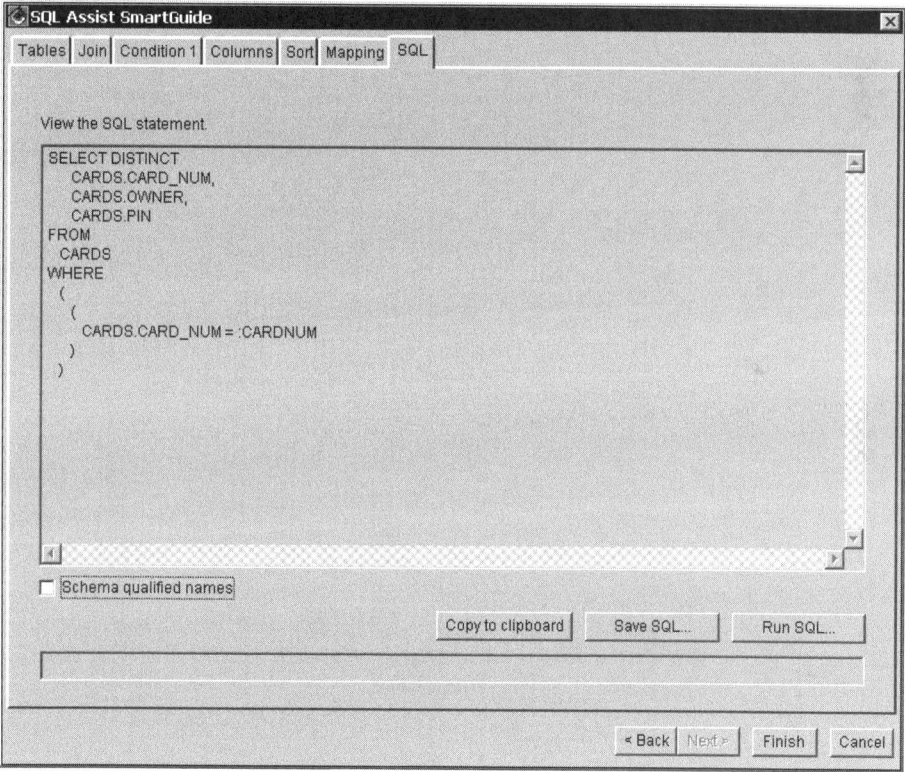

Figure 188. SQL Assist SmartGuide — SQL

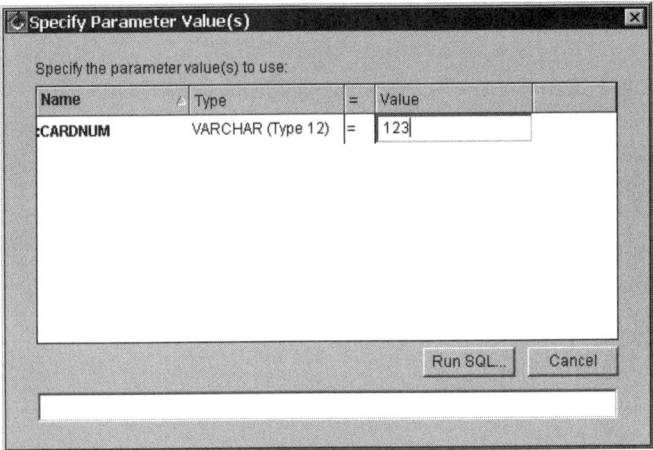

Figure 189. Specify Parameter Values

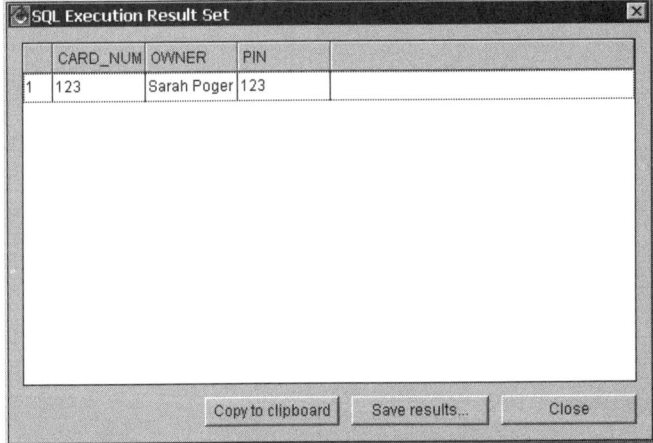

Figure 190. SQL Execution Result Set

Generate your SQL

If you are satisfied with your SQL, close the Result set window and click **Finish** to generate. The SmartGuide generates the ivjCardSelect field, the private getCardSelect method which returns the Select class in the Card class, and the cardSelectSQL method which returns the SQLMetaData class in the CardDAB class. This method contains Java code and binary data which used by **SQL Assist SmartGuide**.

You will see the select SQLs that related to your data access class on your Query Dialog. Figure 191 shows all SQLs that are used in our Card class. Click each SQL to see the actual SQL statement.

```
public static com.ibm.db.StatementMetaData CardSelectSQL() throws java.lang.Throwable {
  String name = "com.ibm.itso.sg245264.atm.database.CardDAB.CardSelectSQL";
  String statement = "SELECT DISTINCT CARDS.CARD_NUM, CARDS.OWNER, CARDS.PIN FROM CARDS
WHERE ( ( CARDS.CARD_NUM = :CARDNUM ) )";

  StatementMetaData aSpec = null;
  try{
    aSpec = new com.ibm.db.StatementMetaData();
    aSpec.setName(name);
    aSpec.setSQL(statement);
    aSpec.addTable("CARDS");
    aSpec.addColumn("CARDS.CARD_NUM", 12,12);
    aSpec.addColumn("CARDS.OWNER", 12,12);
    aSpec.addColumn("CARDS.PIN", 12,12);
    aSpec.addParameter("CARDNUM", 12, 12);
    // user code begin {1}
    // user code end {1}
  }
  catch(java.lang.Throwable e){
    // user code begin {2}
    // user code end {2}
    throw e;
  }
  return aSpec;
/*V2.0
**start of SQL Assist data**
504b030414g08g08g7c80572aggggggggggggg0cggg6275696c64657220646174615bf39681b5b48841
243ada272bb12c512f27312f5d2fb8a428332fdddac897736d8bd193702606868a0206060629a0426
da1da68ea98481d9c8c0b08481d1b0b490a18e810922c66a6c60146f54c220e4e264e4e8e2ebe9a7e
a10ca859044d997fb89f6b108642831206713485203 2de2fd417592dbb918145bc0148359a9b0c0d8c
b00429614d4bcc294e459331051b6980264ac848664b70e818238b319a01b12a8a8869090327cc106b
103604097063081b8004f8501c618ce90866430323f420028a6146a5918119c88f4c46e85e37010973
8a4a53d1e2c61c12371c56208d68fa982d40f663097d4b6038035dcb646884216c885dd8g2c0cg504b
ggf302gg504b010214g14g08g08g7c80572af5c95d012a01ggf302gg0cgggggggggggggggg
gg6275696c6465722064617461504b0506gggg01g01g3aggg6401gggg
**end of SQL Assist data**/
}
```

Chapter 10. Using relational databases

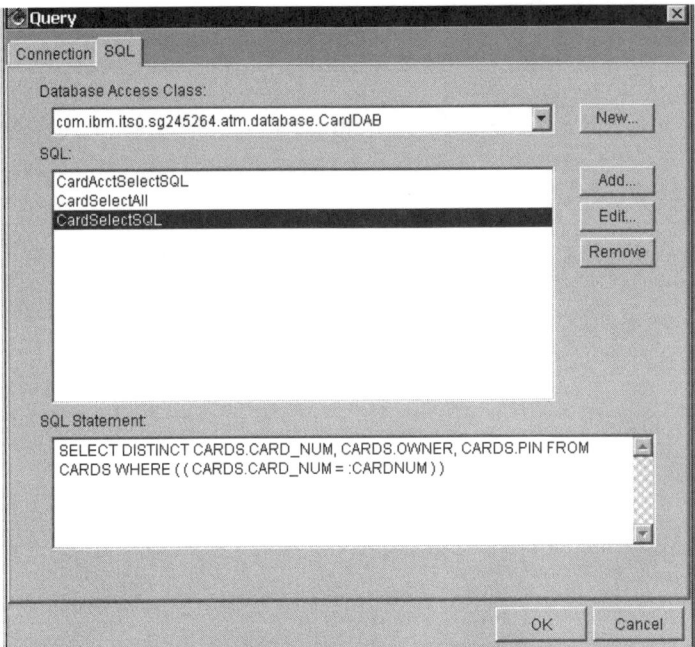

Figure 191. Created SQLs

Other options

While you are working with the SQL Assist SmartGuide, you can join several tables using Join tab or sort the result set by specific order. Mapping can be used when you would like to map manually database data types to Java data types (usually each data type is mapped automatically, and you should not specify them).

Card Select All bean

We created the Card Select All bean to return all cards. Add the Select Bean and create a new SQL definition from the property dialog. You do not have to create a Data Access class and Connection. Reuse those classes and methods created in the Card Select bean. In this case, you do not specify this in the **Condition 1** tab. Figure 192 shows result of SelectAllSQL.

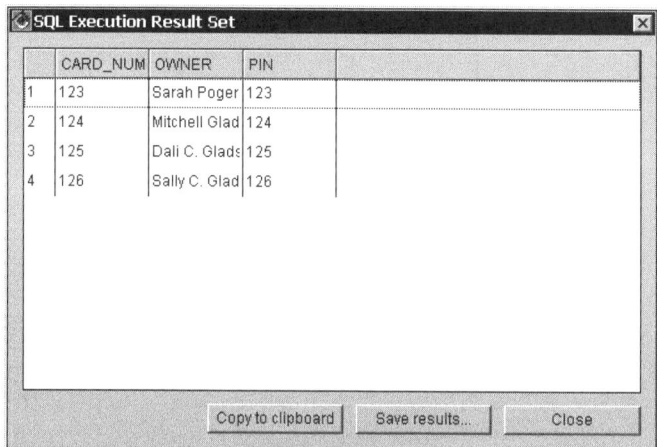

Figure 192. SelectAllSQL Result

CardAcctSelect

CardAcctSelect is a select bean which return Card Account. It is similar to CardSelect but this returns Account number from Card number. Add a Select Bean and create a new SQL using same CardDAB class and conn1 connection. This generates "SELECT * FROM CARDACCT WHERE CARDACCT.CARD_NUM = :CARDNUM" (Figure 193).

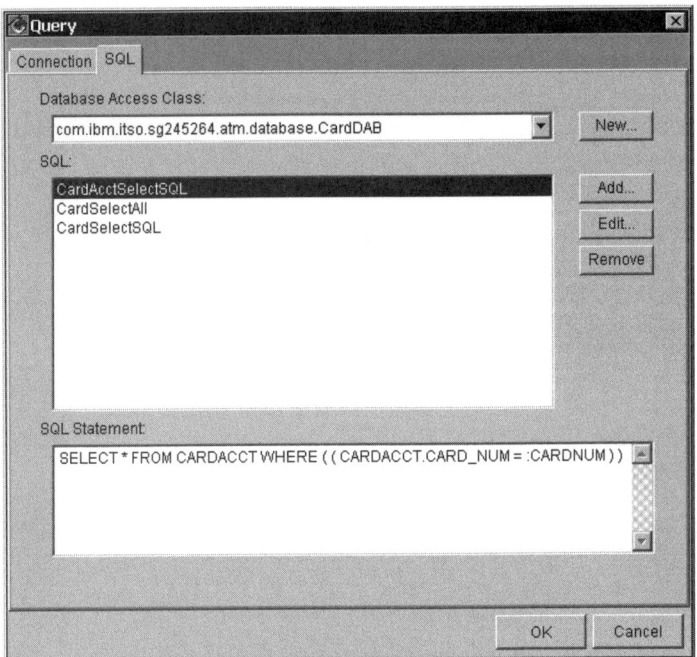

Figure 193. CardAcctSelectSQL

Modify beans

The next step in making the card class persistent is to add Modify beans to the free form surface. Modify Beans allow you to Insert/Update/Delete an operation to your database. We created 5 Modify beans to manipulate CARD and CARDACCT tables.

- Card Insert

    Add a new card.

- Card Delete

    Delete an existed card.

- Card Update

    Update an existed card.

- Card Associated Account

    Add a new associated account.

- Card Delete Attached

    Delete an existed associate account.

Card Insert

Add a Modify bean and name it to CardInsert. Open an Action dialog from the Properties window of Modify bean to define an SQL statement by clicking the square button next to the Action property (Figure 194).

Click the **Add** button to create new SQL from the SQL view. Then select insert as statement type and DB2ADMIN.CARD as table (Figure 195).

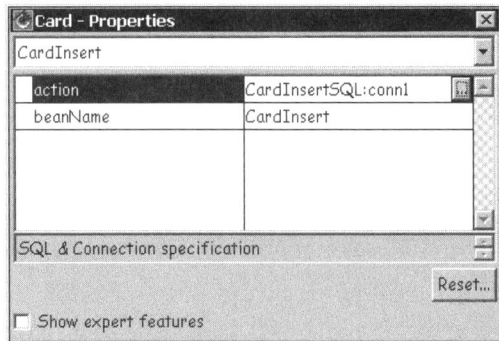

Figure 194. Modify Bean

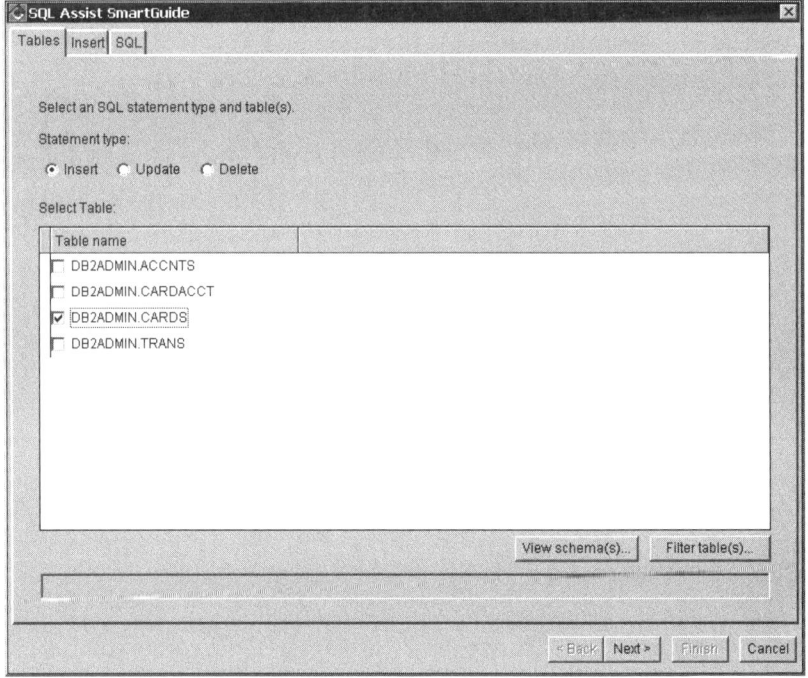

Figure 195. SQL Assist SmartGuide — Insert

Insert values are passed as parameters. Set each value to start with :(colon). See Figure 196.

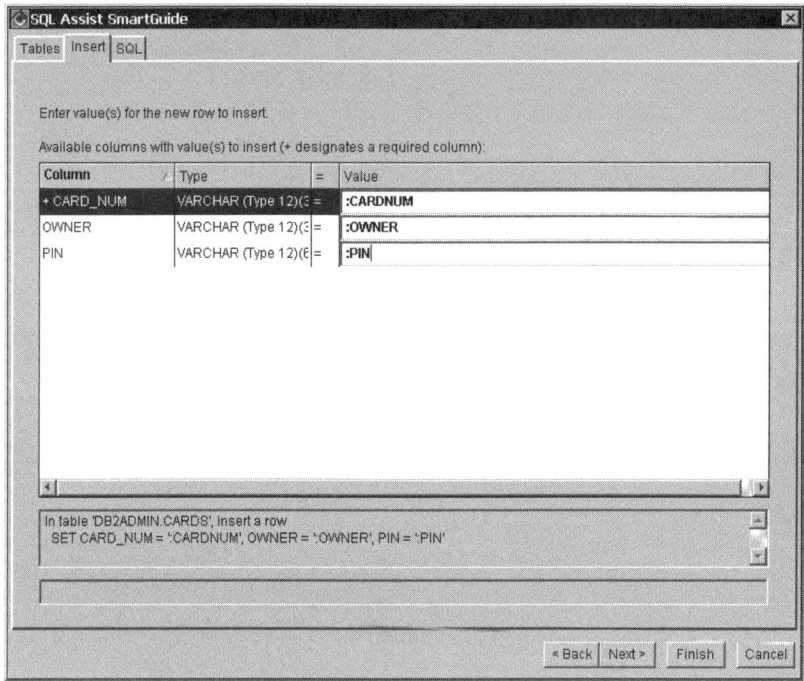

Figure 196. SQL Assist SmartGuide — Insert Value

Check and test your SQL in SQL view (Figure 197).

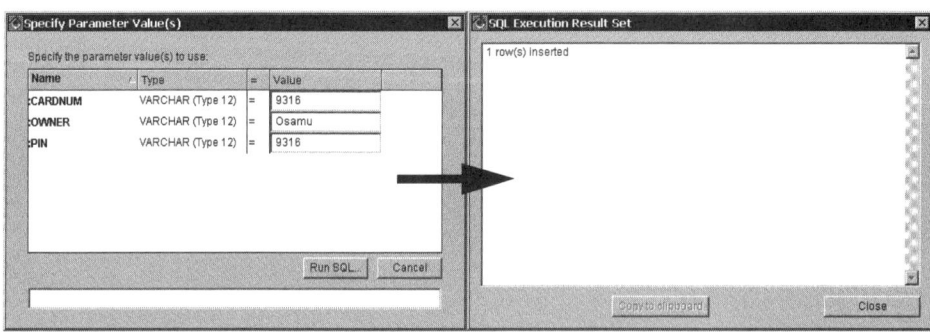

Figure 197. Insert

Card Delete

The Card Delete bean is also a Modify bean. Select Delete as statement type and set :CARDNUM as a parameter (Figure 198).

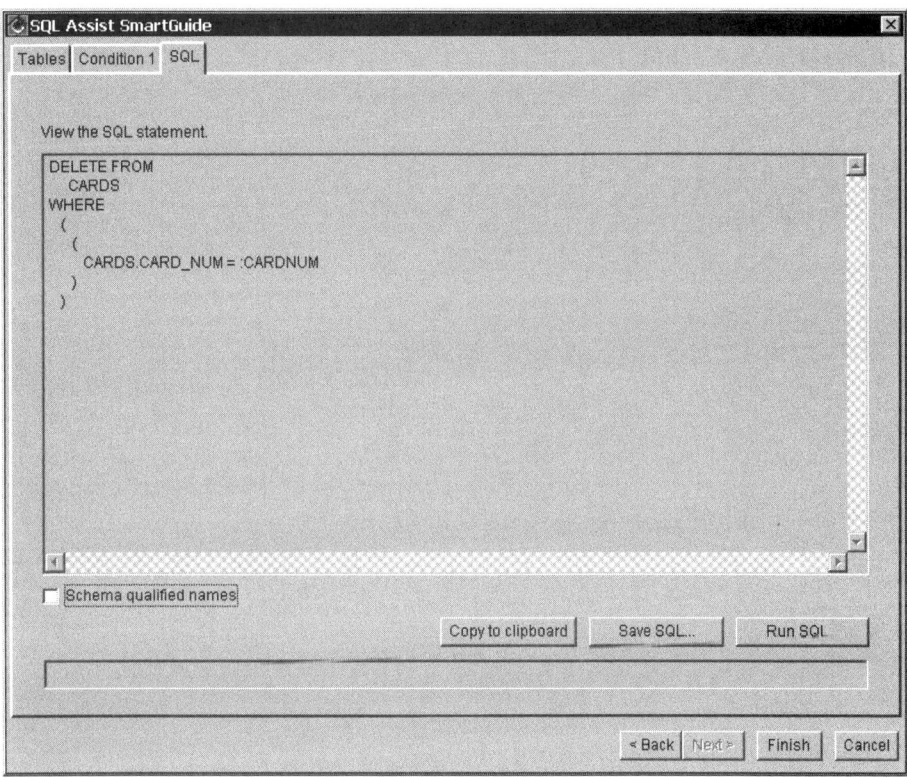

Figure 198. SQL Assist SmartGuide — Delete

Card Update

Card Update is a bean to update a row of card table. Open the update tab and set values as parameters :CARDNUM, :OWNER, :PIN (Figure 199). But Card num must exist before it can be updated, so use condition 1 to set the "where" statement. Figure 200 shows the actual update statement.

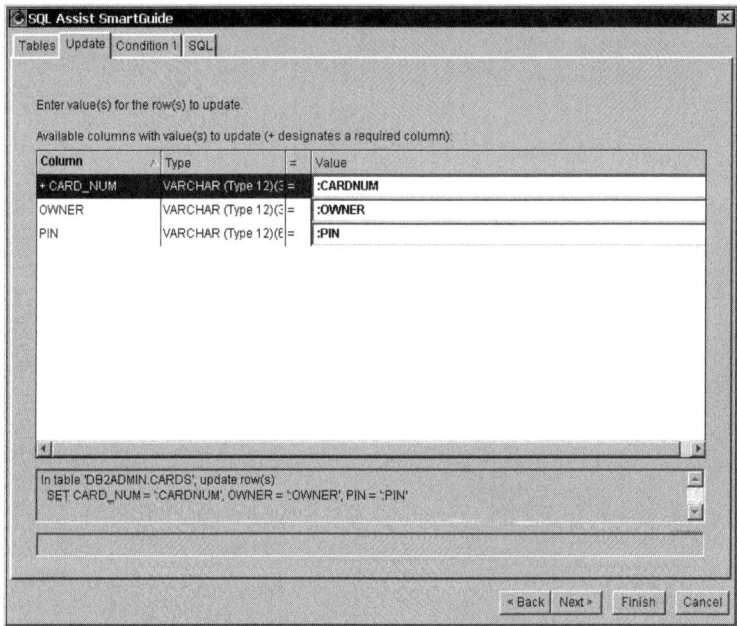

Figure 199. SQL Assist SmartGuide — Update Values

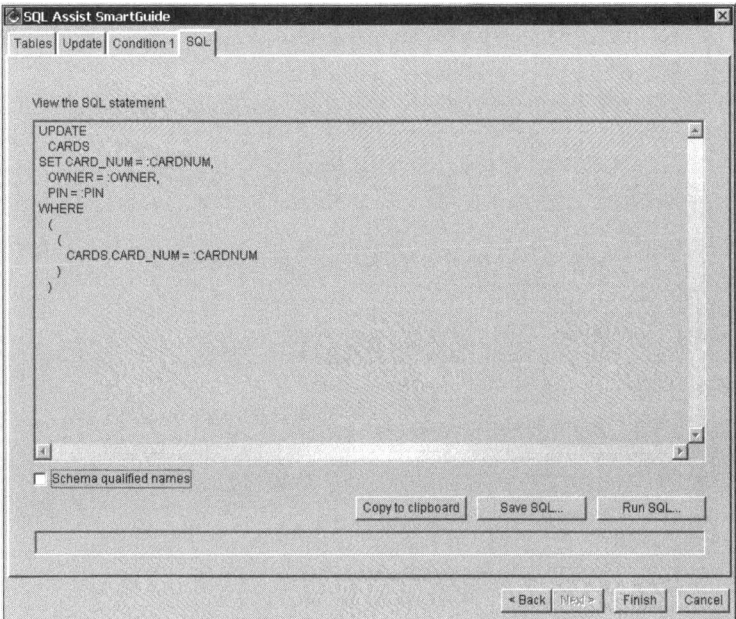

Figure 200. SQL Assist SmartGuide — Update Statement

Card Visual Composition Editor View

After adding all of the Data Access Beans, your VCE looks like Figure 201.

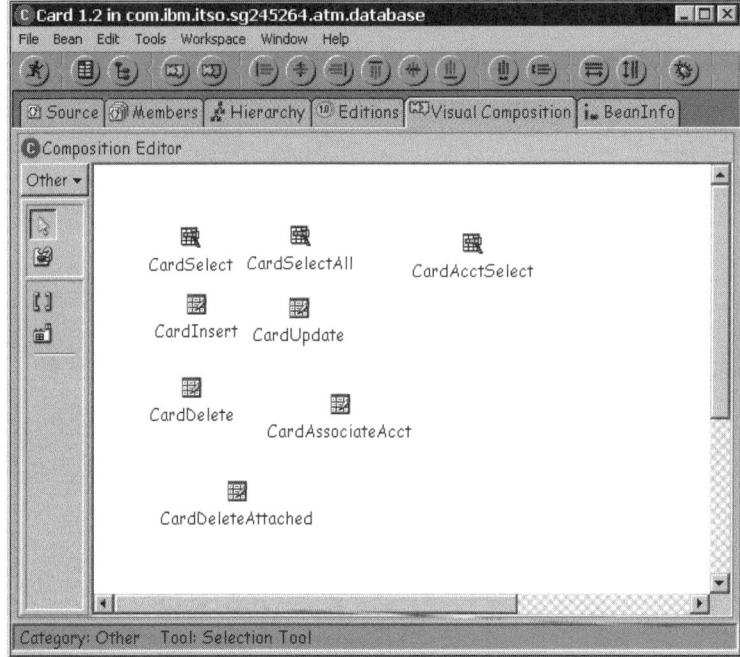

Figure 201. Card Visual Composition Editor

Modifying related methods

Now we need to modify several methods to use with our database. These methods are search, delete or update cards and card accounts.

Find Card method

To find a card, use the CardSelect Select bean. Get an instance of CardSelect bean and set a card number as a parameter using Select.setParameter method. The Select.execute method executes a query and the Select.getRowCount returns a number of results. The findWithCardPK methods execute a query with a specific card number and return all of the card information as an instance of Card class.

```
public static Card findWithCardPK(CardPK anId) throws PersistenceException{
    try{
        Card tempCard=new Card();
        com.ibm.ivj.db.uibeans.Select select = tempCard.getCardSelect();
        select.setParameter("CARDNUM", anId.getIdAsString());
        select.execute();
        if( select.getRowCount() <= 0){
            throw new CardNotFoundException("The card with primary key " +
anId.getIdAsString() + " was not found.");
        }
        select.firstRow();
        String tmpcardnum = (String)select.getColumnValue("CARDS.CARD_NUM");
        String tmpcardowner = (String)select.getColumnValue("CARDS.OWNER");
        String tmpPIN = (String)select.getColumnValue("CARDS.PIN");
        tempCard = new Card((new Card$CardPK(tmpcardnum)),tmpcardowner, tmpPIN );
        return tempCard;
    }
    catch(Exception exp){
        throw new PersistenceException(exp.toString());
    }
}
```

List Card method

The getListOfAllCards methods return all card instances as a vector. This method uses CardSelectAll Select Bean to get all of the card rows.

```
public static Vector getListOfAllCards() throws PersistenceException,
InvalidPINException{
    try{
    Vector allcards = new Vector(0);
    Card tempCard = new Card();
    com.ibm.ivj.db.uibeans.Select select = tempCard.getCardSelectAll();

    select.execute();
    int numrecs  = select.getNumRows();
    if ( numrecs <= 0 ){
        throw new CardNotFoundException("No cards were found.");
    }

    select.firstRow();
    for(int i=0; i< numrecs; i++){
            String tmpcardnum = (String)select.getColumnValue("CARDS.CARD_NUM");
            String tmpcardowner = (String)select.getColumnValue("CARDS.OWNER");
            String tmpPIN = (String)select.getColumnValue("CARDS.PIN");
            tempCard = new Card((new Card$CardPK(tmpcardnum)),tmpcardowner, tmpPIN );

            // add the new acct to the vector holding all accounts associated with
            // this card.
            allcards.addElement(tempCard);
            select.nextRow();
        }
    return allcards;
    }
    catch(com.ibm.db.DataException exp){
        throw new PersistenceException(exp.toString());
    }

}
```

Store method
The Store method is used to update a card row.

```
private void store() throws PersistenceException, InvalidPINException {
    com.ibm.ivj.db.uibeans.Modify modify=null;

    try{
            if (exists()){
                modify = getCardUpdate();
                modify.setParameter("CARD_NUM",this.getId().getIdAsString());
            }
            else{
                //record doesn't exist.
                modify = getCardInsert();
            }


            modify.setParameter("CARDNUM",this.getId().getIdAsString());
            modify.setParameter("PIN",rtPIN());
            modify.setParameter("OWNER",rtOwner());
            modify.execute();
            load();

    }
    catch(com.ibm.db.DataException exp){
        throw new PersistenceException(exp.toString());
    }

}
```

PersistenceException class
Now each method which uses database access throws a PersistenceException. This Exception is inherited from Exception and we allocated it to Database specific exception.

```
package com.ibm.itso.sg245264.atm.database;

/**
 * An instance of this gets thrown whenever there is an issue with persisting an object.
 */
public class PersistenceException extends Exception {
/**
 * Constructor taking a description as argument.
 *
 * @param aDescriptionStr java.lang.String
 */
PersistenceException(String aDescriptionStr) {
   super( aDescriptionStr);
}
}
```

Data Access Beans with an application

If you are planning to use the Data Access bean with an application or an applet, this will be much easier. You can use the Visual Composition Editor to use the select bean and show the results.

Select bean contains a model class for JTable. To show a result set of Select bean, connect Select bean **this** property to JTable model property. To execute query, put a button and connect actionperformed event to execute method of Select bean. If your Select bean need a parameter, put an entry field and connect text property to Param_*NAME* property of Select bean.

Here are the sample steps to create CardQuery applet (see Figure 202) to query a card using CardSelect bean that we created in this chapter.

1. Use SmartGuide to create VCE version of CardQuery Class.
2. Put JTable bean.
3. Put JTextField bean.
4. Put JButton bean.
5. Put Select bean has same setting as CardSelect (See, "Card Select bean" on page 288).
6. Connect actionPerformed event of JButton to execute() method of Select bean.
7. Connect this property of Select bean to model property of JTable bean.
8. Connect text property of JtextField bean to param_CARDNUM property of Select bean.
9. Save and execute.
10. Enter Card number and click button.
11. You will see the result.

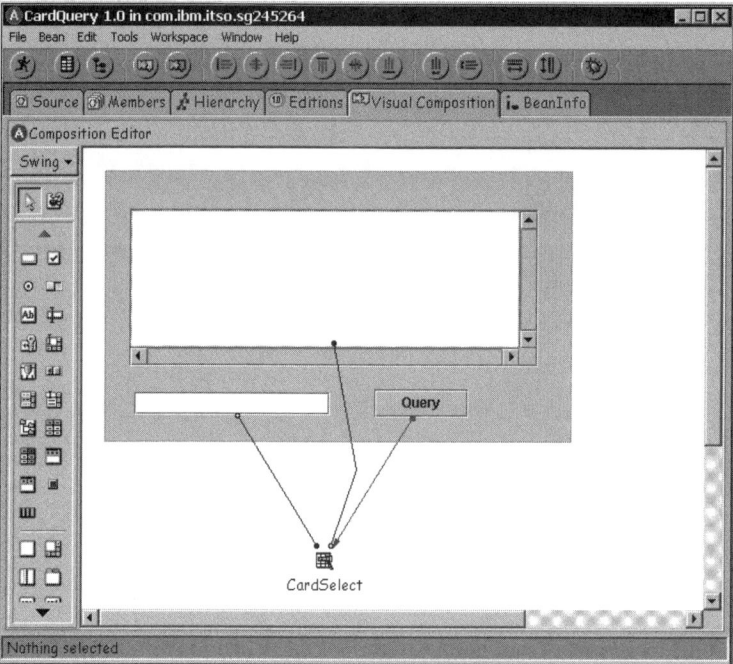

Figure 202. CardQuery Applet — Visual Composition Editor

Chapter 11. Internationalization

With the expansion of the Internet, the whole world can have access to your applet or servlet, and you may want to deploy applications anywhere in the world. Thus, it is important that you provide internationalization support for your programs. By making your Java program international, people all over the world can use it in their own language and with the correct format of specific data such as date, currency, and time.

Programs that support different languages and conventions are usually called *National Language Support* (NLS) enabled or *international* applications.

In this chapter you will learn what the JDK provides to help you write international Java programs, and how international support is integrated into VisualAge for Java.

This chapter explains how you can make your Java programs international. This is not the same as using the international edition of VisualAge for Java that supports developers working in their native languages, including French, German, Spanish, Chinese, Japanese, Korean, Italian, and Portuguese.

Java Internationalization Framework

To simplify the support of international applications, the JDK provides the Internationalization framework. This framework was originally developed in C++ by Taligent, a former IBM company, and has since been ported to the Java environment. Sun adopted this framework without major modifications and made it part of the official JDK since Version 1.1.

The main components of the Internationalization framework are *locales* and *resource bundles*.

Locales

Java uses the term *locale* to identify a geographic or political region for which spoken language and format conventions are specific. The Internationalization framework defines the `java.util.Locale` class to support this framework. Locale objects contain information about supported geographic or political regions.

Classes that provide support for different locales are known as *locale-sensitive* classes. These classes use either a default or a specific locale to determine which locale to support. The approach is very flexible. If the particular locale is not supported, the locale hierarchy is traversed until a supported locale is found or the default locale is reached.

To create a Locale object, you specify a language, and optionally a country and variant. For example, to create a Locale object for British English, you would use the following statement:

Locale myLocale = new Locale ("en", "UK", "");

All locales list sample

The classes in both the java.text and the java.util.Calendar packages provide the getAvailableLocales method that returns an array of all locales that are supported by the class. This list of locales can be used to list different languages associated with the locales.

Follow these steps to create an applet that lists the different languages supported by the NumberFormat class:

1. Create a JApplet named AllLocaleList in a new package named com.ibm.itso.sg245264.nls in the ITSO project and open it in the Visual Composition Editor.

   Drop a JScrollPane on the middle of the applet and drop a JList in the JScrollPane.

2. Drop a DefaultListModel bean and a DefaultListSelectionModel bean on the free-form surface and name them DefaultListModel and DefaultListSelectionModel, respectively.

3. Connect the model of the JList to the this of DefaultListModel (Figure 203).

4. Connect the selectionModel of the JList to the this of the DefaultListSelectionModel (Figure 203).

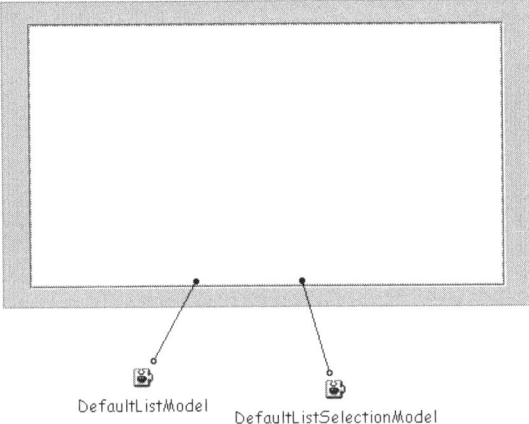

Figure 203. AllLocaleList connections

5. Save the bean.

6. Switch to the Members page and select the init method. Modify it to look like this:

```
public void init()
{
   try {
      setName("AllLocaleList");
      setSize(426, 240);
      setContentPane(getJAppletContentPane());
      initConnections();
         // user code begin {1}
         java.util.Locale[] allLocales =
            java.text.NumberFormat.getAvailableLocales();
         java.util.Locale locale = java.util.Locale.getDefault();
         for (int i = 0; i < allLocales.length; i++) {
         /* Check if it's a valid country */
            if (allLocales[i].getDisplayCountry().length() > 0) {
            /* get name of the current Locale, add it to the list */
               getDefaultListModel().
                     addElement(allLocales[i].getDisplayName());
               /* if it's the current setting, select it */
               if (allLocales[i].getDisplayName().
                  equals(locale.getDisplayName())) {

   getDefaultListSelectionModel().addSelectionInterval(i,i);
               }
```

```
                }
            }
              // user code end
        }
        catch (java.lang.Throwable ivjExc) {
              // user code begin {2}
              // user code end
              handleException(ivjExc);
        }
    }
```

7. Change the applet width in the Properties dialog to 500 and run the applet (Figure 204).

Figure 204. AllLocaleList applet

Resource bundle

Java provides *resource bundle* classes that store and retrieve information, using identifiers or keys. Resource bundle classes (derived directly or indirectly from `java.util.ResourceBundle`) are collections of resources designed to aggregate the resources needed for a specific language. Thus you can separate the program code from the locale-specific data (for example, separate the label of a button from the code that creates it).

A naming convention is used to identify specific resource bundle classes according to their locale, so that the resource bundle methods know which resource bundle classes to select on the basis of the current locale. By using inheritance among locale resources, you can minimize resource duplication across countries and achieve graceful degradation if he exact locale does not have localized resources. For example, your program could use resources from Standard French if there is no explicit support for Canadian French.

Because a locale can be set on a per-object basis, in addition to a default, system-wide basis, it is possible to deal with more than one locale at a time in the same program.

Because `java.util.ResourceBundle` is an abstract class, you must create your own classes that derive from it or one of the abstract subclasses discussed below.

Accessing resource values

The resource bundle classes provide several methods to access resource values:

`getContents`	Return the set of resource key-value pairs.
`getKeys`	Return all the keys.
`getObject`	Return a resource value given the key. You must cast the value to the correct type.
`getString`	Return a resource value given the key. This is a convenience method for string values.
`getStringArray`	Return a resource value given the key. This is a convenience method for string array values.

The two types of resource bundles are List and Property. A `ListResourceBundle` stores the key-value pairs in an array of objects, while the `PropertyResourceBundle` stores the key-value pairs in property files. You may see better performance with a `ListResourceBundle` than a `PropertyResourceBundle` because use of the `PropertyResourceBundle` implies a file access for each bundle. However when you use the `ListResourceBundle`, application code is being modified during translation work, which is not always desirable.

List resource bundles

The `java.util.ListResourceBundle` class is an abstract class that derives from `ResourceBundle`. It stores the localized data in an array of `Object` types. Therefore the localized data can be of any type, for example, `Image`.

When localizing your program, you subclass `ListResourceBundle` with your own classes, that must override the `getContents` method and provide an array, where each item in the array is a pair of objects. The first element of each pair is a `String` key, and the second is the value associated with that key.

A sample ListResourceBundle class might look like this:

```
import java.util.*;
public class MyResources extends ListResourceBundle
{
public Object[][] getContents()
{
return contents;
}
static final Object[][] contents = {
{"GreetingLabel", "Hello World!"},
{"AddButton", "Add"},
};
}
```

Property resource bundles

The `PropertyResourceBundle` class is an abstract subclass of `ResourceBundle` that manages resources for a locale through a set of strings loaded from a property file. Property files must have a `.properties` extension. They contain keys and their corresponding values. You can use those keys in your source code to call `ResourceBundle.getString` in order to retrieve the associated values.

Unlike `ListResourceBundle`, `PropertyResourceBundle` can be used to store strings only, not other objects.

Internationalization in VisualAge for Java

VisualAge for Java supports internationalization through the Externalize String function. Given a string property (in the Visual Composition Editor) or a class containing strings, VisualAge for Java can generate code that references the string indirectly through a resource bundle (property or list) and create the bundle for you. Note that strings that VisualAge for Java generates in user code blocks will not be externalized, and you should move them into separate methods.

VisualAge for Java adds an entry (composed of the key and value) in the array or property file at each point in your code where a string was directly referenced, for example:

```
JTextField1.setText("A string");
```

The string parameter will be replaced by a call to the resource bundle:

```
JTextField1.setText( getResourceBundle1( getString("AStringLabel")).);
```

Externalizing all strings in a class

The steps to externalize all the strings in a class at one time are:

1. From the Projects page of the Workbench, select the class whose strings you want to externalize.
2. Select **Selected**→**Externalize Strings**. Or, click mouse button 2 and select **Externalize Strings** from the pop-up menu.

The Externalizing dialog box appears, with a list of hard coded strings found in the class (Figure 205). As you can see in the figure, not all strings need to be externalized; for example, the "Center" string is a parameter to a call adding the component to a BorderLayout and should not be externalized.

If the same value appears more than once, VisualAge for Java will associate the same key with the value.

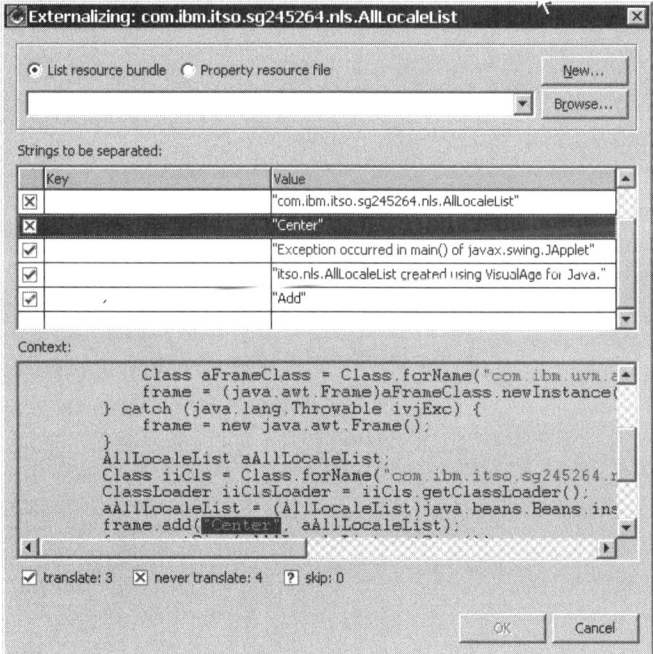

Figure 205. Externalizing strings

3. Specify the type of resource bundle by selecting one of the following radio buttons:
   - List resource bundle
   - Property resource file

4. Specify the name of the resource bundle:
Use the **Browse** button to choose an existing resource bundle, or use the **New** button to create a new bundle.

5. Under **Strings to be separated**, you can mark an item by clicking the iconic checkbox to the left of the column. By default all strings are marked for externalization so no action is required to externalize the string.
   - For strings that are never to be externalized, click once and a red *X* appears (Figure 205). The string will be removed from the *Strings to be separated* list.
   - To leave the string hard coded for now, click twice and a *?* should appear. The string will not be removed from the **Strings to be separated** list.

If you are not sure of a string, review it in the Context field. Then click **OK** to proceed with the externalization.

Removing the externalization information

VisualAge marks each item that you have chosen to externalize or never to externalize with a special comment. To make a string appear in the externalization list once again, find the accessor for the string resource or the string itself in the code and delete the comment at the end of the line: //$NON-NLS-1$. Then perform the steps 1 through 5 again.

Externalizing a string property

If you need more control over the externalization of individual strings, you can externalize each string property separately. The steps to externalize a string property are:

1. In the Visual Composition Editor, open the Property sheet for the bean that contains the string property you want to externalize. Select the value field to the right of the property name. A small button with three dots appears to the right of the text field.

2. Select the button. The Text dialog box appears (Figure 206).

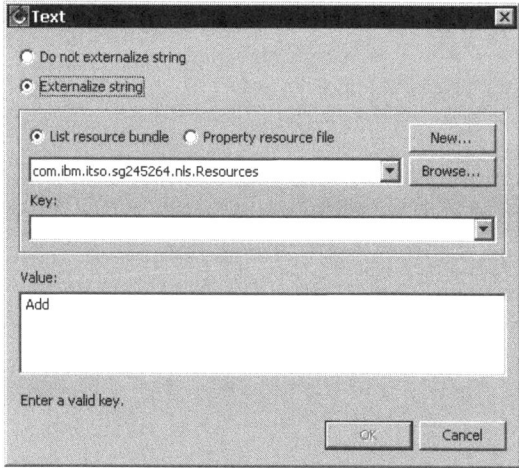

Figure 206. String externalization editor

3. Select the appropriate radio button:
   - Do not externalize string
   - Externalize string

4. If you select **Do not externalize string**, you are finished. Just click **OK** to close the window. Use this selection if the string value is long or runs over multiple lines. You must use the Text dialog to enter the string but you do not have to externalize the string.

5. If you select **Externalize string**, specify the type of resource bundle by selecting one of the following radio buttons:
   - **List resource bundle**
   - **Property resource file**

6. Specify the name of the resource bundle:
   - Use the **Browse** button or the drop-down list to choose an existing resource bundle, or use the **New** button to create a new bundle.
   - The name of the bundle appears in the bundle list.

7. To define a new resource, type its name in the *Key* field. The existing resources can be accessed through the pull-down list on the key field. The *Value:* text area contains the current value of the string property. If a key is selected, the text area contains the current value of the selected key. Click **OK** to close the window.

The next time you save the class, VisualAge for Java modifies the generated `get` methods for the beans so that the `text` property is set from the resource bundle.

Building a language panel

In this section you build a `LanguagePanel` that changes the display on the basis of user input.

First add the three .gif files (`frflag.gif`, `itflag.gif` and `usflag.gif`) from the examples directory into the ITSO project using resources view. You will use the .gif files to display the country flags of the different locales by adding an icon to a JLabel.

LanguagePanel view

1. In the com.ibm.itso.sg245264.nls package create a `LanguagePanel` class that inherits from `javax.swing.JFrame`. Make sure you select the **Compose the class visually** checkbox to open the Visual Composition Editor.

2. Add a `JLabel` to the center of the panel and a `JComboBox` to the bottom of the panel and change the bean names to `SelectLanguageLabel` and `LanguageChoice`.

3. Change the *text* property of `SelectLanguageLabel` to `Select Your Language of Preference`. Change the *foreground* color to `Black` and ensure that *verticalAlignment* and *verticalTextPosition* are set to CENTER, *horizontalAlignment* to LEFT, and *horizontalTextPosition* to RIGHT.

4. Click the field to the right of the `SelectLanguageLabel` *icon* property and then click the button that appears in the right of the field. Select the **file** radio button and click **Browse**. Select **ITSO\usflag.gif** and click **OK**.

5. Resize the frame and the textfield to see the complete text and image (Figure 207).

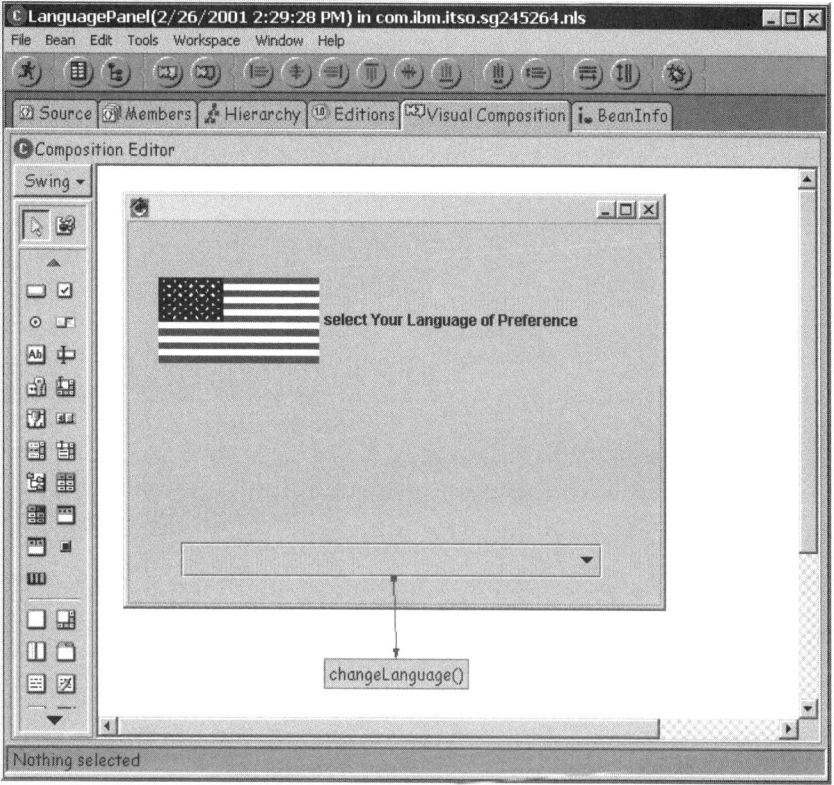

Figure 207. The LanguagePanel in the Visual Composition Editor

Creating the resource bundles

1. Externalize the *text* property of the SelectLanguageLabel (see Figure 208):

    a. Select the **List resource bundle** radio button.

    a. Enter com.ibm.itso.sg245264.nls for the *Package name* and LanguageResources for the *Class Name*.

    a. Enter SelectLanguageLabel in the *Key* field.

    a. The *Value* field should already be filled in with Select Your Language of Preference.

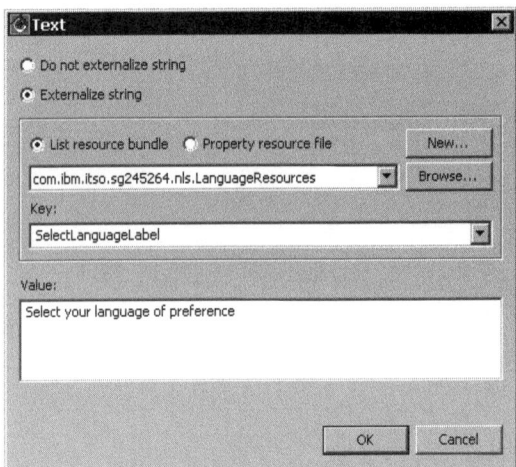

Figure 208. Externalizing the SelectLanguageLabel

You created the alternate resource bundles by copying the created class. You can also use VisualAge for Java to produce the different bundles.

2. Externalize the text property of the SelectLanguageLabel again. This time choose itso.nls for the *Package* and LanguageResources_fr for the *Class name*

   a. Enter SelectLanguageLabel in the *Key* field.

   a. Enter Choisissez une Langue de Préférence in the *Value* field.

   To create an international character, hold down the ALT key and input the ASCII code for the character, using the number pad on the right-hand side of your keyboard, then release ALT. For this example you only need the é symbol: 0233.

3. Repeat the externalization one more time, using itso.nls.LanguageResources_it for Italian:

   a. Enter SelectLanguageLabel in the *Key* field.

   b. Enter Selezionare un Linguaggio dello Preferenza in the *Value* field.

   c. Save the bean. The free-form surface shows the text field with an American flag and Italian text. Don't worry, you will fix that when the application starts.

You now have three resource bundle classes in your itso.nls package: LanguageResources, LanguageResources_fr, and LanguageResources_it. To use the generic resource bundle, LanguageResources, to support the default locale, English, and all the other locales that are not French or Italian, subclass the French and Italian resource bundles from LanguageResources instead of from java.util.ListResourceBundle. Add the icon for the American flag to the default language resources so the LanguageResources class looks like these:

```
public class LanguageResources extends java.util.ListResourceBundle {
    static final Object[][] contents = {
        {"SelectLanguageLabel", "Select your language of preference"},
        {"Icon",new javax.swing.java.swing.ImageIcon("usflag.gif")}
    };
}
```

Modify the two subclasses to match the following code:

```
public class LanguageResources_fr extends LanguageResources {
   static final Object[][] contents = {
      {"SelectLanguageLabel", "Choisissez une Langue de Préférence"},
         {"Icon",new javax.swing.ImageIcon("frflag.gif")}};
}

public class LanguageResources_it extends LanguageResources {
   static final Object[][] contents = {
      {"SelectLanguageLabel", "Selezionare un Linguaggio dello
      Preferenza"},
         {"Icon",new javax.swing.ImageIcon("itflag.gif")}
   };
}
```

Dynamically changing the locale

In "Building a language panel" on page 320, the resource bundle for the default locale was loaded automatically when the program started. To dynamically change the locale, you have to add code to change the locale-specific components.

Loading resource bundles

To load a resource bundle you use the static method, getBundle, from the ResourceBundle with the name of the resource bundle base class (including package information if not in the same package as the calling application) and the preferred locale. For example:

```
ResourceBundle myBundle = ResourceBundle.getBundle("MyResources", aLocale);
```

where aLocale is your Locale object, and MyResources is the name of your resource bundle.

In the `LanguagePanel` applet, you will use only one resource bundle hierarchy. If the current locale is set to French Canadian, the `getBundle` method first looks for a class called `MyResources_fr_CA`. If it does not find the class, it looks for Standard French (`MyResources_fr`). If that search fails, the method loads the generic class `MyResources`. If the method cannot find `MyResources`, it throws a `MissingResourceException`.

Number of resource bundles
In complex applications, you typically define many resource bundle hierarchies; for example, one for each window or one for labels, one for numbers, one for pictures, and one for sounds.

Retrieving resources from resource bundles

Once your resource bundle class is loaded, you can use the keys to access the stored objects. The `getObject` method returns an element of the static array of resources. As the resource is always returned as a `java.lang.Object`, you have to cast it to the correct type of your object. As you learned in "Accessing resource values" on page 315, a `getString` method is provided for convenience. For example, if you want to set a `JLabel` to the "HelloWorld" resource, you use:

```
myTLabel.setText(myBundle.getString("HelloWorld"));
```

When you use the `ListResourceBundle` class, you can also store objects other than strings. For example, you could use myBundle to retrieve the "BigNumber" resource into a variable:

```
Integer myBigNumber = (Integer)myBundle.getObject("BigNumber");
```

Finishing the LanguagePanel

To make `LanguagePanel` a multilingual panel, create two methods:

1. The `changeLanguage()` method is called whenever a user selects a new language from `LanguageChoice`. This method translates the language selected into a supported locale and calls the `setLocale` method by passing the new locale as a parameter.

    - The `updateGui(java.util.Locale)` method retrieves a resource bundle instance and updates the GUI components according to the locale passed as a parameter.

    To create the `updateGui` method:

1. Select `LanguagePanel` and **Selected→Add→Method**. Type in `void updateGui(java.util.Locale aLocale)` as the method name and choose `private` as the access modifier. Click **Finish** to create the method.

2. Select the method and modify its code:

```
private void updateGui(java.util.Locale aLocale)
{
   java.util.ResourceBundle aResourceBundle=null;
      try {
      aResourceBundle=
         java.util.ResourceBundle.getBundle("itso.nls.LanguageResources",
         aLocale);
   }
   catch (Exception e) {
      System.out.println(e);
   }
   getSelectLanguageLabel().
      setText(aResourceBundle.getString("SelectLanguageLabel"));
         getSelectLanguageLabel().setIcon((javax.swing.ImageIcon)
            aResourceBundle.getObject("Icon"));
}
```

At the beginning of the method, a local variable is created to hold the resource bundle object. Then the resource bundle instance is retrieved, using the current locale. Once the resource bundle instance has been retrieved, it is used to get the resources for each label.

To create the `changeLanguage` method:

1. In the Workbench, select the **LanguagePanel** class and **Selected→Add→Method** or click the **M** icon on the toolbar.

2. Enter `void changeLanguage()` as the method name and select `private` as the access modifier. Click **Finish** to create the method.

3. Select the method and modify its code:

```
private void changeLanguage()
{
    if( getLanguageChoice().getSelectedItem().equals(
       java.util.Locale.FRANCE.getDisplayLanguage())) {
          updateGui(java.util.Locale.FRANCE);
    }
    else if(getLanguageChoice().getSelectedItem().equals(
       java.util.Locale.U.S..getDisplayLanguage())) {
          updateGui(java.util.Locale.U.S.);
    }
       else if (getLanguageChoice().getSelectedItem().equals(
```

```
            java.util.Locale.ITALY.getDisplayLanguage())) {
         updateGui(java.util.Locale.ITALY);
      }
   }
```

To change the GUI when the user selects another language, just add an event-to-code connection from the `itemStateChanged` event of the `LanguageChoice` to the `changeLanguage` method (Figure 209). Now save the bean.

Finally, you need to populate the list of languages for the Select language drop-down list and set the GUI to the default locale on initialization. Change the initialize method to look like this:

```
private void initialize() {
      // user code begin {1}
      // user code end
      setName("LanguagePanel");
   setDefaultCloseOperation(javax.swing.WindowConstants.DISPOSE_ON_CLOSE);
      setSize(528, 299);
      setContentPane(getJFrameContentPane());
      initConnections();
      // user code begin {2}

      getLanguageChoice().addItem(java.util.Locale.U.S..getDisplayLanguage())
      ;

      getLanguageChoice().addItem(java.util.Locale.FRANCE.getDisplayLanguage(
      ));

      getLanguageChoice().addItem(java.util.Locale.ITALY.getDisplayLanguage()
      );
         updateGui(java.util.Locale.getDefault());
      // user code end
}
```

Save and run the `LanguagePanel` (Figure 210).

Length of translated strings

One problem encountered when translating user interface elements is the relative length of strings. A translated string can be much longer or shorter than the original string. When you design your user interfaces keep this in mind and use layouts and constraints that will adjust to changing string lengths.

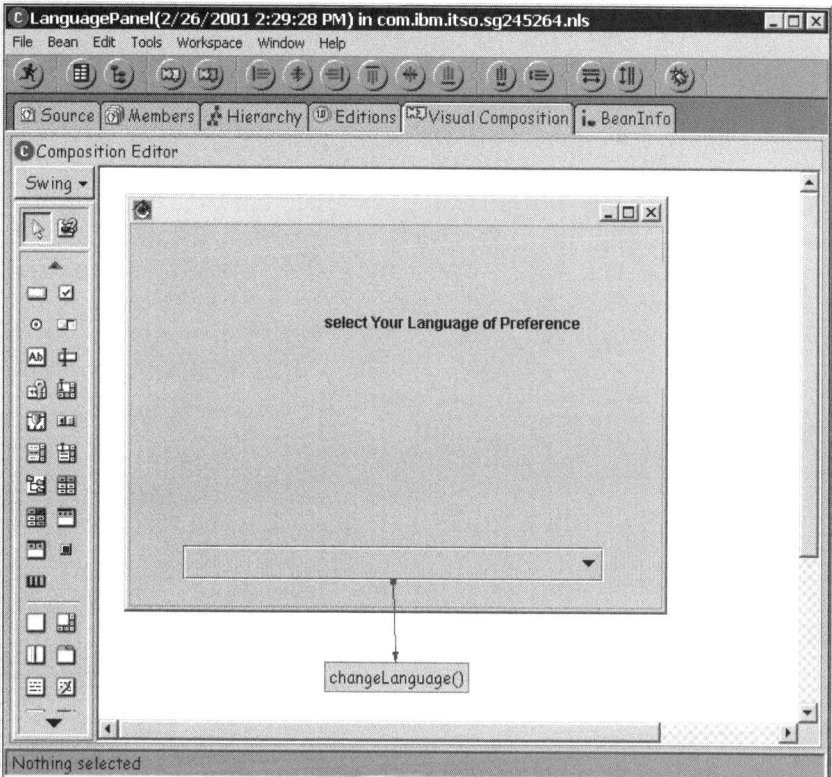

Figure 209. LanguagePanel connection

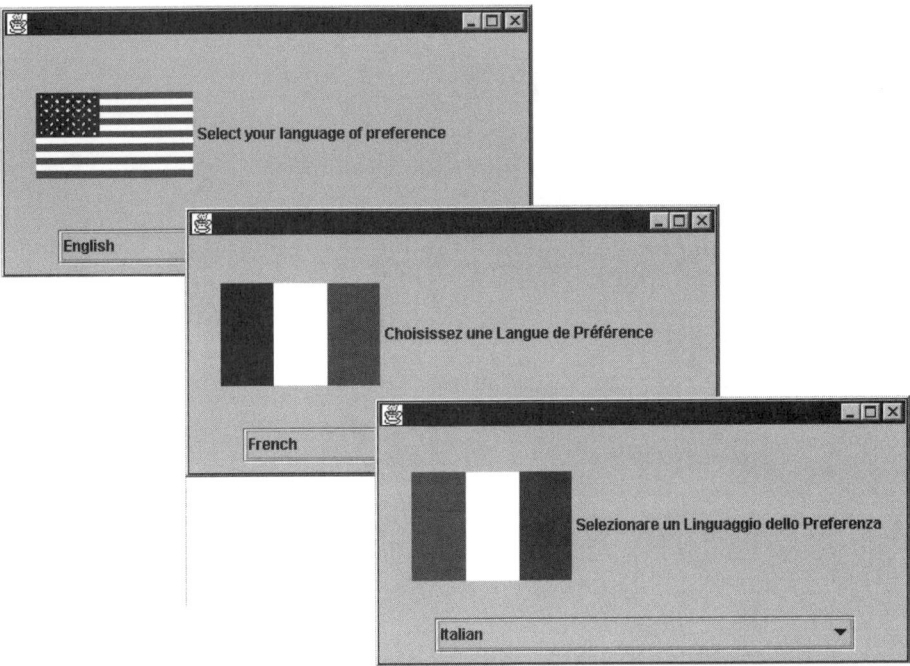

Figure 210. Running LanguagePanel

Formatting dates and times

The `DateFormat` class and its subclasses are used to handle the formatting of date and time information. You have to use the `getDateTimeInstance` method to get the date and time formatter or `getDateInstance` to get only the date formatter. The following code shows you how to use `getDateInstance` for a given `locale` attribute:

```
Date myDate = new Date("31 December 2000");
DateFormat df = DateFormat.getDateInstance(DateFormat.DEFAULT, locale);
String formattedDate = df.format(myDate);
```

The first parameter in the `getDateInstance` method call is used to specify the format of the date or time to be used. Refer to the Java2 SDK documentation for all possible formats.

Adding dates to the LanguagePanel

Follow these steps to update the `Language Panel` with international dates and times:

1. Open your LanguagePanel class and add four JLabels and rename them: TimeLabel, Time, DateLabel, and Date. Set the text properties to Time:, TimeValue, Date:, and DateValue (place them as shown in Figure 211).

2. Save the bean.

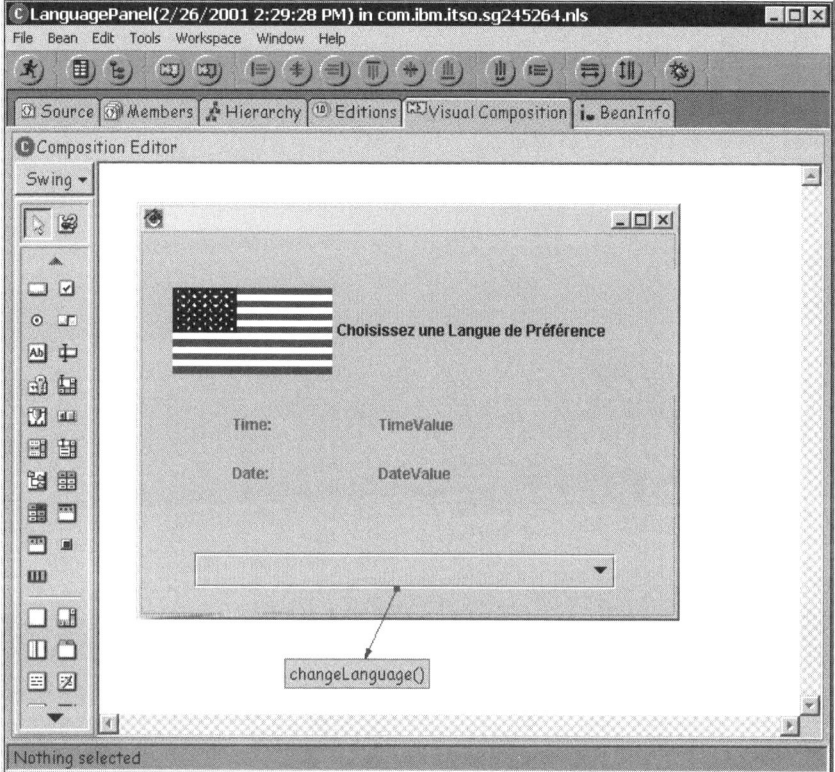

Figure 211. LanguagePanel View2

3. Externalize the TimeLabel and the DateLabel strings through their property sheets to update their appropriate values in the correct resource bundles:

   LanguageResources:

Key	Value
TimeLabel	Time:
DateLabel	Date:

LanguageResources_fr:

Key	Value
TimeLabel	Heure:
DateLabel	Date:

LanguageResources_it:

Key	Value
TimeLabel	Ora:
DateLabel	Data:

4. Modify the `updateGui(Locale)` method in `LanguagePanel`:

```
private void updateGui(java.util.Locale aLocale) {
   java.util.ResourceBundle aResourceBundle=null;
   try {
      aResourceBundle=java.util.ResourceBundle.
        getBundle("itso.nls.LanguageResources",aLocale);
   }
   catch (Exception e) {
      System.out.println(e);
   }
   getSelectLanguageLabel().setText(aResourceBundle.
   getString("SelectLanguageLabel"));
      getSelectLanguageLabel().setIcon((javax.swing.ImageIcon)
         aResourceBundle.getObject("Icon"));
   getTimeLabel().setText(aResourceBundle.getString("TimeLabel"));
   getDateLabel().setText(aResourceBundle.getString("DateLabel"));
   java.text.DateFormat   dFormat, tFormat;
   dFormat = java.text.DateFormat.getDateInstance(
         java.text.DateFormat.DEFAULT, aLocale);
   tFormat = java.text.DateFormat.getTimeInstance(
         java.text.DateFormat.DEFAULT, aLocale);
   java.lang.String timeString = tFormat.format(new java.util.Date());
   java.lang.String timeZone = tFormat.getTimeZone().getID();
   getTime().setText(timeString + "   " + timeZone);
   java.lang.String dateString = dFormat.format(new java.util.Date());
   getDate().setText(dateString);
}
```

5. Save and test your work. Figure 212 shows the output.

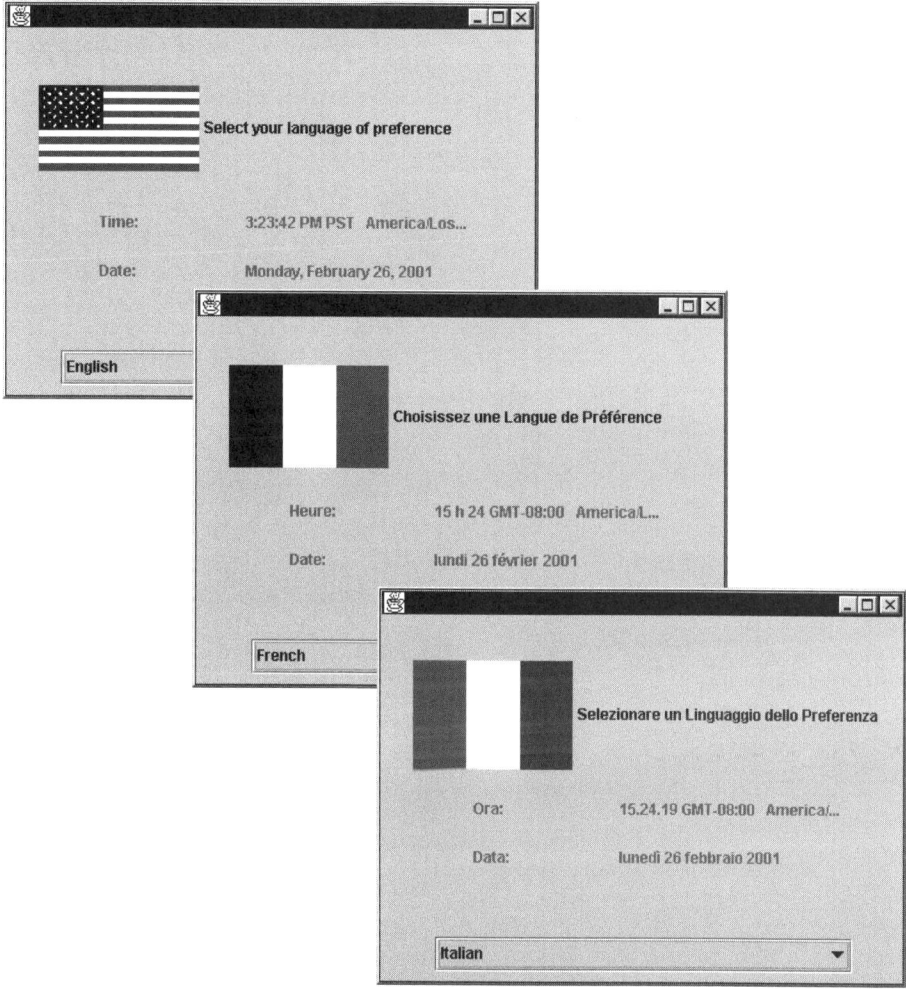

Figure 212. LanguagePanel Output with dates and times

Other internationalization considerations

This section covers resources other than strings and dates that you must consider when internationalizing your Java programs.

Using predefined formats

The JDK supplies the NumberFormat class and its subclasses, ChoiceFormat and DecimalFormat, for the different locale number formats. By invoking the methods provided by the NumberFormat class, you can format numbers, currencies, and percentages according to locale. However, there is a catch: NumberFormat may not support the locale you specify. To find out which locale definitions NumberFormat supports, invoke the getAvailableLocales method:

```
Locale[] locales = NumberFormat.getAvailableLocales();
```

Custom number formats

If NumberFormat does not support a locale that you need, you can create your own formats. You can use the DecimalFormat class to format decimal numbers into locale-specific strings. With this class you can control the display of leading and trailing zeros, prefixes and suffixes, grouping (thousands) separators, and the decimal separator. If you want to change formatting symbols such as the decimal separator, you can use the DecimalFormatSymbols class in conjunction with the DecimalFormat class. These classes offer a great deal of flexibility in the formatting of numbers, but they can make your code more complex. For more details refer to the JDK documentation.

Numbers

You can use the NumberFormat factory methods to format primitives, such as double, and their corresponding wrapper objects, such as Double.

This code example formats a Double according to locale. Invoking the getNumberInstance method returns a locale-specific instance of NumberFormat. The format method accepts the Double as an argument and returns the formatted number in a String.

```
Double amount = new Double(123456.789);
NumberFormat numberFormatter;
String amountOut;
numberFormatter = NumberFormat.getNumberInstance(currentLocale);
amountOut = numberFormatter.format(amount);
System.out.println(amountOut + "   " + currentLocale.toString());
```

The output from this example shows how the format of the same number varies with locale:

```
123 456,789 fr_FR
123.456,789 de_DE
123,456.789 en_U.S.
```

Currencies

You format currencies the same way you format numbers, except with currencies you call getCurrencyInstance to create a formatter. When you invoke the format method, it returns a String that includes the formatted number and the appropriate currency sign.

The following code example shows how to format currency in a locale-specific manner:

```
Double currency = new Double(1234567.89);
NumberFormat currencyFormatter;
String currencyOut;
currencyFormatter = NumberFormat.getCurrencyInstance(currentLocale);
currencyOut = currencyFormatter.format(currency);
System.out.println(currencyOut + "   " + currentLocale.toString());
```

Here is the output generated by the preceding lines of code:

```
1 234 567,89 F    fr_FR
1.234.567,89 DM   de_DE
$1,234,567.89 en_U.S.
```

Converting currencies

At first glance this output may look wrong because all of the numeric values are the same. Of course, 1 234 567,89 F is not equivalent to 1.234.567,89 DM. However, bear in mind that the `NumberFormat` class is unaware of exchange rates. The methods belonging to the `NumberFormat` class format currencies but do not convert them.

Percentages

You can also use the methods of the NumberFormat class to format percentages. To get the locale-specific formatter, invoke the `getPercentInstance` method. With this formatter, a fraction such as 0.75 is displayed as 75%. The following code sample shows how to format a percentage:

```
Double percent = new Double(0.75);
NumberFormat percentFormatter;
String percentOut;
percentFormatter = NumberFormat.getPercentInstance(currentLocale);
percentOut = percentFormatter.format(percent);
```

Messages

Programs often need to build messages from sequences of strings, numbers, and other data. To produce the "The disk 'MyDisk' contains 3 files." message, you would use the following code:

```
int numFiles = 3;
String diskName = "MyDisk",
String message = "The disk" + diskName + " contains"+ numFiles + "files.";
```

The above code, although easy to understand, is extremely difficult to localize because it hard codes both the strings that make up the message and the order in which they are put together. Note, for example, that the French translation of the message, "Il y a 3 fichiers sur le disque 'MyDisk'.", reverses the strings.

The `MessageFormat` class provides a way to build messages in a language-neutral way. It is constructed from a pattern string. The pattern string describes the structure of the message and the substitution order for the parameters. When you use a `MessageFormat`, the code used to create "The disk 'MyDisk' contains 3 files." would look like this:

```
Object[] arguments = new Object[2];
arguments[0] = new Integer(3);
arguments[1] = "MyDisk";
StringBuffer message = new StringBuffer();
MessageFormat fmt= new MessageFormat("Disk {0} contains {1} files.");
fmt.format(arguments, message, null);
fmt = new MessageFormat("Il y a {1} fichiers sur le disque {0} ");
fmt.format(arguments, message, null);
```

The `format` method formats the given arguments and substitutes the result into the pattern string to form the final message. The `MessageFormat` tries to format the given arguments in several ways. An array of `Format` objects can be passed to the `MessageFormat`. If the array is present, parameter n will be formatted using the nth entry of the format array. If an explicit format array has not been passed as a parameter, a default `Format` will be obtained. If the parameter to be formatted is a number, `NumberFormat.getDefault` is called. Otherwise, the parameter's `toString` method is called.

An additional type of `Format`, `ChoiceFormat`, is available for use in formatting the parameters of a message. A `ChoiceFormat` allows text to be associated with a number or range of numbers.

Collations

Applications that search or sort through text perform frequent string comparisons. A report generator performs string comparisons when sorting a list of strings in alphabetical order. However, the order of certain characters in the alphabets of different locales may be significantly different.

If your application audience is limited to people who speak English, you can probably perform string comparisons with the `String.compareTo` method. This method performs a binary comparison of the Unicode characters within the strings. For many languages, you cannot rely on this binary comparison to sort strings, because the Unicode values do not correspond to the relative order of the characters.

Fortunately, the `Collator` class allows your application to perform string comparisons for different languages. You use the `Collator` class to perform locale-independent comparisons. The `Collator` class is locale-sensitive.

To see which locales the `Collator` class supports, invoke the `getAvailableLocales` method:

```
Locale[] locales = Collator.getAvailableLocales();
```

When you instantiate the `Collator` class, you invoke the `getInstance` method and specify the locale:

```
Collator myCollator = Collator.getInstance(new Locale("en", "U.S."));
```

The `getInstance` method actually returns a `RuleBasedCollator`, which is a concrete subclass of `Collator`. The `RuleBasedCollator` class contains a set of rules that determine the sort order of strings for the locale you specify. These rules are predefined for each locale. Because the rules are encapsulated within the `RuleBasedCollator`, your program does not need special routines to deal with the way collation rules vary with language.

You invoke the `Collator.compare` method to perform a locale-independent string comparison. The method returns an integer less than, equal to, or greater than zero when the first string argument is less than, equal to, or greater than the second string argument. For example:

```
myCollator.compare("abc", "xyz"); // returns -1: "abc" is less than "xyz"
myCollator.compare("abc", "abc"); // returns 0: the two strings are equal
myCollator.compare("xyz", "abc"); // returns 1: "xyz" is greater than "abc"
```

You can use the `Collator compare` method when performing sort operations. The sample program (taken from the JDK Demo package) presented below uses the compare method to sort an array of English and French words. It shows what can happen when you sort the same list of words with two different collators.

```
Collator fr_FRCollator = Collator.getInstance(new Locale("fr","FR"));
Collator en_U.S.Collator = Collator.getInstance(new Locale("en","U.S."));
```

The method for sorting, called `sortStrings`, can be used with any `Collator`. Notice that the `sortStrings` method invokes the compare method:

```
public static void sortStrings(Collator collator, String[] words)
{
   String tmp;
```

```
        for (int i = 0; i < words.length; i++) {
            for (int j = i + 1; j < words.length; j++) {
                // Compare elements of the array two at a time.
                if (collator.compare(words[i], words[j] ) > 0 ) {
                // Swap words[i] and words[j]
                tmp = words[i];
                words[i] = words[j];
                words[j] = tmp;
                }
            }
        }
}
```

The English Collator sorts the words like this:

peach
pêche
péché
sin

According to the collation rules of the French language, the preceding list is in the wrong order. In French, "pêche" should follow "péché" in a sorted list. Therefore the French Collator sorts the array of words like this:

peach
péché
pêche
sin

Sample section.

Internationalization in the Web environment

For the Web application, Java VM converts its unicode string to Web server specific code page. This conversion will be done automatically in each conversation. Java VM has various codepage conversion tables, and a particular table is selected based on the locale of the running environment. But even for one language, there are several conversion tables, and Java VM select the default table. However, some default tables are not suitable for the customer, because some characters are not converted correctly, due to the default table. Usually this problem occurs in the DBCS environment, because those languages have so many characters rather than SBCS, and some tables are not large enough to convert special characters.

To specify the conversion table in Java, use codepage parameter:

```
String st = new String( "ABC", [specific encorder]);
```

Encorder is also string. To specify to use eoncorder MS942:

```
String st942 = new String("ABC", "MS942");
```

Note that converter is used by the String constructor to set codepage specific character to unicode.

On the other hand, if your text file is not unicode and would like to read into Java environment through specific converter, you can use following statements.

```
FileInputStream fis = new FileInputStream( [file name]);
InputStreamReader isr = new InputStreamReader(fis, [specific encorder]);
```

To change the default converter, you can specify "file.encoding=" parameter in the property tab of your program.

Character codes on the Web

To build up your Web server environment, you need to consider the character-to-code mapping. Because your server contains multiple products, there are several code conversions that can occur between products, and there could be misconversions by an unsuitable converter.

Web Browser

Typical conversions will occur between the Web browser and the Web server, because the user may be using a different language. Usually the servlet engine converts the character automatically based on the header information of the **Accept-Language** and the **Accept-Charset** tags.

To specify the converter to use with specific language, set command line argument as -Ddefault.client.encoding=CP1252 on the WebSphere Admin panel (see Figure 213).

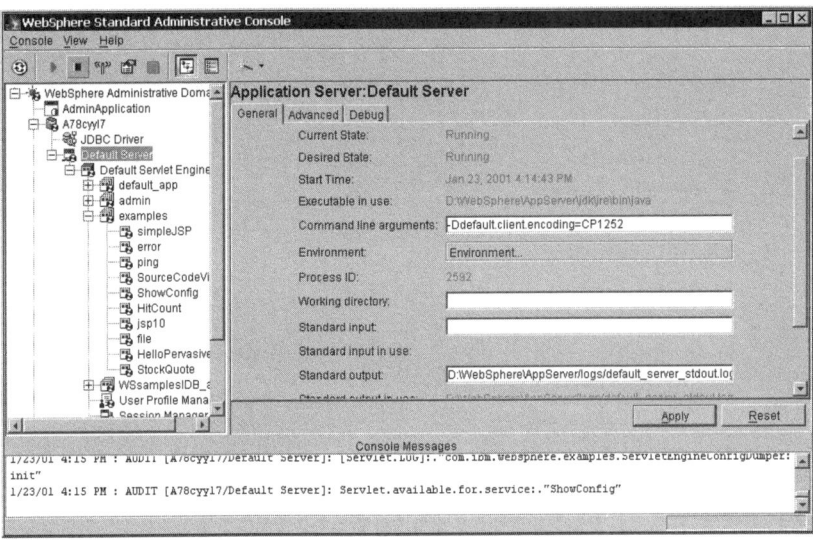

Figure 213. setting up converter manually

You can confirm the setting by ShowConfig servlet. Restart your server and got through with http://[host_name]/webapp/examples/ShowCfg (Figure 214).

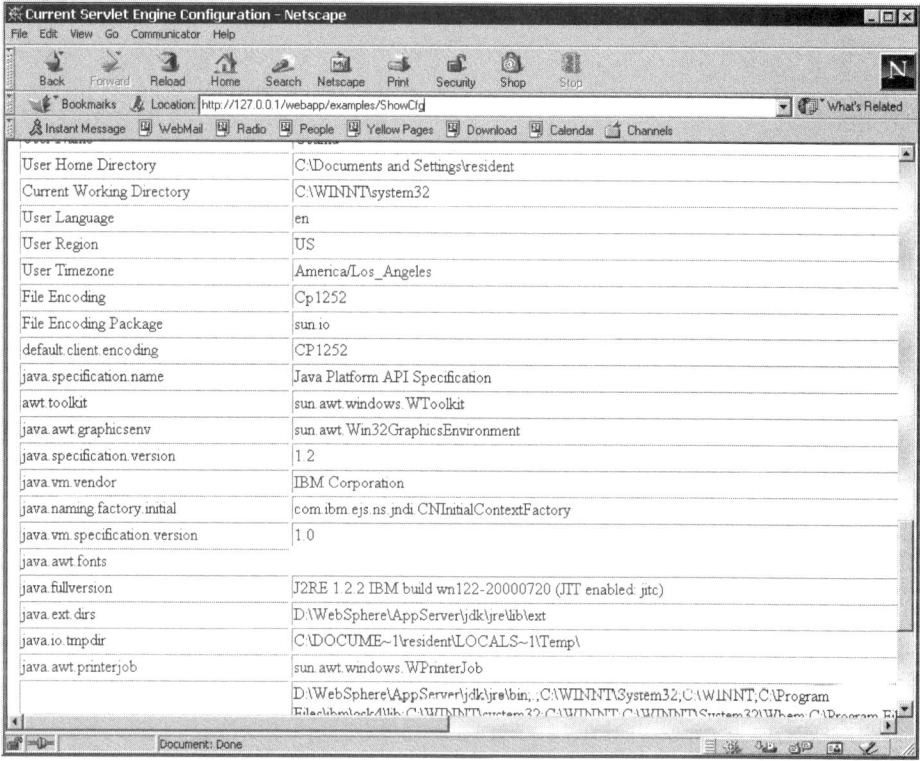

Figure 214. Show Config Servlet

Character conversion in JSP
You can specify the encoder as the parameter of the JSP page compiler if you are using JSP version 0.91. For the JSP version 1.0, you have to specify the encorder as the parameter of the Application Server as above.

Character conversion in servlet
You can specify the encoder when you compile your servlet as follows.

```
javac -encoding [encorder] *.java
```

To compile with a specific converter, you have to compile outside of VisualAge for Java 3.5.

Chapter 12. Deploying the Web application

Traditionally, you develop an application for a specific platform, test it on that platform, and create a platform-specific installation utility to deploy the application. Deploying a Java program is different; the program could be an applet, an application, or a servlet, all with different deployment techniques. In addition, the program is expected to run wherever there is a JVM.

This chapter shows you how to deploy a Java program, whether it is an applet, servlet, or application, to the runtime, or target environment.

Deploying a Java program is usually quite simple. However, because Java is "write once, run anywhere," deployment is not always trivial. The level of JDK, especially when deploying applets, can present problems as can the correct settings for CLASSPATH, and the configuration of the Web server, in the case of servlets.

It is important to test your Java programs on as many JVMs as possible. There are differences in virtual machine implementations, especially in scheduling and time-critical programs.

Deployment can become quite difficult if the Java program contains calls to non Java code or uses nonstandard Java extensions. Writing pure Java code is necessary to ensure trouble-free deployment.

Before you start

To complete the exercises in this chapter, you must set up the correct runtime environments for your Java programs. The requirements for the Java programs are:

Requirements for Servlets
1. IBM HTTP Server 1.3.12

    HTTP server comes with WebSphere Application Server CD.

    A full version of IBM HTTP Server can be download from:

    ```
    http://www.ibm.com
    ```
2. WebSphere Application Server Standard Edition

    ```
    http://www.ibm.com/software/webservers/appserv/download.html
    This trial version includes IBM HTTP Server and IBM DK1.2.2
    ```
3. IBM Developer Kit Java2 Technology Edition 1.2.2

A complete version of IBM DK1.2.2 can be downloaded from:

Requirements for applications
1. Java2 SE 1.2.2 Standard Edition or IBM DK1.2.2 above

   The IBM DK1.2.2 can be downloaded from:

   `http://www.ibm.com/`

Applets
1. A Web browser that supports Java2 SE (1.2.2 above).

   We do not recommend to deploy your Java2 Applet on the Internet. Many of Web browser only supports JDK1.1.x.

   For the intranet environment, you can choose to use Java Plug-in with enables your Java2SE on your favorite Web browser. But you have to install Java2 SE and plug-in on to each client.

   You can download Netscape 6.0.1 which support Java2 SE (as plug-in) from:

   `http://home.netscape.com/download`

   If you wish to use the JavaSoft Java Plug-In you need to download and install it from

   `http://java.sun.com/j2se`

   The JDK, can be downloaded from:

   `http://java.sun.com/j2se`

2. A Web server

   You can use the IBM HTTP server. However, almost any Web server is adequate.

All of the examples in this chapter assume that you are deploying the Java programs on the machine where VisualAge for Java is installed. If you are deploying the programs on another machine, you must transfer the files to the target machine after you export them from VisualAge for Java.

Using WebSphere Application Server

WebSphere Application Server (WAS) allows you to extend the functionality of a standard Web server by enabling Web transactions and interactions with a robust deployment environment for e-business applications. It provides a portable, Java-based Web application deployment platform to support and execute servlets, JavaBeans, and Java Server Pages (JSP) files.

In particular, the **Standard Edition**, for Web site builders, provides:

- Support for Java Server Pages, including:
    - Support for specifications 0.91 and 1.0
    - Extended tagging support for queries and connection management
    - An Extended Markup Language (XML)-compliant DTD for JSPs
- Support for the Java Servlet API 2.1 specification, including automatic user session and user state management
- High speed pooled database access using JDBC for DB2 Universal Database, Oracle and Microsoft SQLServer
- XML server tools, including a parser and data transformation tools
- A Web site analysis tool for developing traffic measurements to help improve the performance and effectiveness of your Web sites
- Machine translation for dynamic language translation of Web page content
- Tivoli-ready modules
- Additional integration with IBM VisualAge for Java to help reduce development time by allowing developers to remotely test and debug Web-based applications

For more information on WebSphere Application Server, see the product documentation and visit the Web site:

http://www.ibm.com/software/webservers/appserv/

Deploying a Web application

To deploy your Web application, you need to create your Web Application (folder) and export your codes then register into the folder.

Creating a Web application

A Web application is a folder which contains your Web applications. Now we will create a Web Application which contain our ATM applications. To create a Web Application, click **Create a Web Application** from the Wizards menu on the WebSphere Standard Administrative Console. Set Web Application name as **ITSO** (Figure 215), be sure JSP 1.0 is selected, then click **Next**.

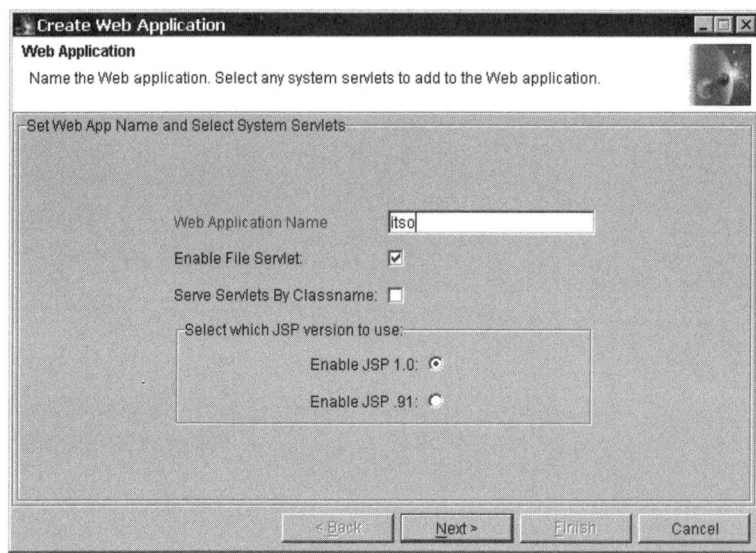

Figure 215. Web Application name

Select **Default Servlet Engine** as parent Servlet Engine (Figure 216), then click **Next**.

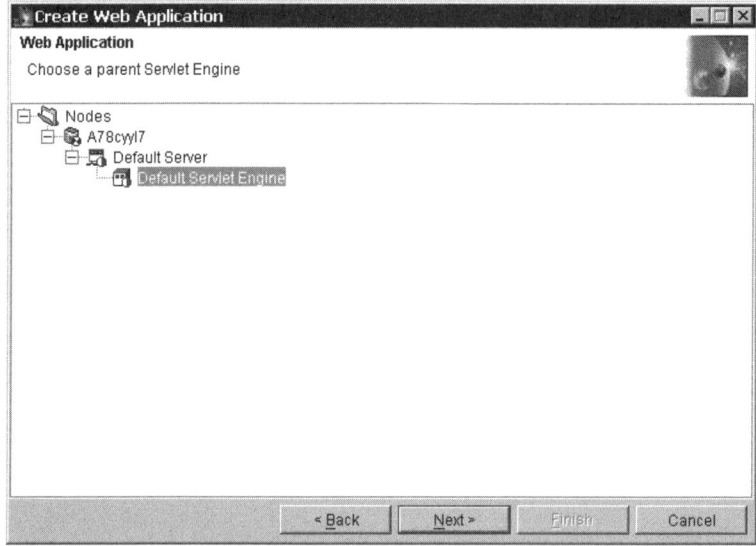

Figure 216. Parent Servlet Engine

Confirm your Web Application name, virtual host, and Web Application Path that are generated, then click **Finish** to create the Web Application. You can click **Next** to see your document root or application class path. The default document root is <WAS ROOT>\hosts\<Virtual Host>\<Web Application Name>\web and default application class path will be <WAS ROOT>\hosts\<Virtual Host>\<Web Application Name>\servlets.

Deploying a servlet

Servlets are typically deployed inside a jar file. The jar file needs to be placed in the root of the servlet path for the Web application. Each Web application defined on a server can have a different servlet path. If the servlets are not placed in a jar, then the .class files need to be placed in a directory structure that is identical to the package name of the class. Placing the classes in a jar file is much simpler to manage. If the classes need to be moved in the file system, it is easier to move 1 or 2 jar files, than a huge amount of directories, subdirectories and class files.

To create a jar file using Visual Age for Java, we use the menu **File** → **Export.** In the **Select export destination** step, choose **Jar file**.

In the WebSphere Application Serve 3.5 running under Windows, the servlet root of the Web application named "itso" is:

C:\WebSphere\AppServer\hosts\default_host\itso\servlets

You have to create the ITSO folder under the default_host directory manually. Web Application Wizard does not create that folder for you.

Defining a servlet

We set up the Web application in such a way that servlets can be invoked by class name. WAS also enables us to invoke servlets by an alias name, and this is the preferred technique.

We deploy the ShowATMServlet servlet to `WebSphere\AppServer\hosts\default_host\itso\servlet` into the subdirectory `com\ibm\itso\sg245364\atm\`servlets.

We define the servlet in WAS by selecting the itso Web application in the Topologies pane and selecting *Create -> Servlet* from the context menu. Answer YES to the question 'Do you want to select an existing Servlet jar file or Directory that contains Servlet classes?' and click **Next**. Select **ITSO Web Application** to add into the ITSO Web Application (Figure 217).

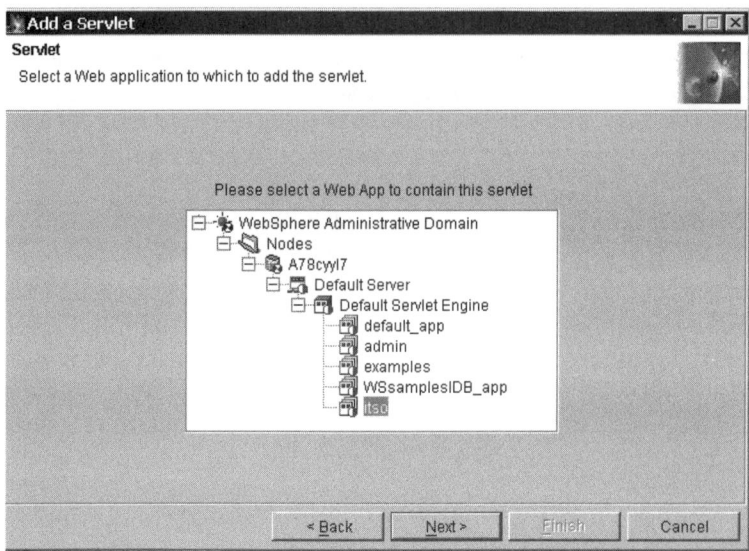

Figure 217. Add a Servlet -— Select the ITSO Web Application

Click the **Browse** button and select **ATM.jar** (Figure 218). Click **Next** and keep the 'Create User Defined Servlet' that is selected. The other options are for WebSphere inner servlets.

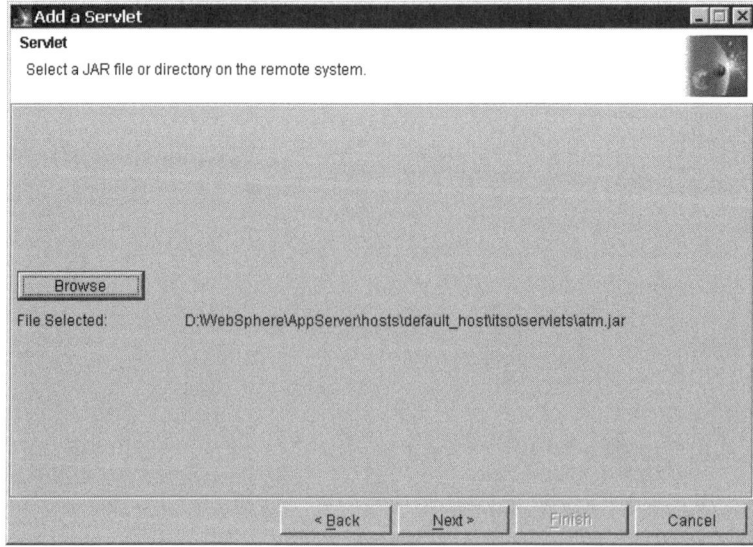

Figure 218. Select ATM.jar

We enter *ATM* as the servlet name, itso as the Web application (preselected), a short description, and finally the class name, which is *com.ibm.itso.sg245264.atm.servlets.ShowATMservlet* (Figure 219).

Click **Add** and enter webapp/itso/*ATM* (webapp/itso is pre-typed and un-editable) as the servlet Web path (this is the alias to be used in the browser). Click **Finish** to define the servlet. This action adds the servlet to the list of servlets under the itso Web application.

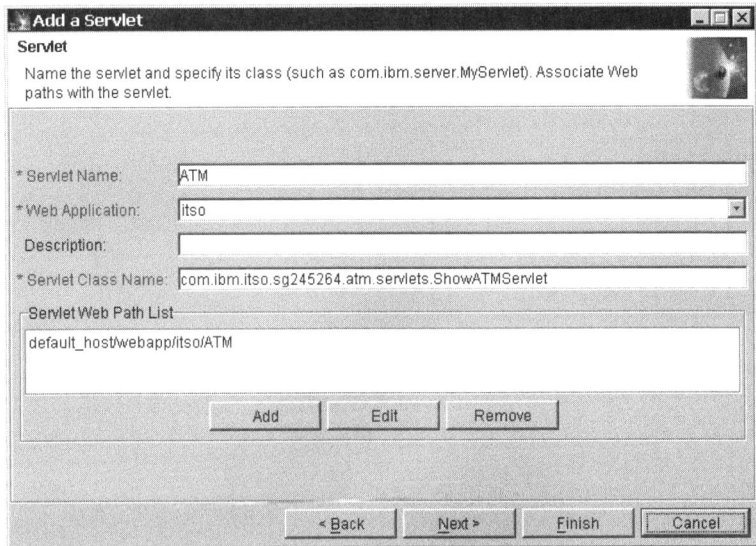

Figure 219. Specify the Servlet class

Start the Web application

If the application server is already running, you can start the new Web application from the console. Right-click on the Web application and select **Restart Web App**. The Web application is also started when the application server is started or restarted (Figure 220).

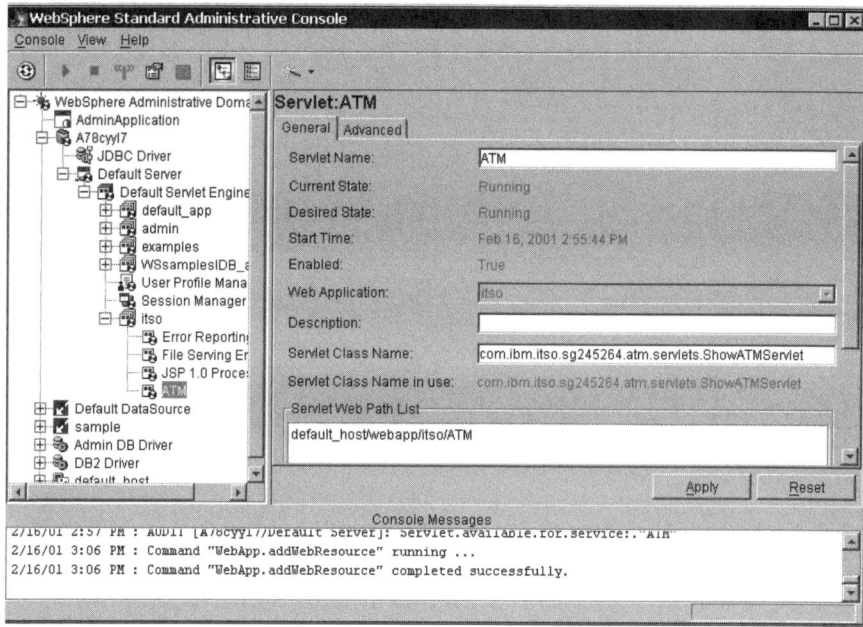

Figure 220. WebSphere Standard Administrative Console

Test the servlet by alias

Open a browser and enter the following URL:

```
http://localhost/webapp/itso/ATM
```

Planning for multiple Web applications

It is important to understand that each Web application has is own servlet root. If there are multiple Web applications on the same server, there are two ways to deploy.

1. Place the jar containing the servlet classes in every Web application servlet path. This is preferred if each Web application is using different servlet classes, or different versions of the servlet classes.

2. Place the jar in a directory of your choice, then add that directory to the classpath of all the Web applications. This is preferred if all Web applications are using the same version of the servlet classes.

So the ATM.jar and ATMServlets.jar files are placed in that location.

Deploying a JSP

Deploy JSPs to the directory <WAS ROOT>\hosts\<Virtual Host>\<Web Application Name>\web. For the ATM, the actual directory will be \websphere\appserver\hosts\default_host\itso\web. Select **Add JSP file or Web Resource** from the Wizard menu on WebSphere Standard Administrative Console. Then select **ITSO WebApplication**. Select your JSP or other HTML file, then click **Finish** when done.

Deploying an application

A Java application is a Java program that is started from a `main` method. A Java object that is to be run as an application must implement a `main` method.

Applications have full access to the host environment. They can start programs and read and write files, and they have the same permissions as native applications. Java applications can be run on any platform that supports a JVM at the correct level.

To deploy a Java application from VisualAge for Java you have to export the Java code:

1. Choose the export type: class files or JAR file.
2. Choose that classes to include in the export:
    - Include referenced types
    - Exclude design time classes
3. Choose whether to include Debug information in the classes. Choose this option only if you are going to debug the application remotely.

Once you have exported the application, you should be able to run it on the target platform provided:

- The target platform has the same or a compatible level of the JDK installed.
- All classes that your application references are either packaged with your application or in the lib directory on the target machine. If you have exported a JAR file, place your jar file into lib\ext folder. Instead of old JDK, you rarely need a CLASSPATH environment at all.

Follow these steps to deploy the ATM Test Application():

1. Install Java2SE on your target machine and add the `bin` directory to your PATH statement as directed in the installation instructions.

2. Export the `com.ibm.itso.sg245264.atm` and `com.ibm.itso.sg245264.atm.database` packages as a JAR file, `Atm.jar` to your `lib\ext` directory. We used `Java2SE Runtime Edition included in WebSphere Application Server` (Figure 221). Click the **Deselect BeanInfo and Property Editor** button.

3. Copy your jdbc driver file and data access Bean to lib\ext directory. DB2 JDBC driver is located on D:\sqllib\java\DB2JAVA.ZIP and Data Access Bean is located on IBMVJAVA\eab\runtime30\ivjdab.jar. Or you can specify the classpath when you run the Application.

Start the application (Figure 222) by entering `java com.ibm.itso.sg245264.atm.TestATMApplication`. Note that the package and class names are case-sensitive. If you receive an error, check all of your jar files and DB2 is started.

You can specify jdbc driver and Data Access Bean by java -classpath d:\sqllib\java\db2java.zip;d:\ibmvjava\eab\runtime30\ivjdab.jar com.ibm.itso.sg24564.atm.TestAtmApplication.

Include Referenced Types

Be careful if you select **Include Referenced Types**. VisualAge for Java adds all the types that your class references to the JAR file or directory export, which may include the complete Data Access Beans or JDBC hierarchies if you use those classes. You may not want to include the classes in your export.

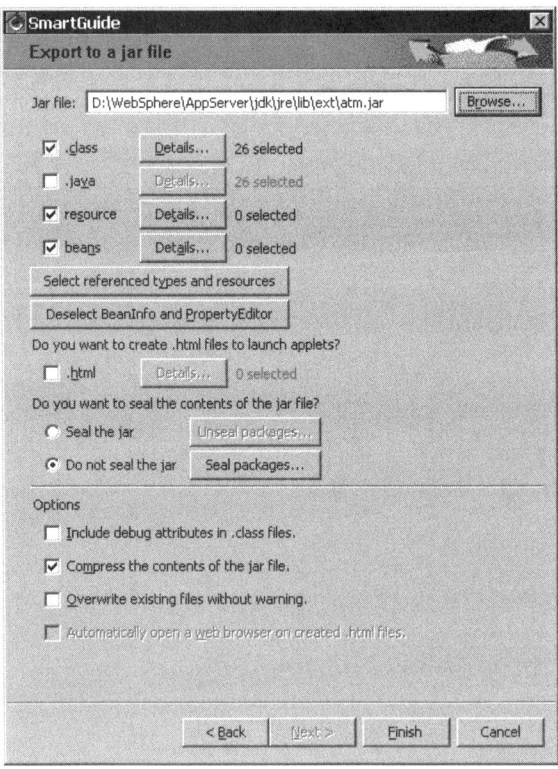

Figure 221. Exporting the ATM to a jar File

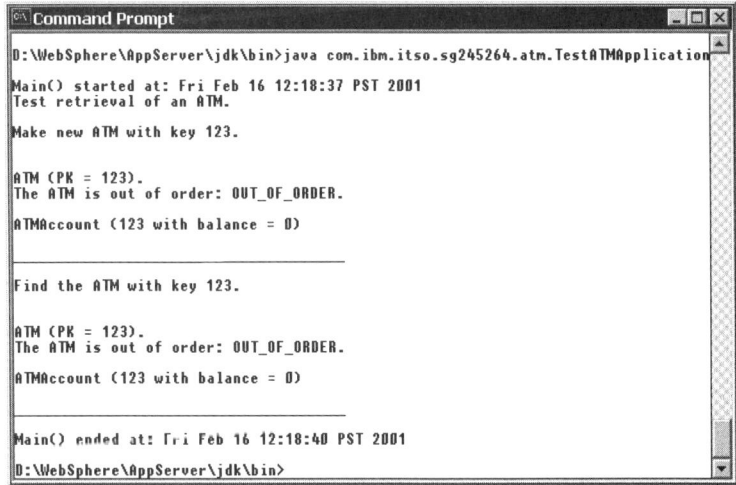

Figure 222. Testing the ATM Application

Deploying an applet

You have probably invoked some applets as you have surfed the Web, whether you were aware of it or not. Applets are Java programs that execute within a Web browser. By default they run in a "sandbox," or protected environment. Also by default, they cannot access files on your machine, and they cannot connect to other machines on the network except to the Web server from which they were accessed.

In Chapter 7, "Creating GUI applications" you created the ATMApplication applet and ran it in VisualAge for Java. VisualAge for Java provides an Applet Viewer to run and test applets within the VisualAge for Java environment. Although the Applet Viewer is good for initial testing of applets, you have to test with Web browsers to see how the applet integrates with HTML pages and whether there are any differences in the way the Web browsers display components or interact with the user.

Deploying an applet consists of two separate tasks:

1. Installing the applet on the Web server, where it can be served to a Web browser.
2. Ensuring that the correct JDK and classes are either supported by the target browsers or available from the Web server.

Web browsers

VisualAge for Java produces Java2SE 1.2.2 code. Your Web browser must be Java enabled and must support Java2 to run the code.

Although there are many Web browsers, the vast majority of users run either Netscape or Microsoft Internet Explorer. Netscape 6 is the only browser that supports Java2 and to use the other browser, you must install Java Plug-in.

CLASSPATH or CODEBASE

A Web server that serves an applet does not need to know anything about Java and therefore does not use the CLASSPATH. When you deploy your applet, you can specify the location of classes through the CODEBASE tag; otherwise the Web server, by default, searches for the classes or JAR files in the same directory as the HTML file that contains the applet. The classes are searched for in a directory relative to the codebase (or current directory) according to the package name of the class.

For example, if you deploy an applet in an HTML page in the /atm directory and the applet class is com.ibm.itso.sg245264.atm.applet.ATMapplication, the Web server attempts to serve the class from the /atm/com/ibm/itso/sg245264/atm/applet directory unless you specify a JAR file through the ARCHIVE tag.

Applet Tags

VisualAge for Java can create a simple .html file for your applet to run in a browser on the Internet when you export your applet. This file simply contains the applet tag and a title. For example:

```
<HTML>
<HEAD>
<TITLE>TestEventQCheck</TITLE>
</HEAD>
<BODY>
<H1>AppletName</H1>
<APPLET CODE=pkgname.Appletname.class WIDTH=250 HEIGHT=300>
</APPLET>
</BODY>
</HTML>
```

The complete syntax for the applet tag ([ ] means optional and the spacing is for readability) is:

```
<APPLET
    [CODEBASE = codebaseURL]
    CODE = appletFile [ALT = alternateText]
    [NAME = appletInstanceName]
    WIDTH = pixels
    HEIGHT = pixels
    [ALIGN = alignment]
    [VSPACE = pixels] [HSPACE = pixels]
    [ARCHIVE = JARFile1, JARFile2 ...]
>
[< PARAM NAME = appletAttribute1 VALUE = value >]
[< PARAM NAME = appletAttribute2 VALUE = value >]
. . .
    [alternate HTML]
</APPLET>
```

where:

- **CODEBASE = codebaseURL** is an optional attribute that specifies the base URL of the server directory that contains the applet's code. If this attribute is not specified, the document's URL is used.

- **CODE = appletFile** is a mandatory attribute that gives the name of the file that contains the applet's compiled Applet subclass. This file is relative to the base URL of the applet. It cannot be absolute.
- **ALT = alternateText** is an optional attribute that specifies any text that should be displayed if the browser understands the APPLET tag but cannot run Java applets.
- **NAME = appletInstanceName** is an optional attribute that specifies a name for the applet instance, that makes it possible for applets on the same page to find (and communicate with) each other.
- **WIDTH = pixels** and **HEIGHT = pixels** are mandatory attributes that give the initial width and height (in pixels) of the applet display area, not counting any windows or dialogs that the applet brings up.
- **ALIGN = alignment** is an optional attribute that specifies the alignment of the applet. The possible values of this attribute are the same as those of the IMG tag: left, right, top, texttop, middle, absmiddle, baseline, bottom, and absbottom.
- **VSPACE = pixels** and **HSPACE = pixels** are optional attributes that specify the number of pixels above and below the applet (VSPACE) and on each side of the applet (HSPACE). They are treated in the same way as the VSPACE and HSPACE attributes of the IMG tag.
- **ARCHIVE = JARFile1, JARFile2 ...** is an optional attribute that specifies one or several archive files to load.

    You can also use .cab or cabinet files to transfer your class files when using Microsoft Internet Explorer.

- **<PARAM NAME = appletAttribute1 VALUE = value> ...** is a tag that specifies an applet-specific attribute. Applets access their attributes with the `getParameter` method.

A Java-enabled browser that understands the <APPLET> tag ignores the [Alternate HTML] part, whereas a browser that does not support Java ignores everything until [Alternate HTML]. Thus Web pages can be created that make sense for both types of browsers.

To specify that the archive file is not in the same directory as the HTML page containing the <APPLET> tag, use the CODEBASE attribute.

Whenever a browser has to load a file needed by an applet, it looks in the directories or archives specified in the CLASSPATH of the browser first. Then it checks the applet's JAR files specified in the ARCHIVE parameter. If the browser fails to find the class file in a JAR file, it looks in the applet's codebase directory hierarchy. Any combination of JAR files and exported .class files can be used.

Deploying the ATMApplication applet

In this section you export the ATMApplication applet as a JAR file and accompanying HTML file and access it from a Web browser.

Follow these steps to deploy the ATMApplication applet:

1. Select the com.ibm.itso.sg245264.atm, com.ibm.itso.sg245264.atm.memory acom.ibm.itso.sg245264.atm.applet packages and select **File→Export**. In the Export to a jar file SmartGuide. Be sure you do not select the com.ibm.itso.sg245264.atm.database package. If you would like to use database from applet, you have to change the JDBC driver to DB2 NET driver instead of DB2 APP driver due to security reason (APP Driver uses DB2 Client and this access path violate the Java security unless you use the signed applet).

   a. Click the **Jar File** radio button and then click **Next>** to continue.

   b. Select the root directory of the Web server that you have installed. For example, if you installed the IBM HTTP Server into C:\IBM HTTP Server, select **C:\IBM HTTP Server\htdocs**. If you are using or are going to use the Web server for production purposes, you may want to configure the Web server for a different directory.

   c. Name the JAR file: `ATMApplet.jar`.

   d. Click the **Deselect BeanInfo and Property Editor** button.

   e. Select the **Do you want to create a .html files to launch applets** and the **Compress the contents of the jar file** checkboxes.

   f. Click **Finish**.

2. Start the Web browser. Enter the URL (`http://hostname/ATMApplication.html`) in the location field and press Enter.

Deploying supporting code

Quite often you have to supply code with your Java programs that you did not create. Typically these are packaged in JAR files. If you are deploying an applet, you can use the ARCHIVE tag to specify these other JAR files. If you are developing servlets or applications, you must place the JAR file in the proper directory of the application server. Deploying a program that uses the Data Access beans in VisualAge for Java is a good example.

To deploy a program that uses the Data Access beans, you must package the required JAR files with the program or make them available to the program. Programs using the Data Access beans and DB2 need access to:

- ivjdab.jar Data Access beans JAR file (found in IBMVJava\eab\runtime30)
- db2java.zip (found in SQLLIB\java)

For example, an applet using the Data Access beans might have an APPLET tag like this:

```
<APPLET CODE=MyDBAccessApplet.class WIDTH=250 HEIGHT=300 ARCHIVE=ivjdab.jar, db2java.zip>
```

In the above APPLET tag the applet class and the two JAR files would exist in the same directory as the HTML file.

Appendix A. JSP tag syntax

In this appendix we review the JSP tag syntax.

JSP tag syntax summary

See Table 13 for a summary of the all tags available in JSP 1.0.

Table 13. Summary of JSP tag syntax

Tag	Description	Syntax
Output Comment	Generates a comment that is sent to the client in the viewable page source	`<!-- comment [ <%= expression %> ] -->`
Hidden Comment	Documents the JSP page, but is not sent to the client	`<%-- comment --%>`
Declaration	Declares variables or methods valid in the page scripting language	`<%! declarations %>`
Expression	Contains an expression valid in the page scripting language	`<%= expression %>`
Scriptlet	Contains a code fragment valid in the page scripting language	`<% code fragment %>`
Include Directive	Includes a file of text or code in the JSP source file	`<%@ include file="relativeURL" %>`

Tag	Description	Syntax

Page Directive	Defines attributes that apply to an entire JSP page	<%@ page [language="java"]
		[extends="*package.class*"]
		[import= "{ *package.class* I
		         package.*} , ..."]
		[session="true I false"]
		[buffer="none I 8kb I *size* kb"]
		[autoFlush="true I false"]
		[isThreadSafe="true I false"]
		[info="*text*"]
		[errorPage="*relativeURL*"]
		[contentType="*mimeType*
		  [; charset=*characterSet*]" I
		  "text/html; charset=ISO-8859-1"]
		[isErrorPage="true I false"] %>

Taglib Directive	Defines a tag library and prefix for the custom tags used in the JSP page	<%@ taglib uri="*URIToTagLibrary*"
		    prefix="*tagPrefix*" %>
		custom tag:
		< tagPrefix:*name attribute*="*value*"
		    + ... />
		< tagPrefix:*name attribute*="*value*"
		    + ... > other tags
		</ tagPrefix:*name* >

jsp:forward	Forwards a client request to an HTML file, JSP file or servlet for processing	<jsp:forward page="{ *relativeURL* I <%= *expression* %> }" />

jsp:getProperty	Gets the value of a Bean property so that you can display it in a JSP page	<jsp:getProperty
		    name="*beanInstanceName*"
		    property="*propertyName*" />

jsp:setProperty	Sets a property value or values in a bean	<jsp:setProperty
		    name="*beanInstanceName*"
		    { property="*"* I
		      property="*propertyName*"
		      [param="*parameterName*"] I
		      property="*propertyName*"
		      value="{*string* I
		        <%= *expression* %> }"}/>

jsp:include	Includes data in a JSP page from another file, without parsing the data	<jsp:include
		    page="{ *relativeURL* I
		        <%= *expression* %> }"
		    flush="true" />

Tag	Description	Syntax

jsp:plugin	Downloads a Java plugin to the client Web browser to execute an applet or Bean	<jsp:plugin type="bean | applet"
		  code="*classFileName*"
		  codebase="*classFileDirName* "
		  [name="*instanceName*"]
		  [archive="*URIToArchive*, ... "]
		  [align="bottom | top | middle |
		      left | right"]
		  [height="*displayPixels*"]
		  [width="*displayPixels*"]
		  [hspace="*leftRightPixels*"]
		  [vspace="*topBottomPixels*"]
		  [jreversion="*JREVersion* | 1.1"]
		  [nspluginurl="*URLToPlugin*"]
		  [iepluginurl="*URLToPlugin*"] >
		[<jsp:params>
		  [<jsp:param name="*parameterName*"
		     value="*parameterValue*" />]
		  </jsp:params>]
		[<jsp:fallback> *text message for
		    user* </jsp:fallback>]
		</jsp:plugin>

jsp:useBean	Locates or instantiates a Bean with a specific name and scope.	<jsp:useBean id="*beanInstanceName*"
		  scope="page | request | session |
		    application"
		  { class="*package.class*" |
		    type="*package.class* " |
		    class="*pkg.cls*" type="*pkg.cls*" |
		    beanName=" { *package.class* |
		      <%= *expression* %> } "
		    type="*package.class* "}
		{ /> | > *other tags* </jsp:useBean> }

WebSphere specific tags

WebSphere Application Server offers a number of tags in addition to the standard tags in the JSP 1.0 specification

Table 14 describes WebSphere specific extensions to the JSP 1.0 syntax.

Table 14. IBM extensions to JSP for variable data

Tag	Description	Syntax
tsx:getProperty	The IBM extension implements all of the <jsp:getProperty> function and adds the ability to introspect a database bean that was created using the IBM extension <tsx:dbquery> or <tsx:dbmodify>.	<tsx:getProperty name="*bean_name*" property="*property_name*" />
tsx:repeat	Use the <tsx:repeat> syntax to iterate over a database query results set or a repeating property in a JavaBean.	<tsx:repeat index=*name* start=*starting_index* end=*ending_index*> </tsx:repeat>
tsx:dbconnect	Use the <tsx:dbconnect> syntax to specify information needed to make a connection to a JDBC or an ODBC database. The <tsx:dbconnect> syntax does not establish the connection. Instead, the <tsx:dbquery> and <tsx:dbmodify> syntax are used to reference a <tsx:dbconnect> in the same JSP file and establish the connection.	<tsx:dbconnect id="*connection_id*" userid="*db_user*" passwd="*user_password*" url="jdbc:*protocol:database*" driver="*database_driver_name*" </tsx:dbconnect>

Tag	Description	Syntax

tsx:userid and tsx:passwd	Instead of hardcoding the user ID and password in the <tsx:dbconnect>, you can use <tsx:userid> and <tsx:passwd> to accept user input for the values and then add that data to the request object where it can be accessed by a JSP that requests the database connection.	<tsx:dbconnect id="*connection_id*"
		<userid>
		  <%= request.
		    getParameter("*userid*") %>
		</userid>
		<passwd>
		  <%= request.
		    getParameter("*passwd*") %>
		</passwd>
		url="jdbc:*protocol*:*database*"
		driver="*database_driver_name*"
		</tsx:dbconnect>

tsx:dbquery	Use the <tsx:dbquery> syntax to establish a connection to a database, submit database queries, and return the results set.	<tsx:dbquery id="*query_id*"
		  connection="*connection_id*"
		  limit="*value*" >
		</tsx:dbquery>

tsx:dbmodify	Use the <tsx:dbmodify> syntax to establish a connection to a database and then add records to a database table.	<tsx:dbmodify connection="*connection_id*" > </tsx:dbmodify>

WebSphere Application Server also extends three JSP 1.0 tags by adding the "language" attribute as shown in Table 15. This enables you to use different scripting syntax for different elements of your JSP.

Table 15. WebSphere scripting language extensions (XML format only)

Syntax
<jsp:scriptlet language="language_name">
<jsp:expr language="language_name">
<jsp:declaration language="language_name">

Appendix B. Using the additional material

This redbook also contains additional material in CD-ROM format, and Web material. See the appropriate section below for instructions on using or downloading each type of material.

Locating the additional material on the Internet

The CD-ROM, diskette, or Web material associated with this redbook is also available in softcopy on the Internet from the IBM Redbooks Web server. Point your Web browser to:

    ftp://www.redbooks.ibm.com/redbooks/SG245264/

Alternatively, you can go to the IBM Redbooks Web site at:

    ibm.com/redbooks

Select the **Additional materials** and open the directory that corresponds with the redbook form number.

Using the Web material

The additional Web material that accompanies this redbook includes the following:

File name	Description
5264samp.zip	Sample code.
readme.txt	Description and latest info.

System requirements for downloading the Web material

The following system configuration is recommended for downloading the additional Web material.

Hard disk space:	20MB
Operating System:	Windows NT or 2000
Processor:	366MHz above
Memory:	256MB Recommended

How to use the Web material

Create a subdirectory (folder) on your workstation and copy the contents of the Web material into this folder.

Unzip the *5264samp.zip* file onto a hard drive. This creates the directory structure:

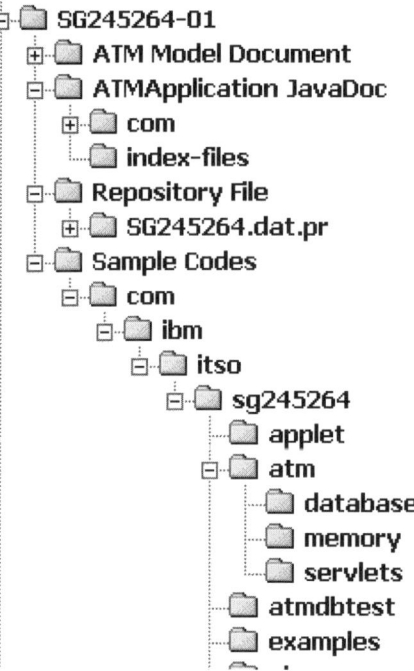

- **ATM Model Document**

  ATM Model Usecase Diagrams. Open root.html to see the documentation (see. Figure 223). This document is generated using Rational Rose and requires JVM enabled Browser.

- **ATM Application JavaDoc**

  JavaDoc Documents. Open index.html in this directory to see the documentation (See. Figure 224).

- **Repository File**

  Import SG245264.dat file as a repository. All related resources are included in SG245264.dat.pr directory will be imported automatically.

- **Sample Code**

  All Java Source code, binaries, JSPs and HTMLs are extracted in this directory.

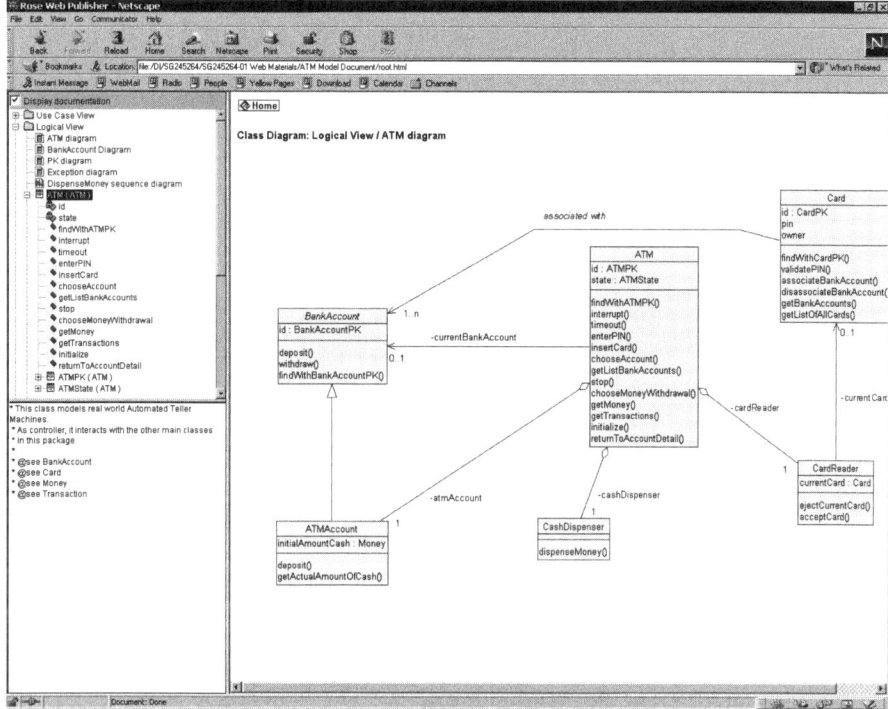

Figure 223. Class diagram

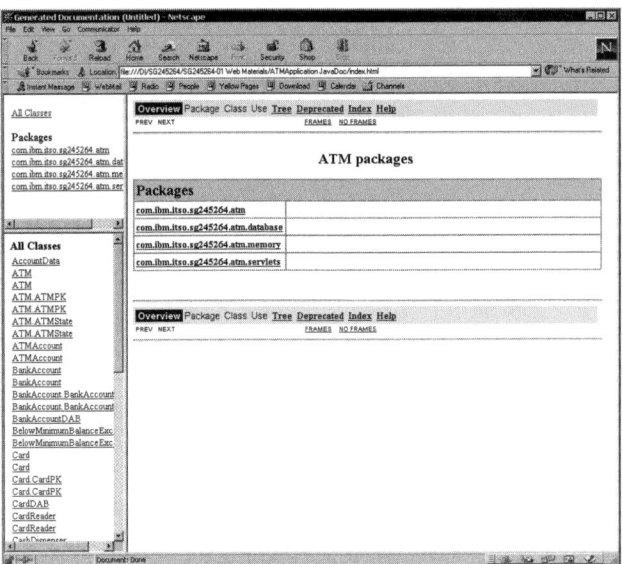

Figure 224. JavaDoc

Appendix C. Special notices

This publication is intended to help VisualAge for Java developers build Java and Web applications using applets, servlets, and JSPs. The information in this publication is not intended as the specification of any programming interfaces that are provided by WebSphere Application Server or WebSphere Studio. See the PUBLICATIONS section of the IBM Programming Announcement for WebSphere Application Server, WebSphere Studio and VisualAge for Java for more information about what publications are considered to be product documentation.

References in this publication to IBM products, programs or services do not imply that IBM intends to make these available in all countries in which IBM operates. Any reference to an IBM product, program, or service is not intended to state or imply that only IBM's product, program, or service may be used. Any functionally equivalent program that does not infringe any of IBM's intellectual property rights may be used instead of the IBM product, program or service.

Information in this book was developed in conjunction with use of the equipment specified, and is limited in application to those specific hardware and software products and levels.

IBM may have patents or pending patent applications covering subject matter in this document. The furnishing of this document does not give you any license to these patents. You can send license inquiries, in writing, to the IBM Director of Licensing, IBM Corporation, North Castle Drive, Armonk, NY 10504-1785.

Licensees of this program who wish to have information about it for the purpose of enabling: (i) the exchange of information between independently created programs and other programs (including this one) and (ii) the mutual use of the information which has been exchanged, should contact IBM Corporation, Dept. 600A, Mail Drop 1329, Somers, NY 10589 USA.

Such information may be available, subject to appropriate terms and conditions, including in some cases, payment of a fee.

The information contained in this document has not been submitted to any formal IBM test and is distributed AS IS. The use of this information or the implementation of any of these techniques is a customer responsibility and depends on the customer's ability to evaluate and integrate them into the customer's operational environment. While each item may have been reviewed by IBM for accuracy in a specific situation, there is no guarantee that the same or similar results will be obtained elsewhere. Customers attempting to adapt these techniques to their own environments do so at their own risk.

Any pointers in this publication to external Web sites are provided for convenience only and do not in any manner serve as an endorsement of these Web sites.

The following terms are trademarks of the International Business Machines Corporation in the United States and/or other countries:

e (logo)® @	Redbooks
IBM ®	Redbooks Logo
DB2	DB2 Universal Database
WebSphere	AIX
VisualAge	OS/2
Wizard	CICS
IMS	MQSeries
MVS/ESA	TXSeries

The following terms are trademarks of other companies:

Tivoli, Manage. Anything. Anywhere.,The Power To Manage., Anything. Anywhere.,TME, NetView, Cross-Site, Tivoli Ready, Tivoli Certified, Planet Tivoli, and Tivoli Enterprise are trademarks or registered trademarks of Tivoli Systems Inc., an IBM company, in the United States, other countries, or both. In Denmark, Tivoli is a trademark licensed from Kjøbenhavns Sommer - Tivoli A/S.

C-bus is a trademark of Corollary, Inc. in the United States and/or other countries.

Java and all Java-based trademarks and logos are trademarks or registered trademarks of Sun Microsystems, Inc. in the United States and/or other countries.

Microsoft, Windows, Windows NT, and the Windows logo are trademarks of Microsoft Corporation in the United States and/or other countries.

Rational Rose, and the Rational logo are trademarks of Rational Corporation in the United States and/or other countries.

PC Direct is a trademark of Ziff Communications Company in the United States and/or other countries and is used by IBM Corporation under license.

ActionMedia, LANDesk, MMX, Pentium and ProShare are trademarks of Intel Corporation in the United States and/or other countries.

UNIX is a registered trademark in the United States and other countries licensed exclusively through The Open Group.

SET, SET Secure Electronic Transaction, and the SET Logo are trademarks owned by SET Secure Electronic Transaction LLC.

Other company, product, and service names may be trademarks or service marks of others.

Appendix D. Related publications

The publications listed in this section are considered particularly suitable for a more detailed discussion of the topics covered in this redbook.

IBM Redbooks

For information on ordering these publications see "How to get IBM Redbooks" on page 373.

- *How about Version 3.5? VisualAge for Java and WebSphere Studio Provide Great New Function*, SG24-6131
- *VisualAge for Java Enterprise Version 2: Data Access Beans - Servlets - CICS Connector*, SG24-5265
- *Servlet and JSP Programming with IBM WebSphere Studio and Visual Age for Java*, SG24-5755
- *VisualAge for Java Version 3: Persistence Builder with GUIs, Servlets, and Java*, SG24-5426

IBM Redbooks collections

Redbooks are also available on the following CD-ROMs. Click the CD-ROMs button at ibm.com/redbooks for information about all the CD-ROMs offered, updates and formats.

CD-ROM Title	Collection Kit Number
IBM System/390 Redbooks Collection	SK2T-2177
IBM Networking Redbooks Collection	SK2T-6022
IBM Redbooks Data Management Collection	SK2T-8038
IBM Redbooks Lotus Collection	SK2T-8039
Tivoli Redbooks Collection	SK2T-8044
IBM iSeries AS/400 Redbooks Collection	SK2T-2849
IBM Netfinity Hardware and Software Redbooks Collection	SK2T-8046
IBM RS/6000 Redbooks Collection	SK2T-8043
IBM Redbooks Application and Integration Middleware Collection	SK2T-8037
IBM Enterprise Storage and Systems Management Solutions	SK3T-3694

Other resources

These publications are also relevant as further information sources:

- *Ackerley, Li. and Parlavecchia, Programming with VisualAge for Java, Version 2*, ISBN:0130212989
- *Hunter, Java Servlet Programming,* ISBN:156592391X
- *White, Fisher, Cattell, Hamilton, and Hapner, JDBC API Tutorial and Reference, Second Edition,* ISBN:0201433281
- *Eckel, Thinking in Java,* ISBN:0130273635
- *Oaks, Wong, Java Threads, 2nd Edition,* ISBN:1565924185

Referenced Web sites

These Web sites are also relevant as further information sources:

- `http://java.sun.com/j2ee/docs.html` Sun's Web site with the complete specification on Java 2 Enterprise Edition, which includes JDBC, servlets, Java Server Pages, and more.
- `http://java.sun.com/j2se` Sun's Web site with the complete specification on Java 2 Standard Edition.
- `http://www.ibm.com/software/vadd` IBM's VisualAge Developer Domain. FAQs, tutorials and more.
- `http://www.ibm.com/software/webservers` IBM's WebSphere related information site.
- `http://www.rational.com/support/downloadcenter/upgrades/rose.jsp` Rational's Rose upgrade information site.
- `http://www.sqlj.org` SQLJ organization main site.
- `http://home.netscape.com/download` Netscape's download information site.

How to get IBM Redbooks

This section explains how both customers and IBM employees can find out about IBM Redbooks, redpieces, and CD-ROMs. A form for ordering books and CD-ROMs by fax or e-mail is also provided.

- **Redbooks Web Site** ibm.com/redbooks

    Search for, view, download, or order hardcopy/CD-ROM Redbooks from the Redbooks Web site. Also read redpieces and download additional materials (code samples or diskette/CD-ROM images) from this Redbooks site.

    Redpieces are Redbooks in progress; not all Redbooks become redpieces and sometimes just a few chapters will be published this way. The intent is to get the information out much quicker than the formal publishing process allows.

- **E-mail Orders**

    Send orders by e-mail including information from the IBM Redbooks fax order form to:

	e-mail address
In United States or Canada	pubscan@us.ibm.com
Outside North America	Contact information is in the "How to Order" section at this site: http://www.elink.ibmlink.ibm.com/pbl/pbl

- **Telephone Orders**

United States (toll free)	1-800-879-2755
Canada (toll free)	1-800-IBM-4YOU
Outside North America	Country coordinator phone number is in the "How to Order" section at this site: http://www.elink.ibmlink.ibm.com/pbl/pbl

- **Fax Orders**

United States (toll free)	1-800-445-9269
Canada	1-403-267-4455
Outside North America	Fax phone number is in the "How to Order" section at this site: http://www.elink.ibmlink.ibm.com/pbl/pbl

This information was current at the time of publication, but is continually subject to change. The latest information may be found at the Redbooks Web site.

IBM Intranet for Employees

IBM employees may register for information on workshops, residencies, and Redbooks by accessing the IBM Intranet Web site at http://w3.itso.ibm.com/ and clicking the ITSO Mailing List button. Look in the Materials repository for workshops, presentations, papers, and Web pages developed and written by the ITSO technical professionals; click the Additional Materials button. Employees may access MyNews at http://w3.ibm.com/ for redbook, residency, and workshop announcements.

IBM Redbooks fax order form

Please send me the following:

Title	Order Number	Quantity

First name   Last name

Company

Address

City   Postal code   Country

Telephone number   Telefax number   VAT number

☐ Invoice to customer number

☐ Credit card number

Credit card expiration date   Card issued to   Signature

We accept American Express, Diners, Eurocard, Master Card, and Visa. Payment by credit card not available in all countries. Signature mandatory for credit card payment.

Glossary

This glossary defines terms and abbreviations that are used in this book.

This glossary includes terms and definitions from the *American National Standard Dictionary for Information Systems*, ANSI X3.172-1990, copyright 1990 by the American National Standards Institute (ANSI). Copies may be purchased from the American National Standards Institute, 1430 Broadway, New York, New York 10018.

A

abstract class. A class that provides common behavior across a set of subclasses but is not itself designed to have instances. An abstract class represents a concept; classes derived from it represent implementations of the concept. See also *base class*.

access modifier: A keyword that controls access to a class, method, or attribute. The access modifiers in Java are public, private, protected, and package, the default.

accessor methods. Methods that an object provides to define the interface to its instance variables. The accessor method to return the value of an instance variable is called a *get* method or *getter* method, and the mutator method to assign a value to an instance variable is called a *set* method or *setter* method.

applet. A Java program designed to run within a Web browser. Contrast with application.

application. In Java programming, a self-contained, stand-alone Java program that includes a main() method. Contrast with applet.

application programming interface (API). A software interface that enables applications to communicate with each other. An API is the set of programming language constructs or statements that can be coded in an application program to obtain the specific functions and services provided by an underlying operating system or service program.

argument. A data element, or value, included as a parameter in a method call. Arguments provide additional information that the called method can use to perform the requested operation.

attribute. A specification of an element of a class. For example, a customer bean could have a name attribute and an address attribute.

B

base class. A class from which other classes or beans are derived. A base class may itself be derived from another base class. See also *abstract class*.

bean. A definition or instance of a JavaBeans component. See also *JavaBeans*.

BeanInfo. (1) A companion class for a bean that defines a set of methods that can be accessed to retrieve information on the bean's properties, events, and methods. (2) In the VisualAge for Java IDE, a page in the Class Browser that provides bean information.

beans palette. In the Visual Composition Editor, a pane that contains beans that you can select and manipulate to create programs. You can add your own categories and beans to the beans palette.

break point. A point in a computer program where the execution will be halted.

browser. (1) In VisualAge for Java, a window that provides information about program elements. There are browsers for projects, packages, classes, methods, and interfaces. (2) An Internet-based tool that lets user browse Web sites.

C

category. In the Visual Composition Editor, a selectable grouping of beans on the palette. Selecting a category displays the beans belonging to that category. See also *beans palette*.

class. A template that defines properties, operations, and behavior for all instances of that template.

class hierarchy. The relationships among classes that share a single inheritance. All Java classes inherit from the Object class.

class library. A collection of classes.

class method. See *method*.

CLASSPATH. (1) In VisualAge for Java the lists of pathnames which will be searched for dynamically loaded classes, BeanInfo information and external source for debugging. (2) In your deployment environment, the environment variable that specifies the directories in which to look for class and resource files.

client/server. The model of interaction in distributed data processing where a program at one location sends a request to a program at another location and awaits a response. The requesting program is called a *client*, and the answering program is called a *server*.

Class Browser. In the VisualAge for Java IDE, a tool used to browse the classes loaded in the workspace.

component model. An architecture and an API that allows developers to define reusable segments of code that can be combined to create a program. VisualAge for Java uses the JavaBeans component model.

composite bean. A bean that is composed of other beans. A composite bean can contain visual beans, nonvisual beans, or both. See also *bean, nonvisual bean,* and *visual bean*.

concrete class. A non-abstract subclass of an abstract class that is a specialization of the abstract class.

connection. In the Visual Composition Editor, a visual link between two components that represents the relationship between the components. Each connection has a source, a target, and other properties. See also *event-to-method connection, parameter connections,* and *property-to-property connection*.

console. In VisualAge for Java, the window that acts as the standard input (System.in) and standard output (System.out) device for programs running in the VisualAge for Java IDE.

construction from parts. A software development technology in which applications are assembled from existing and reusable software components, known as *parts*. In VisualAge for Java, parts are called *beans*.

constructor. A special class method that has the same name as the class and is used to construct and possibly initialize objects of its class type.

container. A component that can hold other components. In Java, examples of containers include Applets, Frames, and Dialogs. In the Visual Composition Editor, containers can be graphically represented and generated.

current edition. The edition of a program element that is currently in the workspace. See also *open edition*.

D

demarshal. To deconstruct an object so that it can be written as a stream of bytes. Synonym for *flatten* and *serialize*.

deserialize. To construct an object from a de-marshaled state. Synonym for *marshal and resurrect*.

double-byte character set (DBCS). A set of characters in which each character is represented by 2 bytes. Languages such as Japanese, Chinese, and Korean, which contain more symbols than can be represented by 256 code points, require double-byte character sets. Compare with *single-byte character set*.

E

edition. A specific "cut" of a program element. VisualAge for Java supports multiple editions of program elements. See also *current edition, open edition,* and *versioned edition*.

encapsulation. The hiding of a software object's internal representation. The object provides an interface that queries and manipulates the data without exposing its underlying structure.

event. An action by a user program, or a specification of a notification that may trigger specific behavior. In JDK 1.1, events notify the relevant listener classes to take appropriate actions.

event-to-method connection. A connection from an event generated by a bean to a method of a bean. When the connected event occurs, the method is executed. See also *connection*.

F

factory. A nonvisual bean capable of dynamically creating new instances of a specified bean.

feature. (1) A component of VisualAge for Java that is installed separately using the QuickStart. (2) A method, field, or event that is available from a bean's interface and to which other beans can connect.

field. See attribute

flatten. Synonymous with *demarshal*.

free-form surface. The open area of the Visual Composition Editor where you can work with visual and nonvisual beans. You add, remove, and connect beans on the free-form surface.

G

graphical user interface (GUI). A type of interface that enables users to communicate with a program by manipulating graphical features, rather than by entering commands. Typically, a GUI includes a combination of graphics, pointing devices, menu bars and other menus, overlapping windows, and icons.

H

Hypertext Markup Language (HTML). The basic language that is used to build hypertext documents on the World Wide Web. It is used in basic, plain ASCII-text documents, but when those documents are interpreted, or *rendered*, by a Web browser such as Netscape, the document can display formatted text, color, a variety of fonts, graphical images, special effects, hypertext jumps to other Internet locations, and information forms.

Hypertext Transfer Protocol (HTTP). The protocol for moving hypertext files across the Internet. Requires an HTTP client program on one end, and an HTTP server program on the other end. HTTP is the most important protocol used in the World Wide Web.

I

IDE. See Integrated Development Environment.

inheritance. (1) A mechanism by which an object class can use the attributes, relationships, and methods defined in classes related to it (its base classes). (2) An object-oriented programming technique that allows you to use existing classes as bases for creating other classes.

instance. Synonym for *object*, a particular instantiation of a data type.

integrated development environment (IDE). In VisualAge for Java, the set of windows that provide the user with access to development tools. The primary windows are Workbench, Class Browser, Log, Console, Debugger, and Repository Explorer.

interface. A named set of method declarations that is implemented by a class. The Interface page in the Workbench lists all interfaces in the workspace.

Internet. The collection of interconnected networks that use TCP/IP and evolved from the ARPANET of the late 1960s and early 1970s.

intranet. A private *network,* inside a company or organization, that uses the same kinds of software that you would find on the public Internet. Many of the tools used on the Internet are being used in private networks; for example, many companies have Web servers that are available only to employees.

Internet Protocol (IP). The protocol that provides basic Internet functions.

IP number. An Internet address that is a unique number consisting of four parts separated by dots, sometimes called a *dotted quad* (for example: 198.204.112.1). Every Internet computer has an IP number, and most computers also have one or more domain names that are mappings for the dotted quad.

J

JDBC. The specification that defines an API that enables programs to access databases that comply with this standard.

Java. A programming language invented by Sun Microsystems that is specifically designed for writing programs that can be safely downloaded to your computer through the Internet and immediately run without fear of viruses or other harm to your computer or files.

Java archive (JAR). A platform-independent file format that groups many files into one. JAR files are used for compression, reduced download time, and security.

JavaBeans. The specification that defines the platform-neutral component model used to represent parts. Instances of JavaBeans (often called beans) may have methods, properties, and events.

K

keyword. A predefined word reserved for Java, for example, *return*, that may not be used as an identifier.

L

listener. A class that receives and handles events.

local area network (LAN). A computer network located on a user's establishment within a limited geographical area. A LAN typically consists of one or more server machines providing services to a number of client workstations.

log. In VisualAge for Java, the window that displays messages and warnings during development.

M

marshal. Synonymous with *deserialize*.

message. A communication from one object to another that requests the receiving object to execute a method. A method call consists of a method name that indicates the requested method and the arguments to be used in executing the method. The method call always returns some object to the requesting object as the result of performing the method. Synonym for *method call*.

method. A fragment of Java code within a class that can be invoked and passed a set of parameters to perform a specific task.

method call. Synonymous with message.

model. A nonvisual bean that represents the state and behavior of an object, such as a customer or an account. Contrast with *view*.

mutator methods. Methods that an object provides to define the interface to its instance variables. The accessor method to return the value of an instance variable is called a *get* method or *getter* method, and the mutator method to assign a value to an instance variable is called a *set* method or *setter* method.

N

named package. In the VisualAge for Java IDE, a package that has been explicitly named and created.

nonvisual bean. In the Visual Composition Editor, a bean that has no visual representation at run time. A nonvisual bean typically represents some real-world object that exists in the business environment. Compare with *model*. Contrast with *view* and *visual bean*.

O

object. (1) A computer representation of something that a user can work with to perform a task. An object can appear as text or an icon. (2) A collection of data and methods that operate on that data, which together represent a logical entity in the system. In object-oriented programming, objects are grouped into classes that share common data definitions and methods. Each object in the class is said to be an instance of the class. (3) An instance of an object class consisting of attributes, a data structure, and operational methods. It can represent a person, place, thing, event, or concept. Each instance has the same properties, attributes, and methods as other instances of the object class, although it has unique values assigned to its attributes.

object class. A template for defining the attributes and methods of an object. An object class can contain other object classes. An individual representation of an object class is called an *object*.

object-oriented programming (OOP). A programming approach based on the concepts of data abstraction and inheritance. Unlike procedural programming techniques, object-oriented programming concentrates on those data objects that constitute the problem and how they are manipulated, not on how something is accomplished.

ODBC driver. An ODBC driver is a dynamic link library that implements ODBC function calls and interacts with a data source.

Open Database Connectivity (ODBC). A Microsoft-developed C database API that allows access to database management systems calling callable SQL, which does not require the use of an SQL preprocessor. In addition, ODBC provides an architecture that allows users to add modules (database drivers) that link the application to their choice of database management systems at run time. Applications no longer need to be directly linked to the modules of all the database management systems that are supported.

open edition. An edition of a program element that can still be modified; that is, the edition has not been versioned. An open edition may reside in the workspace as well as in the repository.

operation. A method or service that can be requested of an object.

P

package. A program element that contains related classes and interfaces.

palette. See *beans palette*.

parameter connection. A connection that satisfies a parameter of an action or method by supplying either a property's value or the return value of an action, method, or script. The parameter is always the source of the connection. See also *connection*.

parent class. The class from which another bean or class inherits data, methods, or both.

part. An existing, reusable software component. In VisualAge for Java, all parts created with the Visual Composition Editor conform to the JavaBeans component model and are referred to as beans. See also non*visual bean* and *visual bean*.

primitive bean. A basic building block of other beans. A primitive bean can be relatively complex in terms of the function it provides.

private. In Java, an access modifier associated with a class member. It allows only the class itself to access the member.

process. A collection of code, data, and other system resources, including at least one thread of execution, that performs a data processing task.

program. In VisualAge for Java, a term that refers to both Java applets and applications.

program element. In VisualAge for Java, a term referring to any of the entities under source control. Program elements are projects, packages, classes, interfaces, or methods.

project. In VisualAge for Java, the topmost kind of program element. A project contains Java packages.

promotion. Within a JavaBean, to make features of a contained bean available to be used for making connections. For example, a bean consisting of three push buttons on a panel. If this bean is placed in a frame, the features of the push buttons would have to be promoted to make them available from within the frame.

property. An initial setting or characteristic of a bean; for example, a name, font, text, or positional characteristic.

property sheet. In the Visual Composition Editor, a set of name-value pairs that specify the initial appearance and other bean characteristics.

property-to-property connection. A connection from a property of one bean to a property of another bean. See also *connection*.

protected. In Java, an access modifier associated with a class member. It allows the class itself, subclasses, and all classes in the same package to access the member.

protocol. (1) The set of all messages to which an object will respond. (2) Specification of the structure and meaning (the semantics) of messages that are exchanged between a client and a server. (3) Computer rules that provide uniform specifications so that computer hardware and operating systems can communicate.

prototype. A method declaration or definition that includes the name of the method, the return type and the types of its arguments. Contrast with *signature*.

R

Remote Method Invocation (RMI). The API that enables you to write distributed Java programs, allowing methods of remote Java objects to be accessed from other Java virtual machines.

repository. In VisualAge for Java, the storage area, separate from the workspace, that contains all editions (both open and versioned) of all program elements that have ever been in the workspace, including the current editions that are in the workspace. You can add editions of program elements to the workspace from the repository.

Repository Explorer. In VisualAge for Java, the window from which you can view and compare editions of program elements that are in the repository.

Repository file. A file that you can export from VisualAge for Java that contains information about selected projects or packages. This file can then be imported into any VisualAge for Java session.

resource file. A file that is referred to from your Java program. Examples include graphics and audio files.

resurrect. Synonymous with *deserialize*.

RMI compiler. The compiler that generates stub and skeleton files that facilitate RMI communication. This compiler can be automatically invoked from the Tools menu item.

RMI registry. A server program that allows remote clients to get a reference to a server bean.

S

Scrapbook. In VisualAge for Java, the window from which you can write and test fragments of code, without having to define an encompassing class or method.

serialize. Synonymous with *demarshal*.

signature. The part of a method declaration consisting of the name of the method and the number and types of its arguments. Contrast with *prototype*.

single-byte character set. A set of characters in which each character is represented by a 1- byte code.

SmartGuide. In IBM software products, an interface that guides you through performing common tasks.

sticky. In the Visual Composition Editor, the mode that enables an application developer to add multiple beans of the same class (for example, three push buttons) without going back and forth between the beans palette and the free-form surface.

superclass. See *abstract class* and *base class*.

T

tear-off property. A property that a developer has exposed as a variable to work with as though it were a stand-alone bean.

thread. A unit of execution within a process.

type. In VisualAge for Java, a generic term for a class or interface.

U

Unicode. A character coding system designed to support the interchange, processing, and display of the written texts of the diverse languages of the modern world. Unicode characters are typically encoded using 16-bit integral unsigned numbers.

uniform resource locator (URL). A standard identifier for a resource on the World Wide Web, used by Web browsers to initiate a connection. The URL includes the communications protocol to use, the name of the server, and path information identifying the objects to be retrieved on the server. A URL looks like this:

http://www.matisse.net/seminars.html

or telnet://well.sf.ca.us.br

or news:new.newusers.question.br

user interface (UI). (1) The hardware, or software, or both that enables a user to interact with a computer. (2) The term *user interface* typically refers to the visual presentation and its underlying software with which a user interacts.

V

variable. (1) A storage place within an object for a data feature. The data feature is an object, such as number or date, stored as an attribute of the containing object. (2) A bean that receives an identity at run time. A variable by itself contains no data or program logic; it must be connected such that it receives run-time identity from a bean elsewhere in the application.

versioned edition. An edition that has been versioned and can no longer be modified.

versioning. The act of making an open edition a versioned edition; that is, making the edition read-only.

view. (1) A visual bean, such as a window, push button, or entry field. (2) A visual representation that can display and change the underlying model objects of an application. Views are both the end result of developing an application and the basic unit of composition of user interfaces. Compare with *visual bean*. Contrast with *model*.

visual bean. In the Visual Composition Editor, a bean that is visible to the end user in the graphical user interface. Compare with *view*. Contrast with *nonvisual bean*.

visual programming tool. A tool that provides a means for specifying programs graphically. Application programmers write applications by manipulating graphical representations of components.

Visual Composition Editor. In VisualAge for Java, the tool where you can create graphical user interfaces from prefabricated beans and define relationships (connections) between both visual and nonvisual beans. The Visual Composition Editor is a page in the class browser.

W

Workbench. In VisualAge for Java, the main window from which you can manage the workspace, create and modify code, and open browsers and other tools.

workspace. The work area that contains all the code you are currently working on (that is, current editions). The workspace also contains the standard Java class libraries and other class libraries.

 Copyright IBM Corp. 2001

Abbreviations and acronyms

API	application programming interface	*RAD*	rapid application development
CGI	Common Gateway Interface	*RDBMS*	relational database management system
DBMS	database management system	*RMI*	Remote Method Invocation
DLL	dynamic link library	*SCC*	software configuration control
EJB	Enterprise JavaBeans	*SCM*	software configuration management
GUI	graphical user interface		
HTML	Hypertext Markup Language	*SQL*	structured query language
HTTP	Hypertext Transfer Protocol	*SSL*	secure socket layer
IBM	International Business Machines Corporation	*TCP/IP*	Transmission Control Protocol/Internet Protocol
IDE	integrated development environment	*UCM*	Unified Change Management
ITSO	International Technical Support Organization	*UDB*	Universal Database
		UML	Unified Modeling Language
JAR	Java archive		
JDBC	Java Database Connectivity	*USS*	UNIX System Services
		URL	uniform resource locator
JDK	Java Developer's Kit		
JFC	Java Foundation Classes	*VCE*	visual composition editor
JRE	Jara Runtime Environemt	*WAS*	WebSphere Application Server
JSDK	Java Servlet Development Kit	*WTE*	WebSphere Test Environment
JSP	JavaServer Pages	*WWW*	World Wide Web
JVM	Java Virtual Machine	*XML*	eXtensible Markup Language
LDAP	Lightweight Directory Access Protocol		
MVC	model-view-controller		
NLS	National Language Support		

Index

Symbols
.cab files 354
.properties files 316

A
Abstract Windowing Toolkit (AWT) 143, 233
Add
    Class 49
    Package 32, 44, 49, 160, 167
    package 164
    Project 44
    Type 160, 164
All Problems 52, 54, 68
Appearance 30
applet 6, 9, 14, 15, 16, 232
applet tags
    ALIGN 354
    ALT 354
    ARCHIVE 354
    CODE 354
    CODEBASE 353
    generated 353
    HEIGHT 354
    HSPACE 354
    NAME 354
    PARAM NAME 354
    VSPACE 354
    WIDTH 354
Applet Viewer 13, 17, 21, 352
application 17, 232
ATM 73, 74, 75, 76, 77, 78, 79, 81, 82, 83, 84, 85, 89, 92, 94, 99, 106, 107, 109, 114, 119, 143, 156, 276, 285, 347
ATM servlets 116
Attribute 6, 49
Automatic Code Completion 26

B
Backup
    repository 189
    workspace 187
Bean
    AppletContentPane 171
    Button 146
    CellRangeSelector 282
    CellSelector 282
    ColumnSelector 282
    JButton 146
    JDialog 173
    JList 146, 172
    List 146
    Modify 282, 300
    Navigation 282
    Procedure Call 282
    RowSelector 282
    Select 282
BeanInfo 62, 69, 161, 350
Breakpoints 236
breakpoints 237, 239
busy 27
bytecode 190

C
cabinet files 354
Cache 29
call stack 234
CGI 110, 112
checking 74
CICS 4
classes 2, 6, 50
    Calendar 312
    ChoiceFormat 331, 334
    Collator 335
    Format 334
    JLabel 320
    LanguagePanel 320
    ListResourceBundle 315
    Locale 311
    MessageFormat 334
    NumberFormat 312, 331
    Object 315
    PropertyResourceBundle 315
    ResourceBundle 314
    RuleBasedCollator 335
    String 248, 334
    StringBuffer 248
CLASSPATH 16, 38, 42, 341, 352
clone 46
Code Assist 26, 56
CODEBASE 352
com.ibm.uvm.* 42
Compact 226

comparison tool   204
configure   266
Connections
   Code   176, 178
   Code (script)   175
   Connectable Features   179, 180
   Event   178
   Event-to-method   175, 176, 177, 178, 179, 180
   Parameter   175, 176, 178
   properties   177
   Property-to-property   175, 177, 179
Console   19, 253
Constructors   19, 98
Control Center   251, 262
Cookie   115
Create
   Applet   44, 169
   Application   44
   Class   44, 164, 167
   Field   44
   Interface   44
   Method   44
   new method feature   165
   Property Feature   162
   Servlet   44

D

DAT file. See interchange files
Data Access Beans   275, 281, 309
DataSource   263, 264, 276, 278
DB2   263, 277, 285, 343, 350
Debugger   44, 231
   Breakpoints page   235
   caught exceptions   241
   class trace   245
   conditional breakpoints   239
   Debug page   231
   external debug   243
Debugging   30
   adding breakpoints   237
   disabling breakpoints   239
   JSP   261
   removing breakpoints   239
   removing external breakpoints   245
   servlets and JSPs   257
debugging   27
declaration   141
default package   48

default.servlet_engine   271
default_app.webapp   267, 272
Deploy   57, 63, 343
   applet   352
   application   349
   JSP   349
   servlet   345
   supporting code   355
Design Time   64
diagram   89
DriverManager   276, 278

E

EAB   4
Edition   44, 191
   Another   213
   Previous   213
edition tab   201
   Packages   210
   Projects   211
   Types   209
EJB   4
Elements   21
English   322
Enterprise Access Builder   4
Enterprise JavaBean   130
errors
   in your code   55
Evaluation   235
event
   mouseClicked   180
exception   88
execution stack. See call stack.
Export   57, 60, 217, 218
expression
   JSP   142, 357
externalize string   316

F

Factory   155
features   42
fields   6, 199
Filter   53
Fix/Migrate   65, 68
Flip Orientation   45, 51
form
   action   132
Formatter   30

formatting
    collations   334
    currencies   332
    dates and times   328
    messages   333
    numbers   332
    percentages   333
forward
    JSP   133
free-form surface   144
French   314, 323
Full source code edit   55

G

garbage collection   112
GridBagLayout   171

H

Hierarchy   50
HTML   41, 62, 77, 91, 93, 109, 114, 122, 129, 138, 261
    page   131
HTTP   31, 78, 93, 94, 109, 115
    GET   116
    POST   116, 123, 125
    request   124

I

IBM Data Access libraries   69
IBM Extension   65
IBM HTTP Server   341
IBM Java Implementation   42
IDE   2, 12, 95, 183, 189, 197, 241
IDL   5
Import   57, 217, 221
Import and export with repository files   218
IMS   4
include
    JSP   132
inner class   3, 103, 199
Inspect   236
Inspectors   26, 102
    changing field values   247
    concepts   245
    navigating   247
    windows   246
InstantDB   263

interchange   58
Interface   6, 52
internationalization
    predefined formats   331
Invoker servlet   269
IP   190
Italian   323
itsoservjsp.webapp   272

J

JApplet   6, 169
JAR   60, 62, 64
JAR files
    importing and exporting   58
Java 2 Platform Enterprise Edition   114
Java 2 SDK   3, 65, 68, 69
Java class files
    importing and exporting   58
Java Class Libraries   42
Java code
    importing   57
Java Foundation Classes   143
Java Server Pages   93
Java source code
    importing and exporting   57
java.*   42
JavaBean   93, 130, 131, 144, 145, 342
Javadoc   30, 99, 100, 197
JavaScript   91, 130
javax.*   42
javax.servlet   33, 114
javax.servlet.http   33, 114
JDBC   95, 262, 275, 276, 277, 279, 289, 343, 350
JDK   47, 65
JSDK   65, 70
JSP   41, 50, 70, 71, 88, 93, 109, 120, 129, 130, 138, 254, 255, 256, 257, 269, 342
    .91 specification   70, 133
    1.0 specification   70, 133, 140
    call servlet   132
    comment   357
    declaration   141, 357, 361
    directive   141
    Execution Monitor   259
    expr   361
    expression   142, 357
    flow   130

forward   133, 358
getProperty   358
include   132, 357, 358
life-cycle   131
overview   129
page   358
plugin   359
root   140
scriptlet   142, 357, 361
setProperty   358
stepping   260
tag syntax   357
taglib   358
URL   132
useBean   140, 359
WebSphere Test Environment   254
JSP 0.91   71
JSP 1.0   71
JVM   22, 110, 241

L

Layout   47
life-cycle   114
Load Left   206
Load Right   206
locale sensitive   312
locales
   concepts   311
   dynamically changing   323

M

mapping tools   4
Maximize   46
Members   194
meta data   64
methods
   compare   335
   compareTo   334
   doGet   34, 114, 118, 122
   doPost   114, 118, 123
   getAvailableLocales   312, 332, 335
   getBundle   323
   getContents   315
   getCurrencyInstance   332
   getDateInstance   328
   getDateTimeInstance   328
   getDefault   334
   getObject   324

   getParameter   354
   handleException   243
   init   131, 178, 252
   performTask   35, 123, 138
   service   131
   toString   334
MissingResourceException   324
model   75
Model-View-Controller   134
MQSeries   4

N

National Language Support. See internationalization
NLS. See internationalization

O

Object   6
open edition   192, 193, 194, 197, 198, 199, 202, 209, 213, 214, 217, 226, 227, 230
Options   28
ORB   5
Orientation   47

P

package   48
Packages   194
packages   6, 41, 42, 46, 96
   creating   47
   default   48
   java.text   312
   java.util   311, 314
page
   JSP   141, 358
Palette   28
path
   Servlet root   253
   Web host   253
Pattern   33
Persistent Name Server   262, 263, 264
Printer   30
problems   53
projects   41, 54, 96, 194
   concepts   41
   default   42
   resources   47
Properties   16, 151

Property Editor   62, 350
purge   225

Q
Queries   278
Quick Start   8, 31

R
RAD   1
Rational Rose   95
Redbooks   1
References   52
Repository   2, 62
repository   50, 57, 190
Repository Explorer   183, 222
request   31, 35, 110, 115
resource   41, 50, 57, 199
resource bundles
    accessing values   315
    concepts   314
    loading   323
    retrieving resources   324
response   31, 35, 110, 114
Restore   46
    repository   189
    workspace   187
restore   225
result sets   278
RMI   31
Root Minus One   48, 51
Run   13, 44

S
savings   74
SCM   217
Scrapbook   22, 25, 26, 27, 232
scriptlet   142
Search   44, 52
server-side include   134
servlet   6, 31, 35, 70, 93, 109, 112, 113, 130, 342
    debugging   257
    ServletEngineConfigDumper   273
Servlet Engine   37, 38, 39, 251, 252, 256, 344
Servlet properties   269
ServletContext   115
session   113
session.xml   269

SmartGuide   3, 8, 9, 18, 19, 31, 34, 58, 65, 66, 98, 101, 158, 283
    SQL Assist   291, 297
Solutions   60, 225, 229, 230
Source View   21, 26, 34, 55, 56
SQLJ   50, 275, 279, 280
stateless   78, 111
Stored procedures   279
strings
    externalization information   318
    length of translated   326
Sun Class Libraries PM Win32   42
sun.*   42
super class   9, 19, 69, 98
Swing   3, 6, 65, 66, 143

T
tag
    FORM   132
    SCRIPT   134
Taligent   311
thread   27, 258
thread-safe   112
Tool Integration Framework   28
Transaction   103
transaction   74, 83
tsx
    dbconnect   360
    dbmodify   361
    dbquery   361
    getProperty   360
    passwd   361
    repeat   360
    userid   361
Types   194

U
UML   78
URL   110, 116, 122, 252, 256, 276
Use cases   76

V
VADD   1, 4, 5
Variable   155, 234
Version   44, 183, 191, 195
    Automatic   196

Name Each   196
  One Name   196
  Show edition names   197
virtual machine   341
Visual Builder   64
Visual Composition Editor   64, 68, 69, 92, 143, 144, 145, 171, 232, 306
  Alignment   149
  Beans List   170
  Browse Connections   153
  Change Bean Name   153
  Change Type   152
  Choose Bean   147, 173
  Choose bean   150
  Connect   153, 178
  Connectable Features   178
  Connections   175
  Delete   153
  Event to Code   152
  Factory   152, 155
  free-form surface   149, 154, 174
  Layout   153
  Modify Palette   147
  Morph Into   153
  Nonvisual beans   146
  Promote Bean Feature   152
  Quick Form   152
  Quick Form Layout window   154
  Quick Form window   154
  Refresh Interface   153
  Reorder Connections From   153
  Save Bean   175
  Save Quick Form window   154
  Selection   147
  Show expert features   151, 171
  Show Properties   151
  Sticky   151
  Tear-Off Property   153
  The Beans Palette   146
  Variable   152
  variable   155
  Visual Beans   146
VisualAge   58
VisualAge Developer Domain   1, 4, 5
VisualAge for Java
  importing   58
  internationalization   316
  projects   41

W

Warning   53, 54
Watches   234
Web   109
Web application   92, 343
Web application server   109, 113
Web browser   17, 31, 39, 110, 111, 113, 122, 342, 352
Web server   109
WebSphere Application Server   1, 2, 31, 70, 341, 342
  Standard Edition   343
WebSphere Test Environment   4, 31, 37, 249, 250, 265, 277
  configuration   266
  Control Center   37
wizards   4
Workbench   12, 19, 28, 34, 42, 43, 68, 95
  All Problems page   52
  Classes page   43, 50
  Interfaces page   43, 52
  Packages page   43, 46
  Projects page   43
  Source pane   43
  toolbar   43
  Unresolved Problems page   43
Working Set   53
workspace   2, 47, 189
WTE   37

X

XMI Toolkit   5
XML   140, 343

IBM Redbooks review

Your feedback is valued by the Redbook authors. In particular we are interested in situations where a Redbook "made the difference" in a task or problem you encountered. Using one of the following methods, **please review the Redbook, addressing value, subject matter, structure, depth and quality as appropriate.**

- Use the online **Contact us** review redbook form found at ibm.com/redbooks
- Fax this form to: USA International Access Code + 1 845 432 8264
- Send your comments in an Internet note to redbook@us.ibm.com

Document Number **Redbook Title**	SG24-5264-01 Programming with VisualAge for Java Version 3.5
Review	
What other subjects would you like to see IBM Redbooks address?	
Please rate your overall satisfaction:	O Very Good O Good O Average O Poor
Please identify yourself as belonging to one of the following groups:	O Customer O Business Partner O Solution Developer O IBM, Lotus or Tivoli Employee O None of the above
Your email address: The data you provide here may be used to provide you with information from IBM or our business partners about our products, services or activities.	O Please do not use the information collected here for future marketing or promotional contacts or other communications beyond the scope of this transaction.
Questions about IBM's privacy policy?	The following link explains how we protect your personal information. ibm.com/privacy/yourprivacy/

© Copyright IBM Corp. 2001

 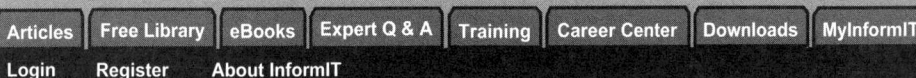

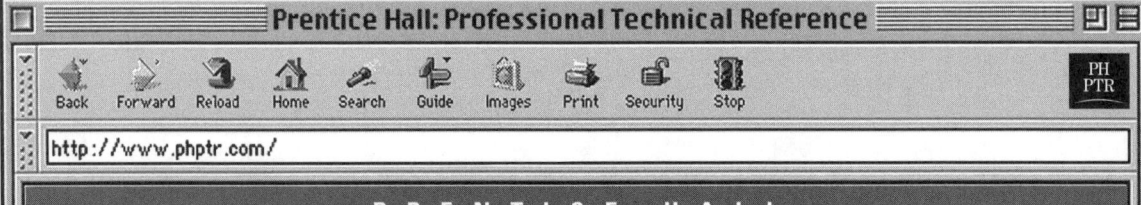

PRENTICE HALL
Professional Technical Reference
Tomorrow's Solutions for Today's Professionals.

Keep Up-to-Date with
PH PTR Online!

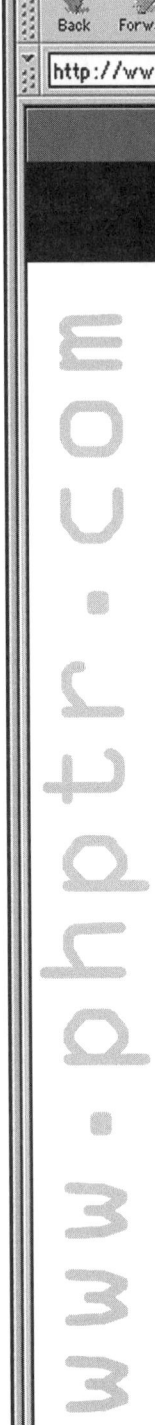

We strive to stay on the cutting edge of what's happening in professional computer science and engineering. Here's a bit of what you'll find when you stop by **www.phptr.com**:

- **Special interest areas** offering our latest books, book series, software, features of the month, related links and other useful information to help you get the job done.

- **Deals, deals, deals!** Come to our promotions section for the latest bargains offered to you exclusively from our retailers.

- **Need to find a bookstore?** Chances are, there's a bookseller near you that carries a broad selection of PTR titles. Locate a Magnet bookstore near you at www.phptr.com.

- **What's new at PH PTR?** We don't just publish books for the professional community, we're a part of it. Check out our convention schedule, join an author chat, get the latest reviews and press releases on topics of interest to you.

- **Subscribe today! Join PH PTR's monthly email newsletter!**

Want to be kept up-to-date on your area of interest? Choose a targeted category on our website, and we'll keep you informed of the latest PH PTR products, author events, reviews and conferences in your interest area.

Visit our mailroom to subscribe today! **http://www.phptr.com/mail_lists**

International License Agreement for Evaluation of Programs

Part 1 - General Terms

PLEASE READ THIS AGREEMENT CAREFULLY BEFORE USING THE PROGRAM. IBM WILL LICENSE THE PROGRAM TO YOU ONLY IF YOU FIRST ACCEPT THE TERMS OF THIS AGREEMENT. BY USING THE PROGRAM YOU AGREE TO THESE TERMS. IF YOU DO NOT AGREE TO THE TERMS OF THIS AGREEMENT, PROMPTLY RETURN THE UNUSED PROGRAM TO IBM.

The Program is owned by International Business Machines Corporation or one of its subsidiaries (IBM) or an IBM supplier, and is copyrighted and licensed, not sold.

The term "Program" means the original program and all whole or partial copies of it. A Program consists of machine-readable instructions, its components, data, audio-visual content (such as images, text, recordings, or pictures), and related licensed materials.

This Agreement includes Part 1 - General Terms and Part 2 - Country-unique Terms and is the complete agreement regarding the use of this Program, and replaces any prior oral or written communications between you and IBM. The terms of Part 2 may replace or modify those of Part 1.

1. License

Use of the Program

IBM grants you a nonexclusive, nontransferable license to use the Program.

You may 1) use the Program only for internal evaluation, testing or demonstration purposes, on a trial or "try-and-buy" basis and 2) make and install a reasonable number of copies of the Program in support of such use, unless IBM identifies a specific number of copies in the documentation accompanying the Program. The terms of this license apply to each copy you make. You will reproduce the copyright notice and any other legends of ownership on each copy, or partial copy, of the Program.

THE PROGRAM MAY CONTAIN A DISABLING DEVICE THAT WILL PREVENT IT FROM BEING USED UPON EXPIRATION OF THIS LICENSE. YOU WILL NOT TAMPER WITH THIS DISABLING DEVICE OR THE PROGRAM. YOU SHOULD TAKE PRECAUTIONS TO AVOID ANY LOSS OF DATA THAT MIGHT RESULT WHEN THE PROGRAM CAN NO LONGER BE USED.

You will 1) maintain a record of all copies of the Program and 2) ensure that anyone who uses the Program does so only for your authorized use and in compliance with the terms of this Agreement.

You may not 1) use, copy, modify or distribute the Program except as provided in this Agreement; 2) reverse assemble, reverse compile, or otherwise translate the Program except as specifically permitted by law without the possibility of contractual waiver; or 3) sublicense, rent, or lease the Program.

This license begins with your first use of the Program and ends 1) as of the duration or date specified in the documentation accompanying the Program or 2) when the Program automatically disables itself. Unless IBM specifies in the documentation accompanying the Program that you may retain the Program (in which case, an additional charge may apply), you will destroy the Program and all copies made of it within ten days of when this license ends.

2. No Warranty

SUBJECT TO ANY STATUTORY WARRANTIES WHICH CANNOT BE EXCLUDED, IBM MAKES NO WARRANTIES OR CONDITIONS EITHER EXPRESS OR IMPLIED, INCLUDING WITHOUT LIMITATION, THE WARRANTY OF NON-INFRINGEMENT AND THE IMPLIED WARRANTIES OF MERCHANTABILITY AND FITNESS FOR A PARTICULAR PURPOSE, REGARDING THE PROGRAM OR TECHNICAL SUPPORT, IF ANY. IBM MAKES NO WARRANTY REGARDING THE CAPABILITY OF THE PROGRAM TO CORRECTLY PROCESS, PROVIDE AND/OR RECEIVE DATE DATA WITHIN AND BETWEEN THE 20TH AND 21ST CENTURIES.

This exclusion also applies to any of IBM's subcontractors, suppliers or program developers (collectively called "Suppliers").

Manufacturers, suppliers, or publishers of non-IBM Programs may provide their own warranties.

3. Limitation of Liability

NEITHER IBM NOR ITS SUPPLIERS ARE LIABLE FOR ANY DIRECT OR INDIRECT DAMAGES, INCLUDING WITHOUT LIMITATION, LOST PROFITS, LOST SAVINGS, OR ANY INCIDENTAL, SPECIAL, OR OTHER ECONOMIC CONSEQUENTIAL DAMAGES, EVEN IF IBM IS INFORMED OF THEIR POSSIBILITY. SOME JURISDICTIONS DO NOT ALLOW THE EXCLUSION OR LIMITATION OF INCIDENTAL OR CONSEQUENTIAL DAMAGES, SO THE ABOVE EXCLUSION OR LIMITATION MAY NOT APPLY TO YOU.

4. General

Nothing in this Agreement affects any statutory rights of consumers that cannot be waived or limited by contract.

IBM may terminate your license if you fail to comply with the terms of this Agreement. If IBM does so, you must immediately destroy the Program and all copies you made of it.

You may not export the Program.

Neither you nor IBM will bring a legal action under this Agreement more than two years after the cause of action arose unless otherwise provided by local law without the possibility of contractual waiver or limitation.

Neither you nor IBM is responsible for failure to fulfill any obligations due to causes beyond its control.

There is no additional charge for use of the Program for the duration of this license.

IBM does not provide program services or technical support, unless IBM specifies otherwise.

The laws of the country in which you acquire the Program govern this Agreement, except 1) in Australia, the laws of the State or Territory in which the transaction is performed govern this Agreement; 2) in Albania, Armenia, Belarus, Bosnia/Herzegovina, Bulgaria, Croatia, Czech Republic, Georgia, Hungary, Kazakhstan, Kirghizia, Former Yugoslav Republic of Macedonia (FYROM), Moldova, Poland, Romania, Russia, Slovak Republic, Slovenia, Ukraine, and Federal Republic of Yugoslavia, the laws of Austria govern this Agreement; 3) in the United Kingdom, all disputes relating to this Agreement will be governed by English Law and will be submitted to the exclusive jurisdiction of the English courts; 4) in Canada, the laws in the Province of Ontario govern this Agreement; and 5) in the United States and Puerto Rico, and People's Republic of China, the laws of the State of New York govern this Agreement.

Part 2 - Country-unique Terms

AUSTRALIA:

No Warranty (Section 2):

The following paragraph is added to this Section:

Although IBM specifies that there are no warranties, you may have certain rights under the Trade Practices Act 1974 or other legislation and are only limited to the extent permitted by the applicable legislation.

Limitation of Liability (Section 3):

The following paragraph is added to this Section:

Where IBM is in breach of a condition or warranty implied by the Trade Practices Act 1974, IBM's liability is limited to the repair or replacement of the goods, or the supply of equivalent goods. Where that condition or warranty relates to right to sell, quiet possession or clear title, or the goods are of a kind ordinarily acquired for personal, domestic or household use or consumption, then none of the limitations in this paragraph apply.

GERMANY:

No Warranty (Section 2):

The following paragraphs are added to this Section:

The minimum warranty period for Programs is six months.

In case a Program is delivered without Specifications, we will only warrant that the Program information correctly describes the Program and that the Program can be used according to the Program information. You have to check the usability according to the Program information within the "money-back guaranty" period.

Limitation of Liability (Section 3):

The following paragraph is added to this Section:

The limitations and exclusions specified in the Agreement will not apply to damages caused by IBM with fraud or gross negligence, and for express warranty.

INDIA:

General (Section 4):

The following replaces the fourth paragraph of this Section:

If no suit or other legal action is brought, within two years after the cause of action arose, in respect of any claim that either party may have against the other, the rights of the concerned party in respect of such claim will be forfeited and the other party will stand released from its obligations in respect of such claim.

IRELAND:

No Warranty (Section 2):

The following paragraph is added to this Section:

Except as expressly provided in these terms and conditions, all statutory conditions, including all warranties implied, but without prejudice to the generality of the foregoing, all warranties implied by the Sale of Goods Act 1893 or the Sale of Goods and Supply of Services Act 1980 are hereby excluded.

ITALY:

Limitation of Liability (Section 3):

This Section is replaced by the following:

Unless otherwise provided by mandatory law, IBM is not liable for any damages which might arise.

NEW ZEALAND:

No Warranty (Section 2):

The following paragraph is added to this Section:

Although IBM specifies that there are no warranties, you may have certain rights under the Consumer Guarantees Act 1993 or other legislation which cannot be excluded or limited. The Consumer Guarantees Act 1993 will not apply in respect of any goods or services which IBM provides, if you require the goods and services for the purposes of a business as defined in that Act.

Limitation of Liability (Section 3):

The following paragraph is added to this Section:

Where Programs are not acquired for the purposes of a business as defined in the Consumer Guarantees Act 1993, the limitations in this Section are subject to the limitations in that Act.

UNITED KINGDOM:

Limitation of Liability (Section 3):

The following paragraph is added to this Section at the end of the first paragraph:

The limitation of liability will not apply to any breach of IBM's obligations implied by Section 12 of the Sales of Goods Act 1979 or Section 2 of the Supply of Goods and Services Act 1982.

Z125-5543-01 (10/97)

LICENSE INFORMATION

The Program listed below is licensed under the following terms and conditions in addition to those of the International License Agreement for Evaluation of Programs.

Program Name: IBM(r) DB2(r) Universal Database(tm) Personal Edition, Version 7.1, Evaluation Version

Specified Operating Environment

The Program Specifications and Specified Operating Environment information may be found in documentation accompanying the Program.

Evaluation Period

The license begins on the date you first use the Program and ends after 365 days.

U.S. Government Users Restricted Rights

U.S. Government Users Restricted Rights - Use, duplication, or disclosure restricted by the GSA ADP Schedule Contract with the IBM Corporation.

About the CD-ROMs

The accompanying CD-ROMs contain VisualAge for Java, Entry Professional Edition, Version 3.5, for Windows 98, Windows NT, and Windows 2000, Evaluation Copy. Please refer to the readme file on the CD-ROM for information on this product. For installation instructions and system requirements for this product, refer to the setup.exe file in the product's directory. A second CD-ROM contains code samples from the book.

Technical Support

Prentice Hall does not offer technical support for any of the programs on this CD-ROM. However, if there is a problem with the CD or it is damaged, you may obtain a replacement copy by sending an email describing the problem to: disc_exchange@prenhall.com